Harvard East Asian Series, 23

FOUNDATIONS OF CONSTITUTIONAL GOVERNMENT IN MODERN JAPAN

1868-1900

THE EAST ASIAN RESEARCH CENTER AT HARVARD UNIVERSITY ADMINISTERS RESEARCH PROJECTS DESIGNED TO FURTHER SCHOLARLY UNDERSTANDING OF CHINA, KOREA, JAPAN, AND ADJACENT AREAS.

George Akita

FOUNDATIONS OF CONSTITUTIONAL GOVERNMENT IN MODERN JAPAN

1868-1900

HARVARD UNIVERSITY PRESS · CAMBRIDGE, MASSACHUSETTS · 1967

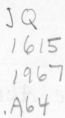
© Copyright 1967 by the President and Fellows of Harvard College
All rights reserved

Distributed in Great Britain by Oxford University Press, London

Preparation and publication of this volume were aided
by grants from the Ford Foundation.

Library of Congress Catalog Card Number 65-13835
Printed in the United States of America

To Akiko

PREFACE

This book has long been in preparation, and in the process I have become indebted to many persons. Special indebtedness is acknowledged to Ambassador Edwin O. Reischauer, who as teacher and thesis adviser, helped shape some of the basic ideas, guided the thesis to completion in Tokyo from Cambridge, and encouraged publication. I am equally obliged to my friend, Professor Albert M. Craig of Harvard University, for his discerning suggestions, unstinting support, and constant encouragement. Professors Benjamin Schwartz of Harvard and Oka Yoshitake (formerly at the University of Tokyo) read the thesis and tactfully commented on arguments I seemed to overstress. Professor Marius B. Jansen of Princeton read the entire manuscript and his comments and corrections have been gratefully incorporated. I wish to thank Professor John K. Fairbank for his interest in the manuscript and the East Asian Research Center, Harvard University, for a timely grant. Dr. Peter Ch'en of Florida State University made useful suggestions to improve sections in the discussion of developments before 1890. Mr. Tetsuo Najita of Carleton College kindly shared with me his knowledge of political developments in the post 1904–1905 period. My colleagues Professors D. W. Y. Kwok and Thomas Murphy generously spent many hours discussing questions arising in the manuscript relating to their respective fields of competence. Miss Nadine Ishitani helped to prepare the Glossary. Miss Ishitani and Miss Patricia Awamura by careful reading prevented many errors from appearing in the final draft.

In Japan I received financial aid from the Harvard-Yenching Institute (1955–1957) and the John Hay Whitney Foundation of New York (1955–1957). A summer (1962) in Tokyo, made possible by support from the University of Hawaii Research Committee, enabled me to work on chapters IX and X. In addition, I received invaluable help and support in many ways in Tokyo from Arai Kōtarō of the National Diet Library, Ikeda Yutaka, James S. Yamada, William Y. Yamamoto, Yutaka Enomoto, and particularly Katsumi Uyemura.

Finally, but not least, I wish to thank Miss Virginia Wharton and particularly Mrs. Elizabeth M. Matheson for editing the manuscript. I am responsible, of course, for all errors in facts and interpretation found in this book.

George Akita

1966
University of Hawaii

CONTENTS

> *[The historian] does not perceive one unique schema as the truth—the only real framework in which alone the facts truly lie; he does not distinguish the one real, cosmic pattern from false ones, as he certainly seeks to distinguish real facts from fiction. The same facts can be arranged in many patterns, seen from many perspectives, displayed in many lights, all of them equally valid, although some will be more suggestive or fertile in one field than in another.*
>
> ISAIAH BERLIN, HISTORICAL INEVITABILITY

INTRODUCTION

When Itō Hirobumi, the chief architect of Meiji constitutionalism, sarcastically referred to "immature students" in Japan who merely dealt in "abstract ideas," he was giving vent to a Japanese politician's contempt for and impatience with Japanese intellectuals. This disdain for the intellectuals' propensity to deal in abstract and "unrealistic" thinking is not limited to Itō and his generation. One writer, touching on the subject in 1910, asserted: "Most of those who are regarded as scholars and intellectuals . . . hate the political parties. And most of those in political parties hate reasoning . . . Little wonder there is no chance for them to understand each other."[1] Yoshida Shigeru, a volatile and cantankerous prime minister in a still later era, followed the traditional pattern; he dismissed as "aimless" the intellectuals' attacks on his efforts to conclude a peace treaty with the United States in 1951. For this he was, as expected, quickly taken to task.[2] This attitude exists even on the other side of the political fence, where intellectuals are supposed to enjoy some esteem. In a rare policy statement, Suzuki Mosaburō, then chairman of the Japan Socialist Party, admonished theoreticians connected with his party by telling them in effect that the intricacies and demands of "practical" politics were beyond them.[3]

This long-standing antipathy between the intellectuals and politicians has had serious implications for the Western student of Meiji political history.[4] There has been in Japan since about the 1890's a deeper gulf between intellectuals and politicians than in most Western countries. And in their appraisal of government and politics, the Japanese intellectuals have seen Japanese reality in terms of Western ideals and models.[5] Consequently their judgment has tended to be unrealistically pessimistic and critical. Pioneer Western scholars in this field, who based many of their interpretations upon the characterizations by the Japanese intellectuals, often reflected this pessimism.

In brief, the traditional interpretations of Meiji constitutional development may be generalized as follows: 1) The Meiji oligarchy, headed first by men like Kido Takayoshi and Ōkubo Toshimichi, and later by Itō and Yamagata Aritomo, reacted with what was essentially a carrot-and-stick policy to the demands of "public opinion" and the so-called Jiyū minken undō (Movement for parliamentary government). The enactment of suppressive laws was matched by timely concessions—establishment of local assemblies and the acceptance of leaders of the Jiyū minken undō into the government. The greatest of these concessions to external pressures were the promises, subsequently fulfilled, to grant a constitution and a parliament. 2) Once the major concessions had been made, the oligarchs took pains to minimize the dangers to their control by strengthening through legal means the absolutist and autocratic tendencies and practices already present in the Japanese body politic. The Meiji constitution, its accompanying laws, and imperial rescripts were masterfully utilized to this end. 3) After constitutional government became a fact, the oligarchs, made even more powerful by the constitution, adroitly manipulated existing institutions such as the emperor and the Privy Council. They also cleverly exploited the inherent weaknesses of the parties—factionalism and the failure to adhere to principles. This two-pronged attack forced the parties to retreat from their primary goal of party cabinets and accept what little in administrative power the oligarchs were willing to grant. The historical consequences of these factors were the effective frustration of democratic government and the party movement in Japan prior to the end of the Pacific War.

A reading of primary sources, as well as a rereading of secondary sources, indicate that Meiji parliamentary development proceeded somewhat differently. To facilitate analysis and comparisons with the traditional interpretations, this book has been divided into three distinct yet overlapping parts. In the first three chapters an attempt has been made to show that constitutionalism was not simply forced on the Meiji oligarchy either by "public opinion" or by the participants in the movement for parliamentary government. The thinking of the oligarchy on the subject plainly antedated the demands of the outs and was at times much more "liberal." Furthermore, the "concessions" may be explained not as capitulations to external pressures but as the flowering, even in hybrid forms, of the ideas and activities of the oligarchs dating from almost the beginning of the Meiji era. Then, too, the stick that the oligarchs wielded during the period preceding the establishment of the Diet, when all things are weighed, was one lightly applied.

The middle part, composed of two chapters, attempts to develop the theme that parliamentary government was not forced on the oligarchs but was freely given. The oligarchs, in establishing constitutional government, accepted the basic premise of this form of government: power-sharing. That the Meiji constitution, which imposed certain clear restrictions on the government and which extended certain rights to the people, was written at all indicates their acceptance of the fact that responsibility should be shared with the people through constitutional mechanism, albeit to a limited extent. The oligarchs, however, were fully cognizant of the accompanying hazards of power-sharing, for this step meant the injection of what they considered irresponsible and selfish elements into the very heart of the administration. Hence the oligarchs were predictably and understandably agreed that this sharing should only be partial, gradual, and carefully hedged. The Meiji constitution represents the primary effort by the oligarchs to control the great experiment legally and rationally; and the other related activities and pronouncements during this period may be interpreted in this light, not as efforts to freeze the status quo.

The oligarchs entered the period of constitutional government with mixed feelings. They were, on the one hand, unhappy and somewhat uncertain about the prospects of party participation in government affairs in the very heart of the nation in Tokyo. On the other hand, they were confident that the controls they had created to neutralize the potential ill effects of this participation would work. For had they not been guiding the development and direction of a growing Japan till that moment?

The final five chapters will indicate how and why the oligarchs were basically wrong in their expectation and in their hopes for a controlled parliamentary experiment. The basic premises are these: First, the Diet, through which the parties worked, instead of being subordinated completely to an oligarchy armed with almost absolute powers—fiscal and institutional—was from the very beginning much stronger than the oligarchs had planned on its being. For one thing, the government had to seek Diet approval for its budget, and the constitutional stipulation that the previous year's budget would come automatically into force was meaningless in an age of rapidly expanding and changing budgetary requirements. In short, the party men now had legally sanctioned footholds in the administration from which to build up their share of public power. The Meiji constitution, then, rather than serving as a tool of the oligarchs to legitimatize authoritarianism, was a weapon fully exploited by the party men to weaken oligarchic control of the government. And it should not be forgotten that the constitution was a gift from the oligarchs themselves.

Second, the oligarchs, though painfully aware of their strategic weaknesses, trod softly in their dealings with the Diet. There were two compelling reasons for their continuing commitment to the success of constitutional government. One was national pride, for Japan was the first non-Western constitutional state. The other was national interest, for the oligarchs were convinced that the West would not consent to treaty revision unless Japan proved itself a modern state, and constitutional government at that time was an indispensable accouterment of an advanced nation.

Third, inherent weaknesses of the oligarchy also subverted its attempts to control and direct the growth of constitutionalism. If the party men were constantly plagued by factionalism, jealousies, and pettiness, the oligarchs were subject to the same debilities. If the party men suffered from a lack or confusion of principles, the oligarchs, too, exhibited a similar defect. For example, the oligarchs were essentially divided in their views on the meaning of constitutional government, with a Yamagata favoring a minimum of concession to the opposition while an Itō was willing to go a long way to accommodate it. The oligarchs, therefore, were unable to present a unified front against the divisive tactics shrewdly employed by the party men. True, the party men were also divided, but perhaps this was fortunate for constitutional development. For there were those who were convinced that only a gradualist approach, meaning compromise with the oligarchs, would enable them to make inroads into the administration. Here is seen the Japanese genius for compromise working in both the oligarchy and parties.

Fourth, the party men came to the first session of the Diet neither overawed nor overwhelmed by the oligarchs. They could boast of several years of experience in local assemblies, and they had used the period since 1881 or even earlier to build up popular support gradually—just as the oligarchs had used the same period to build up their mechanisms of control. These political facts did not go unnoticed by the oligarchs and served as prods for compromise with the party men, which in turn helped the latter slowly but consistently to increase their share of public power.

The book ends with an analysis of the formation of the Rikken seiyūkai (Political Fraternity for Constitutional Government) by Itō in September 1900. This action was the logical culmination of the political realities with which the oligarchs had been contending since 1890. For by the end of only a decade of constitutional experience there had been at least three significant developments: The opposition parties now served as the groups attracting many of the so-called "independent" pro-government politicians, thus increasing their bargaining position with the oligarchy. Bureaucrats of all ranks, shedding or suppressing their traditional distaste for politics and politicians, were joining or openly associating with the parties. All the oligarchs accepted the premise that no reasonably effective cabinet could be formed without at least the tacit consent and cooperation of the parties. These were results unlooked for by the oligarchs, but the measure of their civilization and sense of realism is that they quietly accommodated themselves to these new conditions.

It is sometimes forgotten by the citizens of democratic states that autocratic centralized government, for all its abuses, has played an important part in the history of human development. There is, it is true, a tyranny of misgovernment but there is also a tyranny of chaos, of conditions where government is weak and irresolute or worse still, where there is no government at all. Most men will prefer even harsh government to anarchy.

GEORGE B. SANSOM, JAPAN IN WORLD HISTORY

I

ASSEMBLIES AND CONSTITUTIONS, EARLY MEIJI

A multitude of problems harried the Meiji regime in its early years of rule, but two dangers—anarchy and counterrevolution by the suspicious, jealous, discontented samurai—demanded prompt and decisive measures by the revolutionary regime. These dangers were perceived by Ōkubo Toshimichi, although he seems to have been more apprehensive of the first than of the second, for in 1869 he wrote to Iwakura Tomomi: "There has been an end to hostilities since last year. However, an uneasy peace prevails; the *daimyo* are stricken with doubt and the people are filled with confusion. If . . . we permit the people's feelings to get out of hand, the result will be a situation more fearful than an attack by a huge army."[1]

To fill the vacuum created by the collapse of the Tokugawa government, a body of fixed and basic laws, that is, a constitution, was needed to give direction to governors and governed alike. Assemblies were necessary to provide legitimate outlets for dissatisfaction. Still, assemblies and constitutions were only two of the many necessary steps needed to create a strong, stable, centralized government, and the logic of the times forced the government leaders to recognize and to accept a system of priorities. The inescapable and immediate needs were the creation of a fighting force the government could use to quell and to smash any armed uprising. The han (baronies) had to be abolished and a prefectural system established in order to place administrative control in the hands of the central government. The samurai class,[2] an economic burden and the only real source of physical danger to the authorities, had to be leveled. Revenue sources that were at once steady and fixed had to be found. Compelled to give highest priorities to these requisites, the government thus perforce could allow only a low priority to the introduction of parliamentary forms of government. The exigencies of the times, as well as the alien nature of this form of government, permitted no other alternative.[3]

Miyajima Seiichirō, a section chief in the Sa-in (Left Board)[4] and during this early period one of the leading exponents of the assembly idea, recalls that Itagaki Taisuke remarked on these exigencies when he visited Itagaki about the time of the Korean question in 1873. Miyajima wanted to impress upon Itagaki the importance of creating local assemblies and of enacting a "constitution," but Itagaki parried Miyajima's suggestions and averred that, in order of importance, the concentration of power in the central government preceded the establishment of a national assembly.[5] And even one of the earliest and most perceptive students of Western institutions, Fukuzawa Yukichi, after his trip to England in 1862, was constrained to remark that representative government was "a perplexing institution" and that "election law" and "parliament" were things most difficult for him to understand.[6] These two factors contributed to making everyone in the government who was concerned with this problem a gradualist. All were agreed that broadening the base of power would have to come and all were agreed, too, that the time was not at hand.[7]

That this early, widespread official interest in assemblies and constitutions existed is clearly attested to by an Englishman who spent many hours of conversation with Kido in Hakone. "Through the heat of the afternoon we remained chatting over every conceivable matter grave and gay, but chiefly discussing politics and the application of European principles of government to Japan. Of all subjects this is the favourite among this improvement-seeking class."[8]

Granted the foregoing, it becomes relevant to ask whether this concern was a reaction to demands from those outside the government. Appeasement of "the popular mind" *(minshin)* and the creation of a centralized government, Osatake states, were basic causes for the interest shown in constitutions and assemblies by those in office,[9] and "the people" *(jimmin)* is used by Miyajima in describing those who were advocating a republican form of government.[10]

However, commenting on the word *shomin* [the masses, the people], which appears in Article III of the Charter Oath of 1868,[11] Fukuoka Kōtei, one of the drafters of the Charter Oath declared: "(When I wrote the article), I had in mind the administration of the government by the *kuge* (court nobles) and the *daimyo*. It was not that I held the masses lightly, but I just did not consider them an important political factor."[12]

McLaren, then, was basically correct when he defined public opinion at this time as follows: "The nation politically . . . was synonymous with the feudal aristocracy, and to speak of 'public opinion' was to refer to the opinion of the first group only."[13] Care must therefore be taken against overstressing terms such as "people," "masses," and "public opinion" when these are used, at least during this early period, by Meiji bureaucrats, high and low.

There were, it is true, farmers' revolts and other expressions of dissatisfaction and protest by a bewildered populace swept along by the revolutionary order. A concerted, consistent political movement, however, for the creation of a still newer political order did not emanate from the general population, much less concrete proposals for the enactment of a constitution or the creation of assemblies.[14]

Accepting the definition of public opinion as that reflecting a limited segment of Meiji society, it may still be concluded that before 1874 interest in constitutional government was not the result of any demand from the disparate, loosely knit, and discontented samurai. This interest was limited almost exclusively to those in the government, and this was in part a reflection of the fundamental challenge faced by all revolutionaries —self-preservation.

Definite proposals for broadening the base of Meiji government by creating assemblies and by enacting a constitution were made almost from the start of the Meiji era by prominent and responsible government officials. Etō Shimpei, the star-crossed leader of the abortive Saga Rebellion, is a conspicuous example of the early exponent of the assembly idea in the Meiji government. In October 1870 he submitted his "Kokusei kaikaku an" (Proposal for renovating the national system). The proposal contained, among other things, provisions for a body to discuss "national laws" and for the establishment of a bicameral legislative assembly.[15]

Nearly a year and a half later,[16] in April 1872, Miyajima Seiichirō of the Sa-in presented his "Rikkokuken gi" (Proposal for a national constitution) to the president of the Sa-in, Gotō Shōjirō. In his petition, Miyajima asserted that with the opening of Japan's door to the world, "ignorant and foolish people," exposed to foreign political systems, would in the name of freedom and liberty demand freedom without considering the compensatory obligation of duty. There were even those, he continued, who would mouth the concepts of republican government. He then called for the maintenance of the time-honored system of absolute monarchy. However, since this step, taken alone, would impose restraint on the people, Miyajima urged that both the emperor and the people be governed by the same laws.[17]

A very short time later, in August 1872, the Sa-in submitted its "Kokkai giin tetsuzuki torishirabe" (Studies on the regulations for a national assembly). Nothing concrete resulted from these proposals.[18] However, Sa-in efforts in this field continued. Some time in 1873, for example, Miyajima and Matsuoka Tokitoshi, who in 1872 had himself drafted proposals for a national assembly, were ordered to compile a "constitution." There is no record that the project was carried out to completion.[19]

The first call for drafting a constitution, in the present sense of a national charter, was sounded by Kido Takayoshi, the "soul" of the Restoration.[20] Kido, as stated previously, very early expressed considerable interest in constitutional government. His trip abroad with the Iwakura Mission of 1871–1873 served to heighten his convictions. In fact, for some historians of the Meiji political scene, Kido's increased enthusiasm for constitutional government stands as one of the dramatic results of the mission.[21] In July 1873 he submitted a memorandum requesting the drafting of a constitution to certain other highly placed officials in the government, but his proposal was not accepted.[22]

Kido's effort was followed closely by that of Ōkubo Toshimichi, the iron man of the early and crucial period of the Meiji era. Ōkubo privately circulated his views on constitutional government, possibly in mid-November 1873. As in Kido's case, there were no immediate concrete results.[23]

The following year, on February 28, 1874, the Sa-in petitioned for authorization to draft a constitution. The petition was granted in May 1874. However, like all previous Sa-in attempts, this last proved equally unproductive; the Sa-in was abolished and was replaced by the Genrō-in (Senate) in April 1875.[24]

Interest in constitutions and assemblies, however, persisted among a large segment of officials in the Meiji government. One manifestation of this continuing, and by this time widespread, interest in constitutionalism is the formation of societies by bureaucrats to discuss, study, and propagate, among other things, the problems involved, and to lobby for the acceptance of their views on the subject. One of the earliest of such groups was the Kyōson dōshū (Human Affairs Mutual Study Group) founded by Ono Azusa, Kaneko Kentarō, Shimada Saburō, Hatoyama Kazuo, and others on September 20, 1874.[25] Ōkuma Shigenobu has left a description of this organization, and of the times that permitted and encouraged the growth of these groups:

> The strangest aspect [of the times] was that, while the government has recently begun to look on newspapers as troublesome, in those days the government financed and established newspapers. Bureaucrats also met together. There were a number of these associations of bureaucrats. One of them was known as the Kyōson dōshū. The bureaucrats practiced speechmaking ... Bureaucrats...enthusiastically engaged in political arguments. The government served as the leader, and the people followed. Such was the character of the times.[26]

Even earlier, an organization composed largely of bureaucrats was formed. This was the Meirokusha (Meiji Six Association). Ten men,[27] including Mori Arinori, Nishi Amane, Fukuzawa Yukichi, and Katō Hiroyuki, formed its nucleus. An important item of discussion centered around popular assemblies.[28]

Discussion, argument, and research were, of course, not limited to outside office hours. Yano Fumio recalls that since there was not much to do during the day, he and men like Ozaki Yukio and Inukai Tsuyoshi spent much time discussing constitutions. The aim, according to Yano, was to prepare these bright young men for "great responsibilities" in the future under a constitutional form of government.[29]

Many members of these groups may be identified as advocates of the English school of parliamentarism. The so-called Prussian school seemed to lack articulate public spokesmen. However, a powerful partisan of the Prussian school was another bureaucrat, the brilliant, consumptive Inoue Kowashi, who translated the Prussian constitution in 1875. He was considerably reinforced with the arrival of Carl F. H. Roesler in Japan in 1878.[30] In the end, the views of these two men were to outweigh those of all the proponents of the English school; but this will be dealt with in a later chapter.

Another indication of the added seriousness with which the issue of constitutionalism was being taken was the Meiji government's first real attempt to draft a constitution. At 9:35 on the morning of September 7, 1876, Prince Arisugawa Taruhito, head of the Genrō-in, was received in audience by the emperor. Prince Arisugawa was commanded to proceed with the study of "the laws of various nations" and to draft a constitution based on the results of that study as well as on the national polity.[31] The audience ended, and Arisugawa retired from the imperial chamber. After a brief interlude, he was again summoned to the emperor's study and was told, "Apply yourself diligently to the task and complete it quickly."[32] At the same time, Arisugawa was handed as a reference the work by the librarian of Canada's Parliament, Alpheus Todd's *On Parliamentary Government in England: Its Origin, Development and Practical Operation* (London, 1866), in two volumes.[33] There is evidence that the most powerful men in the Meiji government were behind this development. In a letter by Ōkubo to Iwakura Tomomi, dated September 6, 1876, the former writes of returning the draft of the imperial rescript to Iwakura and then concludes. "When the president [of the Genrō-in] is summoned and is given the imperial command, the state ministers also ought to be present."[34]

A four-man committee, with three secretaries as assistants, was formed by Arisugawa to compile the constitution. The committee completed a draft by December 1876.[35] The drafters apparently were unsatisfied, for the draft was revised several times before it was submitted to Arisugawa as the "Nihon kokken an" (Draft of the Japanese constitution) on June 20, 1878.[36] The committee, however, was ordered by Arisugawa to revise the draft. This was probably because of objections raised by the *udaijin* (minister of the Right), Iwakura Tomomi.[37] Iwakura complained to the *dajōdaijin* (prime minister), Sanjō Sanetomi, in December 1879: "Although the draft has been completed, I have not approved its submission to the emperor because there are parts which do not comport with the national polity."[38] At that time Itō, in reply to Iwakura's queries on the matter said, "After a thorough study of the draft . . . I do not see any indication that [the drafters] paid the least bit of attention to such matters as our national polity and our customs and traditions. They have merely . . . rephrased the constitutions of several European nations."[39]

In the draft, among the points that Itō specifically objected to were: subjecting the revenues of the imperial household to legislative control; dividing the legislative power between the emperor and the legislature, with both parties having the right to submit measures; granting the Genrō-in the power to impeach state ministers and the Daishin-in (Supreme Court) the authority to render judgment in these impeachment cases.[40]

After revision, the draft was resubmitted in July 1880 by Ōki Takatō, who had succeeded Arisugawa as head of the Genrō-in. It was now titled "Kokken sōan" (Draft constitution). A few changes had been made, but they were not of a nature calculated to please either Iwakura or Itō. The controversial legislative provision now read, "The emperor, the Genrō-in and the House of Representatives will jointly exercise the legislative power." The clause granting the Genrō-in power to impeach state ministers merely reappeared in a different section, under "Regulations of the Two Houses."[41] The draft was in turn submitted to the throne in December 1880. This was the last official action on the draft. As a matter of record, it should be noted that for some fifty years the existence of such a draft was unknown even to scholars of Meiji constitutional history.[42]

A reason for the interest shown by the oligarchs in parliamentary government has already been suggested. To Ōkubo, just as to Kido, a government unchecked by laws and a constitution gave only the illusion of strength. Whimsical and arbitrary exercise of power, Ōkubo felt, inevitably invited popular revolt.[43] Kido, citing the example of Poland, had also warned against this danger, but also stressed the added calamity of foreign invasion which inexorably followed anarchy.[44]

The oligarchs did not limit themselves to negative reasons for setting up parliamentary government. For Kido a constitution was a necessary concomitant of centralization.[45] Ōkubo, for his part, believed that a constitutional system insured that all officials would be provided with a fixed and consistent guide for official conduct. This in turn would lead to unity between the people and the government, and then modernization would be possible.[46] Still another point emphasized was that a strong Japan would be able to protect itself from the "insults of neighbors."[47] And with this fear of the West was mixed the realization that the West alone could grant Japan the equal status she sought, and with this, the guarantee of territorial and economic integrity. When Itō, therefore, reminded the privy councilors who met to deliberate on his draft constitution that "There is no nation in Europe which does not have a constitutional form of government,"[48] he was giving voice to a major justification for introducing constitutionalism in Japan. Better still, listen to Itō's plain-speaking confidante, Inoue Kaoru. "Constitutional government was not created simply to satisfy the desires of the people. Those in the government also believed that it was imperative to create a constitutional regime to expedite the revision of treaties and the restoration of equal rights."[49]

To assert, however, that the leaders limited their motives to the demands of *Realpolitik* would be a misinterpretation. There are indications that they were convinced of the intrinsic superiority of the constitutional form of government. "I believe," Itō said one day in 1899, "that since a finer political system . . . has yet to be discovered in human society, there is no course but for us to exert ourselves to the progress and development of constitutional government."[50]

Still, the compulsion to be accepted, and with this acceptance, to be granted equality of status through treaty revision, were basic. Itō's ejaculation of relief after hearing Kaneko Kentarō's report on the reaction of Western scholars and statesmen to the Meiji constitution reminds one of an uncertain college freshman's reaction to his first examination, successfully passed. "Now for the first time I feel relieved . . . There was doubt in my mind whether Europe and America would accept Japan, with a constitution conforming to Japanese national polity and history and yet containing substantial constitutional elements, as a member of the family of Western constitutional states."[51]

It was almost inevitable that these conflicting motives reflecting repulsion and attraction for the West, generated against feelings of inferiority toward and a grating awareness of dependence upon the West, should result in bitter outpourings of national pride. This was the common denominator in most of the justifications for establishing a constitutional form of government. Because the following was written in Europe, by the moderate Itō, while he was studying constitutionalism, the sentiments expressed are especially noteworthy.

I find . . . that the Europeans would harm and deceive us, [and] there is precious little sentiment among them for doing anything to profit or benefit us . . . The European nations, combining together, are trying to outstrip isolated Japan. This feeling, in fine, stems from none other than racial and religious differences . . . If they are going to stress that our level of civilization is not up to their standards, what about their recognizing as civilized and independent states Bulgaria, Serbia, Montenegro, and Rumania? These states are peopled by those who do not differ from wild monkeys. . . . The reason that the Europeans show respect and affection for these uncivilized mountain barbarians and do not recognize the progress of those of us in the East is that there is no fellow feeling between us as between coreligionists.[52]

When Itagaki Taisuke in January 1874 submitted his memorial calling for a popularly elected assembly, he injected a disturbing element into the oligarchs' plans for introducing constitutional government. That the oligarchs' keen interest in constitutional government antedated Itagaki's memorial is plain. That they also anticipated a gradual transition period is also a matter of record. But Itagaki's action injected a new problem. How was the government to control the eventual sharing of power with the intelligent, articulate, and organized elements in society represented by Itagaki and his supporters? This question of control had taken on added urgency by the end of 1877, when the last grave armed threat to the new regime, the Satsuma Rebellion, had been suppressed. The reforms transforming Japan into a centralized state and thus doubly insuring the positions of its leaders were in large measure being successfully implemented. The problems of enacting a constitution and of establishing a national assembly therefore had by this time automatically moved up the scale of priorities.[53] The expressions of dissatisfaction by Iwakura and Itō over the Genrō-in drafts become understandable *in part,* in the light of these new developments. Their complaints against the Genrō-in drafts were that they did not provide sufficient safeguards against this unavoidable future encroachment on the public power domain by the outs. Itō by this time probably was beginning to lean toward the Prussian model of constitutional government as the answer to the problem of controlling participation.[54] However, there were others in the government like Ōkuma Shigenobu, Yano Fumio, and Ono Azusa, who favored the English parliamentary system as an example for Japan to follow. The debate among those in the government over the *type* of constitutional government reached a climax with Ōkuma's memorandum of March 1881 and his subsequent removal from the government later that year. In the meantime, a popular demand for civil rights and democratic forms of government had arisen with some effect on government thinking and policy. Chapters II and III will deal with these two developments.

I do not think it is being captious to demand that Fort Sumter be fired on in April instead of October; to insist that Abraham Lincoln speak in his native nasal treble instead of a deep sonorous voice ... Those are things I just can't stand to see them change.

MCKINLAY KANTOR, NEWSWEEK (FEB. 11, 1957)

II

ITAGAKI AND THE MOVEMENT FOR PARLIAMENTARY GOVERNMENT

The popular movement for parliamentary government, called in Japan the Jiyū minken undō,[1] has been the subject of intense interest among certain Japanese scholars since the end of the Pacific War. Most of these scholars are left of center or Marxist in their ideological bias. Their interpretations, as expected, are deterministic and class-struggle oriented, interspersed with predictable concern for defining terms such as "landlord bourgeois" and "tenant proletariat." And for their basic analytical framework most prefer to conceive of the movement as having developed in three stages, each containing the seeds for the inevitable growth of the one that followed. The three stages have been designated, in order of their appearance: the movement led by the ex-samurai (Shizoku minken undō), the movement led by the well-to-do farmers (Gōnō minken undō), and the movement led by the peasantry (Nōmin minken undō).[2]

The postwar interpreters have done so much serious work that no study of the movement can ignore them or their findings. However, for reasons that follow, their findings cannot be used to check the validity of the basic premises of this chapter, which are: the Meiji government's activities in the constitutional field were not directly traceable to the pressure created by the movement, because for one thing the movement was too weak to offer any real threat to the government; these activities were the outgrowth of the thinking and planning of the oligarchs themselves; the role of the movement in the introduction of constitutionalism into Japan was largely indirect and in a sense negative—its existence served as a constant reminder to the oligarchs that the alternatives to constitutionalism were anarchy or bloody revolution (a conviction, however, which antedated the birth of the movement); the movement was pointed to by certain groups in the government to prod other factions in the government which wanted to delay the introduction of constitutionalism, and it was also held up as a threat to influence the type of constitution to be adopted by the government.

One reason that the results of the postwar school are not applicable is that most of the constitutional developments relevant to the discussion here occurred before the maturation of the movement led by the peasantry, considered to be the most important stage by the postwar students.[3] Another is that most of the standard Western studies have followed the traditional interpretations of Osatake Takeki, Suzuki Yasuzō, and others, with emphasis on Itagaki, his followers, and their efforts.[4] Any reinterpretation, to be sound, should be based on the same major characters and their activities. Thirdly, if one accepts the postulates of the postwar school of interpreters, it would seem that they may be taken to support the thesis that the Meiji government's activities in the constitutional field were not directly traceable to the movement. For example, if Inoue Kiyoshi's interpretation of the postwar school's conclusions is to be accepted—that the leaders were essentially from the same classes and basically shared the same ideology as those who were in the government or who later joined forces with the government—it is to be concluded that the government can hardly be accused of responding to the demands of the movement. Furthermore, the movement led by the peasantry, and considered the most significant phase by this school, was actually too immature to develop into a nationwide movement. Members of this school themselves conclude that the movement was disintegrative, localized in the Kanto area, lacked progressive leadership, and failed in the end.[5]

There is no disagreement on the origins of the movement for parliamentary government. It grew out of the split in the ranks of the Meiji government in October 1873 over the question of sending an expedition to Korea.[6] Itagaki Taisuke and Gotō Shōjirō of Tosa, and Saigō Takamori of Satsuma, advocates of the idea of chastising Korea, left the government[7] when their proposal was blocked by men like Kido, Ōkubo,

Iwakura, and Itō, who favored reform at home over adventure abroad.[8]

Itagaki and Gotō struck back with the first open blow against the government. On January 17, 1874, with six others, they submitted a petition to the Sa-in demanding the establishment of a popularly elected assembly. Government action was limited merely to the Sa-in's accept-ance and transmission of the petition to the Sei-in (Central Board).[9]

This petition, according to Suzuki Yasuzō, created a "sensation" be-cause former councilors *(sangi)* had affixed their signatures to it.[10] Ōkubo Toshimichi, writing at this time, asserted, however: "The submission of the petition was a blunder. No one is impressed by it. Even the unin-formed are contemptuously amused. I understand that even the for-eigners have raised questions. You can generally gauge by the above the seriousness with which the petition is regarded. This is good for us."[11]

The petitioners, joined by others, had formed the Aikokukōtō (Patri-otic Public Party) in Tokyo as a preparatory step for the presentation of their petition. The date was January 12, 1874. This was one of the earliest, if not the first, of public groups pledged to the principles of popular rights and to the establishment of a representative assembly.[12] However, within two months the Aikokukōtō went out of existence, and Itagaki, early in March, left Tokyo for Tosa.

Itagaki late in his life justified his move on the ground that he was convinced that a political party had to have a "grass roots" basis.[13] It is also possible that government surveillance and pressure made his posi-tion in the capital unpleasant. On January 14, three days before he sub-mitted his petition, disaffected Tosa swordsmen attacked Iwakura. The Saga Rebellion erupted in February of the same year. It may be assumed that these events led to a tightening of security measures against all po-tentially dangerous elements in the capital.[14] Osatake, however, probably pointed to the real reason when he wrote that the time was not ripe and that the Aikokukōtō died a natural death from lack of popular interest.[15]

Whatever caused Itagaki to shift his base of operations, his move may be regarded as one of the critical acts in Meiji political history. The full significance of his decision will be evident when the evolution of con-stitutional government in the 1890's is discussed. For the moment, it may be stated that Itagaki's action eventually opened the way for the creation of relatively broad-based political machineries, which enabled elected representatives to battle the oligarchs on not too unequal terms.

The first major step taken in Tosa by Itagaki and his supporters was the founding of the Risshisha[16] in April 1874. Although this society had a political program,[17] in the beginning it devoted its energies almost exclusively to aiding the distressed ex-samurai. For example, it founded tea processing establishments and purchased sixteen "mountains" for timber resources and exploitable lands that were to be resold.[18] Most, if not all, of these projects for the economic rehabilitation of the ex-samurai ended in failure.[19] This turn of events served as a motive for the Risshisha's shift in emphasis from the economic field to the political.[20]

The first attempt at unifying the separate groups advocating popular rights on a supralocal level occurred in 1875, less then a year after the formation of the Risshisha. On February 22 of that year the Risshisha combined with the Jijosha (Self Help Society) of Tokushima to organize the Aikokusha (Patriotic Society) in Osaka.[21] The Aikokusha was a dismal failure, collapsing almost immediately. Itagaki ascribes this failure to lack of funds.[22] Some latter-day interpreters place the responsibility on Itagaki himself. They assert that Itagaki's defection to the government on March 12, 1875, was one of the causes that led to the dissolution of the society.[23]

The demise of the Aikokusha plainly reveals the basically weak and disorganized condition of the so-called movement for parliamentary government at this time. In the first place, as Itagaki pointed out, there was a dearth of capital. Secondly, the movement suffered from the want of a broad base of support. The Aikokukōtō, as Osatake pointed out, had been characterized by this defect. The Aikokusha, similarly, was composed of only some forty members, all of whom were ex-samurai.[24] Itagaki, speaking of the situation in 1875, declared; "At that time, traces of feudal thinking still corroded the minds of the people as a whole. They equated the advocacy of parliamentarism with rebellious conduct. It was not surprising that apart from a few intellectuals, the people simply kept away. Hence, among those who participated in the movement, there was not a single person of wealth or leisure . . . only the ex-samurai."[25]

Thirdly, the movement could hardly qualify as a nationwide movement. In the beginning, membership in the Risshisha was limited to Tosa residents, and the participants in the Aikokusha came mostly from areas west of Osaka. It is true that about this time, 1874–1875, a number of "political societies" made their appearance. However, in the main these were merely small groups of intellectuals, and some could better be described as avant-garde, educational and philosophical groups, rather than political societies.[26] It would be a mistake to assume that the Aikokusha even approached amalgamating these disparate local societies.[27]

In the fourth place, there was a notable lack of understanding, even among the leaders, of the concepts for which the movement was supposed to be fighting. Kataoka Kenkichi and Tani Shigeki, leading spirits in the Risshisha, have left a candid indictment of their own ignorance during this early period. "At that time, we were samurai in the truest sense of the word . . . We did not understand very well what Itagaki was advocating. Besides, we were privately unhappy about the admonition, by Itagaki, that we were to conduct affairs of state together with farmers and merchants."[28] Another participant in the movement recalled that in the 1879 meetings of the Aikokusha, which had by this time been revived, most of those who attended were ex-samurai. Therefore, he reports, the discussions included "much nonsense." He continues: "Even a rather famous person said, 'I'll be satisfied as long as we can revert to the days of the Tokugawa era' . . . So one can deduce from this what went on generally. In any case, there was no one who was satisfied."[29]

This inability to comprehend fundamental guiding principles and the essentially negative attitude of the participants in the movement point to a possible fifth weakness. There were two main alternatives available to the dissatisfied ex-samurai, who sought to regain the social, economic, and political positions to which they were accustomed, in a word, to "revert to the days of the Tokugawa era." One was the traditional method of resort to arms. The other was nonviolent political action—speech-making, pamphleteering, petitioning. It was only after the complete failure of the series of revolts in 1876–1877 that the first method was discredited. It is therefore highly possible that before 1876–1877 internal conflicts over the two choices plagued the more active of the "popular rights" groups, preventing unity of action. The Aikokusha, it is easy to imagine, must have been harassed by this problem, and it could very well have collapsed in part over it. Among its members were some who later participated in the Akizuki Rebellion and in the assassination of Ōkubo.[30]

The pitiably short existence of the Aikokusha, then, clearly reflects the extremely weak position and immaturity of the movement at this time. Moreover, it should be noted that Itagaki's "defection" appears to have very little connection with the failure of the Aikokusha. There are good reasons to believe that Itagaki and his supporters knew *before* the formation of the Aikokusha that he was going to join the government.

The Aikokusha was formally organized in February 1875. It is possible that as early as January 6 of that year Inoue Kaoru had discussed with Kido, in Osaka, the subject of Itagaki's rejoining the government. On January 22 Kido and Inoue called on Itagaki in Osaka for an exchange of ideas on assemblies. By February 11, when Kido, Itagaki, and Ōkubo met, Itagaki's followers must have known that Itagaki was going to participate in the government, for in most of the meetings between Kido and Itagaki held before this date several of Itagaki's supporters were also in attendance.[31] Even if it is granted that Itagaki's switch in loyalties was the main reason for the foundering of the Aikokusha, this only adds further support to the thesis that the underpinnings of the movement were unstable.[32]

A period of armed insurrections, climaxed by the Satsuma Rebellion, followed.[33] On October 24, 1876, the Divine Wind Group (Shimpūren), of about 170 men, attacked the Kumamoto garrison and the Kumamoto prefectural office. This was followed by an uprising on October 26 by some 400 ex-samurai of the Akizaki han. Maebara Issei, a former councilor, gathered a force of over 150 men in Hagi immediately after this. He planned to march to the city of Yamaguchi and then to Tokyo.[34] But these uprisings were easily crushed by the government and by early December of that year the leaders, including Maebara, had been executed.[35] The government did not have such an easy time with the Satsuma Rebellion, which broke out in late January 1877. There were more than six months of bitter fighting before the rebellion was put down. Saigō Takamori, who led the rebellion, died by his own hand on September 24, 1877.[36]

If there is one point of universal agreement in the interpretation of Meiji political history, it is that the Satsuma Rebellion proved that the changes wrought by the Meiji government could not be undone by force of arms.[37] Itagaki, however, needed no such lessons. We have seen that Itagaki was absolved by Kido, for all practical purposes, of any guilt in connection with the attack on Iwakura. In the case of the revolt in Saga, Itagaki did not make any move to act in concert with Etō, and Itagaki is said also to have refused to help Etō when he came to Tosa seeking asylum.[38] Furthermore, Itagaki was not implicated by the government in the 1877 plot by Hayashi Yūzō, Ōe Taku, and others of his followers, to assassinate government officials and to attack the Osaka castle while the government was occupied with the Satsuma Rebellion.[39] Leaving aside the crucial questions of how and why he arrived at his devotion to peaceful political action,[40] Itagaki, by his stand, from the very beginning provided a long-range alternative to a basic, traditional method of political expression.[41] In this sense, Itagaki was truly a revolutionary.

The period following the Satsuma Rebellion saw the so-called flowering of the movement, which reached a climax in 1880 and 1881.[42] On

September 11, 1878, the Aikokusha was resurrected at a meeting in Osaka convoked by the leaders of the Risshisha. Most of the participants were ex-samurai, an indication that the movement still operated from a narrow base.[43] The Aikokusha held another meeting on March 27, 1879, again at Osaka. The third meeting was held also in Osaka on November 7 of the same year. At the November meeting a resolution was approved, calling for the presentation of a petition to the emperor that would ask for the creation of a national assembly.[44] In March 1880 the fourth meeting of the Aikokusha was held in Osaka. One hundred and fourteen delegates, said to represent some 87,000 members in 27 societies and 22 prefectures plus Osaka and Tokyo, came to the convention.[45] The name of the Aikokusha was changed to the League for the Establishment of a National Assembly (Kokkai kisei dōmei kai).[46] In the main order of business, Kataoka Kenkichi and Kōno Hironaka were commissioned to present the petition to the government as representatives of the 87,000 members of the local societies. This they did on April 17. However, no one in the government would accept the petition.[47] The government, nevertheless, was to have no respite from petitioners this year. Osatake lists some fifty-six petitions submitted to the Genrō-in, the majority of them demanding the establishment of a national assembly.[48] In November 1880 the second meeting of the league was held, this time in Tokyo. Sixty-four delegates, representing some 130,000 members of political associations in 22 prefectures and Osaka and Tokyo attended the convention. At this time some of the leaders, in particular Ueki Emori, urged that the league be dissolved and a political party formed. His view was rejected, but in December 1880 Ueki, together with Kōno Hironaka, Matsuda Masahisa, and others, organized the Jiyūtō.[49]

Before the Satsuma Rebellion, limited funds and support seriously hampered the movement for parliamentarism. During the years 1880–1881, however, the movement became noisier and better organized; it spread geographically and drew greater numerical support. Still, one cannot agree with the standard interpretation that government attempts between 1875 and 1881 to liberalize the regime stemmed from the idea of granting "concessions," either in form or substance, to the advocates of parliamentarism. A closer scrutiny of major constitutional developments indicates that most of the changes flowed from long-standing ideas that were considered orthodox by those in the government itself.

Developments most commonly cited to substantiate the standard interpretation are the Osaka Conference (Osaka kaigi) of 1875 and the governmental changes resulting from it, the establishment of the prefectural assemblies *(fu-ken kai)*, and the Imperial Rescript of 1881 calling for the creation of a national assembly by 1890.[50]

The Osaka Conference was held during the first two months of 1875. Two chief results of the conference were the return of Kido and Itagaki to government service and the adoption of a four-point platform. The points were: the establishment of the Genrō-in; the creation of the Daishin-in; the convocation of an assembly of prefectural governors; relief from administrative functions and duties for those with cabinet rank, who would henceforth serve solely as advisors to the throne.[51]

The sickly, idealistic Kido had angrily left the government in May 1874, when his objections to the Formosan Expedition had gone unheeded.[52] His move left only Ōkubo and Iwakura, among the leaders of the Restoration, in the government. In the meantime, Etō's uprising earlier that same year portended more of the same by restless, frustrated ex-samurai. The Formosan Expedition, moreover, had done little to impress Saigō and the more militant of his followers that Ōkubo had seen the wisdom of Saigō's 1873 Korean policy. And in the government, Kido's resignation had caused a conflict of loyalties among rising Chōshū bureaucrats like Itō and Yamagata, and there were also mutterings from this powerful group that Ōkubo of Satsuma was wielding too much power. Even to the forceful and strong-willed Ōkubo, the need to strengthen the government by rebuilding at least the Sat-Chō coalition became obvious. Out of this realization was born the Osaka Conference.

On December 8, 1874, the wheels were set into motion when Ōkubo called Itō to his home and asked him about the feasibility of Kido's returning to the government.[53] Ōkubo made clear his readiness to go to Yamaguchi to ask Kido personally. Itō, however, told Ōkubo that the best thing would be to have the two men meet in Osaka. Ōkubo consented to leave all details to Itō. Late in November Inoue Kaoru, who had discussed Kido's re-entry into the government with Itō even before the Ōkubo-Itō talk, met Komuro and Furuzawa, cosigners with Itagaki of the January 1874 petition, on his way to Osaka. It was at this time that the three decided to persuade both Itagaki and Kido to rejoin the government. It appears, then, that the original plan did not include Itagaki, and that, as Tokutomi Iichirō points out, Itō and Ōkubo were probably unaware of Inoue's unilateral change in the plan.[54]

Without going further into detail, several interrelated generalizations may be made about the conference. There was, undeniably, an awareness of the activities of the proponents of parliamentarism among the participants. Ōkubo, for example, in writing to Kuroda Kiyotaka on January

26 said, "Although I understand that the advocates of a popularly elected assembly are converging on Osaka and seem to be up to something, the matter is not serious."[55] However, the original intention of the conference was to bring about a rapprochement between Ōkubo and Kido, and the fact that Itagaki was finally included may be considered as an extra dividend stemming from the conference. Since the purpose of the conference was to reconstruct the 1868 coalition, Itagaki owes his re-entry less to the fact that he was a leader of the movement for parliamentarism than to his position as one of the leaders of the Restoration. The subject of Itagaki's participation in the government, for instance, was brought up on January 29, *after* general agreement was reached by Kido and Ōkubo on the four-point program Itō had suggested, and after Kido had consented to re-enter the government. On this day Kido asked Ōkubo about Itagaki. Ōkubo replied that he had resolved before the conference to follow Kido's lead and that the choice of personnel was entirely up to Kido.[56] And it was not until the conference was about to end, on February 11, that Itagaki and Ōkubo met for the first time since Itagaki had left the government in October 1873.[57]

This leads to a second point. A look at the record Kido and Ōkubo left reveals that whatever concessions were made were made to Kido as inducements to return to the fold. Kido himself was convinced that the purpose of the conference was to hammer out a political program acceptable to him. On February 9 he recorded in his diary that he had discussed popular assembly ideas with Ōkubo and that Ōkubo had agreed with his views. He also wrote that Itagaki too had earlier agreed to his ideas. Kido then concluded, "Privately, I dance for joy."[58] According to Kido, then, Itagaki was plainly one of the parties making concessions in the conference.

Finally, that Kido already had definite ideas on parliamentarism when he came to Osaka and that Ōkubo did not find it difficult at all to go along with Kido shows that Meiji political history cannot be seen simply as a struggle between a "liberal" opposition demanding political rights and a "conservative" regime bent on maintaining the *status quo* and acquiescing to change only when faced with opposition pressure. The truth of the matter is stated by Maruyama Masao: "The thinking of those in the government up to 1877 was clearly more progressive than that of most of the opposition."[59] This is not to say that a gradual shift did not take place. By the adoption and internalization of alien values which before had been difficult of comprehension even for the leaders, the parties became "liberal"—more so than the oligarchs. This development does not mean that the oligarchs were reactionary. It does suggest, however, that without changing they were less liberal in 1881 or 1885 than in 1872 or 1877, because "liberal" is defined relative to the climate of thought, and this had changed.

The establishment of prefectural assemblies in July 1878, often cited as a concession to the movement for parliamentarism, is still another indication of the liberal thinking of the oligarchs. In the first place, the concept of local assemblies was being advocated among leaders even very early in the Meiji period. In 1870, for example, Etō Shimpei submitted several proposals that called for the creation of local assemblies.[60] Furthermore, on January 29, 1874, Kido recorded a talk with Itagaki in which they discussed the subjects of assemblies of prefectural governors and prefectural assemblies, which subjects, Kido told Itagaki, were being discussed in the government.[61] Secondly, although the prefectural assemblies were established in July 1878, two months after the assassination of Ōkubo, regulations governing the assemblies had already been considered and decided on during the second assembly of prefectural governors in April and early May of that year. So neither the assassination of Ōkubo in May, nor the revival of the Aikokusha in September, later that year, had much direct bearing on the establishment of prefectural assemblies.[62]

To state that the government's program for introducing constitutionalism was not a response to outside pressures *is not, of course, the same as asserting that the movement for parliamentary government had no influence.* There were ample expressions of concern over the movement, and the government took enough cognizance of it to react with restrictive laws. Before it is possible, however, to discuss the influence of the movement on the thinking and activities of those in the government, it is important that these expressions of concern be explained.

A quick perusal of the pertinent documents on the subject reveals the following: none regards the movement as presenting any real, immediate danger to the Meiji regime; the threat presented by the movement, or in many instances, what is merely designated as a misguided and aroused "public opinion," is but vaguely described and placed in the indeterminate future, and is usually presented as an alternative to government indecision and inaction; and none of the proposals opposes a constitutional form of government, and the point usually raised is not whether the government is going to adopt this form of government, but what type of constitutional system the government should adopt. Ōkuma

Shigenobu, for example, describing the movement during its apogee writes:

After the Satsuma Rebellion, there was formed, amidst a great deal of enthusiasm and excitement, what was known as the Gikai [sic] kisei dōmei kai. This was a rather enlightened movement. Hence there was no danger involved, as was the case with the movement by the proponents of "oust the barbarians" (jō-i), and there was no threat to life. However, the movement gave extreme pain to those in the government. The tranquillity of the authorities was disturbed. This Dōmei kai which sought to reform the government was quite vigorous.[63]

There is also the oft-quoted letter, used to buttress the thesis of government alarm over the movement, in which Yamagata says that those in the movement "hoped to overthrow the government at the opportune moment," and that with each delay, "the evil poison will spread more and more over the provinces, penetrate into the minds of the young, and inevitably produce unfathomable evils."[64] It should be noted, however, that in the same letter Yamagata says that those in the movement were limiting themselves to "slanderous and irresponsible utterances" and that there was no evidence that they would mount any attacks against the prefectural authorities or resort to arms. Yamagata then says that to treat the problem lightly would only invite further verbal attacks against the government, and that there might be the possibility that the government would be overthrown. Yamagata, it should further be noted, like all leading figures in the Meiji government, did not doubt the eventual creation of a national assembly. He wrote to Suematsu Kenchō on May 17, 1880, "It does not take an intelligent person to perceive that someday, eventually, there will have to be a national assembly."[65]

Writings of Sasaki Takayuki,[66] a person close to the court, also reveal the three traits mentioned above. In his widely cited petition of September 9, 1881, in which he complains about the government's action involving the properties of the Hokkaido Colonization Commission, Sasaki writes:

I recognize that in the future you [Prime Minister Sanjō] will establish a national assembly. However, I believe that if they [the advocates of parliamentarism] at this time use this mistake of the government [in approving the sale of Hokkaido Colonization Commission properties] as a pretext to underscore their demands for establishing a popular-rights-oriented national assembly... to excite the national temper, and to cause turmoil, and if we are compelled to give in to their demands, violent and perfidious men will have their way.

And if perhaps we repeat the experience of the French Revolution, our bitterest regrets will be in vain.[67]

Earlier, on March 4, 1881, Sasaki saw Itō to ask whether he favored a constitution enacted with popular participation or one which was an "imperial gift." Itō, of course, answered that he favored an imperially granted constitution. Sasaki, pleased, said: "If we speedily enact an imperially granted constitution we need not fear any attack. However, if we let things drift as at present, and do not decide on a national policy for a year or two, the argument for a popularly enacted constitution will gain strength, and we will probably not be able to do anything about it."[68] When Sasaki referred to those proposing a popularly enacted constitution, he was not limiting himself to those outside the government. He prefaced his remarks with the observation that while the popular parties were demanding a constitution written with the participation of the people, "there were those even in the Genrō-in, like Asano Chōkun, who support this view." Sasaki added an even more significant statement: "Among the junior secretaries are also advocates of the radical line."[69]

This, then, suggests one of the ways the movement for parliamentarism exerted influence on constitutional development in Meiji Japan. As stated previously, and at the risk of repeating material that will be fully covered in the next chapter, it may be said that following the Satsuma Rebellion, after the danger of revolts had waned, there evolved, within government ranks, the beginnings of a "great debate" over the timing and type of constitutional government. Two major groups emerged, one supporting a Prussian type of constitutional government and another urging the adoption of a system based on the English experience. The first group also supported the gradual introduction of the new system while the second group favored the almost immediate establishment of parliamentarism. A case will be made to show that the conservatives who favored the gradual introduction of the Prussian type of constitutional government in many cases were stressing the "dangers" of the movement to forestall the demands of those, also in the government, who were seeking to establish an English-modeled constitutional system. Furthermore, the proponents of the English school, by a sort of "guilt by association" process, were also lumped together with the advocates of extreme parliamentarism, and in certain instances were depicted as dangerous. Inoue Kowashi, for example, in a letter to Iwakura, probably only a few months after the Sasaki-Itō meeting, warned: "The Risshisha and others who last year petitioned the government have organized the Kokkai kisei kai in the metropolitan area. Fukuzawa is vigorously advocating a radical line. *Their parties are composed of three or four thousand members* and extend throughout the whole nation, and already have even extended into Kagoshima . . . If we let this pass we will see incalculable disturbances.''[70]

The proponents of the English school similarly touched on the potential dangers posed by the movement. Ono Azusa, a gifted bureaucrat and one of the most consistent and vociferous spokesman of this school, on February 2, 1878, wrote: "Since the introduction of the issue of a popularly elected assembly, the fever for self-government has gradually heightened, and the requests by the people for the right to participate in the government have daily become louder. It is practically impossible to determine where this will stop. *I believe that at this time, the government's only recourse is to conform to the national trend and to settle the problem on this basis.* This was, in all likelihood, the reason why the Rescript of April 14, 1875, was handed down." And Ono went on to complain that in spite of the rescript there were those in and out of the government who insisted that the government should not immediately establish a popular assembly and who advocated gradualism.[71]

To place Ono's concern over the movement in perspective, a revealing glimpse of the movement by Fukuzawa Yukichi himself can be cited.[72] Fukuzawa writes about a certain student from the provinces who came to Tokyo at the time when the movement was at its height. This student called on a certain teacher to discuss national affairs and on taking leave said that he was going to call on prince so-and-so and the state minister so-and-so to argue the issue of a national assembly. The teacher tried to discourage him on the ground that a person from the provinces without an introduction or a letter of recommendation could hardly expect to get past the guards, and advised the student to go straight home. The student laughed and said that he realized only too well that he could not get to see the prince or the state minister, but that he only intended to see the receptionists and to talk to them. The student also said that if he was stopped by the guards he hoped to make enough of a scene so that if by chance the incident got in the newspapers this would be a good "present" for those at home. The teacher, Fukuzawa says, was speechless with exasperation. Fukuzawa then concludes: "This may merely be a curious anecdote, but if one desires further proof that the political views expounded at that time were cynically motivated, there are many incidents that can be cited to bear this out."[73]

If Fukuzawa's description is correct and if the assumptions made about the movement, especially as it was constituted around the years 1878–1879, are sound, a partial explanation of Ono's expression of concern is that he, like his more conservative colleagues in the government, was using the movement to justify the speedy adoption of his views on constitutionalism.

The movement made itself felt in the government in still another manner. The birth and continued existence of the movement *confirmed* what the top bureaucrats had already been aware of through their "feel" of history. This was that constitutionalism was the "wave of the future," a wave that was sweeping inexorably from the West; that arbitrary government inevitably gave rise to bloody revolution and a republican form of government; and that these repugnant developments could be forestalled by the judicious establishment of a constitutional system.

It is probably safe to state that the Japanese have as keen a sense of history and appreciation of the lessons it teaches as do any comparable group of people in the world. The oligarchs in their early lifetime were less than a half century removed from the French Revolution. The revolutions that swept through Europe in 1830 and 1848 occurred in their lifetime or within the lifetime of those only one generation before them. When Ōkubo, therefore, in presenting his views on constitutional government, asserted that "lessons may be learned from Cromwell in England and the revolution of eighteenth-century France,"[74] he was saying so with what must have been for him a deep and real appreciation of the dangers of suppressive government. When Kido, too, touched on a similar theme in his petition, he cited with obvious feeling the example of a once free and independent Poland devastated by revolution and anarchy and carved by powerful neighbors.[75] And the words that sent a "thrill" through him were spoken by a scholar in France who told him: "Not only are the French deprived of more than half their legal rights given by his [sic] government, but many of them are eager wrongfully to seize privileges never granted them. This has been the sure cause of the frequent revolutions which have kept our country in a state of weakness."[76]

What the appearance of the movement for parliamentarism did was to impart a sense of reality and some urgency to these allusions to mobs and barricades. It served as a constant reminder to those in the government of the convulsions in Europe and thus helped to keep the oligarchs from wavering from their original decisions to establish a constitutional system. These reminders can be seen in Sasaki's petition cited earlier as well as in an Ono memorandum of later 1879.

Those who are zealous about popular rights are more and more becoming excited and extreme... I feel that if the present trend continues, after a few years the government will become all the more arbitrary and the people more than ever fervent in their demands for liberty. At the height of the friction, in the end, mobs will rise and the virulence of the [revolution] in Paris will make its appearance in Japan. We would then experience not only the needles folly of officials being slaughtered, but, what is more horrible to contemplate, the imperial house would be endangered.[77]

For all these expressions of concern, however, the leaders in the government did not have any real doubts about their control over the overall march toward constitutional government. Each step, each move, was made more in response to the needs and objectives of the oligarchs than as a reaction to the demands of the advocates of parliamentarism outside the government. Itō leaves the clearest exposition on the thinking of the oligarchs on all this.

The present political disturbance is symptomatic of a general trend sweeping the whole world and is not limited to a single nation or province. About a hundred years ago the revolutions in Europe started in France and spread gradually to other European nations. The momentum of these revolutions gained strength and has come to constitute a tremendous force. Sooner or later practically all nations... will feel the impact of this force and change their form of government. The change from old to new was accompanied by violent disturbances. The disturbances have lasted to this very day. An enlightened ruler and his wise ministers would control and divert the force toward a solidifying of the government. To achieve this, all despotic conduct must be abandoned, and there can be no avoiding a sharing of the government's power with the people... When we look at the roots of these ideas we see that they are all nurtured by the general trends of the times sweeping the whole world, and they spring forth just as the grass grows when fed by the rain... The method to be adopted by the government today is to follow the trends of the time to take advantage of opportunities when they appear. So, even as we control the trends, there will be no violence, and even when ideas are given free rein they will not lead [people] astray. Progress will be orderly and we will set the pace of progress, and the passage of time will bring about the normalization of the trends... Your Majesty has earlier graciously granted a rescript stating that constitutional government will be gradually adopted. The complete achievement of constitutional government must await the passage of some time. In the meanwhile, everything will be under control.[78]

One measure of the confidence with which the oligarchs faced the movement is the concrete acts it took against it. The government's activities were essentially limited to the passage of restrictive press and assembly laws against the movement.[79] The hand of the government, however, was lightly applied, as Osatake indicates. He says: "Despite the facts that the opposition was almost unanimous in upholding the thesis that sovereignty did not reside in the emperor and that there was strict control over speech, we must fully take into consideration that it was possible to debate [the subject] freely. This is deeply stirring."[80] If the government's treatment of the movement was, all things considered, humane and not severe, this is in part a reflection of the weakness of the movement, which obviated the need for sterner measures. It also reflects the fact that, in the main, the Meiji government itself was committed to the same goals as the opposition. The leaders in the government were concerned first not with the advocates of parliamentarism among the outs; they wanted to devise means to control these men who would some day take part in the government.[81] This is the lesson of the purge of Ōkuma Shigenobu, or the Crisis of 1881.

III

ITŌ AND ŌKUMA: THE CRISIS OF 1881

By the end of the 1870's the Meiji leadership group was still burdened
by fiscal problems and haunted by the existence of unequal treaties. The
dangers of anarchy and counterrevolution, however, lay behind them.
The consolidation of the accomplishments of the first decade, the
strengthening of Japan so that it would not suffer the "fate" of China,
and the acceptance of Japan as a member of the civilized community of
states on an equal basis—these were the challenges that the oligarchs
faced at this point of history.[1] These goals, of course, were legacies from
the first Meiji decade and the original Meiji leadership group. Still, there
were significant and noticeable shifts in emphasis in the specific programs
through which these general aims were to be accomplished. For example,
the oligarchs could now afford the luxury of thinking about taking the
last great strides toward the establishment of a constitutional form of
government. These shifts in priorities grew out of changes in the situa-
tions that the oligarchs confronted. However, by a historical coincidence,
the shifts can also be exemplified by the changes in the personalities composing the highest brackets of the Meiji leadership group, and by the
manner in which the original leaders departed from the scene. Ōkubo
Toshimichi, the most powerful figure in the government, was assassinated by disaffected ex-samurai. Kido Takayoshi, the sensitive and

highly-strung idealist from Chōshū, probably died as much from frustration and bitterness as from illness—over the ineffectuality of his protests against the reforms of the government, which he felt were criminally unjust to the ex-samurai. In the place of these men appeared men like Itō Hirobumi and Ōkuma Shigenobu.

Itō and Ōkuma were second-generation leaders who had experienced the daily administrative routine required in running a government—in a word, they were bureaucrats before they assumed their positions of leadership in the Meiji government. And they were, as one contemporary source states, "able and active officers."[2] One can also see in Itō and Ōkuma (perhaps more in the former than in the latter) highly skilled practitioners of the art of the possible.[3] Neither could boast of truly outstanding contributions to the Restoration,[4] and Ōkuma was burdened by the added handicap of coming from Hizen.[5] So both had to rely on their wits to compensate for their lack of prestige. These two, then, were the major protagonists in the Crisis of 1881, and the fact that they were bureaucrat-politicians had some influence in shaping the nature and outcome of the crisis.[6]

Ōkuma and his supporters were ousted from the government. From that moment, Satsuma-Chōshū domination of the Meiji government was firmly established and *hambatsu seifu* (clan government) became a pejorative phrase in the Japanese language. Where Saigō, Etō, Itagaki, Gotō, and Kido resigned from the government and many of their followers voluntarily went with them, Ōkuma and his clique had the dubious distinction of being victims of the first and only major government purge in the Meiji era. This was one result of the crisis.

The issues of the date for establishing a national assembly and the type of constitution to be enacted were decisively settled in favor of Itō. This was the other result of the crisis.

Though Ōkuma later said that only the emperor stood between himself and the executioner,[7] and his opponents in the government made rather overelaborate preparations to counter possible attacks by Ōkuma partisans,[8] the purge was singularly free from bloodshed. This was one distinctive feature of the crisis.

The issues were raised by and fought among bureaucrats, with the nongovernment advocates of parliamentarism and their activities playing at best a secondary role in the final resolution of the questions. This was the other significant characteristic of the crisis.

Iwakura Tomomi unwittingly set the stage for the purge of his good friend Ōkuma. It will be recalled that in December 1879 Iwakura expressed dissatisfaction with the draft constitution produced by the Genrō-in. At that time, he also proposed to Sanjō and Arisugawa that the councilors be asked to submit their ideas on the constitutional question to Arisugawa. This proposal was given imperial sanction.[9] In December 1879 Yamagata Aritomo submitted his memorandum. He was followed by Kuroda Kiyotaka on February 12, 1880, Yamada Akiyoshi in June 1880, Inoue Kaoru in July 1880, Itō on December 14, 1880, Ōkuma in March 1881, and Ōki Takatō in May 1881.[10]

There is some confusion about the next major development following Itō's submission of his draft memorial. The story, according to Itō's biography, is that in January 1881 the state ministers Sanjō, Arisugawa, and Iwakura met and decided to call an imperial conference to discuss the proposals submitted by the councilors. However, Councilor Kawamura Sumiyoshi (Jungi) just about this time had happened to suggest that it would be wiser to coordinate and collate all the views and to bring about a general area of agreement before bringing up the matter in an imperial conference.[11] This suggestion was adopted and the senior councilor, Ōkuma, was entrusted with the task of coordinating the suggestions. Accordingly, Ōkuma, on January 12, 1881, went to see Itō and Kuroda, who were at Atami, to discuss the matter.[12]

Biographies of Ōkuma, however, say that the talks at Atami were between Itō, Inoue, and Ōkuma. These three, proponents of "progressive ideas," are said to have felt that the establishment of a national assembly was inevitable and thus had decided to meet at Atami to discuss this and related issues. In January they met at the Fujiya Hotel and talked freely and frankly over cups of sake and Saga and Nagasaki dishes offered by Ōkuma.

The details of the talks are unknown. Even Yano Fumio, who accompanied Ōkuma, could only say that it could be surmised that the vital question of the day, that of establishing a national assembly, was discussed.[13] One thing seems certain. Itō, at this time, showed Ōkuma the views of himself and the other councilors on the constitutional question.[14]

The events after the Atami talks are somewhat clearer. Sometime during the first three months of 1881 Arisugawa asked Ōkuma why he had not submitted his ideas on constitutionalism.[15] Ōkuma replied that he wanted to wait till the imperial conference to present his opinions orally.[16] Ōkuma justified his position by saying that he could not do merit to his views in writing. Moreover, he continued, there was a danger of leakage if his ideas were committed to writing. His protestations were not allowed, so in March he submitted his proposal.[17]

When Ōkuma submitted his proposal he asked that no one be allowed to see it before the emperor had read it. Arisugawa agreed.[18] However, when Arisugawa read Ōkuma's petition he was "shocked" at what he believed to be radical proposals. In sum, Ōkuma was calling for an election by the end of 1882 to fill the national assembly, which would be convoked during the early part of 1883. Moreover, those entrusted with the highest positions in the government would be leaders of the party controlling a majority in the national assembly. Arisugawa, in spite of his promise to Ōkuma, showed the draft to Sanjō and Iwakura.[19] The three then concluded that the position taken by Ōkuma made it impossible to harmonize the views of the councilors. Therefore, they decided to call off the projected imperial conference and to ask the councilors to submit their views individually to the emperor. Yamagata appeared before the throne on June 4, 1881. On June 22 Itō presented his ideas.[20]

In the meantime, during early or mid-June, Iwakura called on Ōkuma and told him that Arisugawa had shown his petition to both him and Sanjō. Iwakura added that no one else had seen it.[21] He then told Ōkuma that their views differed greatly and that he doubted that "the groundwork" could be completed by 1883, when Ōkuma hoped to see the establishment of the national assembly. Iwakura asked him how he justified his whole position. Ōkuma replied:

The situation has already developed to a point where temporizing measures will not suffice to placate the people's sentiments. When a group of people desire something, satisfying their desire piecemeal only serves to whet their appetites and they eventually become uncontrollable. The wiser method is to anticipate their demands and to satisfy them fully... My motive for suggesting 1883 as the date for establishing the national assembly stems from the above conviction, and [my petition] is presented with the aim of taking the initiative away from the opposition.[22]

Iwakura finally asked Ōkuma if there were any differences between his proposal and Itō's. Ōkuma replied, "there are no appreciable differences."[23] A few days later Iwakura suggested to Sanjō that Itō be shown Ōkuma's petition. On June 27 Sanjō "borrowed" Ōkuma's petition from the emperor and showed it to Itō.[24] Itō read it and then copied it.[25]

The question now arises: why did such a long time elapse between the submission of Ōkuma's memorandum and Itō's copying of it?[26] Two reasons may be given.[27] The first is that the state ministers were deeply concerned about the possibility of a split between the two most powerful councilors, Itō and Ōkuma, if the latter's views became known to Itō.

Itō, as we have seen, said that the state ministers were very reluctant to show Ōkuma's memorandum to him. Iwakura's visit to Ōkuma in early or mid-June, and Itō's letter to Iwakura on May 29, can in part also be interpreted as indicating the state ministers' awareness of the explosiveness of Ōkuma's views. Hence, it was not strange that the state ministers delayed as long as possible the confrontation between Ōkuma and Itō or sought ways to avoid it.

The second reason is that Itō, on his part, was not concerned with Ōkuma's views. He had been working closely with Ōkuma and Inoue Kaoru on the constitutional question and was convinced, as we shall see, that Ōkuma's ideas did not radically differ from his. Itō's efforts before June were primarily directed toward two other tasks. The first was the attempt to bring Kuroda and other highly "conservative" councilors into line.[28] The other was even more difficult. This was to counter the ideological "threat" posed by men like Ōki Takatō and Motoda Eifu, who heavily stressed the "national polity" and "personal or direct rule" by the emperor. Their views disturbed Itō to the point where he directed Inoue Kowashi to prepare a "critique" of their ideas. It is believed that Inoue handed in his paper to Itō in June 1881. It should be recalled that Ōki's memorandum was submitted in May 1881.[29] Therefore, until June at least, Itō had his hands full trying to counter the "conservatives" in the government. We shall see that this was neither the first nor the last time that Itō had to spend time and effort fighting off harassment from this source.

Itō's attention, however, was dramatically shifted toward Ōkuma's direction when he read the latter's memorandum. Itō's reaction was the one the state ministers had expected: he was angry. He told Sanjō that when he had shown his memorial to Ōkuma, Ōkuma had said that his views were the same. Itō declared that he was therefore completely in the dark as to Ōkuma's intentions in submitting his memorandum.[30] Itō followed this outburst with a letter to Iwakura.

I have read Ōkuma's memorial thoroughly. It is an unexpectedly radical proposal. One as dull as I am will not be able to go along with my colleague. Moreover, we differ greatly in our appraisal of the present and future state of affairs. From a reading of history, and considering the evolutions and changes in Europe, I do not believe that we can easily attain the goals he has outlined in his memorial. Since Ōkuma's views and mine are absolutely irreconcilable on most essential points...I have no other recourse but to resign from my posts.[31]

When Iwakura received this letter he asked Itō to see him. At their meeting, on July 3, Iwakura tried to placate the angry Itō by saying that although he also disagreed with Ōkuma's views, he saw no reason for Itō's resigning over the memorandum. Iwakura failed to convince him, and on the ground of illness, he stopped attending to his official duties.[32]

Iwakura, continuing his mediative efforts, told Ōkuma on July 4 to see Itō.[33] Ōkuma assented, but still insisted that there was no great difference in their views. He called on Itō on the same day and explained his position. Itō remained suspicious and angry. He reminded Ōkuma that when Ōkubo died they had both promised to resolve together the problems facing the nation. He asserted that it was really difficult to understand why Ōkuma, on such a vital matter as the establishment of the national assembly, had not even hinted at what his approach in the petition was going to be. To this Ōkuma replied that he had had no other motive than a desire to keep his views secret until the emperor had a chance to read his memorial. On this day the two did not delve into the contents of the memorial, and after agreeing to meet again the next day Ōkuma took his leave.[34]

When they met again the following day, Ōkuma was greeted with this outburst from Itō:

Your memorial calls for selecting the heads of ministries and imperial household officials from political parties. In the final analysis this is equivalent to transferring the imperial prerogatives to the people. Such heretical views should not be held by any subject. I too, in conformity with the Imperial Rescript of 1875, some day hope to see the establishment of a national assembly. However, I desire first to place the imperial prerogatives on a firm, unshakeable foundation. Since you have your own ideas about this, however, you may assume the burden of carrying out state affairs from this day.[35]

Ōkuma replied that he did not aspire to run the government by himself and that Itō should calm himself. In spite of his pleas for self-control, Itō continued, "With your fourteen years of experience in the government, did you think for a moment that, with only the approval of the minister of the Left you would be able to settle such a grave matter of state? . . . What on earth drove you to take such a unilateral step?"[36] Ōkuma's answer was that his only motive was fear of brewing an argument before an imperial decision was made. Itō remained unconvinced and angry.[37] On July 8 Arisugawa called on Itō, and Itō on this day finally decided to return to his official duties.[38]

However, before Itō consented to return to his duties, he had moved swiftly and resolutely to have gradualism and his ideas on the constitution accepted by the three state ministers, Iwakura, Sanjō, and Arisugawa. This noteworthy development can be traced by following the words and actions of Inoue Kowashi, one of the lesser known but indubitably one of the most influential figures in the Meiji period.

Inoue Kowashi, according to Ōkubo Toshiaki, just prior to June 19, 1881, seems to have submitted to Iwakura, for the first time, his views on the constitutional issues. Ōkubo believes that Iwakura was not informed on this subject so, when Inoue stepped in with his ideas, Iwakura in effect made him his adviser on constitutional problems.[39] On June 21 Iwakura called on Inoue and told him to submit concrete plans for the drafting of a constitution. Inoue complied by submitting the next day a memorandum he had already prepared.[40] This relationship between Iwakura and Inoue is drawn by Ōkubo to show that from about mid-June 1881 serious and conclusive discussion on the enactment of a constitution had begun. Ōkubo makes the point that Iwakura and Inoue first got together and that Itō was brought in later.[41] Ōkubo's reasoning is that Itō was "nothing more than a councilor." Above the councilors, Ōkubo continues, stood the *sandaijin* (three ministers of state) and "these men held the greatest power." On constitutional problems, the *sandaijin's* and in particular Iwakura's, influence and power were widespread, and Itō could best be described, according to Ōkubo, as one who merely stood ready to answer questions asked him by Iwakura. And when Ōkuma submitted his radical proposals Iwakura was shocked into taking firm steps toward enacting a constitution. On June 28 Iwakura and the other two state ministers selected Itō to assume working responsibility for this purpose. By this act, asserts Ōkubo, Itō was "launched on his way to greatness."[42]

To continue Ōkubo's description of the developments at this time, on July 5 Iwakura wrote to Sanjō and Arisugawa, urging the "fixing of the fundamental principles of the constitutional system," and proposing three possible methods for drafting the constitution.[43] This letter was accompanied by the "Daikōryō" (General Principles), "Kōryō" (Principles), three "Iken" (Opinions), and several memoranda.[44] The "General Principles" and "Principles" provided the basic guidelines for the constitution. Ōkubo feels that they were in effect the first drafts of the Meiji constitution.[45] The two documents, for example, proposed that the constitution be imperially granted; that gradualism be the guiding principle in its enactment; that a strong monarchical system, with the retention of the traditional prerogatives of the throne, be written into the constitution; that the cabinet be made independent of the national assembly; that the franchise be limited; and that the previous year's budget become effective if the government and the elected body could not agree on the current budget.[46]

According to the above recitation, Iwakura was the principal guiding hand and the ultimately responsible figure in resolving the issue of gradualism versus "radicalism," and in clarifying and articulating the bedrock principles that were to be incorporated into the Meiji constitution. Furthermore, Itō is pictured as a Johnny-come-lately into the Iwakura-Inoue combination. A case may be made, however, to show that Itō, and not Iwakura, was the pivotal figure in the constitutional question, and that Itō was ultimately responsible for the triumph of gradualism and the writing of the basic constitutional principles.

The relationships between Itō and Iwakura (and the two other state ministers), and between Itō and Inoue Kowashi must first be clarified. It is undeniable that in rank Iwakura and the two state ministers stood above the councilors. They also had direct access to the emperor. In prestige they overshadowed the councilors, for they were from the nobility. Iwakura and Sanjō also had illustrious pre-Restoration records, and had served in the highest posts from the inception of the Meiji government. In other words, their rank and prestige were such that all major policy decisions had to have their official and public consent. However, their consent generally could not be withheld against the combined wishes of the councilors or against the strong desires of a few councilors.[47] Several examples may be cited to show that the councilors could either overrule the state ministers or compel them to comply with their decisions. On August 23, 1878, an artillery battalion of the Imperial Division mutinied in Tokyo.[48] The mutiny was put down by 4:00 a.m. on August 24. Earlier in the month, it had been planned that the emperor would tour the Hokuriku and Tōkai regions. Now, however, with the mutiny, and because "in the provinces the movement for parliamentary government was very active," Iwakura and most of the imperial attendants urged postponement of the tour. But Itō and Sanjō pushed for the tour on the grounds that the mutiny was only a passing incident and the movement for parliamentary government was not the least bit dangerous. The emperor "agreed" and the tour proceeded as scheduled on August 30.[49] In the incident closest at hand, Sasaki Takayuki recorded in his diary on October 11: "It appears that the councilors have combined and have applied pressure on the three state ministers on the ouster of Ōkuma. Because it would be troublesome if the state ministers do not act decisively, it seems that the councilors are wielding their authority as usual."[50] Therefore, while Idditti may have somewhat overstated his case, I believe that he is essentially correct when he asserts that: " . . . the influence of the two men [Sanjō and Iwakura] was rather passive than active. Their value lay in holding together the members of the cabinet, composing differences and maintaining peace at the council table."[51]

Inoue Kowashi's relationship to Itō is equally complex. There is no question that Inoue was highly talented, respected, and influential. Tokutomi, describing Inoue's role in the crisis says, "It is rare to find a comparable case where the efforts of one individual have so influenced a nation's political ideology."[52] Moreover, the power exercised by the subordinate bureaucrats was, and is still, widespread and great. Ozaki Yukio tells us that at this time, "It was bruited about that the ministers-councilors were figureheads. Although they talked importantly, they were really not great. The secretaries below them were important and were arbitrarily manipulating the ministers-councilors as puppets."[53]

For all the above, it would still be hazardous to overstress Inoue's influence. The arguments for Inoue's preponderant role in the crisis are essentially two. One, in the aftermath of the presentation of Ōkuma's memorandum Iwakura first approached Inoue and only later brought Itō into his confidence. The implication is that the Iwakura-Inoue duo was ultimately responsible for the crucial decisions on constitutionalism, that only because Iwakura placed his hand on Itō's shoulder was Itō able to join the twosome. Furthermore, it is postulated that the "close" relationship between Itō and Inoue began from about June or July 1881.[54] The foregoing is based on the further premise that Iwakura was the most powerful single person in the government. Two, the documentary evidence reveals that the fundamental ideas that were ultimately incorporated into the Meiji constitution were penned by Inoue. Moreover, many of the moves made by both Iwakura and Itō were suggested by Inoue, such as the urging of Itō to assume responsibility for drafting the constitution and for rescinding the decision to sell the properties of the Hokkaido Colonization Commission. Inoue is also revealed in the documents as a key figure in solidifying the support of other councilors around Itō.

I have accepted, for general purposes, Idditti's judgment on the role of Iwakura and the other state ministers in the government. It can also be shown that Inoue was working "closely" with Itō long before June 1881 on constitutional and related problems, and that consequently he did not need a summons from Iwakura to be "launched on his way to greatness." It has already been pointed out that Itō had asked Inoue Kowashi to draft the April 14, 1875, rescript, considered by the Meiji leadership group as a major landmark in Japan's march toward the establishment of constitutional government.[55] Itō also had Inoue draft the December 1880 memorandum, another key document in the constitutional history of the Meiji era.[56] We have already pointed to the drafting of a "critique" by Inoue of the views of Motoda and Ōki, at Itō's behest. This was in 1881. Earlier, in 1879, Inoue had drafted for Itō a long memorial on education which in turn was rebutted by Motoda.[57] It is plain, therefore, that Inoue was serving Itō in a valued way before June 1881. It must be further added that Itō was "launched on his way to greatness" not by Iwakura, but by Ōkubo Toshimichi, and that Itō in turn owed his rise to native ability, hard work, political talent and sagacity, a liberal helping of luck, and his birth in Chōshū.

If we accept at face value the documentary evidence of the period June–October 1881, Inoue emerges as a manipulator of men and events. A gifted subordinate like Inoue was an extremely rare and precious asset, and Itō's reliance on him made him highly influential. But this is not the same thing as having the ultimate power of decision-making. This Itō possessed by virtue of his position as one of the most powerful men in the Sat-Chō clique.[58] Itō, by temperament—and perhaps this is another measure of his political ability—was willing to trust his subordinates and to give them a great deal of autonomy. This may in turn give the impression that Itō was easily moved by his subordinates. However, Itō was also known as a proud, vainglorious man who certainly would not have tolerated any of his secretaries going beyond a certain point, and this fact too was apparently recognized by Inoue Kowashi.[59]

There is one further point to consider. That Inoue urged Itō to become the drafter of the constitution and that he helped to rally support for Itō is understandable, I think, in terms of Japanese-Confucian patterns of political behavior. It is hard to conceive of Itō writing to anyone and saying: "I will draft the constitution." The documents were written, in part, for a purpose: to show that Itō, in his public words and deeds, was acting in a manner expected of a proper and humble servant of the emperor who knew his place. Analogies are tricky to handle but one can say that Inoue and Itō were displaying, in part, what I would designate as the Wang Mang syndrome.[60] On the other hand, hints of words and behavior contrary to political mores are often found in the unguarded expressions or unsympathetic reports of the opposition—for it is humanly impossible to be constantly and consistently maintaining proper postures. During the crisis itself several such instances may be cited. The first is the conversation with Itō recorded by Sasaki on October 4. In this exchange

Itō revealed that he too had direct access to the emperor and that he was not above threatening the state ministers in order to get his way. Another is Itō's petulant outburst prior to Ōkuma's ouster and reported by an Ōkuma sympathizer: "I am going to establish the assembly. Why should I yield to another the position of leadership?"[61] Still another is the statement by Sasaki, mentioned earlier, of the pressures exerted by the councilors on the state ministers on October 11.

A recasting of the narrative, this time accepting the premise that Itō was *de facto* superior to Iwakura, would read as follows: when Itō discovered that Ōkuma had submitted his memorandum calling for the immediate establishment of an English-model constitutional system, he reacted quickly and violently. Ōkuma, by setting definite dates, forced Itō to think about the problem of enacting a constitution in more concrete terms than he had proposed in his own petition. Itō therefore had Inoue, one of the very few in the government espousing the Prussian constitutional system, submit definite ideas to Iwakura on the methods of enacting a constitution. Itō Miyoji later recalled: "[Itō] showed his [Ōkuma's] *Shigi kempō* (privately drafted constitution) to Inoue Kowashi and me. We were ordered to draft a detailed refutation. Inoue and I therefore discussed the problem and drafted the rebuttal."[62]

Iwakura's activities in the short period between his own awareness of the nature of Ōkuma's memorandum and Itō's realization of it can be described as temporizing, holding actions. He was fully aware that Itō would have to be informed, could easily guess at his probable reaction, and was mightily disturbed by the prospect. His words and actions after Itō discovered the contents of Ōkuma's memorandum were aimed at restoring harmony and peace in the shattered councilor ranks. When he realized that he could not succeed, he tried to remain away from the scene of impending battle. Ono Azusa, writing sometime in September or October 1881 says as much: "In the cabinet Sanjō already does not have the ability to refute their [the councilors'] demands and intends to resign. Iwakura is dodging [the issue] and is not taking part in the affair. Rather, he inclines toward taking advantage of this opportunity to form a political party."[63]

The immediate agreement by Iwakura, Sanjō, and Arisugawa, then, to a definite method of enacting the constitution and to the basic principles of the constitution was the price Itō exacted for his return to his posts in the government. It is not a coincidence that Iwakura sent his letter embodying these principles on July 5, and that Itō consented to resume his duties on July 8. The full significance of this fateful development became clear when in little over a month the storm over the sale of the properties of the Hokkaido Colonization Commission broke.[64]

The Hokkaido Colonization Commission was established in 1869, when it was budgeted a sum of about 400,000 yen to expend yearly. The primary purpose for the development of Hokkaido was strategic. The Japanese feared Russian encroachment.[65] In 1870 Kuroda Kiyotaka petitioned for the expansion of the colonization project in Hokkaido. His petition was accepted. It was decided that from 1872, with a ten-year limit, a sum of 1,000,000 yen would be allotted yearly for this purpose. In 1880, with the ten-year limit approaching, the question of abolishing or continuing the commission was debated in the government. Kuroda strongly opposed abolition. However, Kuroda finally consented to abolition, after his fellow clansman Matsukata Masayoshi supported Ito's plea for discontinuing government support for the commission.[66]

On July 21, 1881, Kuroda submitted a petition to Sanjō, on behalf of four secretaries of the commission. This request was accompanied by a memorandum by Kuroda explaining the aims of the group. The group proposed to purchase for 387,082 yen government properties on which the government had expended over 14,096,800 yen. This sum was to be payable over a period of thirty years without interest.[67] The petition was discussed at a cabinet meeting on July 28. Minister of the Left Arisugawa, Councilor Ōkuma, Minister of Finance Sano Tsunetami, and several others voiced disapproval. Kuroda threatened to resign and was reported to have later underlined his demand for approval by flinging a candlestick at Sanjō. In any case, imperial consent was obtained on July 30, the day the emperor left on a tour of northern Japan.[68]

The first public voice raised against the proposed sale was in the form of an editorial in the Tokyo-Yokohama *Mainichi,* dated July 26. This was followed by two more editorials in the same newspaper,[69] and in others appearing in the Tokyo *Nichi nichi* on August 10 and 11.[70] Rallies were also held to protest the proposed sale. The most famous one was the one held on August 25 at the Shin tomi za in Tokyo. This was attended by all the leading opponents of the proposed sale, including Fukuchi Gen'ichirō, editor of the Tokyo *Nichi nichi,* and Numa Morikazu, editor of the Tokyo-Yokohama *Mainichi.*[71]

Elements within the government also protested. Sasaki Takayuki, vice-president of the Genrō-in, as well as other members of that organ, submitted memoranda protesting the sale.[72] Four generals, Torio Koyata, Miura Gorō, Tani Kanjō, and Soga Sukenori, jointly submitted a petition expressing opposition. The generals did not seem overly concerned with the sale itself. Rather, they were accusing the cabinet of practicing arbitrary, oligarchic rule in the name of the emperor.[73]

In the meantime, Ōkuma became the target of rumors that he was utilizing the uproar with the aim of overthrowing the Sat-Chō group in the government. He was being abetted, the rumors charged, by Fukuzawa Yukichi and the Keiō gijuku or Mita faction on the one hand, and by Iwasaki Yatarō and his Mitsubishi money on the other.[74]

The August 29 entry of Sasaki Takayuki's diary reveals that Itō "believed" the rumors that Ōkuma had joined forces outside the government.[75] In fact, it appears that about this time most of the key personnel in the government "believed" the rumors. On September 6, 1881, Sanjō wrote to Iwakura.

After that, Itō, Inoue, Yamagata, Yamada, and Saigō [Tsugumichi] held confidential talks, and generally agreed with Inoue's views. They want to bring the matter to a head immediately after the return of the imperial tour and have resolved to exert their all to this end, and to resign if they fail. Consequently, there is no question but that there will be a great upheaval when the imperial tour returns to Tokyo. With the internal situation rapidly drawing to a climax, I cannot but be deeply concerned. Ōkuma, since his petition, has completely gone over to the Fukuzawa camp, and this has angered everyone. Thus there is hardly any likelihood that peace can be made with Ōkuma.[76]

It is obvious that the decision to oust Ōkuma had been made in Tokyo. Two problems remained. One was to get Iwakura's concurrence. The other was to persuade Kuroda to support the plan to abandon the proposed sale. To accomplish the first task, Councilor Yamada Akiyoshi was dispatched to Kyoto.[77] Yamada, in his meeting with Iwakura on September 18, repeated the rumors surrounding Ōkuma, and he made the point that it would be an error to believe that the differences in views between Itō and Ōkuma over Ōkuma's petition were healed. Yamada followed up with a discussion of the problem raised by the projected sale of the commission's properties and said:

The matter of the sale is of *minor importance. The basic issue is the enactment of a constitution and the setting of the date for establishing the national assembly.* We must settle these problems immediately after the return of the imperial tour. At that time, the question will be whether we will adopt Ōkuma's views or the ideas of the other cabinet members... If we are to take the latter course, we must resolutely dismiss Ōkuma from his posts and oust his followers. (italics mine)[78]

Iwakura in reply said that he had taken the lead in advocating the enactment of a constitution since the year before last and that he was willing to go along with setting the date for establishing the national assembly. However, he said, he could not assent to the dismissal of Ōkuma because he had been led to believe that Itō and Ōkuma had come to an understanding. Therefore he would withhold a decision until he spoke with Itō.[79]

To convince Kuroda, Matsukata, who was with the imperial party, met Kuroda in Sapporo.[80] Itō, and later Kuroda's compatriots, Saigō and Kabayama Sukenori, saw Kuroda and finally convinced him to go along with the majority.[81]

Meanwhile, Navy Minister Kawamura Sumiyoshi was delegated to "escort" the reluctant Iwakura back to Tokyo on a naval vessel.[82] This step was necessary, for the imperial tour was rapidly drawing to a close. Kawamura met Iwakura on October 1. Kawamura repeated many of Yamada's arguments, saying that the enactment of a constitution and the establishment of the national assembly were the most pressing matters at hand. He also gave assurances to Iwakura that Kuroda would eventually concede on the matter of calling off the proposed sale.[83]

Iwakura, though still unhappy, nevertheless left Kyoto on October 4 and arrived in Tokyo on October 6.[84] The next day Itō visited and showed Iwakura a draft of an imperial rescript calling for the establishment of the national assembly. He also went over Ōkuma's recent alleged activities and demanded that Iwakura support their plan to purge Ōkuma. Iwakura, after his talk with Itō, finally decided to go along with the plan to oust Ōkuma.[85]

The imperial entourage arrived at the Senjū Station on October 11. It was 3:30 in the afternoon when the party reached the Imperial Palace in the heart of Tokyo.[86] That night, State Ministers Sanjō, Arisugawa, and Iwakura, and Councilors Terajima Munenori, Yamagata, Itō, Kuroda, Saigō, Inoue, and Yamada met at the Imperial Palace.[87] One of the first items of business was the submission of a memorial signed by all seven of the councilors in attendance. It was an unequivocal statement on gradualism. The memorial began by recounting the steps taken by the Meiji government to lay the groundwork for constitutional government. It then condemned those who sought to establish the national assembly with precipitous haste, but added that a definite date for its establishment had to be set to convince the people that the government's policies were clear and fixed.[88] When imperial sanction was granted to this memorial, gradualism became the official guideline.

The problem of Ōkuma's ouster was taken up. Sasaki Takayuki leaves us a description of what occurred. The emperor is said to have questioned the lack of substantial grounds for ousting Ōkuma. It was probably Iwakura who replied to the effect that if the emperor did not have confidence in the leaders from Satsuma and Chōshū who were behind this move to purge Ōkuma, the cabinet would collapse. The emperor then asked about the sale. The answer was that if Ōkuma was dismissed, Kuroda would go along with the decision to suspend the sale. The emperor was puzzled. He said that that remark was difficult to understand, for the *problems were not related*. Iwakura was a little put out and replied that he had not phrased the matter precisely enough. What he meant, he said, was that Kuroda was willing to follow the imperial decision on the matter.[89]

Imperial sanction was granted, and Ōkuma's bureaucratic career was dealt a stunning blow. Ōkuma's own words poignantly summarize the completeness of his defeat. "The situation had changed so radically that I was reduced to being treated as a criminal. I, who had till only yesterday attended His Majesty and had accompanied the prince, was today firmly rejected by the guards and could not even be received in audience."[90] The same day, October 12, 1881,[91] an imperial rescript was handed down calling for the establishment of the national assembly in 1890.[92]

It may help to illuminate the activities and motivations of the major protagonists and the conflicts among them, if we first spotlight Ōkuma the man and his position in the government. Ōkuma Shigenobu was born on February 16, 1838, the eldest son of a retainer in the service of the daimyo of Hizen, Nabeshima Naomasa.[93] Although Ōkuma is not credited with any major contribution toward bringing about the Restoration, he had, by all accounts, a brilliant career in the government from the onset of the Meiji era.[94] By early February 1869, he was vice-minister of foreign affairs; in July of the same year he was appointed vice-minister of civil affairs, and in August vice-minister of finance. He held the latter two posts concurrently. Ōkuma was, by Western count, a youthful thirty-one at this time.[95] On September 2, 1870, he was promoted to the position of councilor. He resigned in June 1871 but was reappointed almost immediately in July 1871. He continued to serve in this capacity until his ouster in October 1881.[96] After the death of Ōkubo in May 1878, Ōkuma and Itō assumed the leading positions in the government. Itō succeeded Ōkubo as head of the Home Ministry, while Ōkuma became the "senior" councilor. Idditti, however, is probably correct in describing the period between Ōkubo's death and Ōkuma's ouster as a time when "Ōkuma's sun was in the zenith."[97]

Ōkuma could not have carved such a brilliant bureaucratic career had he not been an exceptionally talented and capable person. His biographers naturally depict an Ōkuma of rather heroic proportions.[98] There is, however, no doubt of his abilities. Miyake Setsurei, for example, has characterized Ōkuma as a man of uncommon intelligence.[99] *Nippon* considered him, along with Itō and Matsukata, "superior to the other *genkun* (elder statesmen)."[100] Among foreigners Ōkuma was probably the most highly regarded of the Japanese statesmen. One who interviewed him reported, "Throughout, I was impressed with the rare penetration, grasp, philosophic candor and statesmanlike sense of proportion of an unusually elevated and courageous thinker."[101] The measure of Ōkuma's abilities is this—he commanded the respect and admiration, even if not the affection, of his contemporaries, while spending most of his political life after 1881 in the opposition, which gave him little opportunity for concrete political achievements.[102]

Ōkuma, naturally, did not stand alone in the government. In the period under consideration, Sano Tsunetami succeeded him as head of the Finance Ministry.[103] And in the newly created Agriculture and Commerce Ministry was Ōkuma's good and trusted friend, Kōno Togama. Ono Azusa was a leading official in the Audit Bureau and wrote the regulations governing the bureau.[104] Yano Fumio headed the Statistics Bureau, and had as subordinates two young, promising officials, Ozaki Yukio and Inukai Tsuyoshi.[105] Ozaki leaves a description of Ōkuma's position at this time.

In the cabinet were a very small number of councilors. A single councilor supervised two or three ministries. Ōkuma supervised the Finance, Agriculture-Commerce and Justice ministries. And, although covertly, he also appeared to have been supervising the Foreign Ministry. Beyond the fact that he controlled four ministries, since he was the director of the newly established Statistics Bureau, which stood above all the ministries, this was the time when Ōkuma's influence was extremely powerful.[106]

Ōkuma, then, was at the height of his power and was like "an Arabian charger carrying all before him."[107] He could not only boast of rare ability, experience, power, and a growing coterie of friends and young talent placed in strategic positions, but he possessed the confidence of Iwakura and the support of Itō and Inoue. Why then did Ōkuma submit a proposal so out of line with the openly expressed views of Itō and by this action threaten the very core of his powerful position?

The reason accepted by Ōkuma apologists is that he did so in the belief that his views were substantially the same as those held by Itō.[108] Yano Fumio, for example, while admitting that his failure to consult with Itō was a *faux pas,* attributes this to Ōkuma's "simply believing that their views were the same."[109]

The aim of Ōkuma's biographers in stressing the "Atami Conference," at which time Ōkuma, Itō, and Inoue discussed the problems of constitutionalism, seems to be to indicate that the trio worked closely together.[110] Still another project involving the triumvirate is cited to substantiate this point. In the latter part of December 1880, just before the "Atami Conference," Fukuzawa Yukichi met Itō and Inoue at Ōkuma's house. There Inoue asked Fukuzawa to publish a newspaper. Fukuzawa did not commit himself. He and Inoue met again in the beginning of January 1881 at Inoue's home. Fukuzawa had gone there with the intention of declining the same request. At this point Inoue shocked Fukuzawa by stating that the three, Itō, Inoue, and Ōkuma, were determined to establish a national assembly. Inoue at this time also made a statement that did not differ from one of Ōkuma's basic premises. Inoue told Fukuzawa, "No matter what parties emerge, we are resolved to hand over the reins of the government fairly and openly to the majority party." Inoue also told Fukuzawa that Itō and Ōkuma were in agreement with the matter at hand. Fukuzawa then agreed to publish what was going to be essentially a government organ.[111]

Others, on the other hand, have ascribed to Ōkuma an unscrupulous motive for his step. They believe that Ōkuma's aim was to enhance his own position at the expense of his colleagues, by submitting a "superior" petition, and that his ultimate objective was to do away with Sat-Chō influence in the government through the effecting of his proposals.[112]

Actually, the motive or motives for what was in the final analysis a personally catastrophic step must remain shrouded in mystery for the present. Ōkubo Toshiaki concedes that he cannot fathom Ōkuma's intentions and calls his action "a riddle."[113] However, Ōkubo casts some doubt on the thesis that Ōkuma acted because he was under the impression that his ideas and Itō's were similar. Ōkubo says that Ōkuma was far too intelligent not to have been aware of the differences.[114]

With the outcry against the government's action on the properties of the Hokkaido Colonization Commission, Ōkuma was again accused of sinister and selfish designs. He was said, as we have noted, to be taking advantage of "public" dissatisfaction with the proposed sale in order to overthrow Sat-Chō influence in the government and to be aided and abetted by Fukuzawa and Iwasaki to attain this objective.

In spite of the unquestionably close relationship that existed between Ōkuma and the groups that formed the vanguard of the attack against the government, evidence suggests the following two propositions: (1) Ōkuma and most of his followers were not aiming at effecting a "palace revolution," and (2) the rumors, if not actually instigated by the highest authorities in the government, were encouraged and fanned by this small group to justify the purge of Ōkuma and his clique. Restated, Itō skillfully used the extraneous issue of the protests against the proposed sale to settle conclusively the questions of the timing and the character of constitutionalism.[115]

Accepting these premises will compel a reassessment of one of the most widely held beliefs in connection with the crisis. This is that the public protest against the government's proposed sale became interlaced with the popular movement for parliamentarism and that this double-barreled attack represented a pressure that the government could not ignore. There is some divergence among the interpreters of the Meiji political scene in the importance they attach to this development. However, there is general agreement that the government's promise in October 1881 to establish the national assembly was a direct result of the conflux of these two forces.[116]

To return to the first proposition, Ōkuma was with the imperial entourage throughout the disturbance.[117] Yano Fumio, one of the closest, if not the most intimate, of Ōkuma's supporters, was in Ōita when the issue of the sale of commission properties boiled over.[118] It is highly questionable that Yano would have left his post in Tokyo if he had known in advance of such a development. He also seemed genuinely dismayed when he first heard that the younger members of the Keiō gijuku were leading the assault against the government.[119] It is, of course, possible that elaborate plans could have been made before the departure of Ōkuma and Yano from Tokyo. The words and activities of Ōkuma's active supporters, and of those who can reasonably be designated as Ōkuma sympathizers, however, show too great a confusion, too much a working at cross purposes to indicate the existence of a well thought out, elaborate plan.[120] Such a plan would have been a *sine qua non* for the execution of what Ōkuma was accused of attempting—the downfall of the Sat-Chō clique. And Ōkuma was much too intelligent, even granting his impetuosity, not to have recognized this fact.[121] Yano Fumio sums up the case with what appears to be considerable logic. He recalls:

Basically we had no reason even to consider the overthrow of Sat-Chō influence in the government. We were as much a part of the government as they were. It was already no secret that a majority of the cabinet was in favor of constitutional government. Why should we then go to the trouble of combining with the "outs" and in this way undermine our own position in the government? I was fully convinced that rather than going with the "outs," it would be more advantageous and simpler to achieve the goal of constitutional government by sticking with the government and going along with it.[122]

Watanabe Ikujirō, the dean among authorities on Ōkuma, is therefore justified in dismissing as plain nonsense the charge that Ōkuma and his active supporters were plotting to overthrow the Sat-Chō faction.[123]

An even better case may be made for the second proposition. The immediately striking aspect surrounding the rumors is that they did not make their appearance until late August 1881 at the earliest. None of the letters addressed to Ōkuma, quoted in *Ōkuma monjo* and dated in July and August, makes any mention of the rumors.[124] The first letter containing a reference to the rumors is from Gō Junzō, a senior secretary in the Finance Ministry, who dismissed them as laughable.[125] The letter is dated September 11. In contrast, the first reference to Ōkuma's complicity in a plot appears in a letter from Kuroda to Terajima Munenori dated August 21.[126] Sasaki Takayuki records that Itō repeated the rumors to him on August 29.[127] The diary of Kabayama Sukenori, a Satsuma man and at that time superintendent of the Metropolitan Police, also reveals the same time pattern. There is no reference in his diary for the month of August to the protest against the proposed sale. In fact, on August 21 he left Tokyo for the Atami hot springs area for a vacation. He was recalled to Tokyo on August 30, and from September 1 the issue of the proposed sale becomes the main topic in his diary.[128]

That the rumors apparently first circulated among anti-Ōkuma forces in the government takes on added significance when seen against two prior developments. The first is that by August 2, 1881, key members of the ruling group, including Itō, Inoue, Matsukata, Kuroda, and Saigō, were agreed that the Meiji government was going to enact an imperially sanctioned constitution based on the Prussian model.[129] The second is that the first editorial against the proposed sale appeared in the pro-Ōkuma Tokyo-Yokohama *Mainichi* on July 26, and by mid-August even the normally pro-government *Nichi nichi* was commenting on the same subject. Add to this the fact that Ōkuma was absent from the capital and the soil was fertile for planting and nourishing anti-Ōkuma rumors.

Fukuzawa's writings also lend support to the thesis of the "inner circle origins" of the rumors. Almost immediately after Ōkuma's ouster Fukuzawa wrote a bitingly critical paper entitled "Meiji shinki kiji"

(Account of 1881). In this Fukuzawa postulated two possible origins of the rumors: either Inoue and Itō were the instigators of the rumors, or Inoue and Itō took advantage of the anger and doubt of the Satsuma clique *vis-à-vis* Fukuzawa, which were prompted by the attack against the sale by Fukuzawa disciples and the writing of the "Shigi kempō" by members of the Kōjunsha.[130] In other words, Itō and Inoue fanned these already existing feelings of anger and suspicion. In this case, Fukuzawa said, they had merely skillfully combined with the Satsuma clique. He concluded, "Only time will tell which is the truth."[131]

The enormity of Ōkuma's blunder in introducing his highly impractical memorial now becomes apparent. For Itō, who had acted as a buffer between Ōkuma and his enemies in the government, particularly the Satsuma faction, had turned against him and was actively directing the campaign to purge Ōkuma. Itō, as we have seen, reacted with bitterness and anger over Ōkuma's memorial. There is the possibility that Itō and Ōkuma being after all politicians, these reactions were expressed by Itō to disguise or justify power moves against his most serious rival for the top position in the Meiji government.[132] Itō, being both vain and conscious of his role in history, must also have been stung by what he regarded as an unprincipled attempt by Ōkuma to do him one better. The records further indicate that Itō's anger was occasioned by a real disagreement over the constitutional problem. It is this aspect of the crisis that interests us most. Itō found two faults with Ōkuma's proposal.

The first was with Ōkuma's suggestion that the national assembly be immediately established. It is true that Itō, Ōkuma, and Inoue Kaoru shared the belief that a national assembly was inevitable. However, there is no evidence that the trio had agreed on the matter of timing. According to Fukuzawa, when he met Ōkuma in February 1881 he asked Ōkuma when the national assembly would be established. Ōkuma replied that the date would probably be decided in the fall of that year. When Inoue was asked the same question by Fukuzawa the answer was three years, but this was merely another way of saying that preparations would prove difficult. Itō was also asked. Itō did not mention a date and talked about reforming the Genrō-in and the problem of the ex-samurai.[133] To Itō, timing was a most vital factor. In his angry letter of July 2, 1881, he had explicitly stressed this point to Iwakura when he declared, "I do not believe that we can easily attain the goals he [Ōkuma] has outlined in his memorial."[134] To Itō, Ōkuma's sin was this: Ōkuma knew that the Meiji leadership group had committed itself to the eventual sharing of power and responsibility. Yet, he called for opening the way to admittedly divisive outside elements into the heart of the government in Tokyo before the government could set up the necessary controls to cope with these elements.

Itō's second basic point of disagreement with Ōkuma was the latter's "heretical" suggestion of a cabinet system based on the English model.[135] Itō, who had earlier opposed the Genrō-in draft constitution primarily on the ground that it endowed the legislature with too much power, could hardly be expected to agree publicly with Ōkuma on this crucial point.

There is hardly any question that Itō, Ōkuma, and Inoue Kaoru were holding serious talks on the constitutional problem at this time. Therefore, if Ōkuma wanted to establish a national assembly earlier than Itō and Inoue deemed advisable, the two knew of this and probably believed that they had talked him out of it. It has also been shown that Inoue agreed in principle with British constitutional practice. In fact, in the memorandum he submitted in July 1880 he suggested that *sometime in the future* the British and American practice of having parties peacefully effect change of power in the government was possible.[136] However, Ōkuma took the first step toward his political suicide when he spelled out the English system *in detail* and tied it with *a specific date in the immediate future*.[137] This appears to be Itō's version of the crisis.

Naturally, we all accepted the premise that the establishment of a national assembly was inevitable. The fundamental problems were, under what type of constitutional system was this national assembly going to be established, and once we had decided to create a national assembly, how could we go about achieving it. However, Ōkuma, with whom we had been frankly exchanging our views, undercut us. He came up with a hastily written draft constitution (*shigi kempō*) and submitted it to minister of Left Arisugawa. And for him to submit a petition to the emperor calling for the immediate establishment of the national assembly the following year [sic] was truly an act of betrayal of his friends. It was an unspeakable act ... If Ōkuma were to persist in carrying out his views, we would have no alternative but to resign. On the other hand, if our views were to be accepted by the throne, Ōkuma's position in the government would be untenable. The resolution of this dilemma was the Crisis of 1881.[138]

It was one thing to disagree in private, which left the door open for compromise and the eventual putting forward of a unanimous public front. It was quite another matter to expose private disagreements—in this case, over the type and timing of constitutionalism—and thus force an either/or public position. This was the meaning of Itō's words on July 5 when he castigated Ōkuma, who, according to Itō, with fourteen years of experience in the government should have known better than to try unilaterally to "settle such a grave state matter." The period of calm that followed Itō's return to his official duties, then, was superficial and deceptive. Itō could hardly consider the constitutional issues settled simply because Iwakura, Sanjō, and Arisugawa agreed to support his petitions on the issues.

Itō did not find it difficult to rally support for the grave decision to purge Ōkuma. In fact, Yano writes that about this time Ōkuma was "sitting atop a seething volcano, and it was only a question of when [the volcano] was going to explode."[139] Ōkuma always seemed to pose a threat to one or another faction in the government. Probably no single major figure in the Meiji government was so consistently the object of attack on the part of so many. Ōkubo Toshimichi demanded Ōkuma's resignation from the government in 1870.[140] In 1874 Shimazu Hisamitsu did the same and in 1875, Itagaki and Kido.[141] Ōkuma's personality and talents must have contributed to his lightning-rod-like capacity to attract these threats. His confidence in his own abilities could easily have been taken for arrogance and superciliousness by the less talented. The quickness of his intellect could have been construed as craftiness by the jealous. His courage and boldness could have signaled dangerous ambition to the suspicious. Even Ōkuma's biographers are forced to concede that his personality traits were not such as to endear him to his colleagues in the government. "Ōkuma," they say, "unlike the affable person he was in later years, was hard to please, stubborn and brusque in his manner of setting about his business. Others consequently were ready to regard him as a crafty and designing person."[142]

Furthermore, Ōkuma's relatively enlightened views must have aroused much suspicion and fear among the conservative group in the government. Shimazu Hisamitsu's antagonism toward Ōkuma can be traced in part to this.[143] Those close to the throne, like Sasaki Takayuki, could hardly be sympathetic with Ōkuma's progressive ideas on constitutional government.[144]

An even more ominous development, as far as Ōkuma was concerned, was the growing hostility he faced from the Satsuma faction. This was in part a reflection of ideological differences. As Fukuzawa had pointed out: "The military faction's influence is rather strong, and they are hardly sympathetic with the progressive principles advocated by Ōkuma and Itō . . . They are . . . in the majority and have [great] influence, so there is danger that all the progressive policies will come to no good end. This is why at present Ōkuma and Itō cannot achieve anything."[145]

The basis for the Satsuma faction's vindictive animosity toward Ōkuma, however, is traceable to the faction's anxiety about its deteriorating influence in the government, which was compounded by jealousy of the Ōkuma group's increasing strength. The Satsuma faction, as Fukuzawa stressed, cannot be said to have been weak at this time.[146] Still, relative to the unquestioned position of eminence it held under Ōkubo, its influence in the government was undoubtedly on the wane. Ono Azusa, in his memorandum to Ōkuma clearly points to this fact.[147] Furthermore, it did not help Ōkuma's cause at all that he came from Hizen and not from the two leading clans represented in the government—Satsuma and Chōshū.[148] This anti-Ōkuma sentiment was strongest where perhaps it counted the most: among the nameless but powerful junior bureaucrats of Satsuma and Chōshū origins. Yano recalls: "Among the most prominent of the members of the Sat-Chō there was no particular ill-feeling. There is no doubt, however, that all those from the middle ranks and below harbored dissatisfactions."[149] In another work Yano says that some of Itō's followers were unhappy about Ōkuma's gradually increasing influence,[150] while Ōkuma's recollection also is that "Itō's underlings" were dissatisfied with his growing power.[151]

Here then is a picture of rising young men in the Sat-Chō faction angered and frustrated with every new appointment by Ōkuma from among his own followers. In a political system that placed a premium on personal relationships and in which subordinates exercised power out of proportion to their status, it would have been strange indeed if these subordinates had not demanded of their superiors the removal of the source that threatened to close, or at least narrow, the avenues of their advance.

So great was the Satsuma clique's antipathy toward Ōkuma that Ōkuma, Fukuzawa, and Yano all believed that Itō and Inoue submitted to Satsuma pressure for Ōkuma's ouster. This is Ōkuma's interpretation of the crisis. "[Our meetings] became the object of suspicion of the others [in the government] . . . We were uncertain as to how mistrustful the Satsuma militarist clique would be, [so] we took extra precautions to meet secretly . . . However, Itō and Inoue allowed themselves to be intimidated by the reactionary Satsuma men. As a result, my neck was forfeited—they had surrendered to the Satsuma militarist faction."[152] Ōkuma and Fukuzawa were in one sense correct. Itō, it can easily be imagined, told the Satsuma councilors who were for delaying the establishment of a national assembly far beyond the period Itō regarded as reasonable, and who held conservative constitutional views,[153] "If you do not go along with me on the constitutional question, you will have to deal with Ōkuma's proposals." This, I think, is the meaning of Itō Miyoji's words when he told Watanabe Ikujirō years later, "Because [Ōkuma] presented his memorandum, the establishment of constitutional government was speeded up and the emperor handed down the rescript setting the ten-year [*sic*] target date for the establishment of the national assembly."[154]

In any case, once Itō and Inoue combined with the anti-Ōkuma Satsuma faction, Ōkuma could do nothing to counterattack. This explains in large part Ōkuma's quiet acceptance of his ouster. As Yano sagely observed: "The Sat-Chō had great influence in the Army and Navy . . . On the surface Ōkuma's power was flourishing and was at its peak. Actually, the roots [of his power] were shallow and the bases insubstantial. That Ōkuma's position was dangerous should have been clear."[155]

What of the role of Itagaki and his supporters? As stated earlier, many believe that the conjoining of the protests against the proposed sale and the demands by the advocates of parliamentarism proved too much for the government. A closer scrutiny of the record, however, shows that the leading figures in all three camps—the anti-Ōkuma forces in the government, the Ōkuma faction, and the Itagaki group—minimized the role of the movement for parliamentary government in the crisis.

Ono Azusa, for one, thought of the problem of the sale of commission properties as mainly involving those in the government. In the long memorandum cited earlier he limited his head count of prospective supporters to government personages and groups and dismissed "outside" support almost unceremoniously with the words: "Although we may have the support of certain representatives of the people, their power is negligible."[156] Fukuzawa and Yano too laughed at the suggestions that Ōkuma had anything to do with the advocates of parliamentarism. Fukuzawa charged in his "Account of 1881" that Itō and Inoue dragged his name in because there was no evidence that Ōkuma had anything to do with the proponents of parliamentarism.[157] Yano's contention that they would have been foolish to have undermined their own position in the government by combining with the outs best summarizes the stand of most of Ōkuma's faction.[158]

Yet, there were a few among Ōkuma's supporters who sought to combine with Itagaki and his forces. And Itagaki for a moment evinced some interest. However, in the course he ultimately chose and the reasons he gave for that choice can be found strong rebuttals against the thesis that the movement for parliamentarism played a meaningful role in the crisis.

According to Itagaki's version, Ōkuma at this time found that his views did not agree with those of the other councilors, so he raised the matter of the proposed sale and was trying to stir up the political world. Ōkuma's disciples thus were hardly interested in the problem of forming a political party with him, but, by directing all their energies on the sale issue, wanted to "renovate the cabinet." In other words, Ōkuma's followers, by making use of the "popular" forces led by himself, wanted to launch a two-pronged attack—from within and without the government —to bring the government down. To these suggestions Itagaki says he replied: "That something like the proposed sale of Hokkaido Colonization Commission properties should arise under the present form of government should not surprise us. Hence my desire is to go to the root of the matter and remedy the situation. I not only disdain combining forces with one segment of the bureaucracy to attack still another section of the administration . . . [I am convinced] that this is not the path by which we will achieve our aims." With these words, Itagaki asserts, he washed his hands of the entire matter and left Tokyo for the north on September 26.[159]

Inoue Kowashi also did not think of the Itagaki forces as the primary source of danger. It has been postulated that as the Meiji regime stabilized, attention to the problem of constitutionalism increased, and that some of the most openly articulate expounders on this topic were supporters of the English school. It was from these eloquent and promising proponents of the English school of constitutionalism, and not from the participants in the movement for parliamentarism, that Inoue felt the most threatening challenge to his concepts of constitutional government.[160] Inoue in a letter cited earlier wrote:

I have kept a close watch on the present state of affairs. Those who have been petitioning for the establishment of a national assembly are now not so noisy. However, this certainly does not indicate that they are idle. In other words . . . they have now all shifted their energies to the study of constitutions. And this study of constitutions is based essentially on Fukuzawa's privately drafted constitution. Fukuzawa's Kōjunsha is now the leading instrument for the formation of a political party by the seduction of the majority of the people. Its influence is being exerted *sub terra* and is quietly at work on the people's sentiments . . . If those in the government are really going to accept Fukuzawa's ideas and are thinking about conforming to his precepts, it would be proper to use him unhesitatingly and to have his party become the government's party. If, however, this is not the intention, and if the government plans to reject popular government, which grants power to the nameless masses, such as is found in England, and to support a monarchy like that found in Prussia, should we delay even one day in...carrying out the Imperial Rescript of 1875 ...and drafting a government-centered constitution...?[161]

The three "Opinions" presented by Iwakura on July 5 make it even clearer that the ideological conflict was between the Prussian and English schools within the government. In "Opinion No. 1" Iwakura (or more strictly, Inoue Kowashi speaking for Iwakura) explained the English and Prussian constitutional systems. The choice facing Japan, according to Iwakura, was either "at one great leap" to adopt the English system, in which the majority party controls the government, or "on the basis of gradualism" to accept the Prussian system, in which the parliament possesses only the legislative prerogative and the power to organize the administration is entirely in the hands of the ruler. Iwakura also expounded on other disadvantages of the English system.[162] In "Opinion No. 2" he laid down the three crucial elements necessary for a Prussian-type system. First, the ruler would have the prerogative of appointing and dismissing ministers and officials of the *chokunin* rank; second, the system of joint responsibility for cabinet ministers—an English constitutional practice—would be rejected; third, the previous year's budget would come into effect if the government and the legislature could not agree on the current budget—a stipulation found in the Prussian constitution.[163] "Opinion No. 3" contained further elaboration of points raised in "Opinion No. 2," as well as a rebuttal against portions of the Kōjunsha's "Shigi kempō" and the Genrō-in's "Kokken-an."[164] In view of the above, it is easy to agree with Tokutomi's judgment that Inoue "felt a compulsion to do way with Fukuzawa's political ideology."[165]

Even the move to rescind the decision to sell the properties of the Hokkaido Colonization Commission can be explained without too much reference to the movement for parliamentarism. True, the petition by those in the government against the proposed sale cited the "uproar" outside.[166] However, the four "dissident" generals seemed to be less interested in the sale than in taking the opportunity to diminish Sat-Chō influence in the government. In fact, Ōkubo feels that this flanking attack by the generals and others against the Sat-Chō was a "directly important" cause of the crisis.[167]

Certain members of the Ōkuma clique, like Ono, also viewed the proposed sale as a subordinate issue, to be used to renovate the government and to establish a constitutional government. And the anti-Ōkuma group too saw the sale issue in basically this same way. This is why Yamada and Kawamura, in trying to persuade Iwakura to return to Tokyo, dismissed the matter of the sale and emphasized the importance of setting a date for the national assembly. This is also why the emperor expressed confusion when Iwakura linked the demand for Ōkuma's ouster with Kuroda's concurrence to rescind the decision to sell. In fine, Itō, by demanding that Kuroda submit, took away the one issue that the anti-Sat-Chō groups in the government could bring to bear against the Sat-Chō clique and that the Ōkuma group could continue to use from outside the government. This is clear proof that Itō had the situation under complete control, and it further reveals him as the master political strategist among the Meiji oligarchs. Itō, throughout his political career, manifested this ability for the adroit, carefully thought out, cleverly executed maneuver, based on a sensitive and precise understanding of the political tangibles and intangibles with which he had to deal.

The crisis, then, had its genesis in the rash act of Ōkuma early in 1881 and resulted in the resolution of problems created by this act. The main characters were Meiji bureaucrats and the issues were primarily those affecting them. The movement for parliamentarism, therefore, can only be assigned a peripheral role in the crisis. Its existence served Inoue's purpose, for he could link Ōkuma's and Fukuzawa's ideas with irreverent radicalism. And if Sasaki Takayuki associated Ōkuma supporters with the movement, it must have been easy for others in the government to do the same.

Still, the basic choice Itō held before the Satsuma forces, whose support he required, was not that between Itagaki's or Ōkuma's brand of "radicalism," but between Ōkuma's ideas on constitutionalism and his own. Moreover, it would have been strange indeed if those who counted in the government had been overly concerned about the movement. They had purged with impunity one of the most powerful figures *in the government,* who had followers placed in strategic administrative posts. They had little cause to be sleepless over a weak, divided movement that had been committed to nonviolent political action from the beginning.[168]

One final point to remember. It speaks eloquently of the enlightenment and humaneness of the Meiji government that Ōkuma, who presented a threat to the stability of the regime, was merely ousted and not eradicated. The Meiji leadership, from the beginning of the Meiji era, generally levied the gravest penalty only when the party concerned actually took up arms against the government.[169]

*My way of evaluating the nature [of the average man]
differs from that of Mencius. Mencius evaluates it in
comparison with the doings of birds and beasts below,
and therefore he says that the nature [of the average
man] itself is good. I evaluate it in comparison with the
doings of the sages above, and therefore I say that the
nature [of the average man] is not good.*

TUNG CHUNG-SHU, IN FUNG YU-LAN,
A HISTORY OF CHINESE PHILOSOPHY

IV

ITŌ AND THE DRAFTING OF THE MEIJI CONSTITUTION

In the years 1876–1880 the Genrō-in proved that a constitution could be drafted in Japan which scholars later would consider to be creditable. The Meiji oligarchs, however, still felt it necessary to send one of their members abroad to sit at the feet of leading European constitutional specialists. This move was impelled in part by the peculiar nature of the threat posed by the outs, which now included the highly articulate Ōkuma partisans.

It has been argued that the movement for parliamentarism had but a peripheral role in the government's key decisions concerning the acceptance of a constitutional form of government and the timing of its establishment. In what may be regarded as the middle period of Meiji parliamentary history—the period of the actual preparations for parliamentary government—the premise that the outs had neither immediate nor direct influence on major issues and decisions in this area is still applicable.

The significance of the opposition to the government lay elsewhere. The one important early influence of the movement for parliamentarism was that its very existence served as a reminder to the oligarchs of the potential dangers of ignoring constitutionalism as the wave of the future. The pertinacious presence of the opposition in this period made the oligarchs uneasy because of the dangers it threatened once the constitution was promulgated. There were two ways in which the outs could cause mischief after 1890. One was to attack the constitution itself; the other was to act in an unrestrained and undisciplined manner once they became sharers of the public power. The constitution was drafted with these two possible threats in mind.

Perpetuation in power is the first law of politics, and the Meiji constitution predictably weighted power overwhelmingly in favor of the administration and against the Diet.[1] Indeed, it would have been surprising had the reverse been the case, for the Meiji leaders from Satsuma and Chōshū had what to them were excellent reasons in support of this axiom. The Meiji oligarchs, as revolutionaries in the truest sense of the word, were driven by a form of collective Messianic complex. They were thoroughly convinced that it was both their mission and responsibility to lead Japan out of the wilderness of backwardness and weakness toward the green pastures of civilization and power. Their contributions in bringing about the Restoration, they felt, fully justified their assumption of this role, and each successful step toward a stable and powerful Japan served to bolster this conviction.[2] Kabayama Sukenori, navy minister in the first Matsukata ministry, gave the most famous expression of this faith. "Who would accuse us of defiling the national honor?... The present government is the government which has succeeded in overcoming all external and internal difficulties the nation has confronted. Call it the Sat-Chō government, or designate it by whatever name you wish; but who would deny its achievement in maintaining the security and well-being of 40,000,000 souls?"[3]

A corollary of this Sat-Chō article of faith was the conviction of the Meiji oligarchs that the parties, the only other groups with the potential for eventually challenging their claim as directors and guardians of Japan's destiny, fully disqualified themselves by their conduct and avowed goals. An ideal party, according to Itō, was one that would conduct the affairs of the nation for all the people.[4] It seemed to him, however, that the parties failed in this one basic requirement, and consistently sacrificed national interests for selfish party interests. This viewpoint is clearly expressed in Itō's bitter complaint about the members of the Seiyūkai, a party formed by Itō himself. "The one thing that drives me to distraction is that there is none among them who thinks of the nation above self... I cannot visualize any one of them working out with any enthusiasm administrative plans and measures on the basis of true concern for the country."[5]

The oligarchs in the decade after the Rescript of 1881 thus faced a real dilemma. On the one hand, they were impelled by their desire for Japan to become a modern and powerful state, and by their reading of Europe's history and experiences, to create a constitutional form of government; on the other hand, as enlightened and realistic men they realized that the ineluctable condition for the institution of such a regime was the sharing of power and responsibility with men and groups they believed lacked the qualifications for running the state. Furthermore, this sharing, as far as they were concerned, threatened to inject instability, disunity, and unseemly grasping for personal gains and benefits in the highest places. Such a state of affairs, they believed, would hinder and even subvert the very purpose for which constitutional government was to be established—the creation of a stable, powerful, and modern Japan. So the essential problem facing Itō in his task of drafting the constitution was to seek means of controlling and rendering as harmless as possible this encroachment into the public power area by the parties. This is the second special characteristic of the challenge posed by the outs to the Meiji government. But it was a danger and challenge that lay largely *in the future.*

Itō's trip to Europe to study constitutions can be explained partially on this basis. The fundamental elements of what was to be incorporated in the Meiji constitution were decided upon before the trip, the final product faithfully reflecting the stipulations contained in the Iwakura memoranda of July 5, 1881.[6] The only mystery is why under the circumstances the oligarchs should have granted leave to the most powerful man in the government and permitted him a liberal expenditure of time and currency, both then in extremely short supply.

The constitution, after its promulgation, was to become "public" property, in the same way that the private preserve in Tokyo that was the pre-1890 Meiji government was going to be opened for limited exploitation after 1890. The constitution, in a word, was going to be fair game, and, as Suzuki Yasuzō put it, "if theoretically unsound, would enable the opposition to tear it apart or make fun of it."[7] And those in the government were keenly aware that they generally lacked the theoretical shield necessary to deflect the possible attacks on the constitution. Itō recalls: "There were many types of constitutional governments . . . I was completely at a loss as to what constitutional government, or whatever it was called, stood for. The situation was such that one classical scholar asked whether Shōtoku Taishi's constitution would suffice."[8]

The leaders in the government were not only on uncertain theoretical footing; they were manning a lonely, embattled rampart. Itō Miyoji later recalled: "Before the enactment of the constitution, in the days when the parliamentary government movement was vigorous, the French and English constitutional concept that sovereignty resided in the people or in the parliament was popular. The impact of those of us who said that sovereignty was located in the emperor or who advocated a strong monarchy was extremely weak, and it seemed that we were lonely and isolated voices."[9]

One way to forestall this future challenge to the constitution by the opposition was to link it with the emperor. "If the constitution is known to the people as having been drafted by a given individual," warned Itō, "not only will this give rise to much public comment and criticism, but also the constitution will lose the people's respect. It may [even] come to be said that it would be better not to have a constitution than to have a constitution unrespected by the people."[10] At this time, however, there was no guarantee that coupling the emperor with the constitution would make the document automatically immune to attack. For if a tentative generalization about the role of the emperor may be permitted, it is that at least until some time after 1890 the emperor still had not become an unquestioned public symbol of reverence and awe. In the early 1880's, for example, the question of the locus of sovereignty was the object of a raging public controversy.[11] And Dr. Erwin Baelz, perhaps less biased than most Japanese reporters on this subject, was constrained to record in his diary even as late as November 3, 1880: "The Emperor's birthday. It distresses me to see how little interest the populace take in their ruler. Only when the police insist on it are the houses decorated with flags. In default of this, house-owners do the minimum."[12]

Nothing less than a pilgrimage to the fountainhead of constitutionalism, then, with the prestige and theoretical fortification that would result from it, would suffice to silence the potential challenge from the outs. Itō's letters to colleagues remaining in Japan sometimes turned to the subject of acquiring theoretical support to counter the possible attacks by antigovernment forces. In a letter to Iwakura, he wrote:

Thanks to the famous German scholars Gneist and Stein, I have come to understand the essential features of the structure and operation of states. In the most crucial matter of fixing the foundations of our imperial system and of retaining the prerogatives belonging to it, I have already found sufficient substantiation ... The situation in our country is characterized by the erroneous belief that the words of English, American, and French liberals and radicals are eternal verities. This misplaced enthusiasm would practically lead to the overthrow of the nation. I have acquired arguments and principles to retrieve the situation ... I face the future with pleasant anticipation.[13]

There are reasons to suspect that Itō felt that Ōkuma's group would be more formidable than Itagaki and his followers on the verbal front. For one thing, Itō and Inoue encouraged Itagaki to take a trip to Europe at this time. And the evidence is that Itō urged Gotō, who also made the trip, to listen to lectures by Stein.[14] Furthermore, Saionji Kimmochi, who was in Paris, sought to have Itagaki see as much of the political situation in France in the hope that Itagaki would thus be able to discern the difference in the theory and the practice of the French political system. Perhaps one of Itō's aims in supporting the Gotō-Itagaki trip was that he believed he would be able to convert these two men to his political views.[15]

Secondly, the Ōkuma faction enjoyed a widespread and justified reputation for wit and eloquence.[16] The *Japan Weekly Mail,* for example, early in 1891 compared the Kaishintō and the Jiyūtō in the following manner: "In discipline, in intelligence, and in wealth, the Progressionists are upon the whole far ahead of their allies—the Radicals ... The Kaishin-tō journals, the *Mainichi,* the *Yomiuri,* and the *Hōchi* occupy front rank in the press of the capital; while the single organ of the Jiyū-tō, the *Jiyū,* is regarded at best as a second rate paper. The Kaishin-tō organs write on the situation in a calm and confident tone, while the Jiyū-tō paper resorts to childish displays of braggadocio and passion."[17] It is no wonder, then, that Itō, in a letter reminiscent of Inoue Kowashi's attacks against Fuku-zawa, bitterly criticized both Ōkuma and the "callow students" who surrounded him, as well as the English constitutional system.[18]

One more possible motive exists for Itō's sojourn in Europe. Itō was well known among his contemporaries for his overweening and passion-ate drive for fame.[19] Whether this striving stemmed from a feeling of insecurity,[20] a sense of destiny, or both, is difficult to determine. Oka Yoshitake, however, has written a rather convincing article in which he attributes many of Itō's public acts to this personal trait.[21] Itō's earnest application to his studies and the fantastic pace he set for himself through-out his stay in Europe[22] indicate the seriousness with which he regarded his task of drafting a constitution that would at once be above criticism and remain a lasting and immutable monument to him.[23]

The lessons learned in Europe were gratifying to Itō. Yet, it would be a mistake to lose sight of the crucial fact that he fully accepted a basic premise of constitutionalism: the sharing of power. "Itō," Kaneko re-members, "sought rule by both the monarch and the people, the grant-ing by the monarch to the people of the right to participate in govern-ment." "This," Kaneko continues, "was Itō's injunction to us in the writing of a constitution for a constitutional state."[24] Moreover, Itō may have been more liberal than Gneist on this point. In a rather intriguing passage of a letter to Matsukata, written shortly after he had met Gneist, Itō reported that the German professor's principles, at first glance at least, were "extremely authoritarian" when viewed in the context of the situation existing in Japan.[25]

On June 23, 1883, some thirteen months after they had arrived in Europe, Itō and his party left Rome for Japan. At Hong Kong Itō learned for the first time of Iwakura's death, which had occurred on June 20. The party arrived at Yokohama on August 3, 1883, slightly over a year and a half after they had first turned toward Europe.[26]

Three months after his return to Japan Itō established the Office for the Study of the Constitution (Kempō torishirabe jo). On March 17, 1884, the Bureau for the Study of Administrative Reforms (Seido tori-shirabe kyoku) was also established, and it absorbed the Office for the Study of the Constitution.[27] The creation of these offices was not followed by serious work on the drafting of the constitution, for Itō, as the leading figure in the government, was occupied with other state matters, foreign and domestic. For example, he made a trip to China lasting two months to settle differences between Japan and China arising over their growing mutual interest in Korea.[28] At home, Itō, as holder of three high administrative positions,[29] undertook administrative reforms as necessary first steps toward constitutional government. On July 7, 1884, the Peerage Law was revised to establish the basis for the House of Peers. In December 1885 the Dajōkan was abolished and replaced by a cabinet.[30] Work on the constitution, however, was not entirely in abeyance. From March 1884 to the winter of 1885 Itō discussed in detail with Inoue Kowashi, Itō Miyoji, and Kaneko Kentarō his studies in Germany.[31] From about the beginning of 1886, after the creation of the cabinet system, drafting the constitution was given top priority by Itō.[32]

Much attention has been directed by scholars to the process of drafting the Meiji constitution.[33] Hence it is sufficient here to note that the constitution was drafted essentially by five men—four Japanese and one foreigner: Itō,[34] Inoue Kowashi,[35] Itō Miyoji,[36] Kaneko Kentarō,[37] and Carl Friedrich Hermann Roesler.[38] An aspect of the drafting process that seems to have been given less scrutiny is the constant pressure applied by those in the government to influence Itō's efforts—indeed, even to the extent of trying to undermine his efforts.

Itō took elaborate measures to safeguard his secrets and to forestall potential opposition attacks.[39] The stringent security measures he took[40] were more than ample to meet the "danger" from without. In fact, the success of these measures was such that throughout the 1880's the outs, in their attacks against the government in this field, concentrated their efforts primarily on clandestine publications of what they asserted were drafts of the constitution.[41] It is true that there was vigorous public opposition to Inoue's and Ōkuma's treaty revision attempts in the years 1887–1889 which culminated in a bomb attack on Ōkuma. However, the failure to revise the treaties can be explained as much by looking at the conflicts within the government as by focusing on external pressure. In a word, it would be hazardous to gauge the strength of the political "parties" on the basis of the loudness of their opposition. It may be closer to the truth to say that Itō, while displaying some concern over the threats posed by the outs, was able without much difficulty to control and minimize these dangers, as he did in the Crisis of 1881. Until the day when the opposition was to partake of public power, through the Meiji constitution, Itō's primary concern was not the harassment by the outs but the demands of the various and constantly clashing factions composing the Meiji government. He attempted to keep these within manageable limits, by an adroit balance of compromise, firmness, and patronage.[42]

The threat from the "Left" in the government was personified by Terajima Munenori, head of the Genrō-in. Terajima wanted to be named envoy to the United States in 1882 so that he could duplicate Itō's efforts in Europe. He was named minister to the United States in July 1882, but was not able to fulfill his desire.[43] The antagonism between those in the Genrō-in and Itō is traceable, as we have seen, to the time when the Genrō-in was commissioned to draft a constitution, an effort roundly criticized by Itō.[44] Moreover, as mentioned earlier, it was the Genrō-in's attempt to outdo Itō that had the unlooked-for result of bringing Itō and Kaneko together. This zeal for constitution-making remained undiminished even in 1887, when Itō was already deep in his work.[45] Finally, one of the reasons for specifically creating the Privy Council to deliberate on the draft constitution, according to Osatake, was to bypass the Genrō-in, which claimed the deliberative right. As Osatake puts it, "The fate [of the Itō draft constitution] would have been a foregone conclusion if the Genrō-in had been allowed to discuss it."[46]

Itō also expressed some concern about the charge made by still other proponents of parliamentarism that he was drafting a "Bismarckian" constitution that would serve as the basis of an authoritarian regime.[47] Ōkuma Shigenobu, for example, who was foreign minister at this time, in the company of Prime Minister Kuroda Kiyotaka one day personally called on Itō to make this charge and asked that certain elements of the English constitution be included in the draft.[48]

However, it appears that what troubled Itō most were the attacks from the conservatives in the government. Imperial Household officials were especially vocal in their fears that Itō was a blind worshipper of the West and that he intended to establish the parliament-centered system of England. A leading figure in this group was Motoda Eifu, a scholar in Chinese learning.[49] Itō later commented: "In spite of the fact that in and out of [the Privy Council] there was an undercurrent of extreme conservatism, the emperor's wishes almost invariably were liberal and progressive."[50] And years after the enactment of the constitution Itō was still fighting this battle against the Chinese scholars. He described them as having "narrow and limited" views on government because they insisted that the only form of government that conformed to Japan's polity was absolutism.[51]

These internal pressures may have compelled Itō constantly to seek precedents for ideas that he sought to incorporate into the draft. Kaneko remembers once suggesting that representatives of the merchant, industrial, and farming classes be permitted to sit in the House of Peers. Itō agreed but told Kaneko that he did not relish facing later charges that this was a "frivolous idea, typical of Itō." To forestall such charges, Itō told Kaneko to find a precedent and was mightily pleased when Kaneko succeeded.[52]

Itō successfully weathered most of the challenges from within the government,[53] and the Meiji constitution bore Itō's unmistakable imprint. Needless to say, in no instance can any major concept or principle embodied in the constitution be said to have reflected the demands or pressures from the outs.[54] Hence, just as Itō and the oligarchs had almost complete control over the questions of the *introduction* of constitutional government and the *timing* of the introduction, they exercised as firm a control over the *type* of constitutional government Meiji Japan finally adopted. Political phenomena, it is true, are not always susceptible to logical or even reasonable interpretations. Still, it is difficult to follow the widely accepted argument that in the matters of the introduction and timing of constitutionalism the government bowed to external pressure, but that in defining the substance of Meiji constitutional government the oligarchs were able to withstand and even ignore outside influence.[55]

The attacks against the Meiji constitution by the outs were loud but not vigorously pressed.[56] A reason that may be cited is that the opposition was fully aware of the immense number of theoretical arguments Itō could bring to bear in any debate. Another and more important reason may be that those in the opposition, after seeing the product, realized that the constitution offered it the opening to public power in Tokyo that they had been seeking,[57] and the opportunities for later expanding and exploiting this wedge—a fact fully realized by the oligarchs themselves. Some years after the promulgation of the constitution, Kaneko asked Ōkuma why he did not attend the sessions in which the Privy Council deliberated on the draft constitution.[58] Ōkuma's reply was that he felt that his presence was not necessary, for the draft contained three important provisions for the Diet: the right to petition the throne; the power to initiate legislation; and the guarantee that the budget would be presented to the House of Representatives before the House of Peers.[59]

The measure of the enlightenment of the oligarchs is that they themselves accepted the fact of real participation in the government by the outs as an irreducible minimum for constitutional government, in spite of the fact that the revolutionary government was only twenty-two years old and they had very serious misgivings about the ability of both the opposition and the general public to handle public responsibilities. Given this premise, the Meiji constitution, through which the oligarchs hoped to control and soften this future challenge by the outs, should not, as is often the case, be construed as a symbol of illiberality and reaction, but rather as an expression of a clear-sighted leadership, willingly embarking on a bold and revolutionary experiment.

One of the worst indictments of the Soviet system is that after 40 years they have not worked out a means of transferring power without conspiracy, exile and violence.

ADLAI E. STEVENSON, FRIENDS AND ENEMIES:
WHAT I LEARNED IN RUSSIA

V

PREPARING FOR "PARLIAMENTARY" GOVERNMENT

The decision to enact a constitution and the constitution itself indicated that the oligarchs felt that responsibility should be shared to some degree with the people through parliamentary mechanisms. The problem was how much sharing there should be. The Meiji oligarchy was not a tightly knit group, but a loosely-held body of jealous and proud individuals, each with his specific ideas on how best to achieve the goal of a strong and independent Japan. On the question of sharing, at one end were men like Yamagata who deplored any real sharing of responsibility. On the other were men like Itō and Inoue Kaoru who believed that party governments might develop some day when political conditions were somehow more favorable. And on the outside was an ex-oligarch, Ōkuma, who had foolishly expounded the radical view of immediate parliamentary responsibility. In any case, the general approach was that "parliamentary" government should only be partial, very gradual, and carefully hedged around. The oligarchs therefore took precautions to strengthen their position in all ways *vis-à-vis* the parliamentary forces.

The Meiji constitution represented the oligarchs' primary answer to the problem of controlling the participation of political parties in the government after 1890. An earlier move in this direction had been the elimination of the Dajōkan system and its replacement by the cabinet system. Under the Dajōkan system, only the three state ministers were legally empowered to decide on state matters. On the other hand, the councilors, like Itō, who were the men of ability in the government and who exercised real power, had in theory neither the decision-making prerogative in state affairs nor the right to advise the throne.[1] Theoretically, also, the councilors served simply as consultants to the three state ministers. Moreover, the heads of ministries, who made policy decisions, were an entirely separate group, and they could not carry out anything on their own initiative, the consent of the Dajōkan being necessary on all matters. In effect, the Dajōkan system represented an unwieldy and inefficient three-headed administrative monstrosity.

Under the cabinet system, formally established on December 22, 1885,[2] the position of prime minister was created; this minister was empowered to select the heads of each ministry and to exercise supervision and control over them. The councilors, who in fact took over the cabinet, absorbed the functions of the three state ministers as well as those of the heads of the ministries, and in their new role as ministers were empowered to supervise and control administrative departments and to advise the throne. The state ministers, who had furnished only a weak, symbolic leadership,[3] especially since the death of Iwakura, were thus replaced by the group of men who held real power and who were considered a match for the leaders of the prospective opposition parties.[4] In brief, the reform, by concentrating power and authority, by streamlining administrative lines of responsibility, by combining in the same persons *de jure* as well as *de facto* powers, contributed to the strengthening of the executive branch and created a major bulwark against the expected assault by the outs.[5] Furthermore, by replacing what must have been a strange façade to Western eyes with a modern system, the oligarchs presented an administrative structure understandable and "acceptable" to the nations of the West. Saionji Kimmochi, in a letter to Itō from Europe, best expressed the motives for this change: "Your reform plan, which went beyond my expectations, and which was so positive, made me literally jump for joy . . . I believe that this reform will be the first step in proving that our national government has real power and responsibility . . . Now we may take our place as equals among the civilized states; now we need not be worried about the establishment of the national assembly in the [near] future."[6]

Mutsu Munemitsu's entry into the first Yamagata cabinet is cited by two leading Meiji political historians as another example of the oligarchs' careful preparation for "parliamentary" government.[7] Mutsu was one of the most brilliant men in public life.[8] According to Osatake, when the government planned, as a measure against the expected attacks by the opposition in the Diet, to try to capture the presidency of the House of Representatives, they chose Mutsu, who was then minister to the United States.[9] Inoue Kaoru, probably Mutsu's closest friend in the government, urged him to return to Japan to run for a seat in the Lower House. Mutsu declined. He was apparently holding out for a position in the cabinet, and if he could not get it was not prepared to relinquish his post as minister to the United States.[10] Mutsu remained obdurate until he received a letter dated November 29, 1889, hinting that a cabinet seat was available.[11] Mutsu returned to Japan in January 1890, only to find that the cabinet post he thought was his was already occupied by some-one else. In the end, however, after a bit of political in-fighting that forced the reluctant incumbent out, Mutsu became minister of agriculture and commerce.[12]

These efforts to have Mutsu occupy a strategic position in Tokyo are symptomatic not only of the oligarchs' desire to use Mutsu's unquestioned political talents "against" the prospective opposition,[13] but also of a flexible and realistic state of mind. The oligarchs, it appears, valued Mutsu's "contacts" with the then dormant Jiyūtō, and sought to maintain through him a line of communication with that "party."[14] The oligarchs, then, did not conceive of the confrontation after 1890 in terms of a clash between two rigid, immovable power blocs. With typical foresight, they were preparing the ground for compromise.

Still another major move made by the oligarchs to temper the shock of the first impact between the government and the opposition in the Diet was to have Itō Hirobumi serve as president of the House of Peers. The government's plan, according to Osatake, called for standing fast in the House of Peers if "defeated" in the Lower House.[15] Itō at this time was without any official post, and his biography describes at length the attempts of nearly everyone in the government to have him take over the presidency of the House of Peers.[16] Itō finally accepted, but only on condition that he would serve for just one session and that he would thereafter be "allowed" to take a trip to China.[17]

Itō's patent reluctance to assume any responsibility at this time also underscores the growing antagonism between Itō and Yamagata. In a letter to Nakai Hiroshi, Itō complained: "Although I greatly deplore stepping forward as president [of the House of Peers], we have exhausted all possibilities for a compromise solution and the only alternative left is to open a major [political] fight. I would like to have you look with sympathy upon the unavoidable situation mentioned above."[18] It is rather obvious that Itō begrudged anything he did to help Yamagata achieve success as the first prime minister in the parliamentary era. Only Itō's fear of splitting the oligarchy on the eve of the great experiment prompted his decision to serve as president of the House of Peers. Yamagata, on his part, while pleading incompetence as "a mere soldier," must have been strongly motivated to show Itō that he could succeed, and well.[19] This phenomenon of oligarchs, who by virtue of grating personalities and clashing philosophies found each other almost unbearable, yet nearly always accommodated each other, is a recurrent one. The oligarchs acted, in short, as civilized men. This factor explains in some measure the peaceful, evolutionary nature of Meiji political development.

Immediately after the promulgation of the constitution, the Meiji oligarchs propounded the principle of *chōzen naikaku* (nonparty cabinets).[20] Kuroda Kiyotaka, speaking on February 12, 1889, to the prefectural governors meeting in Tokyo, outlined this principle. "It is inevitable that people differ in their views on how to run the government. It is equally unavoidable that there exist in society what we can designate as political parties, which are formed by those of similar views. However, the government must constantly maintain a fixed course, and by standing apart from and aloof from political parties, adhere to the path of impartiality and fairness."[21] Itō immediately followed Kuroda's pronouncement with a speech before the presidents of the prefectural assemblies on February 15.

To the extent that we have enacted a constitution and are aiming to establish a Diet, it is natural that political factions appear ... Although it is impossible to avoid the rise of political groups in any parliament or society, a government party is most improper ... The emperor stands above the people and apart from every party. Consequently, the government cannot favor one party above the other. It must be fair and impartial. And the prime minister...who assists the emperor, must not allow the government to be manipulated by the parties.[22]

These words by Kuroda and Itō caused not a little confusion and consternation, even among Itō's closest followers. Itō's exchange with Inoue Kowashi, Itō Miyoji, and Kaneko Kentarō, which followed his speech, is perhaps one of the most revealing episodes in Meiji political history. According to Kaneko, the three were stunned when they heard Itō's speech. They waited until the dinner guests had departed before they converged on Itō. Inoue Kowashi was first to speak.

Inoue: According to your speech, you intend to apply completely the

     Bismarkian absolute state to Japan. Is this really what you have in mind? We have frequently argued with you about the principle of ministerial responsibility, but I believe that your thesis today is a little different from your usual views.

    Itō: Different in what respects?

Itō Miyoji: It is wholly different. We, who had had our doubts when we heard Prime Minister Kuroda yesterday...find it positively surprising that you repeat his words.[23]

    Itō: The views expressed are absolutely no different from my original thoughts.

  Kaneko: Haven't you constantly instructed us to the effect that all measures are to be decided by public opinion? . . . However, what do you mean by declaring today that the state ministers have nothing to do with public opinion and are responsible only to the emperor?

    Itō: Then you are saying that the state ministers must be responsible to the Diet?

  Inoue: Absolutely not. The ancient philosophers of Greece said, "The voice of the people is the voice of the gods." And the enlightened emperors of China declared, "We will make the people's will our will." Moreover, the Meiji emperor *[sic]* has asserted, "All measures are to be decided by public opinion." These three pronouncements attest to the same principle without reference to country or time. There is no justification for the emperor to place confidence in a cabinet that has nothing to do with public opinion. Therefore, I believe that, though from the point of legal theory the state ministers are responsible to the emperor, actually they are responsible to the people through the Diet. However, to declare publicly that state ministers have no connection with public opinion and that even though they have received the emperor's confidence they need not resign [is to make mockery of the sentiments expressed by the enlightened rulers].[24]

 At another occasion, recalling the same incident, Kaneko placed a different emphasis on the reason for their opposition to the principle of nonparty cabinets. Inoue Kowashi is quoted as saying:

There are to be 300 members in the House of Representatives . . . It is a foregone conclusion that...the majority will be elected from among the Jiyūtō and Kaishintō. On the other hand, there is not a single person who can be designated a member of the government party. In other words, is there any reason to hope for success in containing the Jiyūtō and Kaishintō and in controlling the situation in the Diet by jumping stark naked into the 300-man House of Representatives? . . . So long as we have adopted a parliamentary system of government, the natural course of development would produce party government. This is why I believe it necessary for the government to have its own party by all means.

Itō protested that if the government would face the Diet in complete good faith and sincerity, without a shadow of malicious intent, or design, no party would react unreasonably. Inoue is the one who presumably made the reply. He said, "The parties are driven by a variety of personal considerations, habits, and most important of all, by emotional factors . . . They will turn a deaf ear to any approach by the government, no matter how grounded in sincerity and good faith. The issue must be resolved by the possession of real power."[25]

In view of the confusion expressed by these three, it is not surprising that there has been a tendency to interpret the principle of nonparty cabinets as a disavowal of parties under the constitutional regime Japan was to adopt. Uyehara Etsujirō, one of the earliest commentators on Meiji political history writes: "They [the oligarchs] invented, issued, and propagated a political doctrine so that they might be able *permanently* to keep the administrative power of the State in their hands exclusively, independently of *any* political party" (italics mine).[26] And Osatake said: "It is evident that at least he [Itō] became convinced *after years of actual experience* with parliamentary government that to the extent that parliamentary government was to be carried out, the *existence* of political parties was inevitable, that it was difficult to expect the completely smooth development of constitutional government by ignoring political parties. However, at the beginning he believed that he could carry out parliamentary government by adhering to his principle of nonparty cabinets" (italics mine).[27]

If all the words and actions of the oligarchs described so far have any meaning, it is that no major, responsible figure in the Meiji government disavowed the necessary, although limited, role of political parties in a constitutional system.[28] Furthermore, if the reports on the exchanges between Itō and his followers are reasonably accurate, the possibility of party cabinets was not overlooked.[29] Still, the party that came to power had to be one that had the best interests of the whole nation at heart, rather than one with selfish, narrow interests, as characterized, the oligarchs believed, by the antigovernment "parties." An implied premise was that only the members of the oligarchy, who had so far proved themselves loyal, conscientious servants of the emperor, with broad national welfare in mind, were qualified to create and to lead a national party.[30] All these feelings may be deduced from the words of two of the leading men in the government, Itō and Inoue Kaoru. Itō's views at this time were:

Even with the forthcoming establishment of the Diet and with the government prepared to be conducted on the basis of public opinion, to hope for the immediate consummation of parliamentary government—in other words, to have parties organize the cabinets—is extremely dangerous. Although there are not a few who stress the benefits of party factions because the constitution has already been enacted, it is necessary that the parties develop sufficient discipline before we entrust the government to the legislative branch. If without fulfilling this necessary condition, the parties were to disturb the foundations of the nation, how bad it would be for the future. This is what causes me much anxiety.[31]

Inoue, probably the most enlightened among the Meiji oligarchs,[32] spoke out even more plainly, as was his wont. He asserted that Itō's espousal of the principle of nonparty cabinets was "only an expression of opinion" and that no one could foresee the course of development of "parliamentary" government. Inoue then declared that he looked forward to the day when political parties "which are sufficiently well organized and representative, will be entrusted with the control of state affairs," and predicted that "the time may come when changes of cabinet will be quietly effected through their influence as in England."[33] Inoue had obviously missed the crucial aspect of the principle of nonparty cabinets, for on a later occasion he qualified the above remarks and said that the parties he had in mind were "national parties" that had the nation's total interests at heart and were not to be used as personal instruments of individual leaders.[34]

The principle of nonparty cabinets as enunciated by Itō and supported by Inoue, then, was essentially made up of two policy statements. The first was that "parliamentary" government entailed only a partial sharing of the public power; in a word, cabinets could and should be above party control. Yamagata subscribed to and consistently adhered to this principle throughout his post-1890 political life.[35] However, because Itō was perhaps a deeper thinker than Yamagata,[36] he qualified the principle of nonparty cabinets with the second policy statement. This was that when political parties, in the indeterminate future, became responsible "national" parties, party cabinets would be possible. It was on this issue that Yamagata fought a continuous battle with Itō after 1890. Yamagata never once conceded that political parties, no matter how defined, should ever be entrusted with the responsibility of governing the nation. Yamagata, moreover, always had the better of Itō in the often bitter behind-the-scenes arguments on this question, for his position was the only one that could logically be deduced from the basic proposition that the imperial prerogative, with respect to the appointment and dismissal of ministers, was indivisible. His was therefore an easier theoretical stand to take and defend.[37]

Itō, however, was perpetually plagued by his seemingly untenable theoretical stand. On the one hand he agreed with Yamagata. "The position of the monarch is similar to that of a deity and is thus inviolable. What I mean by inviolability is that he cannot be held accountable to Japanese law . . . a part of the imperial prerogatives, the legislative prerogative is entrusted to the Diet. The administrative prerogative is entrusted to the government . . . the appointment of ministers . . . is completely in the hands of the monarch, and the dismissal of ministers depends entirely on the pleasure of the emperor."[38] Itō also adhered to this interpretation of the role and nature of the emperor throughout his political life. "I have never yielded on the question of responsibility. The Japanese constitution plainly states that we are responsible to the emperor . . . Therefore, we cannot say that we are responsible to the Diet. It is axiomatic that we can owe responsibility to only one source."[39]

Still Itō realized that if "parliamentary" government was to have any real meaning, the possibility of the eventual development of party government had to be considered. However, because he was unwilling or unable, perhaps because of pressure from other oligarchs, to concede *in practice* immediately what he was propounding in theory, Itō often sounded ambiguous and contradictory.[40] Little wonder, then, that the trio of Itō's closest followers were perplexed.

For all his ambiguity, Itō enunciated the principle of nonparty cabinets in a spirit of confidence and assurance. Implicit in the principle was the premise that the prerogative to lay down the definitions of an acceptable party and of the conditions under which party government would be allowed to exist was retained by the oligarchs.[41]

The moves made by the oligarchs in preparation for "parliamentary" government, as outlined in this chapter, were based on the fundamental proposition that constitutional government meant a limited and gradual sharing of power and responsibility by the oligarchs with the people they ruled. It takes little imagination, then, to understand Itō's stunned and angry reaction to Ōkuma's call for the immediate establishment of a national assembly. For Ōkuma was proposing that the step be taken before institutions and conditions could be created to minimize and soften the inevitable dislocation. The oligarchs, as intelligent and perspicacious men, were certainly aware of the dangers of granting a little freedom.[42]

The ultimate significance of these preparatory steps, however, is that they plainly reveal the oligarchs' acceptance of the right of an opposition to exist and also the flexibility of their approach to a new and uncharted area of political experience. This meant that the oligarchs would use every means possible to overwhelm the opposition, but that all efforts would be made in accordance with the ground rules recognized by and acceptable to *both* sides. And a constitutional system of government, based on the Meiji constitution, was accepted as the basic framework within which the game of politics was going to be played. It is true that the rules were weighted heavily in favor of the ins and that, as Uyehara has stated, the oligarchs hoped to keep administrative power permanently in their hands. However, no one in politics is likely to give up power unless in the relinquishing he gains or expects to gain more than in the retention. Moreover, the oligarchs at this time were truly embarking on a revolutionary step and, to them, one fraught with grave dangers. It is unfair to expect them to have conformed to Western ideals of constitutionalism and to heap condemnation on them for not measuring up to this standard. They were practical men, faced with certain practical demands and goals, and they were trying to cope with these demands and goals in a practical, realistic way.

The subsequent story of "parliamentary" government in Meiji Japan is the story of the failure of the oligarchs to accomplish their purpose: to contain and control the new sharers of the public power. The irony of it all is that the oligarchs typically had made careful preparations to prevent any dangerous incursions by the outs into the public power domain and had thus entered the period of constitutional government with considerable confidence that the Diet's share of power could be kept small. The next three decades, however, were to show that they were basically wrong in their expectations.

VI

THE CONSTITUTION IN PRACTICE: THE FIRST DIET

The first general election, held on July 1, 1890, was quiet and orderly.[1] The results of the election were disappointing to the government. Out of the 300 elected, it could count on the support of 129 representatives, a bare and tantalizing 22 votes short of a majority. The combined strength of the Jiyūtō and the Kaishintō was 171.[2] This state of affairs may have been a motive for one of the final moves to neutralize the opposition. On July 25, 1890, Prime Minister Yamagata Aritomo revised the Regulations for Public Meetings and Political Associations, which forbade any party from combining or communicating with another party.[3]

Tuesday, November 25, 1890,[4] was beautiful and fair as only an autumn day in Japan can be. At nine o'clock the tall iron gates fronting the Diet were opened, and Japan began its days as a constitutional state. As Wigmore says of the revolutionary development symbolized by the opening of the gates: "The change from the old and the new in Japan is a trite subject, but to my mind, this was the occasion which most marks the turning point. Until today these men had entered those doors only by leave of others; henceforward they were to enter in their own right, and in that of the nation."[5] Then on Saturday, November 29, the first

This chapter appeared as an article in the *Journal of Asian Studies,* 22: 31-46 (Nov. 1962). Since then it has been revised.

Diet session was formally opened by the emperor. The budget immediately proved to be the issue over which the frontal clash between the government and the opposition parties occurred. The House of Representatives selected sixty-three of its members, headed by Ōe Taku, a leading figure in the Jiyūtō, to form the Budget Committee on December 6.[6] The committee produced a seven-point "Policies to Guide the Revision of the Budget," and it was on the basis of these policies that the famous "revised draft" was formulated. The "revised draft," passed by the committee on December 27, called for a cut of some 11 per cent, or 8,880,723 yen, from the budget submitted by the government.[7]

On January 9, 1891, Finance Minister Matsukata Masayoshi, speaking in the House of Representatives, warned the members that the government could not approve the revised budget, as this would cause a deterioration in the functions of the administrative branch of government.[8] From the moment Matsukata announced the government's position the battle commenced. The skirmishes were fought on two interrelated grounds. The first was the reduction demanded by the opposition and vigorously rejected by the government; the second was the constitutional question on the interpretation of Article 67. The article read: "Those already fixed expenditures based by the constitution upon the power appertaining to the emperor, and such expenditures as may have arisen by the effect of law, or that appertain to the legal obligations of the government, shall be neither rejected nor reduced by the Imperial Diet, without the concurrence of the government."[9] The constitutional problem arose because part of the projected cuts came under the scope of this article.[10]

On February 10 Yamagata made a short speech. He declared that in spite of Matsukata's words outlining the government's position on the constitutional problem[11] it could be surmised that the Lower House had chosen to ignore the government's stand. Such being the case, he continued, the government could not reply to questions related to the budget items falling within the meaning of Article 67. The opposition rose in anger after the speech, and the House was thrown into utter confusion, forcing the president temporarily to suspend its proceedings.[12]

When Itō heard about the speech he was "beyond himself with anger." He complained to Itō Miyoji: "Yamagata's speech seems to reveal that he does not realize that actually the revised budget is progressive. Furthermore, by not revealing the government's views on the budget beforehand he has failed to prevent the government from falling into a dangerous position. It is inexcusable and absurd to say that the government will foreswear all explanations simply because the government and the House of Representatives have clashed [over the revised budget]. If the opposition tells the government that it will not listen to the government, do you suppose that the government will meekly submit? Yamagata truly made a foolish statement. The prime minister's speech was ill-timed. Instead of meeting the fundamental problems, he has gone off on a useless tangent."[13]

Itō was here giving Yamagata low marks in political generalship and castigating him for antagonizing the opposition purposelessly. These remarks also reflect the basic attitude of the two men toward the opposition. From the beginning Itō conceived of it as something with which the oligarchs must learn to live, whereas Yamagata, somewhat reluctant even about the wisdom of permitting it to exist, tried to ignore its existence insofar as this was feasible.

Six days later, on February 16, Yamagata and Matsukata both spoke. Yamagata in essence declared that the government could not condone the Lower House's attempt to reduce the budget drastically.[14] Matsukata, who followed Yamagata to the rostrum, made a thinly veiled threat to dissolve the House: "Gentlemen, this Diet session is the first attempt at constitutional government in the Orient. Since the success we have with constitutional government is intimately related to the honor of our nation, the government, with your reasonable and steadfast support, hopes to achieve consummate success. If by chance, however, the revised budget passes, the government will be forced to take appropriate measures, to make clear its disagreement, and to realize its objects."[15]

It appears that Yamagata also gave some thought to the possibility of dissolving the Diet. In the letter from Itō Miyoji to Itō dated February 13, Itō is quoted as saying:

A few days ago, the prime minister sent Komiya [Mihomatsu] ... to tell me that the present state of affairs in the Diet was extremely alarming. [Yamagata, he said], felt that it was difficult to predict what kind of disorder was still in store, that the opposition might even contravene the constitution or violate laws. Moreover, if there was absolutely no hope of seeing an amicable solution, there was no other recourse but to resort to the final step of dissolution. [I was asked] what my views were. When I heard these words, I was positively shocked by the prime minister's superficiality and rashness. So I angrily turned to Komiya and said, "Tell the prime minister that Itō merely said, 'Is that so?'" But Komiya was not on his toes and did not seem to understand. So I had to elaborate. I said that dissolution is the ultimate measure to be employed when the government finds itself in a dangerous position where it can do nothing else. However, I cannot be sympathetic to any proposal that includes the suggestion for a dissolution, simply because the prime minister, on observing the situation, gets excited and feels that there possibly will be in the future a violation of the constitution or a contravention of laws. Even should the situation develop to a point where a dissolution becomes mandatory, the government must exhaust all possibilities in an effort to avoid taking that step. Only then should this ultimate move be made. And then it should be done quickly and decisively. I refuse to be dragged into a purposeless discussion of dissolution merely on a pointless conjecture of future events. In the first place, the action of the prime minister in sending a person like Komiya to discuss a matter of such gravity as dissolution leaves me speechless.[16]

Talk of dissolution apparently ended at this point. The only move remaining was compromise, if the government was unwilling to dissolve the Diet. According to Itō's biography, Itō was the moving spirit behind this effort at compromise. Minister of Communications Gotō Shōjirō and Agriculture and Commerce Minister Mutsu Munemitsu were chosen to work out the compromise with the Jiyūtō.[17]

Among some of the Jiyūtō sentiment favoring compromise with the government was revealed even before the first session was called to order. Just prior to the opening of the Diet, Ōe Taku, Takeuchi Tsuna, Kataoka Kenkichi, Nakajima Nobuyuki, and Kōno Hironaka called on Yamagata and Matsukata and "expressed the hope" that the first session of the Diet would not be ended by dissolution.[18]

On February 20, even as the Tokyo *Nichi nichi* was reporting that the Yamagata cabinet had decided to dissolve the Diet,[19] the Tosa faction of the Jiyūtō was supporting a motion in the Diet which in effect upheld the government's position on the constitutional question.[20] It is an almost universally accepted belief that the Tosa faction was bribed to support the government.[21] However, Oka categorically states: "To this date no historical material has been discovered to substantiate this rumor."[22]

On February 24 Mutsu reported to Matsukata that forty-one members of the Jiyūtō had bolted the party, thus doubly assuring that there would be compromise on the budget issue also.[23] The first phase of the government-opposition conflict, then, really had been resolved when the Tosa faction of the Jiyūtō had voted with the government forces in the Diet on the constitutional issue. The battle over the budget in the first session ended on March 2, 1891, when a reduction of 6,510,000 yen was passed by the House of Representatives by a vote of 157 to 125, again with the help of the Tosa faction's votes.[24]

One traditional interpretation of the conflict over the budget is that the final result was a government victory. The government, according to this view, had managed to limit the reduction to a mere 6,510,000 yen instead of the 8,880,000 yen the opposition had first demanded. Moreover, the method by which the government had achieved this victory—dividing the opposition by corrupting it—was to become an accepted and common practice, adding further stresses to the already weak position of the opposition. In other words, venality[25] and lack of principles and ideals among those in the opposition, and the legal obstacles created by the Meiji constitution, made it almost impossible for democracy to take root and flourish in Meiji Japan. The pattern of failure was already discernible in the first session of the Diet.

The above interpretation, however, is valid only if it is assumed that in 1890 Japan at one great leap should have achieved full democracy, and that "progress" can be achieved only through "revolution." Actually, the Diet showed much greater power than even the cabinet moderates like Itō had anticipated or desired, and as a result steady strides toward parliamentary responsibility were begun.

A crucial argument for holders of the traditional view is that the Diet was powerless because it lacked control over the purse strings. A standard text on Japanese politics is an excellent example of this viewpoint.

Even with such limitations, the Diet could have been an important branch had it held even one string of the public purse. But the Constitution and the Law of Finance removed public monies from popular control. The bulk of the budget consisted of "fixed expenditures" which could be neither rejected nor reduced; the Government had a "continuing expenditure fund," with a "reserve fund," for deficiencies; when the Diet was not in session, the Government could take "all necessary financial measures" by means of Imperial ordinances. And if for any reasons the Diet failed to vote on the budget, the Government could carry out the previous year's schedule.[26]

Here then is a picture of the overwhelming superiority of the government over the Diet on the matter of control of public funds. It is easy, in a descriptive effort, to come to such a dismal conclusion, especially when one is familiar with constitutions with more liberal stipulations.

The difficulty that the government had with the budget, however, may be used to support the proposition that the Diet's control in this area was greater than the framers of the constitution had realized. In the very first test of strength, the opposition, by exploiting fully the provision that "The expenditure and revenue of the State require the consent of the Imperial Diet by means of an annual Budget,"[27] presented the government with only two real choices: dissolution or compromise.

The oligarchs were to be faced with these two unhappy alternatives consistently in the first decade of the constitutional experience. Dissolution was resorted to, but this final step could be taken only on a limited scale if constitutional government was to succeed, and this was a goal to which all the oligarchs were publicly committed. Moreover, Itō had emphatically stated that dissolution was not to be frivolously or lightly ordered.[28] Yamagata himself pronounced the soundest judgment on the effect of Article 64 when he wrote to Finance Minister Matsukata, "No matter what is decided as a result of the debate [over the budget] I am apprehensive that this will be a source of grave difficulty in the future."[29]

Furthermore, it can well be argued that some of the checks in the hands of the government served the cause of the opposition rather than that of the government. A case in point is the much quoted stipulation providing for carrying over the previous year's budget should the Diet fail to pass a budget for a given fiscal year. A constantly expanding budget was necessary for a Japan driving herself to become a first rate power,[30] so that any time the Diet forced the government to work with the previous year's budget it in fact won great budgetary and political victories.[31]

The difficulties the oligarchs met in the enactment of the budget in the first session draw our attention to a question intimately related to the suggestion made above. This is the view of some historians and political scientists that the Meiji constitution imposed an institutional strait jacket on the political aspirations of the opposition parties. One of the leading Western interpreters of Meiji political history writes: "The hold of the Oligarchy was intact and was to remain so. In fact one could say that its hold had been strengthened, for now the autocratic practices which had been developed in the Meiji era were legitimatized and sanctioned by the Constitution."[32]

The untenable position in which the government found itself in the very first session of the Diet, however, is clear indication of how difficult it is in politics to "freeze the *status quo.*" Moreover, the Meiji constitution, by the very fact that it legitimatized, sanctioned, and thus institutionalized the machinery of parliamentarism, actually provided a boost to the growth and strength of the political parties. This argument, in part, was made by many contemporary observers of the Meiji political scene. The *Japan Weekly Mail* pointed to the fact that since the constitution, under ordinary circumstances, would make it impossible for the government to obtain funds without the concurrence of the Diet, the Diet was "practically master of the situation." The paper continued:

"Nothing can be more certain than that, if the provisions of the Constitution are carried into effect, government by party will become an accomplished fact in Japan as soon as party supremacy becomes a reality in the Diet."[33]

Inoue Kaoru even earlier had expressed some fears about the potential strength of the Diet. He had predicted that future government-Diet relations would be characterized by friction. To cope with the problem the government would have two alternatives. The first, he said, would be a "policy of firmness" and dissolution of the Diet. The election that followed, he continued, would return many of the members to the Diet, so there would be a recurrence of friction, followed by another dissolution. The result of this policy of firmness, Inoue ventured, would see popular feeling across the country turning against the government. The alternative course that could be adopted by the government, according to Inoue, would be to go along with the Diet. If the government concurred with the views of the Diet, however, on such matters as the reduction of the budget and administrative reform, then the government would in effect be consenting to the assumption by the Diet of important administrative rights and duties.[34] In short, Inoue was predicting that in the practical application of the constitution the government would be immediately placed in the most unenviable and unappealing position of having to choose between popular anger and recognition of the Diet's demands on the administration. It was a situation in which the parties could hardly lose.

It must be noted that Inoue almost matter-of-factly mentioned that the election following a dissolution would return many of the members of the opposition to the Diet. This is the second reason why the Diet possessed greater strength than the oligarchs had planned on. For the parties had gained experience in locally elected bodies and had used the period since 1881 to build up popular support, just as the oligarchs had used the same period to build up their mechanisms of control. The result of the efforts of the outs was that powerful antigovernment voting strength was accepted as inevitable by both sides.[35] *Chōya* early in 1892 stated:

What is the greatest mistake ever committed by the government since the Restoration? [This has been] its failure to cultivate public opinion. Plans for the present should have been made as early as 1881 . . . The continued silence of the government . . . and its generosity in permitting the opposition parties a free hand are its greatest mistakes, among many . . . The so-called popular parties have been energetic in imbuing the people's minds with their principles and have succeeded in creating a climate of opinion favorable to them . . . In many localities merely belonging to a "popular party" assures support of the voters.[36]

The politicians did not, of course, confine their efforts merely to talk. In a valuable contribution to an understanding of Meiji political history, Joseph L. Sutton has shown how Inukai Tsuyoshi built up his highly successful and powerful political machine in Okayama.[37] While Inukai's efforts began with the first general election, they may probably be legitimately taken as indexes of the groundwork laid by other politicians in the decade preceding the first general election when they were running for prefectural assemblies. Sutton shows how Inukai and his adherents adopted and carried out tactics familiar to any student of American political campaigns, but geared to capture what Sutton designates as the "feudal institutions" of the Japanese body politic.[38] The person-to-person canvass,[39] electioneering speeches, campaign managers, and campaign organizations were used. Moreover, Inukai cultivated the organs of local power, such as the prefectural assembly and the cooperatives and the Kurozumi sect of the Shinto "church," as well as the Buddhist church.[40] He also appealed to special groups in his constituency, such as the *eta*,[41] the tenant farmers, and small poor landowners.[42] The opposition not only had an organized basis of power, but its members, when they sat in the Diet, were already veterans at parliamentary maneuvering and political in-fighting. They had mastered these valuable political lessons in the prefectural assemblies.[43]

Most commentators have looked upon the prefectural assemblies as merely extensions of the power of the central government and as the tools for the control of the political life of the nation by the government in Tokyo. One such description reads: "Since the participation of the people in local administration was very limited, the local government system in its modern garb became a main pillar of the absolute political power of the central government. The reorganization of local government presaged the form of the national assembly, which in a sense, became an extension of the powerless local assemblies."[44] As the following quotation attests, however, the prefectural assemblies, though legally restricted, did not take kindly to central government attempts at control, fought the government all the way, and enabled their members to build up experience for the confrontation on the national level. "The Assemblies proved troublesome bodies, so much so that in 1881 a Board was created in the Dajōkan called the Board of Adjudication, the purpose of which was to settle disputes between local governors and the assemblies."[45]

There is a third reason for the unexpected edge the opposition enjoyed in the Diet. The oligarchs wanted to show the rest of the world, particularly the advanced states of the West, that the Japanese were capable of running a constitutional regime. There were two dimensions to this concern, one of which was the drive to be accepted as civilized, modern people, and the fear of being laughed at by the foreigners for failing in the attempt.[46]

The intensity of this compulsion to succeed and by this success to make a place for Japan in the community of civilized states is indicated by the immense pride in constitutional government exhibited at this time by Japanese of all political shades.[47] It is of course difficult, if not impossible, to gauge accurately the effect of national pride on constitutional development. This seems to have been a situation, however, in which nationalism, instead of hindering the development of constitutional government, gave it a boost. Kaneko Kentarō, who was at this time a member of the House of Peers, recalled:

Then [at the time of the promulgation of the constitution] certain European people ridiculed the idea of Japan's adopting a constitutional government, saying that a constitutional system of government is not suitable for an Asiatic nation and is only adapted to the cool-headed people of northern Europe; even the southern European nations have failed in establishing constitutional government. How can an Asiatic nation accomplish what southern European nations have found impossible? So it was thought that if the Diet was dissolved in its very first session, unpleasant comments would be made by foreign critics. And, in consequence, a compromise was effected between the government and the Diet.[48]

Itō, for one, carried out his role as a constitutional statesman with one ear constantly attuned to criticisms from the West. "If there is one mistake," he said in 1899, "in the progress and direction of constitutional government, there will be those who will question the suitability of constitutional government for the Orient. This is what concerns me."[49]

The desire to make the experiment work and thereby satisfy national pride was a goal in itself. The second dimension to the concern about the success of constitutional government was the aim of treaty revision. Treaty revision, as stated in an earlier chapter, was one of the basic reasons for establishing constitutional government in the first place, and this factor exerted a continuing and powerful influence in compelling the oligarchs to save the experiment. And party leaders too, especially

Itagaki, felt that in the national interest constitutional government had to be made workable. This theme recurs consistently in Itagaki's political thinking. Cody writes: "Itagaki stressed the need for bold and unusual decisions by Japanese leaders if the treaties were to be revised. He suggested two alternatives, or perhaps supplementary plans, for achieving this aim: (1) to carry out reforms to create an excellent governmental system which even Europeans would be forced to admire, and (2) to develop the military strength of Japan."[50]

A fourth reason may be cited for the relatively advantageous position in which the opposition found itself *vis-à-vis* the oligarchs. This is that the oligarchs were basically divided in their opinions on the role of constitutional government. In fact, one of the most striking aspects of the budget squabble in the first Diet was that it further revealed the antagonism between Itō and Yamagata. There were disagreements not only on day-to-day matters such as the timing of speeches, but on fundamental issues such as the government's attitude toward the Diet, the opposition parties, and the vital question of dissolution. The split between the two was aggravated by an intense emotionalism; Itō is seen as being angry, exasperated, and even contemptuous of Yamagata's views and policies and of Yamagata himself.[51] It would be too much to ask that the highly sensitive Yamagata not be affected and not reciprocate these feelings.[52]

The description of Japanese political parties as "exclusive clubs, yet . . . clubs lacking any real unity, torn by violent internal struggles for power which frequently had little or no connection with consideration of public policy"[53] can be said to apply with equal validity to the oligarchy.[54] It should be re-emphasized, however, that strong personal animosities were secondary and in part derived from basic, substantive differences in political philosophies. Any other view, it seems, would be doing an injustice to the intelligence and patriotism of the oligarchs. If the oligarchy, like the opposition, was divided, this does not necessarily compound the causes of "the failure of democracy in Japan." It may simply mean that the parties were not as much at a handicap with respect to the oligarchy as heretofore assumed. The division among the oligarchs, together with the legal openings provided by the constitution, created opportunities which the politicians seized and exploited, until within a decade no government could be formed without at least their covert cooperation.

In spite of the rude shock the oligarchs must have suffered in the first test of strength, none of them suggested radical changes in the body politic to redress further the balance in their favor. Rather, by accepting the reduction in the budget, they indicated that compromise would be a standard operational procedure governing the relationship between the government and the opposition.[55] This is clear evidence of how surprisingly "enlightened" and "liberal" the oligarchs were.

The existence of the compromise faction within the Jiyūtō was another factor which almost assured that constitutional government in Japan would be carried out through a series of compromises. The rationalization offered by Gotō in his acceptance of public office—to work for the fruition of constitutional government from within the oligarchy—was in the best tradition of this compromise faction.[56] This faction was composed of men like Itagaki, Hayashi Yūzō, Hoshi Tōru, and Ōe Taku, and their actions revealed that they believed that stubborn frontal assault against the government was not the way to public power. These politicians had a vital stake in the success of constitutional government, for constitutionalism legitimatized their participation in government. This, after all, was the goal they had aimed at for nearly two decades. In this sense, the factionalization of the parties was based not only on the propensity toward atomization along personal lines; an equally strong force was the differences that arose on policy matters.

The above leads to the proposition that the division and fragmentation characteristic of the opposition parties were fortunate for the development of constitutional government. If the opposition had been able to present a unified, uncompromising front from the beginning, the resulting stoppage of the parliamentary process would have given the oligarchs little choice but to question the wisdom of their decision to establish a constitutional form of government. By bringing to bear the total military and police resources at their command, the oligarchs, if so inclined, could have snuffed out the constitutional experiment. If the opposition was split, however, the oligarchy also suffered from the same weakness. This must have loomed large in the calculations and aspirations of the party men, who must have been able to discern the disunity among the oligarchs. Then, too, the "compromise" faction faced two men who were as pliable as they were. We have already seen Itō characterized as one who would avoid a fight, "even at the cost, when necessary, of making a dignified retreat."[57] Yamagata also was described by his biographer not as an inflexible, obdurate oligarch, but as a rather astute politician able to withdraw at the strategic moment: "Much of the skill claimed for Yamagata as a political tactician rested on the instinct he showed for the correct moment to pull one step backward before taking two steps forward. He never attempted to move recklessly when prospects for advancing were slim. He always prepared his withdrawal even as he calculated his maneuvers."[58]

The objective situation in the Diet also favored compromise. The government could muster some 129 votes in the first session; control depended on swinging only a few votes. This elemental fact certainly did not escape the preceptive, realistic Itō and Yamagata. Just as important, the oligarchs were assuredly aware of the easily fragmented nature of the opposition and could not have been ignorant of the willingness of part of the opposition to compromise. In short, we see here the Japanese genius for compromise working in both the oligarchy and the Diet.

The first Diet session set the stage for a steady expansion of the Diet's share in power, at a more rapid rate than even the gradualists had expected. Actually, contemporary commentators saw this, or had even foreseen it, much more clearly than more recent interpreters. Even before the first session, the *Japan Weekly Mail* in an editorial drew this discerning and penetrating picture of the practical implications of constitutional government:

It is very easy to conceive what will happen when opinions begin to divide under the influence of parliamentary discussion, the Cabinet itself not being a party Cabinet, but a coterie of statesmen who, although united in the cause of general progress, hold various views with respect to methods and measures. Divisions in the Diet, if it does not immediately produce division in the Cabinet, will inevitably have the effect in the course of time. A section of the Ministers will drift into the ranks of the Opposition, and thus supply the latter with the official experience essential to political efficiency.[59]

Chōya, though blunter, was no less perceptive. Discussing the principle of nonparty cabinets and the division within the oligarchy, the newspaper stated:

Although Premier Yamagata is sincere in his belief in the principle of nonparty cabinets, not a few of the other ministers know that this policy cannot be maintained under a constitutional form of government. Therefore, even though they are members of the cabinet, in spirit they have in part become members of the opposition party, forming a hostile faction [in the cabinet]. In this way they hope to maintain their positions. As long as things go smoothly they will assist Premier Yamagata and defend the present cabinet, but as soon as the situation becomes unfavorable to them, there is no question but that they will unite with the opposition party and turn their bayonets on their chief. We have seen this situation repeat itself consistently in the past ten years or so . . . If the opposition party concentrates its strength on the vulnerable part of the present government, how can the party in power, divided and weak, cope with the attack? Furthermore, the supporters of the opposition party outnumber those in the party in power. These are the reasons why we are very sorry for the present cabinet.[60]

In sum, the first session of the Diet gave vivid hints about the manner in which constitutional government would develop in the first decade of its implementation. These patterns were dictated partly by the division and factionalism within the ranks of the oligarchy. Such splits were common enough phenomena even before 1890. Before the opening of the Diet, however, they were in the nature of family quarrels, for no nongovernment third force came close to breaking oligarchic monopoly of the vital areas of public power. The great political significance of the creation of constitutional government is that its very nature meant the opening of the doors to outside forces heretofore so skillfully and effectively contained. In this situation, the division among the Meiji leaders, stemming from the same roots that caused the splits among the opposition parties, was a luxury the oligarchy could ill afford. The minimum requirement necessary to control and contain the opposition was the firm, consistent unity of the oligarchs; yet there was a conspicuous and persistent lack of this unity. Moreover, the opposition was now in a position to exploit fully the differences among the oligarchs, for they were now legitimate sharers of the public power.

It is in this light that the strength of the parties becomes a weighty factor. They had had over a decade and a half to propagate their views and to win converts to their cause. They were also skillfully and effectively organizing and strengthening their basis of power in the provinces, as well as gaining precious experience in local assemblies. Consequently, once the constitution sanctioned and legitimatized the participation of the parties in the government and made their consent mandatory for adopting the budget and passing laws, the fact that they could come to the Diet with a relatively powerful position of strength was a factor that the government could not and did not ignore.

All this talk about the strength of the opposition, of course, cannot obscure the fact that it was, more often than not, divided. And if it appears that the strength of the opposition is exaggerated, this is a reaction to the traditionally accepted interpretation that would see all the cards—in terms of legal, economic, and political power—stacked overwhelmingly against it.

The really important thing to remember is that for all the reasons mentioned there were those in the government and the opposition who realized that compromise offered a realistic approach to the new legal and political order, and that both sides from the very beginning acted, when necessary, on the basis of this conviction. At no time was an implacable, unyielding position maintained by all the oligarchs or all those in the opposition. The question is which group—the oligarchy or the opposition—gained more by the compromises. The experience of the 1890's shows that the gains of the opposition, relative to their position at the beginning of the decade, were significant to a striking degree. In this decade, the politicians were to pursue every advantage, gradually but persistently, realistically, and relentlessly, turning every small opening into everwidening beachheads. Having said this, however, it must be stressed that the fundamental political decisions were still in the hands of the oligarchs, and the role of the politicians was basically one of reacting to these decisions. For this reason the words and actions of Itō and Yamagata are crucial to an understanding of constitutional development in the 1890's. This is why so many of the following pages will be devoted to these two men.

*In our day, "politics" and "power politics" have be-
come terms of implied condemnation. Politics and politicians are contrasted with statesmanship and statesmen;
international issues are framed as peace and humanity
versus power politics. . . . The only real sense which
can be attributed to these distinctions lies in the manner
in which power is exercised.*

RICHARD C. SNYDER AND H. HUBERT WILSON,
ROOTS OF POLITICAL BEHAVIOR:
INTRODUCTION TO GOVERNMENT AND POLITICS

VII

ITŌ AND YAMAGATA: THE NATURE AND ROLE OF PARTIES

The first session of the Diet, which ended on March 8, 1891, was in a
sense special. It now appears that the oligarchy and the opposition sought
to avoid dissolution, and both sides refrained from raising and pursuing
issues to a point that would have precipitated this action. Therefore,
while the oligarchs had expressed their philosophy on the nature and role
of parties in terms of the principle of nonparty cabinets, this principle
was not put to a real and practical test. During the Matsukata ministry
(May 6, 1891 to July 30, 1892), Itō and Yamagata proposed different
answers to the question of the role of parties in the constitutional state
which was now Japan. The question arose because the oligarchs were
quick to perceive that the controls they had created to contain the parties
were not as effective as they had anticipated. Itō therefore demanded a
chance to form a government party with himself as the head, but he was
out-voted by his fellow oligarchs. Yamagata suggested election interference to gain a parliamentary majority but with the crucial qualification that the government would not and could not recognize this majority as the government party. Yamagata narrowly missed getting his
majority in the Diet. So, strictly speaking, neither proposal was put to
the full test. However, because of Yamagata's "failure," and because the
oligarchs were "obligated" to let Itō try his way, a debt he was to collect

a few years later, the nature of constitutional government to an important degree was shaped by Itō. This is the legacy of the Matsukata ministry to Japanese constitutionalism.

Two factors, among others, which made up the political structure of post-1890 Meiji Japan, were to facilitate Itō's task of guiding and molding constitutional government. One was the nature and role of the emperor, and the other the existence of a moderate group in the opposition. And during the Matsukata ministry there evolved in an interesting and significant manner political expressions of these two factors. In the first instance, the oligarchs momentarily lost control of the emperor, whom they had been nurturing as the symbol of the omnipotent state, to a non-Sat-Chō group in the government. This meant that the emperor was a neutral force that could be used and managed by whoever could impose his will on him at any given time. It is commonly acknowledged that Itō, after the deaths of Ōkubo and Kido, developed manipulation of this symbol to the level of a fine art. Also during the Matsukata administration, a moderate faction within the Jiyūtō unabashedly approached the government with a proposition for compromise. The successful ending of the third session of the Diet is attributable to the acceptance of this offer by the oligarchs. By continuing the precedent of compromise set in the first session, the oligarchs were preparing the ground for making compromise with the hated parties an accepted standard of behavior. And by the time of the second Itō ministry, which succeeded Matsukata's, Itō was willing to try the expedient of granting a cabinet post to the head of one of the parties.

About a month after the end of the first session, Yamagata revealed to the emperor his intention to resign.[1] Itō was notified of Yamagata's action while he was in Kobe with his wife and daughter. Later he was commanded by the emperor to succeed Yamagata, but he firmly declined.[2] Itō in turn suggested Saigō Tsugumichi and Matsukata, but the former refused on the ground that he should not be considered for the position merely because his name happened to be Saigō.[3] Matsukata, too, declined at first but accepted after pressure was applied by Itō, Inoue, and Yamagata. Thus, on May 6, 1891, the first Matsukata ministry was formed.[4]

Matsukata was probably chosen as a sop to the sensibilities of the Satsuma faction. By this time the locus of power in the government had shifted from the Satsuma to the Chōshū faction. However, the Satsuma faction was still strategically positioned and powerful enough to compel Chōshū to have at least outward fidelity to the principle of "maintaining the Sat-Chō balance."[5] *Jiji shimpō's* remarks after the fall of the Kuroda cabinet are just as applicable to this time.

Count Itō's resignation at this time may come as a shock to the people . . . There has been a reshuffle in the cabinet, and those who had opposed his views on the treaty revision question have resigned [and his position on the question vindicated] . . . It is widely known that the present government is in fact a coalition of clans. Under no circumstances must this coalition ever be endangered. The statesmen in power do everything possible to maintain this coalition in a proper state . . . for they are convinced that if this coalition is not preserved the strength of the government cannot be continued. For the count to resign when his views were not accepted was proper. For him to have remained in his post after the opinions of those who disagreed with him had been rejected and after these men had tendered their resignations would not have been proper . . . The count's resignation is indicative of the strength of the practice of maintaining equilibrium of power between clans.[6]

This self-imposed wait in the wings was to have serious repercussions. Itō, in his anxiety to hurry his grand entrance on the parliamentary stage, was to say and do things calculated to crush Matsukata, making of the latter a bitter political enemy.

While Matsukata was forming his ministry a dramatic historical incident was being shaped. The military services demanded of Matsukata that the military establishment be enlarged. They let it be known that if these demands were not met, the posts of the service ministers would remain unfilled. Here, then, is probably the earliest such threat made by the military against a prime minister.[7] Matsukata acted with a firmness that belies the accusations that he was an indecisive weakling. In July 1891 he undertook a revision of the "Table of Organization for the War Ministry," enacted in June 1888, which provided that the war minister and vice-minister must be officers of the grade of general. Matsukata wanted this changed so that it would be possible for "those other than generals" to be service ministers. The revolutionary implications of this move cannot be minimized, for independence of the military was one of the fundamental and sacrosanct principles held by the oligarchs, and Matsukata, at this very early date, was trying to tamper with it.[8] The ensuing arguments over Matsukata's proposal became so heated that the emperor "consulted" Itō. Itō replied:

If it is our desire to support the principles of constitutional monarchy and to prevent the transfer of the imperial prerogatives to the people, we should not make the military prerogative a plaything of the Diet and the political parties . . . If the sovereign wishes to control the military prerogative directly, rather than entrust ministerial responsibility for controlling it to the political parties and those who . . . are called ordinary politicians and are motivated only by the lure of office, we should entrust it to officers of the rank of general. These officers are, by virtue of military training, proficient and knowledgeable in the conditions of the military system, discipline and personnel . . . It is of the utmost importance that the discords of the political world not extend to military matters.[9]

This pronouncement presaged the death of Matsukata's radical suggestion, and this was but one of many occasions during his tenure when he was to find himself isolated and embattled on crucial issues. As important as this incident is in terms of modern Japanese history, Itō's advice is cited because it reveals that on the eve of his first proposal to form a government party, Itō had the opportunity to restate his views on the nature of the opposition parties officially. His deep-rooted conviction on this point was one reason for his desire to create a "national" party.

Itō, in his memorandum, also emphasized the dangers that would result if the "discords of the political world" were to disturb the smooth functioning of Japan's military establishment. He was speaking from bitter experience, for already, as the *Japan Weekly Mail* had clearly foreseen, "division in the Diet" was producing "divisions in the Cabinet." Ito's attempt to check this insidious development, which threatened to make a mockery of the oligarchs' goal of a controlled constitutional experiment, was another reason for his decision to form a party.

Almost immediately after the formation of the Matsukata ministry, Agriculture and Commerce Minister Mutsu Munemitsu proposed the creation of an organ within the cabinet to control the clashes and disunity among cabinet members which were driving the executive branch into a state of near anarchy. *Nichi nichi* spoke of conditions in the government about this time which may very well have motivated Mutsu's move.

No matter who organizes the cabinet, there are persons whom the cabinet members must be able to influence and move. Granting this necessity, there is no guarantee that these people will follow the policies of the prime minister and work in unity. It does not take a discerning person to realize that the prime minister cannot fulfill his duties to the emperor and satisfy the demands of the Diet if he has to lead cabinet members who are not united in action . . . The most difficult [obstacle] of all is that there are no allies of the cabinet in the Imperial Diet . . . The supporters of the government . . . are exceedingly few and unreliable.[10]

Shortly before August 11, 1891, Mutsu and Itō Miyoji, after prior consultation with Itō, completed the drafts of two documents, the Cabinet Resolution ("Naikaku giketsusho") and the Cabinet Covenant No. 1 ("Daiichi naikaku kiyaku"), and presented them to Matsukata.[11] The "Resolution" contained pledges to eliminate "weakness and disunity" in the government and to work for the unification of government policies. It also called for the "consolidation" of administrative functions and the "strengthening" of the foundations of the government. Three basic steps toward achieving these goals were then cited: a cabinet minister, in discussing government policies and political moves with those outside the cabinet, must first secure the concurrence of the other ministers; the Diet speeches by ministers must be in agreement; there must be consistency in the views of the cabinet ministers when their views were expressed in newspapers and magazines.[12] The "Covenant" provided for the establishment of a Political Affairs Bureau (Seimubu) within the cabinet, responsible ·for carrying out the goals spelled out in the "Resolution." According to the "Covenant," the head of the bureau would be a state minister thoroughly informed on all cabinet plans and policies, and on the conditions existing in each political party. He would also be charged with the responsibility of "anticipating" all matters of explosive political potential and of devising countermeasures. Other state ministers, in turn, were to clear all Diet speeches with the bureau head, and to reveal to him the substance of their opinions prior to public expression. The bureau head was also given the tasks of supervising government-controlled newspapers and magazines and of editorial control over essays and articles appearing in them.[13] In short, the Seimubu was conceived as a secret organ, and its aims were to *control* as well as to coordinate cabinet views. It is even possible that it could have evolved into a government within a government if the principles of the "Covenant" had been pushed to logical extremes.

Itō Miyoji, in a letter dated August 13, 1891, informed Itō of the purpose and results of a meeting held on August 11 between Inoue Kaoru, Matsukata, and Shinagawa Yajirō.[14]

The morning before last, Matsukata, Shinagawa, and Inoue met at the prime minister's residence to discuss the "Cabinet Resolution." Shinagawa gave expression to various disagreements. However, Inoue strongly pressed Shinagawa with a minute exposition on the existing evils and the urgent need for unity. Furthermore, Inoue stressed that a precise and detailed plan such as the one at hand was a step toward preventing future discord and would serve to forestall arguments and contention. Inoue also emphasized that the plan would suppress discontent and discord. He then laid two choices before Shinagawa: superficial unity while disastrous results accrued from vagueness and indecision, or benefits from this plan by defining precise areas of competence.[15]

Shinagawa finally agreed with Inoue, and at the cabinet meeting held on August 14 he undertook to explain the "Covenant" and to recommend Mutsu as the head of the Political Bureau.[16] Both the "Resolution" and "Covenant" were then approved unanimously, and Mutsu was selected bureau chief. On August 17 the emperor granted imperial sanction, and the Political Affairs Bureau was formed a week later. Hara Kei and seven others were appointed members.[17] Less than a month later, on September 15, Mutsu resigned as bureau chief. Itō Miyoji again serves as the source for clarifying the motives. The day after Mutsu resigned, Itō Miyoji wrote Itō:

[Mutsu] could not put into effect the "Cabinet Resolution" and the "Covenant" of the Political Affairs Bureau. For example, the ministers would neither hand over their secret funds when asked nor permit inspection of their accounts. Superficially, the ministers do not seem to reject any request, but actually they ignore the agreements. Realizing that there was absolutely no hope for substantially strict compliance, he resigned yesterday. At yesterday's budget meeting, at the height of a vituperative argument, Viscount Shinagawa turned to Mutsu and said, "If you're going to be so demanding, why don't you try and be the home minister." Enomoto [Takeaki] also declared, "Even though you are the head of the Political Affairs Bureau, I don't like to be told what to do as if commanded" . . . There is nothing we can do but express words of great regret. Here we have a major government organ with imposing goals . . . [Moreover], Imperial sanction . . . [has been] granted to the cabinet agreements. Still, we cannot put into practice these agreements, preparing them for burial even before the ink on them is dry.[18]

Some weeks after the collapse of his plan, Mutsu gave vent to his bitterness in a letter to Itō. His views, though jaundiced, may serve as a barometer of the discord and conflict in the government. He revealed first that he had called on Inoue Kaoru and had found him extremely worried; Inoue, unlike his usually vigorous self, "presented a sorrowful appearance." Mutsu then said that Inoue voiced fears that no remedial measures would be effective with the situation having degenerated to this point. Inoue complained to Mutsu that men like Yamagata and Matsukata did not seem to feel that the government was in any particular danger. Inoue's suggestion, reported Mutsu, was to let Matsukata "go his way" and experience a failure and make him learn from it. Mutsu's comment on Inoue's views was that they were indeed "penetrating insights into the present situation." Mutsu then continued: "In my humble

opinion . . . today, when we are faced with a Diet controlled by the opposition parties, and with the cabinet split as it is, we present not the
sight of defeated troops, but the unseemly spectacle of an army in flight.
Even a sage cannot remedy the situation. To permit a government which,
since the Restoration, has made wonderful progress to degenerate into
anarchy is a great crime."[19]

Itō's decision to form a party must be seen against this background of
oligarchic disunity. In late November 1891, Itō went to Yamaguchi and
he seriously discussed with his friends and supporters the organization of
a political party.[20] Two months later, on January 22, 1892, he formally
submitted a memorial in which he petitioned for permission to carry out
his plan.

The difficulty involved in expelling the present party members as Diet members and of replacing them with good people is already known to Your Majesty. Accordingly, there is but one way to cope with this problem: that is,
Hirobumi, of his own free will, must relinquish his titles and become a commoner, and by using the Taiseikai as a basis, organize a political party. This
party will pledge itself to the great principle of imperial supremacy and will
strive to overwhelm the parties espousing liberal-democratic doctrines and in
this manner aid the cabinet.[21]

Itō's basic characterization of political parties remained unchanged. A
good party was one that pledged itself to the principle of imperial supremacy. A bad party was one that espoused liberal-democratic doctrines, one peopled by "ordinary politicians motivated only by the lure
of office." Moreover, Itō foresaw the day when the lack of government
efforts to build up a party would mean loss of control over the administration by default to the tyranny of numbers. This had been precisely
what Inoue Kowashi had so strongly stressed in his argument with Itō
over the principle of nonparty cabinets. In a reply on December 10, 1891,
to an imperial inquiry about the political situation, Itō declared:

After careful consideration [I have come to the conclusion] that if by chance
we are satisfied merely with the passage of the budget, and that if this year's
Diet, like last year's, presents a picture of dispute and confusion, the momentum for growth generated by the parties will be increased all the more. We
will find that by next year's session there will be much insinuation and argument for joining the opposition. Local popular sentiment will be gradually de-
ceived and attracted to the opposition. What is called constitutional government will degenerate into a mere contest among political parties, and the nation will have to submit to the oppression of numbers . . . Once people join
the ranks of the parties, it will be difficult for them to secede . . . The situation

of the past two or three years is this: the government does not have a fixed policy and the ranks of officialdom are torn asunder, with no unifying principle to hold them together. Officials flatter the leaders of political parties to insure themselves of a position at some future date. Therefore, there is no state secret that does not leak out, and party spies without any effort are able to discover state secrets.[22]

In this reply to the emperor Itō gives a hint as to why he felt it necessary for him to become the first commoner prime minister. Itō was plainly disgusted with the petty wrangling among high government officials. Even more grave, Itō saw signs that this administration disunity would enable the "popular parties" to control the government. Top-level bureaucrats were trying to build cliques of party members and were flattering the "leaders of political parties" as insurance against just such a development. Itō, then, was seeking to create a strong, personally controlled government party that would obviate the need for administration officials to make unnatural allies. In a message to Tokudaiji Sanenori, Itō complained:

If, in spite of the aforementioned weaknesses, the government manages to win a majority, how can we expect a unified course of action? For each cabinet member, and this is the customary practice, desires to enlist Diet members secretly and to control them. This in turn has led to conflict among the members of the cabinet. In extreme instances there has been the unseemly sight of squabbling over the sharing of funds, over whether funds are available, or over the size of funds. The alternative to unity is disunity—a disorderly mob. What benefit will arise from acquiring a majority? There is rather the danger that a majority will be the cause of bringing about a great failure.[23]

After Itō submitted his January 22 memorial asking for imperial sanction to form a party, he approached Matsukata, Inoue Kaoru, Kuroda, Shinagawa, and Enomoto with his plans. None of them approved.[24] Inoue Kaoru wrote Itō on January 26 expressing disagreement with Itō's "unorthodox" approach for solving the political crisis and suggested that Itō's entry into the cabinet would be more to the point.[25] Itō replied that "ordinary solutions" would be ineffective in rooting out the evils inherent in the political situation. This was the time, he continued, to throw oneself wholeheartedly into carrying out one's plans.[26]

On February 1, 1892, Matsukata called a meeting of the *genrō* at his Mita residence. Kuroda, Yamagata, and Inoue, who were present, disagreed with Itō. Shinagawa, who came at the express invitation of Inoue, also disagreed. The discussion next turned to Shinagawa's projected plans for interfering with the forthcoming general elections, but a violent argument between Itō and Shinagawa ensued, which ended only when the meeting was adjourned.[27] On February 4 Matsukata reported to the throne on his failure to change Itō's mind. He then recommended that Itō be appointed prime minister. This may have been a face-saving recommendation, since Itō had failed to convince his colleagues, and the cabinet had decided to try election interference instead, in an effort to cope with the lack of majority control in the Diet.[28]

The government earnestly and ruthlessly embarked on an attempt to see that only those "loyal and sympathetic"[29] to it were elected. Bribery, strong-arm thugs, police, gendarmes, and even troops were used.[30] It was a bloody affair from the beginning, and a glimpse of the situation may be seen in a letter Shinagawa wrote to Matsukata on February 1. "Blood has already flowed in Kōchi, Osaka, and Toyama. I am afraid that 'flowers of blood' will bloom in the dead of winter, between now and the fifteenth. Circumstances make this inevitable."[31] The government had every expectation of winning the election. War Minister Takashima Tomonosuke on the day of the election wrote: "Since we have received forecasts of complete victory, this is truly good fortune for the nation, and it is something to be deeply grateful about. Please accept my humble felicitations on this occasion."[32] But the results were disappointing for the government. The opposition parties, obtaining a return of 163, captured a majority of the seats, with the government's supporters totaling 137.[33] It may be said that the election interference was an important factor in turning the election toward victory for the opposition parties.[34]

The problem facing the Meiji oligarchs after the first two sessions of the Diet was as painful as it was elementary. A smoothly functioning administration was an irreducible prerequisite for fulfilling their goal of a strong and independent Japan. However, as pointed out clearly by the *Nichi nichi* article, the lack of "allies" in the Diet made it difficult, if not impossible, for the government to carry out its administrative programs. Compromise was not overlooked as one way to solve this dilemma.[35] Still, compromise was not a permanent solution, for it meant increasing the opposition parties' share of the public power. An attempt at least had to be made to eliminate this unpleasant alternative to the full and continuing control of both the executive and legislative branches of government.

It was at this point that different approaches were suggested by the two giants among the oligarchs. The approaches reflected the temperaments as well as the political *Weltanschauung* of the two. Yamagata's method was direct and simple: election interference. The reasons for his position, however, were less simple. For one thing, he must have felt that it would be unnecessarily foolhardy for the oligarchs to substitute "unorthodox" and complicated moves for tried and proved tactics. Yamagata must also have sensed that the government's public endorsement of a party could be taken as government recognition of the principle of party cabinets.[36] Consequently, being even more prudent and circumspect than the cautious Itō, he must have felt it unthinkable to risk this possibility by associating openly with the Taiseikai before the election results were known. Then, too, there was really no guarantee that even if the government won this specific election it could win all the subsequent ones. To these pragmatic considerations must be added what appears to be Yamagata's most important reason for opposing Itō's suggestion. By countering Itō's plan with his own, Yamagata was asking Itō to go back to basic principles. Yamagata, like Itō, fully appreciated the need for a working majority in the Diet. What he was saying, however, was that while the government should and could get a working majority, the oligarchs should above all remain true to fundamental principles. And Yamagata's concept of constitutional government, according to one of his biographers, was as follows:

Within the new framework of Western political forms, the traditional absolute power of officialdom was to continue to operate. The Diet's powers were narrowly restricted so as not to undermine this predominance. As representatives of the people, the Diet members were to be consulted and allowed to advise and give support to measures proposed by the government. That they should question the essential rights of the executive and deny officials the ultimate power of decision was not a part of this scheme. To insure this unequal relationship the first principle was for all cabinets to remain outside the parties. To Yamagata, a conflict of loyalties was involved in the notion that parties should lead the government. The party member, he felt, was pledged to support a program, his first loyalty was to his party, whereas an official or cabinet minister was pledged to support an official policy as a servant, not of the people, but of the Emperor.[37]

Yamagata's position was that once *de jure* recognition was granted to political parties as equal partners in decision-making, the theoretical underpinnings of the Meiji governmental system would become untenable. And once penetration of the theoretical bulwarks that the oligarchs had built up with so much care and effort was permitted, total surrender to the attacking opposition forces was inevitable.[38]

Itō, on the other hand, came out for a government party because he was fully cognizant of other practical sources of danger besides the lack of a Diet majority. These were: the almost complete lack of harmony and unity among the highest functionaries in the government, and the tendency among these functionaries to build their own empires in the Diet with consequent aggravation of the chaos among their ranks. Itō obviously felt that only personal intervention by a man of his stature, prestige, and dignity, whose feet were implanted in both the Diet and the administration, could eliminate the destructive factionalism in the government and unite and revitalize the government's supporters in the Diet.

Itō, of course, never conceded to Yamagata that he was departing from basic principles. Itō was asserting that if a party fulfilled the qualification he laid down for a "national party," then the government would not be recognizing party government. Essentially, whereas Yamagata in effect was maintaining that something must be given a name before it exists, Itō was stating that defining a thing differently changes its character. This was the measure of the unpleasant reality that the oligarchs had to face so early in the constitutional experiment.

Itō gave up his plan after the election results were known.[39] He had insisted all along that election interference was a negative approach and would be unrewarding, and he had won his point. Persisting with his plan would only run the grave risk of further humiliating Yamagata and his faction. Itō must also have believed that Matsukata's days as prime minister were numbered, and that open and direct control of the government would enable him to carry out his ideals.[40]

On the same day that he expressed willingness to shelve his plan to form a party, Itō submitted his resignation as head of the Privy Council. This was apparently a move designed to hasten the resignation of Home Minister Shinagawa, who was directly responsible for election interference.[41] Yamagata, Inoue, and Kuroda opposed Shinagawa's resignation, but in the end Itō had his way.[42] Agriculture and Commerce Minister Mutsu also became a casualty of cabinet discord and dissension.[43] Shinagawa was succeeded by Soejima Taneomi, and Mutsu by Kōno Togama. The appointment of these two men, who were intimate with those in the opposition ranks, was an indication that the government was predisposed to revert to compromise.[44]

The third session of the Diet was convoked on May 2, 1892. On May 11 the House of Peers passed a resolution demanding that the government "resolve the election interference problem properly." The next day, in the House of Representatives, a memorial to the throne impeaching the government for election interference was submitted, but this measure was defeated, 146–143. On May 14 the Lower House passed by a vote of 154–111 a resolution calling on the government to take responsibility for election interference and resign. The House was prorogued for one week, beginning May 16.[45] On this day the dissolution of the Lower House was discussed among those in the government.[46] However, neither the Jiyūtō leadership nor the oligarchs really relished the prospect of dissolution.

The willingness of men like Itagaki, Hoshi Tōru, Kōno Hironaka, and Takeuchi Tsuna to compromise becomes understandable in part against the background of a bitter struggle for power in the Jiyūtō ranks. Generalized, it may be said that Ōi Kentarō, long an advocate and practitioner of "direct action," had about this time organized a group of non-Diet members in the Jiyūtō into the Two-Seven Society (Ni shichi kai), so named because it met on the second and seventh days of each month. This society formed a vociferous and powerful lobby in the Jiyūtō. On the surface its aim was to pressure the Jiyūtō Diet members into taking strong and uncompromising stands against the government and in this way bring about "responsible cabinets." The real aim, however, was to force the government, through unremitting pressure, to dissolve the Diet, the purpose being to give non-Diet members of the party a chance to be elected into the House of Representatives.[47] Hoshi Tōru and his supporters opposed this attempt to compel Diet members to submit to the control of Ōi Kentarō and his followers, and at a party general meeting in Osaka in 1891 Hoshi won control of the party machinery.[48] It was the need to protect this recently gained control over the party that impelled Itagaki and Hoshi to be amenable to compromise.[49] For, while they were confident that the party would win the election, they entertained some fears about the gains that the Ōi faction could make at their expense.[50]

The Itagaki group, in seeking compromise, left nothing to chance and made its intention clear to the government. Takeuchi Tsuna and Kōno Hironaka of this group took pains to inform Suematsu Kenchō, a leading progovernment Diet member, that their faction was willing to compromise. These overtures were immediately relayed to Itō.[51] Furthermore, the Jiyūtō organ, *Jiyū*, on May 20 carried an article quoting Itagaki and his "soft" line.[52]

And on the other side, in spite of the talk of dissolution, sentiments in the highest government ranks almost unanimously favored taking a moderate position toward the Lower House. Yamagata, though coming out for dissolution if no other course was available, still was unconvinced of the wisdom of Matsukata's prorogation order, and it is fairly plain that he did not consider dissolution the alternative answer.[53] Itō, on his part, stressed the disunity among Diet members supporting the government and warned that the government had to be extremely careful about depending on them to carry out its policies.[54] Itō Miyoji best summed up the feelings of both sides when he wrote Itō that "with this moderate government and this moderate Diet, neither side cares for a head-on clash."[55]

The Lower House reconvened on May 23, and by a series of compromises the supplementary budget for fiscal 1892 was passed, permitting the Diet to adjourn on June 15, 1892.[56] The day after the Diet adjourned Matsukata revealed his intention to resign. This move brought into being and pitted against each other a rather unusual grouping of power blocs. Itō was asked in the meantime to succeed Matsukata, and on June 29 he expressed his readiness to accept on condition that all the *genrō* participate in his cabinet. Yamagata refused to accede to this demand, but the next day, after a heated argument and a threat by Itō that he would retire permanently from all activities connected with the government including that of advice-giving, Yamagata yielded.[57] Itō was now fully prepared to take over from Matsukata.

However, a minor revolt arose among the junior members of the cabinet. War Minister Takashima, Navy Minister Kabayama, Foreign Minister Enomoto, Education Minister Ōki Takatō, and Agriculture and Commerce Minister Kōno declared that there was no reason for the cabinet to resign since it had safely weathered the third session of the Diet. Moreover, they attacked the "tyranny" of the *kuromaku genrō* (behind-the-scenes elder statesmen), who had arrogated to themselves the right to make and unmake cabinets. Matsukata, emboldened by this support, on July 10 called Itō, Yamagata, Kuroda, Inoue, and Ōyama Iwao to his residence and informed them that he would not resign after all. Itō could do nothing but tell Matsukata to remain in office.[58]

On July 14 Agriculture and Commerce Minister Kōno was offered the post of home minister. This move was plainly made to settle the election interference problem. It is also possible to say that it was directed against the Shinagawa-Shirane-Takashima axis in the government.[59] When Kōno accepted, the strongest group within the cabinet was composed of Kōno, Gotō,[60] Enomoto, and Sano Tsunetami, who had succeeded Kōno as minister of agriculture and commerce. Immediately after his acceptance Kōno forced Shirane to resign because of his role in election interference. Prefectural governors who had been overly conspicuous in their zeal for election interference were transferred or compelled to submit resignations.[61]

War Minister Takashima and Navy Minister Kabayama struck back by refusing to attend cabinet meetings and finally by submitting their resignations on July 27. Matsukata, about 6:00 p.m. on the same day, also submitted his resignation. However, the emperor, after consulting with Gotō, Kōno, Enomoto, and Sano, told Matsukata that the resignation of the two service ministers was no reason for him to resign.[62] Thus, at this time, secondary figures in the government who were closely associated with the opposition parties were actually advising the throne. A power vacuum had been created by Itō's refusal to deal with Matsukata because of the latter's refusal to resign and by Yamagata's supporters' boycott of cabinet meetings because Matsukata was working with the Kōno-Gotō-Sano combination. This vacuum the trio had quickly filled. This meant that the emperor, like the Meiji constitution, could also be used by non-Sat-Chō groups to further their own ends. In the very near future, during the Itō ministry, there were to be two more such attempts.

Matsukata, armed with the "advice" from the emperor, again changed his mind and began to look for successors for the service ministers. He sought Itō's help on July 29, but Itō refused, saying that this was a matter on which Matsukata should consult the military.[63] The following day General Ōyama Iwao, accompanied by Lt. General Kawakami Sōroku and Vice-Admiral Nirei Kagenori, called on Matsukata. They told him that while it was proper for a subject to obey the emperor's will, the basic cause of his troubles was his reliance on men like Gotō and Kōno and his rejection of the service ministers' advice. They then informed him that it was impossible to find generals who were willing to step forward as successors. Matsukata saw the hopelessness of his position and turned in his resignation for the final time the same day, July 30, 1892.[64]

In retrospect, the first Matsukata ministry was in many ways the most interesting and revealing of the cabinets in the first decade of parliamentary government. The very fact that Matsukata was chosen indicated that there had to be at least outward compliance with the practice of maintaining the balance between the Sat-Chō factions. His appointment, however, had all the traits of an interim appointment between two Chōshū cabinets, evidence that Satsuma was no longer the force in Japanese politics that it once was. Hence the weakness of his cabinet, for he had only as much support and sympathy as any lame duck politician could expect. Another source of Matsukata's weakness was that since the battle lines were drawn primarily between Itō and Yamagata, not between Satsuma and Chōshū, the support that he should normally have received from the Satsuma faction was given to Yamagata instead.

Matsukata had ideas, radical ones for his day and for one in his position. His suggestion for revising the "Tables of Organization for the War Ministry" is an example. He was also capable of acting, as witness his attempt to form an independent non-Sat-Chō locus of power in the government. But when Yamagata turned against him and used Satsuma men like Takashima, Kabayama, Ōyama, Nirei, and Kawakami as his political shock troops, Matsukata was crushed. Furthermore, it is pertinent to wonder how different the development of constitutional government would have been if Itō, who was actually closer in temperament and ideas to Matsukata[65] than he was to Yamagata, had supported Matsukata. Instead, it was Itō, no friend of Yamagata, who paved the way for Matsukata's downfall by rejecting Matsukata's plea for assistance.

The antipathy between Itō and Yamagata mirrored the deep-rooted disunity and discord within government ranks. The situation was so chaotic, in the eyes of Itō and his supporters, at least, that they created a special organ with special rules to cope with it. Their failure shows only too clearly that the government and the parties were equally harassed by factionalism: the laws of Meiji political behavior were universal in their application. And if the government was quick to take advantage of the splits in the opposition ranks,[66] it was in turn, as Fukaya has emphasized, "subject to the mischief-making of the parties."[67] In fact, many in the government had already gone so far as to "flatter the heads of political parties" to insure against a future time when the parties would conceivably wield public power. *Chōya's* prophecy that members of the Yamagata cabinet would "turn their bayonets on their chief" as soon as it was to their advantage to do so seemed by the time of the Matsukata cabinet to be bearing fruit.

Lack of unity and harmony was not the only major weakness plaguing the government. It lacked the essential condition to carry out its long-range plans and goals, that is, a majority in the House of Representatives. This deficiency was quickly and sorely felt during Yamagata's tenure, but a desire on the part of both the government and the opposition not to mar the very first session with a dissolution probably prevented this issue from being brought to a climax.

The second session of the Diet had barely gotten underway when it was dissolved. It was as if the oligarchs were anxious to experiment with their ideas on solving the problem of the lack of a Diet majority. Yamagata and his followers, like Shinagawa and Shirane,[68] felt that corruption and violence would not only win the election but so decisively that their efforts could very well insure a continuing majority. The Yamagata approach failed, and he has since been branded as an anticonstitution statesman. This is a patently unfair charge and this distinction must be made: Yamagata interfered in the *election* but he did not tamper with the constitution itself.[69] The point must be brought up, for it reveals that there was at least a tacit acceptance by all the oligarchs that constitutional government was in Japan to stay. Yamagata and his supporters battled the opposition on their grounds, if not on their terms. Thus, when election interference proved unsuccessful, the alternative was compromise with a group within the opposition, not the altering of the constitution.

The oligarchs were highly practical and realistic men. They had just lost an emotion-charged, hard-fought and bloody election. But they rolled with the blow and dispassionately returned to the business of running the government, even if this meant compromise with their bitter antagonists. This did not mean that the oligarchs were cynics; they were utterly loyal to what they believed were first principles. The great battle during the Matsukata ministry, in fact, was not between the oligarchs and the opposition, but between Itō and Yamagata on the question how best to square these principles with the political realities they faced.

The real significance of the conflict between the two men, therefore, can be stated as follows. The Yamagata formula of election interference came very close to succeeding. The margin of difference between the opposition parties and those who supported the government was narrowed in the second election from forty-two seats to twenty-six. If Itō and Yamagata had been agreed on this method, very possibly the government could have won. If it had not, another attempt would have been made immediately. It is not difficult to imagine the type of constitutional government that would have developed with the oligarchs in firm control of the Diet and the government. As it was, Itō strongly espoused a different course of action, and when election interference failed, the parties were given a breathing spell. Itō had to be given his chance, and his was the softer approach. This is one way the disunity among the oligarchs contributed to the growth of constitutional government in Japan.

Itō, by his passivity, helped to bring down the Matsukata cabinet. He was eager to test his reputation as the "greatest" constitutional statesman in Japan by openly taking over the reins of government[70] and by directly dealing with the parties on his own terms. Chapter VIII will discuss the first stages of the Itō approach to constitutional government.

A political party exists primarily to obtain power through accession to office and only secondarily to effectuate idealistic notions of self-sacrifice for a great common good.

HAROLD S. QUIGLEY,
JAPANESE GOVERNMENT AND POLITICS

VIII

THE SECOND ITŌ MINISTRY: ITŌ AS A CONSTITUTIONAL STATESMAN

Itō Hirobumi, the author of the constitution, was fully confident that he would be able to bring under control the parliamentary experiment.[1] He had been almost contemptuous of what he believed were Yamagata's bumbling and naïve tactics against the Lower House and of his lack of understanding of constitutionalism. After Yamagata's resignation he had been forced a second time to make way for one he considered a mediocrity, one completely incapable of handling the responsibilities of a prime minister. Thus, as far as Itō was concerned, the direction of and efforts at constitutional government in Japan had been in the hands of two men not competent for the tasks. The formidable array of elder statesmen and non-Sat-Chō talent[2] in Itō's cabinet indicated that he was prepared to make a real attempt at forging constitutionalism, as he conceived it, into a viable system of government, productive of the ends for which it was created. And the characteristic that was most conspicuous in Itō in his efforts to achieve these aims was his ability to compromise.

In spite of some failures, Itō was already famed for his skill in preserving a working balance between contentious and jealous individuals and cliques in the government—a result of his willingness to compromise. In his first try as a constitutional statesman, he used this talent in dealing with his political opponents in the Diet. This enabled him to weather successfully the fourth and ninth sessions of the Diet.[3] He also compromised on priorities or ends. During his first administration under the constitution, he postponed the consummation of his ideals on constitutionalism to expedite revision of the unequal treaties. Furthermore, he compromised on methods. Before he resigned as prime minister he tested Itō Miyoji's plan for joining hands with the Jiyūtō, rather than attempt to form his own "national" party hurriedly. Finally, he compromised on the use of the emperor, the cornerstone of the constitutional monarchy created by the oligarchs. Early in his second tenure as prime minister Itō in effect permitted the Jiyūtō to hide behind this symbol. Itō's mastery of the art of the possible, as revealed during his second administration, and the implications of this mastery for Meiji constitutional development form the major theme of this chapter.

The fourth session of the Diet was convoked on November 25, 1892. The opening ceremonies were scheduled for November 29. On Sunday, November 27, Itō decided to visit his parents. Just as his personal jinrikisha turned the gate, a speeding carriage bearing Princess Komatsu hit it from the side. Itō was thrown off and struck his head on a wheel of the swerving carriage before he fell to the ground. He suffered a severe laceration on his forehead and lost six or seven of his upper teeth. He had to go to Ōiso to recuperate from his severe injuries.[4] Inoue Kaoru was designated provisional prime minister.[5] It is ironic that at the moment Itō had chosen to emerge with almost indecent haste from behind the scenes, he was compelled to play again the part of a *kuromaku genrō*.

The budget once more served as the focal point of the clash between the government and the Lower House. Watanabe Kunitake submitted a budget calling for an expenditure of 83,750,000 yen. The budget committee of the Lower House slashed 8,840,000 yen, or approximately 11 per cent, from the budget and presented the revised budget to the Lower House on December 19. Before the House of Representatives could act on it, the Diet adjourned for the year-end holidays.[6] During the recess the government deliberated on the policies to be adopted against the Diet. Inoue Kaoru, writing to the convalescing Itō, outlined the steps the government should take in meeting the Lower House's challenge on the budget. Three points in his letter are worth noting. The first is his recommendation that the Lower House should not be dissolved. The second is his suggestion that the administration officials responsible for presenting the government's budgetary case to the Diet go along with the reductions and be apprised of the reasons for this necessity. The third is the revelation that cabinet disunity remained a nagging problem. "On this occasion," Inoue wrote, "what demands greatest attention is to see that the cabinet works together in harmony. We should see to it that everyone makes concessions whenever differences occur. Furthermore, everyone must be extra careful to keep whatever occurs within the cabinet from becoming known to the outside."[7]

Itō's reply was also marked by a conciliatory attitude toward the Lower House. He said that the government ought to concede where concessions were called for, and that both sides ought to show magnanimity. He then hinted that Itagaki was amenable to compromise. "On looking back, in the spring of 1875 Kido and Ōkubo met at Osaka and in the end returned with Itagaki. Although the situation at that time naturally differs . . . from the present, the conditions now are the same when measured by the need for tolerance and magnanimity."[8] Itō could well afford to express these generous sentiments. He had sufficient evidence that an important segment of the Jiyūtō was willing to compromise with the Itō cabinet. Even while Matsukata was prime minister, Kōno Hironaka told Suematsu Kenchō of the need for "fresh air" to circulate in the government, an obvious reference to Itō.[9] On August 31, 1892, a few weeks after Itō became prime minister for the second time, Inoue Kaoru wrote Itō that Matsuda Masahisa, another leading light in the Jiyūtō, expressed the view that the prospects for constitutional government would darken if the "present cabinet did not do well." Matsuda was also quoted as saying that the Jiyūtō intended to split with the Kaishintō as soon as possible.[10] Then, on November 26, the day after the Diet was convoked, Inoue Kaoru again wrote to Itō that Hoshi, Kōno, Matsuda, and Takeuchi Tsuna had met at Itagaki's home on November 9 and pledged that they would ignore critics who asked whether the Jiyūtō was a government party or an opposition party, and they would support the government whenever the government ought to be supported.[11]

The Diet reconvened on January 9, 1893. After one month of jockeying between the government and the Lower House, including a prorogation ordered by the former and the submission of a draft memorial by the latter, the budget was settled. The issue was resolved when the emperor handed down an imperial rescript commanding all government officials, civil and military, to pay the national treasury one-tenth of their salaries for six years to help cover expenses for naval construction. The emperor on his part promised to contribute the sum of 300,000 yen yearly for the same period.[12] On February 15 Itō also promised a "reorganization of the administrative branch by the time the fifth session of the Diet was convoked" and a "sweeping" reform of the Navy. These two moves made the passage of the budget for the fiscal year 1893 a certainty, and the Diet adjourned on March 1, 1893.[13]

The fourth session has been characterized as follows:

The injection of the Throne into politics was a great victory for the ideas of Itō and spelled a major defeat for the liberal parties. Its immediate effect was to force the parties to compromise with the government despite their realization of the true nature of events. Its long-run effect was even more serious. Professor Fukaya . . . has remarked that from the end of this Diet session, the Jiyūtō tended to lose its pure *mintō* [antigovernment party] character. The major reason for this was the discouraging fact that although a popular party might oppose the Peers, the Privy Council and even the Genrō in the cabinet or out, it could not oppose the Emperor, and a spirit of defeatism was certain to arise among the party men which would hasten the day toward compromise and corruption . . . The most significant factor . . . was that *mintō* unity, which had been exceptionally strong up to this point, began to crack under the terrific pressure of these first years.[14]

The above may be questioned on several accounts. In the first place, issue can be taken with the statement that "*mintō* unity . . . exceptionally strong up to this point began to crack under the terrific pressure of these first years." The proposition was advanced in an earlier chapter that part of the Jiyūtō expressed willingness to come to terms with the government before the first session of the Diet was convened. Even if this is not conceded, the evidence is ample that during the first and third sessions compromise between some members of the Jiyūtō and the government made possible the passage of budgets in those sessions. It has also been sufficiently demonstrated that this state of affairs continued during the fourth session. The very fact that the Jiyūtō itself was hopelessly divided makes a myth of the concept of "*mintō* unity."[15]

Secondly, to think of compromise in Meiji politics as an unhealthy development is to condemn the Japanese practitioners of this art on the basis of an unrealistic and unfair measuring stick. Perhaps it is enough to quote the life-long champion of parliamentarism in Japan, Ozaki Yukio. While he is speaking of "moderation" and not "compromise," his sentiments are appropriate enough to make the point.

If I were to point out the failing of the Seiyūkai, it would be the vagueness of its platform. However, for a major party, a party which seeks to carry out its policies, or one which possesses administrative power, or one which is about to grasp administrative power, this is unavoidable. It cannot afford the luxury of a minor party with little expectation of coming into possession of public power, which can speak clearly and loudly of its convictions. This is true anywhere in the world . . . A party with responsibility, or one which is about to assume responsibility, cannot but become moderate in its words and speeches.[16]

Thirdly, "injection of the Throne" has been pictured with perhaps too much emphasis as a completely one-sided factor in Meiji politics, as though only the oligarchs benefitted from the use of the emperor.[17] Just about this time Inoue Kaoru wrote to Itō saying that there were those in both the Kaishintō and Jiyūtō who hoped for some sort of settlement of the budget question and were *exerting all* efforts to this end.[18] If we accept the fact that segments of the government and the Jiyūtō were amenable to compromise, the intervention of the throne, rather than *forcing* compromise or *compelling* the opposition to submit, offered a way out for shifts in public position by both sides. In other words, the rescript in this instance provided a cover for compromise.

Fourthly, and this is related to our third point, it is difficult to concede that the immediate, direct result of the rescript spelled a great defeat for the "liberal parties." The rescript called for a flat ten-per-cent reduction in the salaries of bureaucrats for six years, which first of all satisfied one of the major demands of the opposition voiced since the first session.[19] More importantly, the budget in effect was reduced, and the use of the emperor enabled both the government and the opposition to save face in the process.[20]

From the end of the fourth session, the groups in and out of the Diet pledged to unbending opposition to the government changed the focus of their attack from the budget to foreign policy. This was good politics, for the government was in the midst of treaty revision negotiations with Britain. Spearheaded by the Japan League (Dai Nihon kyōkai), composed of men like Ōi Kentarō, Abei Iwane, and Ōtake Kan'ichi, the antigovernment movement was joined by the Kaishintō, Dōmei kurabu, and the Kokumin kyōkai.[21] The actions of the Japan League were in some ways simply expressions of splits within Jiyūtō ranks.[22] Hence, during the first days of the fifth session the fighting resembled not so much something between the unyielding opposition and the government, as a clash between Hoshi and his enemies in the Diet, which included supporters of Yamagata.

The fifth session was convoked on November 25, 1893. On November 29, the day after the opening ceremonies, a motion of nonconfidence against Hoshi, the president of the Lower House, was submitted by Abei Iwane.[23] The motion passed by a vote of 166 to 119. No one expected Hoshi to take the president's chair again after the vote. When he did, the Lower House adjourned to give Hoshi time for "self-reflection." Hoshi was not the type to take this kind of advice too seriously and he calmly occupied his chair the next day. This action caused the anti-Hoshi forces to decide to expel him from the House by submitting a memorial of nonconfidence to the throne.[24]

Itō's countermeasure against the memorial, presented below in detail, shows without doubt that Itō was closely allied with Hoshi, and that the emperor merely parroted the "advice" of the person or persons who happened to have his ear at a given time. It is also evident that the anti-Hoshi faction was outmaneuvered by Itō. This is only to be expected, since the anti-Hoshi faction was carrying the fight into grounds controlled by Itō.

Itō wrote to Minister of the Imperial Household Hijikata Hisamoto instructing him how to handle the presentation of the memorial by the Lower House.

1. When the president of the Lower House [in this case, the vice-president, Kusumoto Masataka] seeks the audience with the emperor, the minister of the Imperial Household should, through his private secretary, inform the president of the following facts: memorials to the emperor are covered by Article 51 of the Laws of the Houses. All memorials are made in the form of documents. Now, since the purpose of an audience is to present a document, he is expected to present the memorial with the knowledge that he is not to make an oral report apart from the document he is to present. Inquire, as a precautionary measure, whether he has any objections to this. If he does not, that is fine. If he has objections, the private secretary is to record the opinion of the president right then and there and report it to the minister of the Imperial Household. If he answers that he has an oral report over and above the document to be presented, it would be better not to grant him an audience.

2. During the audience, the minister of the Imperial Household and the grand chamberlain shall be in attendance.

3. After the audience, when the vice-president retires after presenting the memorial, there will be the following words by the emperor: "I will read it carefully." The possibility that the vice-president will read the memorial aloud in the presence of the emperor must not be discounted . . . In this case, it would be enough for the emperor merely to receive the memorial.

If by chance the president says that he would like an imperial reply to the memorial, the minister of the Imperial Household will caution the president as follows: "Whether or not the emperor answers depends on his gracious will, so you need not concern yourself about it."

[The emperor's questions on the memorial will be]:

"Is the object of the memorial to petition His Majesty to change the president of the House of Representatives? Or is the object of the House to volunteer an apology to His Majesty for its lack of sagacity? You should consider which of the two the memorial seeks to establish and then report back."[25]

On December 2 Vice-President of the House of Representatives Kusumoto Masataka presented the memorial. The emperor replied: "Is the object of the memorial to petition His Majesty to change the president of the House of Representatives or is it the object of the House to volunteer an apology to His Majesty for its lack of sagacity?" The emperor then commanded Kusumoto to consider which of the two the memorial sought to establish, and then to report back. After considering the matter, the Lower House answered that the real intention of the memorial was to apologize for its lack of sagacity.[26]

The question then is why did those who opposed Hoshi resort to a step which they, veteran politicians as they were, ought at least to have guessed would rebound unfavorably upon them? The answer seems to be that even while realizing that the chances of real success were small, the politicians from this very early stage were experimenting with how best to use the emperor for their own ends. They were probing this possibility as carefully and assiduously as they were testing the Meiji constitution; they sought to exploit any opportunity to enlarge the small foothold that the oligarchs had relinquished them in the administration. As the party men refined by experimentation the use of memorials to the throne, the memorials became a weapon to harass, inconvenience, and embarrass the government. In addition, the tactics of presenting memorials afforded Diet members a chance to "play to the gallery." Uyehara, who later became a politician, describes the motivations behind the addresses to the throne.

The right of address to the Crown is often exercised by the Diet, especially the House of Representatives, to embarrass the government; and it is of great political value . . . It ought not, however, to be inferred that the Diet advises the Emperor by means of addresses to interfere with or to change the policy of the State. Far from it. The real value of this right is not any force it brings to bear upon the Emperor, but the peculiar effect produced in the minds of the people . . . Indeed, addresses to the Emperor by the Diet . . . are usually presented for the sake of pointing out the defects and unsatisfactory conditions of the administration, and of making the Cabinet Ministers appear to the people as thwarting the will of the Emperor.[27]

The use of the memorial, therefore, as it developed, was more for effect than for precipitating significant alterations in the existing political situation. Those in the opposition parties, as politicians having to account to the electorate at certain intervals, found the memorial of immense practical use. The submission of a memorial linked them indirectly to the highest symbol of state authority. This had some value in terms of reflected glory. The action invariably became widely known, and in most instances the contents of the memorial put them squarely on public record on issues popular with the electorate. And if the issues happened to clash with personal convictions, preferences, or ambitions, the memorial could be used to proclaim a public stand while permitting pursuit of private goals. The memorial, then, is another illustration of how political instruments created by the oligarchs to render party participation in government harmless eventually turned out to be double-edged swords in the skillful hands of the party politicians.[28]

After the "failure" of its move in memorializing the throne, the anti-Hoshi faction succeeded in forming a disciplinary committee which voted a week-long suspension for Hoshi. After the week was over Hoshi unconcernedly resumed his chair. This time the disciplinary committee recommended expulsion, which was approved by the House by a vote of 185–92.[29]

On the foreign policy front, the attacks against the government centered on the accusation by the Groups Demanding a Firm Foreign Policy (Taigai kō ha), as the antigovernment faction was also known, that the government was failing to enforce its rights under the treaties for fear that this would inconvenience or embarrass foreign powers. On December 8, 1893, the Taigai kō ha introduced three measures in the Lower House, all of which in essence called upon the government to define clearly the rights and duties of the signatories of treaties and to enforce the treaties strictly.[30] Mutsu, as stated earlier, was at this time in the midst of treaty-revision negotiations with Britain. Feeling that the passage of the above measures would inject unnecessary obstacles into the talks, he suggested in a secret memorandum that the Diet be prorogued on the day the measures were brought up for debate. He further proposed that the Lower House be dissolved if it persisted in pushing the measures after the prorogation. On December 19 the measures were brought up for discussion. The Diet was then prorogued for ten days. At the end of the period Mutsu took to the rostrum and spoke against the measures. Immediately after the speech the Diet was again prorogued, this time for fifteen days. The next day, December 30, the emperor issued a rescript dissolving the fifth session of the Diet.[31]

The special election was held on March 1, 1894, and the Taigai kō ha won 130 seats, supporters of the government 168.[32] The basic issue in the sixth session, as it was in the fifth, was foreign policy. This was reflected in the speech delivered by Itō on May 16, 1894, the day after the opening ceremonies.

The policies on treaty revision have remained fixed and unalterable since the Restoration . . . The reason for dissolving the previous session was this problem of treaty revision . . . The most important factor contributing to the conflict between the government and the Diet is the measures calling for the strict enforcement of treaties . . . The policies since the Restoration, as you well know, are to uphold the principle of "open country" and to acquire the rights of an independent nation. And once the latter are won, to have intercourse with all nations on the basis of international law . . . To secure the revision of treaties is considered by the government its greatest responsibility. We are exerting ourselves in this direction, and we are now making progress . . . We intend to overcome all obstacles. Moreover, we intend to accomplish our aim . . . I believe that the achievement of concrete results is not distant . . . I would like to ask you to refrain from using this problem for selfish political purposes. I come in sincerity to ask you to reconsider your position.[33]

The antigovernment forces, however, ignored Itō's pleas and the next day introduced a draft memorial impeaching the cabinet on the grounds of maladministration in internal and external affairs. The measure was defeated by the slim margin of five votes, 149–144. The Jiyūtō and the Independents supported the government.[34] On May 18 the Jiyūtō introduced a resolution condemning the "unfair" dissolution of the fifth session. The Jiyūtō was charged with making this move "merely to preserve the appearance that it was still an opposition party."[35] The antigovernment forces, not satisfied merely with criticizing the injustice of the dissolution, added a revision impeaching the cabinet. Both the original measure and the revised bill were voted down. A resolution condemning the government for the unconstitutional act of dissolving the previous Diet without giving formal reasons was passed on May 21. On May 31 the antigovernment faction succeeded in pushing through, by a vote of 153–139, a draft memorial on nonconfidence in the cabinet.[36] On June 2, 1894, the sixth Diet was dissolved.[37]

It may seem strange that Itō sanctioned two consecutive dissolutions of the Lower House.[38] He was the father of constitutional government in Japan and epitomized moderation in his relationship with the Diet. Moreover, he had begun his tenure as prime minister with high hopes that harmony and cooperation between the executive and legislative branches could be achieved if he dealt with the Lower House personally and with sincerity. And if, as Inoue Kowashi had warned, sincerity was not enough, Itō had powerful allies in the House of Representatives in the form of Jiyūtō members. Furthermore, he had been extremely critical of both Yamagata and Matsukata for their handling of the Diet and he had assumed the prime ministry with confidence that he would succeed where they had failed.

The principal reasons for the dissolutions lay outside the Diet chambers. It is true that Itō faced the same basic problem that plagued Yamagata and Matsukata—a lack of a *consistent* majority in the Lower House—and that this was an important cause for Itō's actions. However, Itō and his foreign minister, Mutsu, were concerned primarily with the effect that dissolutions would have on representatives of foreign powers in Japan.

Japan was on the verge of realizing the overriding goal of Japanese statesmanship since the Restoration, in Itō's words, of acquiring the "rights of an independent nation."[39] The opposition was preaching what was basically antiforeignism to attack the government at this critical juncture. If the government were unable to show that it could control this group, this would be a revelation that it could not shield the rights of foreigners who would be without the protection afforded by the existing treaties. Consequently, Itō's actions can be said to have been taken to reassure the foreign diplomatic representatives that the Japanese government could act with firmness and dispatch in safeguarding the rights of foreigners residing in Japan in the event the treaties were revised. Mutsu's correspondence with Itō amply bears this out. In one letter Mutsu reported that the French minister voiced dissatisfaction about the antiforeign sentiment. Mutsu's reply is noteworthy, not only for its support of the premise made above, but also as an indication of the basic philosophy that governed the oligarchs' attitudes and actions toward antigovernment forces and their activities throughout the Meiji era. Mutsu first began with what appears to be a bald attempt at flattery by expressing surprise that the French minister, a long-time resident of Japan, should even bring up the subject. The minister should be aware, Mutsu averred, that in the twenty years of rapid development in Japan reactions were frequent. Mutsu said that Japan was now experiencing one of these periods. However, he assured the minister that "On this too, the government certainly does not intend to remain passive once it reaches a certain point," and he promised that the Japanese government had absolutely no intention of losing control of the situation.[40]

Furthermore, there was one factor that added urgency to the demands of the foreign ministers. This was the petticoat influence existing in the foreign community. Mutsu wrote to Itō that both the German and

French ministers had complained about the "fears" that antiforeignism was generating among the female sector of the European community. Mutsu conceded that the views of the British, French, and German ministers were proper.[41]

The effect of the dissolutions was precisely the one desired by Itō and Mutsu. When the fifth session was dissolved, for example, the acting minister from Britain wrote to Mutsu: "Your speech before the Diet can be taken as sufficient proof of the sincerity of your government's progressive policy. The dissolution of the anti-foreign Japan League and the measures taken against the Diet are evocative of our deepest emotions."[42] And in a letter sent by Mutsu to Inoue Kaoru on January 2, 1894, Mutsu reported that all the ministers from Europe that he met at the Palace on New Year's Day expressed satisfaction with his speech of December 29. They were full of praise, Mutsu said, for the "resolute action of the cabinet in dissolving both the Diet and the Japan League."[43]

The dissolution of the sixth session can also be explained largely in terms of foreign policy demands on the Japanese government. Opposition attacks against the government's foreign policy, in and out of the Diet, had continued unabated, and there was at least one serious instance of manhandling of foreigners.[44] However, in spite of all this, the activities of the antigovernment forces during the sixth session were not so threatening that a dissolution was justified as a punitive and retaliatory measure.[45] Passage of the draft memorial of nonconfidence by the Lower House may have given the government the excuse it needed to dissolve the House, but there were other countermeasures available to the government if it desired them. In fact, many representatives, according to Hara Kei, were caught unawares by the government's action because it was unexpected.[46]

The talks with Britain were approaching the climactic stage in the summer of 1894, just about the time of the dissolution, and the antiforeign activities in Japan were probably furnishing Britain with an excellent talking point in the negotiations. Even as late as two days prior to the final signing, Foreign Secretary John W. Kimberley reprimanded the minister to Britain, Aoki Shūzō, on the matter. He told Aoki that the Japanese government had chosen to ignore the antiforeign movement in Japan which had been in existence for several years and had failed to suppress it. This was an indication, Kimberley added, that the Japanese government lacked international morality and was lukewarm on the matter of treaty revision.[47] Fortunately, however, the last-minute agonies suffered by the Japanese were short-lived, for the final signing took place in London on July 16, just a month and a half after the dissolution of the sixth session. After the successful signing Mutsu boasted, "I achieved success in treaty revision by giving primary attention to domestic politics rather than to diplomacy."[48]

All the while the situation in the Korean peninsula was deteriorating, and Japan formally declared war on China on August 1, 1894.[49] The general election following the dissolution of the sixth session was held a month later, on September 1.[50] Hiroshima, which served as the imperial headquarters for the duration of the war, was the site of the seventh session, convoked on October 15 to pass on military expenditures. There were some fears that the government would encounter opposition even on the war budget. These fears proved groundless as the Diet in record time, and in complete agreement, passed the war budget.[51] The *Japan Weekly Mail,* commenting on the situation, wrote: "All the parties received the Premier's address with applause and passed the War Budget without a dissentient voice. The task the House had been asked to achieve in seven days it accomplished in three, a striking contrast to its custom on previous occasions . . . The House has acquitted itself so well, there will be less disposition to assert that the Japanese are unfit for constitutional government."[52]

The eighth session was convoked in Tokyo on December 22, 1894.[53] On February 20 Itō presented a supplementary military budget for 100,000,000 yen which unanimously passed both Houses. The 1895 budget passed with few reductions. The session ended on March 27, 1895.[54] Less than a month later, on April 17, the Shimonoseki Treaty was signed, restoring peace between China and Japan. On April 23 representatives of Germany, Russia, and France demanded that Japan retrocede the Liaotung Peninsula to China. Japan complied, and on May 10 this step was formally revealed to the Japanese people through an imperial rescript. For the Taigai kō ha, about this time known as the Association of Political Friends (Seiyū yūshi kai), retrocession became one of the main issues with which to attack the government after the honeymoon that had lasted for two sessions.[55]

The government, however, was not completely isolated, for even while the Jiyūtō sent representatives to meet with the Association of Political Friends, the executive committee of the Jiyūtō was secretly making overtures to the government. There are varying accounts of the steps that eventually led to the publicly acknowledged rapprochement between the Jiyūtō and the government in 1895. One of the key figures in the negotiations, Itō Miyoji, offers this recollection of the events.

Itō Miyoji states that on May 13, a few days after the rescript made public the retrocession, he told Itō, who was in Kyoto, to assume responsibility for the retrocession by resigning. Itō Miyoji then returned to Tokyo where he witnessed the antigovernment forces' attempts to take political advantage of the retrocession. According to Itō Miyoji, this caused him to write back to Itō and rescind his advice, for, as Itō Miyoji says, "If the government did not eliminate the antigovernment movement, this would permit the roots of calamity to flourish in the future." It was then that he saw Itagaki, telling the latter that the continued existence of the Itō cabinet was imperative if the government was to carry out its plans for postwar development.[56] He further emphasized in the strongest possible terms, in the conversation with Itagaki, the necessity of party support to achieve the goals of postwar construction. Itō Miyoji says that an "understanding" was reached with Itagaki. Itō, in the meantime, had returned to Tokyo. Itō Miyoji laid down his proposals, actually already accomplished, to Itō. Itō approved. It was only after this that Itō Miyoji revealed his secret talks with Itagaki. Itō, according to this account, "was overjoyed" and gave his consent to the rapprochement with the Jiyūtō.[57]

On July 9, 1895, the Jiyūtō gave a hint that it had reached some kind of working relationship with the Itō cabinet. On this day the party made the following policy announcement: "Our party has for years advocated the downfall of clan cabinets and the establishment of responsible cabinets. We yield first place to no other on these aims. However, today the whole nation must unite and strive for the enlargement of the military establishment and resolve to face the difficult problems facing us from without. Therefore, we must temporarily put off pressing for responsible cabinets."[58] About four months later, on November 22, 1895, the Jiyūtō finally made public the details of the agreement reached between the government and itself. At this time the Jiyūtō demanded that Itagaki be appointed home minister. However, opposition by the incumbent, Viscount Nomura Yasushi, and Vice-Home Minister Shirane threatened a breakup of the cabinet as well as Itō's resignation, so the Jiyūtō contented itself merely with the public announcement of the rapprochement.[59]

The coalition was fruitful. The government introduced a record budget of 200,000,000 yen in the ninth session, which was convoked on December 25, 1895. The Jiyūtō combined with the Kokumin kyōkai and pushed through the budget without much difficulty by February 4, 1896.[60] When the session ended on March 29, 1896, it had passed a huge total of ninety-three bills. Hara Kei thought the ninth session's record noteworthy enough to write about. "This year's Diet has done an amount of work not seen in recent years . . . One reason is that it was not popular to oppose matters coming under the scope of 'postwar development.' Also, the government and the Jiyūtō had concluded an alliance, with the result that the government's bills always had the backing of a majority in the Diet."[61]

Home Minister Nomura Yasushi, a member of good standing in the Yamagata faction, was less than enthusiastic about the Itō-Jiyūtō coalition.[62] Perhaps his unhappiness resulted as much from an awareness that his post was being covetously eyed by the Jiyūtō as from his conviction that compromise with the Jiyūtō was undesirable.[63] In any case, shortly after the end of the ninth session Itō was clearly aware that the time had come for making good on the political debt to the Jiyūtō incurred during the session. This meant a place in the cabinet for Itagaki. On April 4, 1896, he wrote to Inoue Kaoru:

We have survived the session with the passage of all the measures submitted by the government . . . There is no question but that this result was due to the efforts of Itagaki's group. Among party members there are many who are pushing Itagaki's entry into the cabinet. There are those in the government who are also strongly inclined . . . [to have Itagaki in the cabinet]. Although I have admonished them not to air their request publicly, it appears that it would be difficult to delay this matter [of a cabinet seat for Itagaki] much longer . . . I have briefed Kuroda on this situation. He also said that the demand is most proper.[64]

Ten days later, on April 14, Itagaki was appointed home minister. The chief of the Prefectures Bureau in the Home Ministry and the private secretary to the home minister were also appointed from among Jiyūtō ranks.[65] However, as a condition for joining the government, Itagaki and others from the Jiyūtō who were given official appointments removed their names from the party list.[66] Furthermore, the organ of the Jiyūtō, the Tokyo *Shimpō,* on April 15 instructed the members of the party against demanding the resignations of officials of the Home Ministry in the central government as well as in the provinces. They were also enjoined not to bother Itagaki with requests for appointments. The party's original goals, it said, should be pursued "quietly and steadily."[67]

Itagaki was not destined to remain in office for long. On May 30, a month and a half after Itagaki's entry into the cabinet, Itō lost his strong right arm when Mutsu resigned because of illness.[68] Furthermore, Finance Minister Watanabe Kunitake indicated his intention to resign over differences with other members of the cabinet on fiscal matters. Inoue Kaoru suggested that Matsukata be brought in as finance minister and Ōkuma as foreign minister.[69] On August 16 Itō, President of the Privy Council Kuroda, War Minister Ōyama, Navy Minister Saigō, Colonization Minister Takashima, and Home Minister Itagaki met to discuss Inoue's suggestion. Itagaki strongly opposed Ōkuma's entry and threatened to resign if this happened.[70] Itō adjourned the meeting and entrusted Kuroda and Takashima to sound out Matsukata about joining the cabinet. Matsukata evinced interest but held out for Ōkuma's participation. In all likelihood, Matsukata and Ōkuma already had a tacit agreement to hold out for joint entry into the cabinet.[71]

The cabinet met on August 27 to discuss Matsukata's refusal to enter the cabinet alone. At this meeting Itagaki persisted in opposing Ōkuma's appointment. Itō, unable to fill the positions of foreign and finance minister without incurring the loss of Jiyūtō support, resigned on August 28. His resignation was accepted on August 31, 1896.[72]

Itō's biography stresses his inability to settle the imbroglio over cabinet posts for Ōkuma and Itagaki as the reason for his resignation.[73] Other reasons may be adduced. One is that he may have been exhausted from his long tenure as prime minister, already the longest and most trying to date. He also must have felt the loss of Mutsu sorely. Another reason is that neither Itō nor his greatest and oldest friend, Inoue Kaoru, was fully convinced that open alliance with the Jiyūtō offered a permanent solution to the problem of unstable Diet-government relations. The Itō-Itagaki rapprochement was a victory for the ideas and efforts of Itō Miyoji, who believed that without a coalition with the Jiyūtō the government could not carry out its administrative programs. Inoue Kaoru, on the other hand, seems to have felt strongly that Itō should try to form his own party in order to free himself from reliance on an untrustworthy ally in the Lower House. Hence, Itō may have acted in order to break the chain binding him to the Jiyūtō.

Whatever the reasons for Itō's resignation, his second tenure as prime minister sheds light on Japanese political behavior during the last decade of the nineteenth century. The imperial institution, for example, cannot be seen simply as the ultimate, unbeatable shield held up by the oligarchs against the attempted incursions by the outs into the government. The emperor could be used by both party men and oligarchs as a useful and acceptable façade for covering political machinations and arrangements. During the fourth session of the Diet, "intervention by the throne" enabled the Itō cabinet to give in to opposition demands for a reduced budget. The imperial command also offered the Jiyūtō a graceful, public re-treat from its platform, which demanded nothing less than the complete overthrow of clan government, and enabled the party to maintain its public image of an opposition party, though somewhat hazily. The injection of the emperor into politics would have been difficult, of course, if the Itō cabinet had not accepted and continued the arrangement begun during the Matsukata and Yamagata ministries: *de facto* compromise and coalition with part of the opposition, even while proclaiming adherence to the principle of nonparty cabinets. In other words, the oligarchs had to give at least tacit consent to the use of the emperor in the manner de-scribed.

The fifth and sixth sessions also witnessed a somewhat O. Henry-like twist in constitutional government. Itō, the author of the constitution, regarded by his contemporaries as the leading advocate and supporter of constitutional government, and who sincerely believed that he could bring about a harmonious working relationship between the government and the Diet, dissolved the Lower House twice in quick succession. Itō, by temperament, inclination, and convictions, would have preferred not to take the drastic step of dissolution, much less twice in a row. More-over, the sensitive and proud Itō must have been fully cognizant of the comparison that would be made between the "successful" Yamagata ministry and a dissolution-racked Itō ministry.[74] Itō, however, was twice compelled to stage a dramatic show of firmness, to convince representa-tives of foreign powers that Japan was ready to assume responsibilities as an independent state. He could not have been unmindful that he stood on the threshold of grasping that greatest prize of Meiji statesmanship—treaty revision—one that had been eluding all the giants among the Meiji government. He could wait to earn his laurels as a constitutional statesman, for constitutionalism was an internal matter over which he had greater control. Favorable foreign sentiment toward treaty revision took years to develop and success was contingent on factors to some ex-tent beyond his control. It must be emphasized, however, that the oli-garchs' commitment to constitutional government was such that even while sanctioning two consecutive dissolutions they did not consider elimination of this form of government, nor did they believe that the dissolutions would work irreparable harm to the system.

The show of firmness by the Itō administration and the use of the emperor by both the oligarchs and the opposition indicate the great and necessary role of rituals in politics. These rituals may be simple, trans-parent, or complex; they may be cynical in conception or serious in performance. In many cases the actors and the audience may be fully aware of the ritualistic nature of a given political act, but both parties recognize the act as a prerequisite to the ends for which the performance is played. Itō, the master politician who detested fighting and preferred, more than did Yamagata, to take one step backward in order to advance two forward, understood and appreciated the necessity of ritual. The adherence to outward forms, he knew, provided him with opportunities for backstage maneuvers and opened possibilities for compromise. And what was the practice of constitutional government but a continuing series of political activities requiring practical solutions consented to by the parties concerned? More importantly, it would perhaps be legitimate to measure the sensitivity of the oligarchy to "public opinion" by the elaborateness and lengths involved in the performance of these rituals; and if the attempt to measure were made, surely an index would show that the trend became markedly pronounced after 1890.

A noteworthy development along constitutional lines during the Itō ministry was the *public* acknowledgement by the government of the working relationship it had been maintaining with part of the opposition. A contemporary of Itō, Hayashida, stresses the openness of the rapprochement and considers this a departure from the principle of nonparty cabinets.[75] However, the oligarchs, strictly speaking, did not renounce this principle. They still did not regard the existing parties as responsible, selfless groups capable of administering the state. Itagaki and the other members of the Jiyūtō had to leave the party when they entered the government. Furthermore, as stated earlier, Itō was not fully satisfied that this arrangement with the Jiyūtō was a happy alternative to an Itō-formed and Itō-led "national" party. Then, too, it can be and has been argued that the positions given to party members were few in number and insignificant.

For all these reasons the Jiyūtō's accomplishment cannot be denied. In the short space of five years it had been openly accepted as a needed, if undesirable, appendage of the executive branch. It had a potent ally in Itō Miyoji,[76] at this time one of Itō's few really close followers.[77] The bureaucratic ramparts had been breached.

The significance of this breakthrough was that it heralded a gradual but definite shift of "loyalties" from the government to the political parties among two broad groupings of people. One was composed of those who could be identified as progovernment or neutral party men. These men actually very early displayed their chameleon-like ability. In July 1892 the *Japan Weekly Mail* editorialized:

There was a semblance of a Government party in the first session, but it became entirely invertebrate after the Budget compromise, and when the second session opened, only one member of the whole House of Representatives ventured to openly declare himself a pro-government man . . . Dissolution materially changed the complexion of affairs. Politicians saw that the Cabinet was in earnest, and when the Diet reassembled, there was found in the Lower House, some ninety members who, though not openly organized as a Government party, did not hesitate to vote consistently with the Government and to identify themselves with official measures.[78]

The progovernment politicians who could balance the pluses and minuses of their political loyalties and make a decision after one test of strength could be expected to sense with characteristic accuracy the shifts in political trends after the second Itō ministry.

The second group, perhaps more important than the first, was composed of bureaucrats from the highest to the lowest ranks. Itō Hirobumi, Katsura Tarō, and Saionji Kimmochi represent the top-stratum bureaucrats who moved to align themselves with the parties. Hara Kei may be considered an example of officials of the middle to upper level. Mizuno Rentarō, the author of the article cited earlier on home ministers under whom he served, exemplifies the lesser known bureaucrats who turned politician.[79]

By the end of the first five years of Meiji constitutional government, then, the signs were abundant that the oligarchs were inexorably losing control over the constitutional experiment. By the end of the second five years, the culmination of these developments was the creation of a *de facto* party government, headed by Itō himself. The events leading to and the factors involved in the establishment of the Rikken seiyūkai will form the basic themes of chapters IX and X.

*Inoue and Yamagata had many interests . . . Itō was
extremely skilled in calligraphy and in composing Chinese poems. Yet it was strange that Itō actually had no
real interests aside from politics . . . Wine and women
served merely as a necessary concomitant to politics or
as a safety valve. In short, Itō lived and breathed
politics.*

TOKUTOMI IICHIRŌ,
"ITŌ, ŌKUMA, AND YAMAGATA"

IX

ITŌ AND HIS "NATIONAL PARTY"

The formation of the Rikken seiyūkai in September 1900 represents a
triumph by Itō, who believed in accepting political reality, over Yamagata, who insisted on maintaining political ideals. But this is something
of an oversimplification: Itō succeeded only because Yamagata intrin-
sically was a realist and had accepted Itō's views of the political situation
even while he was rejecting Itō's values.

Two events in 1898 presaged and determined the formation and nature
of the Seiyūkai in 1900. In the summer of 1898, Itō made an unsuccessful
second bid to organize a party. He was unable to create a new government party based on a combination of nonparty members, that is, on
bureaucrats, industrialists, and intellectuals. He was compelled, therefore,
to look to the alternative suggested by Itō Miyoji, that of basing his new
party on an established party, the Kenseitō. This decision helped set the
pattern for the Rikken seiyūkai and all subsequent major parties of an
open alliance between bureaucrats and politicians. Then, also in 1898,
Itō outmaneuvered the other oligarchs in a swift and surprising move to
permit the two major parties to form a party cabinet. This second development was crucial, for when Yamagata reluctantly acceded to Itō's suggestion in 1898 for an Ōkuma-Itagaki cabinet he helped set a precedent
which enabled Itō to form his own government party in 1900.

The circumstances surrounding the formation, tenure, and downfall of the second Matsukata ministry (September 18, 1896–December 28, 1897) made it even plainer to the party men and oligarchs that party support of the government continued to be the minimum requirement for a successful administration—as long as a powerful government party did not exist. At the same time, however, the party men also revealed themselves as being extremely eager to compromise, for as long as the government was controlled by the oligarchs, compromise provided the only way through which party men could widen their foothold in the government provided by the constitution.

When Itō resigned in August 1896, his action resolved the problem of Itagaki's opposition to Ōkuma's entry into the government. Matsukata, after taking over the reins of government, quickly sought Ōkuma's participation.[1] Ōkuma accepted, but only after Matsukata agreed to accept three conditions. These were: only those who possessed the confidence of the people were to be appointed state ministers; freedom of speech, assembly, and press were to be respected; and men of talent from among the people were to be appointed to government posts.[2]

Actually, the Matsukata-Ōkuma cabinet came close to not being organized at all. Shortly before the formation of the cabinet Ōkuma met with Matsukata, Kabayama Sukenori, and Takashima Tomonosuke. Ōkuma proceeded to lecture the trio from Satsuma on the causes of cabinet weakness, stressing that lack of unity within cabinets, not attacks from without, was the basic cause. He then suggested that the cure lay in the creation of responsible cabinets. A few angry words were exchanged at this meeting, probably on the meaning of responsible cabinets. Whether because of this rather heated discussion, or because he was being bothered by a toothache, Ōkuma left in the midst of the meeting and returned home. There he found Ozaki and others from the Shimpotō (Progressive party).[3] In an unpleasant mood, Ōkuma told them that he would not join the cabinet after all. Ozaki protested strongly, asking Ōkuma to reconsider his decision on the grounds of duty and obligation, for there was "deep commitment" on the part of all the parties concerned to form a Matsukata-Ōkuma cabinet. Ōkuma remained adamant. The equally strong-willed Ozaki threatened to leave the party and to support the Matsukata cabinet alone. As Ozaki prepared to leave, Ōkuma's wife saw him and told him to leave the matter to her. She assured Ozaki that as soon as Ōkuma's toothache became less painful she would talk to her husband. She then went to see Ōkuma, returned, and informed Ozaki that her husband had consented to enter the cabinet.[4]

The foregoing incident is cited only secondarily for the insight it gives into Ōkuma's private life and primarily to indicate the tremendous pressure exerted by his subordinates who hoped to share in administrative power.[5] Therefore, the impetus to compromise, though for different reasons, came from both sides of the political fence. For if Matsukata fully realized that the cooperation of the Shimpotō was imperative for pushing through his legislative program in the Diet, the members of the party were eager for office and were clearly aware that Matsukata and the oligarchs still had essential control of the administrative sector of the government.

The government, with Shimpotō support,[6] successfully weathered the tenth session of the Diet (December 22, 1896–March 25, 1897).[7] After the end of the tenth session there occurred a series of incidents, involving lower-level bureaucrats, which had a direct impact on the breakup of the Matsukata-Ōkuma cabinet.[8] The rupture finally occurred on November 6, when Ōkuma resigned. Ōkuma's resignation was preceded by a Shimpotō declaration on October 20 dissolving the alliance and Matsukata's dismissal from their government positions on November 2 of several highly placed Shimpotō members, including Ozaki Yukio.[9]

Since the Shimpotō no longer provided him support, Matsukata sought a coalition with the Jiyūtō. The Jiyūtō, split into pro- and anti-coalition factions, finally decided to attach three conditions to cooperation with Matsukata. It demanded: two cabinet posts; appointment of more than five Jiyūtō men as prefectural governors; and adoption of the Jiyūtō platform by the Matsukata cabinet. The cabinet rejected these demands and the Jiyūtō immediately announced its opposition to the government.[10] The eleventh session of the Diet was convoked on December 22, 1897. On December 25 a nonconfidence motion was introduced. However, the Lower House was dissolved just as it was about to debate the motion. Matsukata submitted his resignation on December 28.[11]

Katsura Tarō, a rising junior member of the Chōshū clique, writes in his autobiography that the history of party cabinets starts with the Matsukata-Ōkuma cabinet.[12] There is much truth in this observation. As Lebra has pointed out, Itagaki had joined the second Itō cabinet after it had been formed, whereas Matsukata actively sought Shimpotō support in organizing his cabinet.[13] And the withdrawal of Shimpotō support was the chief and direct cause of the downfall of the cabinet. The Shimpotō and its predecessor, the Kaishintō, moreover, had up to the end of the ninth session stood and acted on the principle of inveterate opposition to "clan" government. Hence, when the Shimpotō accepted and conformed to the political pattern created by the Jiyūtō, and when men like Kabayama and Takashima, though unhappy and reluctant, participated in open alliance with the party, this marked the general acceptance in practice of the premise that henceforth no government could stand without the active cooperation of a majority in the Lower House. The speedy dissolution of the eleventh session was emphatic proof of this political development.

However, compromise, covert or overt, was at best unsatisfactory. The oligarchs found that the parties sought a greater share of the public power with each agreement of cooperation. Itō's biography, for example, graphically describes the inroads made into the administration by the members of the Shimpotō. "Ōkuma [after the tenth session], on the ground of opening the road for the advancement of men of talent, appointed many vice-ministers, bureau chiefs, and prefectural governors from the ranks of the Shimpotō. Moreover, he established the new position of councilors of the *chokunin* rank, and appointed Shimpotō members as councilors."[14] There was, furthermore, the even greater danger, perceived by *Chōya* and the *Japan Weekly Mail* very early in the decade, of officials and government supporters defecting to the "enemy." The degree of accuracy of the prediction by the two newspapers may be gauged by the description left behind by a contemporary observer of the Matsukata-Ōkuma cabinet. "Many politicians of influence who hitherto have kept out of parties are said to be now thinking of enrolling themselves as members of the different parties . . . And the change from a Transcendental Cabinet to one in which the Ministers are avowedly or tacitly responsible to the majority in the Diet will take place sooner than many think."[15]

The only solution to what seemed to the oligarchs grave defects in the constitutional structure was the one proposed earlier during the first Matsukata ministry by Itō: a government party controlled by a powerful and respected person with feet implanted firmly in the Diet and in the administration.

The suggestion that Itō take over the prime ministry was made even before the fall of the second Matsukata ministry.[16] Following the collapse of the second Matsukata cabinet, Itō negotiated with both Ōkuma and Itagaki for their support. Ōkuma's price was three cabinet seats for members of the Shimpotō, plus the home minister's portfolio for himself. Itō could hardly be expected to comply with these demands.[17] Itagaki also asked for the home minister's position. Itō, however, refused to concede the post to Itagaki. Itō's reason was that, if he gave that cabinet seat to a party man on the eve of a general election,[18] he would be accused of rigging the election in favor of the incumbent's party. The negotiations broke off when Itō, for the same reason, refused to agree to appoint Hayashi Yūzō, a Jiyūtō member, as vice-home minister.[19]

Itō formed his cabinet on January 12, 1898, without including a single party member. However, Agriculture and Commerce Minister Itō Miyoji was busily engaged in trying to bring about a rapprochement between Itō and the Jiyūtō before the twelfth session of the Diet. According to Itō Miyoji's biography, "an understanding" was achieved between the two parties and Itagaki was "tacitly" promised the home ministry. Tokutomi, however, says that Itō was at best unenthusiastic about a coalition.[20]

In the general election, the Jiyūtō and the Shimpotō emerged with nearly the same numerical strength, capturing ninety-eight and ninety-one seats, respectively.[21] Hayashi Yūzō called on Itō after the election and asked that Itagaki be given a cabinet post. Itō said that he had no particular objections to Itagaki but requested delay since there was no vacancy in the cabinet. Hayashi replied that if Itagaki's entry into the cabinet was deferred this would raise problems of control over party members.[22] The fruits of administrative power were just as sweet and desirable to Jiyūtō members as they were to Shimpotō followers. The same day, April 13, Itō called a cabinet meeting to discuss Hayashi's request. Itō Miyoji strongly supported the Jiyūtō demand, saying that when he had negotiated with the Jiyūtō he had tacitly promised Itagaki a cabinet post.[23] Finance Minister Inoue Kaoru opposed Itō Miyoji's stand vigorously on the ground that Itagaki's entry would cause "internal dissension." The argument was heated and bitter. Itō Miyoji finally turned to Inoue and asked point-blank, "Is there any possibility of success in the Diet without taking the Jiyūtō into consideration?"[24] Itō, however, agreed with Inoue and decided to reject the Jiyūtō request. When Hayashi called on Itō on April 16 he was given the cabinet's decision.[25] Itō Miyoji submitted his resignation on April 14.[26]

Itō's decision to reject Itagaki reveals certain facets of the constantly evolving drama that was the Meiji constitutional experience. In the first place, Itō appears to have been unable to keep his own house in order. While he complained about the self-seeking, jealousies, and backbiting that characterized other factions in the government, those closest to Itō were not immune to the same faults. Itō Miyoji and Inoue Kaoru on this occasion clashed over policy differences. However, long-standing ill feeling exacerbated their argument over Itagaki's place in the new Itō cabinet.[27]

Secondly, the confrontation at this time represented something more basic than a cabinet seat for Itagaki. Itō Miyoji represented the group that favored compromise with the Jiyūtō. Itō Miyoji must have urged that it would be more realistic to depend on an already established party than to try to organize one from the ground up. This is the significance of his riposte to Inoue that the government could not expect to achieve anything in the Diet without Jiyūtō help. Inoue Kaoru, on the other hand, propounded the view that Itō had to free himself from reliance on a party with such an insatiable appetite and try to form his own party.[28] This may explain the famous and oft-quoted remark that Itō made when he decided in favor of Inoue's position: "It is not enough to depend on mercenary troops. I must have my own army."[29] In other words, Itō, by siding with Inoue on the Itagaki issue, made it clear that the government party he had in mind did not include Jiyūtō members.

Thirdly, after this incident Itō Miyoji was less close to Itō, despite Itō Miyoji's protestations to the contrary.[30] This drifting apart of Itō and his long-time supporter and disciple, Itō Miyoji, may reflect in part a phenomenon that began to be very apparent about this time. This was the growing impatience among the younger men in the government with the ideas and leadership of the oligarchs. Itō Miyoji, for example, made a quicker adjustment than did either Itō or Inoue to the new political situation brought into existence by the open alliance with the parties. He became extremely close and friendly with the Jiyūtō leaders. Hara Kei was still another bureaucrat who was developing ideas and methods that differed meaningfully from those of the oligarchs.[31] Even Yamagata, who was reputed to have the largest, most closely knit, and most loyal personal following, could not escape this development. Katsura Tarō, his most talented political chief of staff, eventually broke with him.

The twelfth session of the Diet was convoked on May 14, 1898. Very early the Shimpotō introduced an impeachment memorial, charging that the government lacked "positive" policies to counter the carving up of China by the Western powers. The Jiyūtō, however, did not go along with this move and the measure was defeated, 172–116.[32] The government's principal worry during the twelfth session was a growing deficit, one expected to reach 35,000,000 yen in fiscal 1899. The government could not resort to floating any more public loans for fear of shaking the confidence of financial circles. The only alternative was the politically unpopular device of tax increases. Itō's plan called for raises in land, income, and brewery taxes.[33] Itō, however, by introducing an election reform bill, made sure that he would receive the support of the opposition parties in the Diet.[34] The reform was a rather liberal concession. The enfranchised at this time numbered between 400,000 and 450,000 in a population of 42,000,000. The reform, if passed, would increase the number of voters to 2,000,000, a fivefold increase.[35] At this point the government seems to have made a tactical error. Instead of pushing through the election reform bill, it sought first to pass measures for increasing taxes. By doing this it forced the Jiyūtō to take a public stand against the increases. Perhaps, as Maeda says, the government was overconfident because it had received Jiyūtō support on the impeachment resolution. If the government had received approval for the election reform bill first, then the Jiyūtō, assured of one plum for the electorate, might have backed the tax bills. In any event, the tax measure was defeated on June 10, 1898, by a vote of 247–24.[36] Never before had the government been in such an isolated position. The Lower House was dissolved on the same day.

In the next twenty days events within and without the government marked a historic turning point in the development of Meiji constitutionalism. The first step in this climactic development had been taken on or about April 16. On this day Itō had made his remark about "mercenary troops." This indicates that Itō may have been making some effort to create his own party even before the dissolution of the twelfth session.[37] Itō is also said to have revealed to the emperor his intention to form a party when he asked for the rescript to dissolve the twelfth session.[38] Itō discussed his plans to form a party at a cabinet meeting following his meeting with the emperor. This meeting presumably took place on or about June 10. Finance Minister Inoue Kaoru and Agriculture Minister Kaneko Kentarō gave their immediate approval. Kuroda Kiyotaka, head of the Privy Council, also supported Itō's plan. However, when Yamagata heard of the discussions, he met with Inoue and Home Minister Yoshikawa and voiced strong opposition.[39] Itō was undaunted by Yamagata's opposition and continued to push for his party, which was to be based on the intelligentsia from the ranks of the universities and on the rich from industrial circles. Watanabe Kōki was to bring together the university group and Inoue Kaoru the industrialists.[40]

In the meantime, on June 3, 1898, the unification of the Jiyūtō and the Shimpotō had been discussed by certain Jiyūtō leaders. Members of the two parties had their first meeting on June 7, and by June 22 the parties were amalgamated to form the Kenseitō (Constitutional government party). The union of the two parties must have compelled Itō to move even more quickly to bring together his party.[41] Itō therefore met with the industrialists at the Imperial Hotel on June 14 to "promote his ideas." On June 19, again at the Imperial Hotel, he saw Shibusawa Eiichi and about ten other important businessmen.[42] Inoue, on his part, was meeting with indifferent success in his attempts to rally business groups around Itō. A letter Inoue wrote to Itō on June 19 predicted the failure of Itō's project. "The industrial circles," said Inoue, "seem to follow Iwasaki Yanosuke's views [on this matter]. The other night I had a talk with Iwasaki. After I left Iwasaki gave the matter deep thought, and finally he made this much clear. He would be impartial and avoid being entangled with a political party . . . His association with Ōkuma is based on a friendship of many years. He is [also] closely associated with the Progressive faction, many of whom are graduates of Fukuzawa's school . . . We can scarcely expect the solid backing of the industrialists."[43]

The following day, on June 20, 1898, at an organizational meeting with prospective participants, Itō was confronted with three problems. The Kokumin kyōkai had arrogated to itself the central position in the planned party, "pushing the other groups aside," causing unhappiness among some of Itō's supporters. This dissatisfaction with the Kokumin kyōkai's move probably stemmed from the fact that during most of its existence it was pro-Yamagata. There was also a noticeable dampening of the "initial enthusiasm" among many industrialists who discovered that the party was not going to be formed on the basis of a coalition between Itō, Ōkuma, and Itagaki. And among the university group the argument was voiced that for a statesman of Itō's stature to become the head of a political party would cause an imbalance between the two Houses in the Diet, resulting in the "despotism of the House of Representatives" and endangering the "foundations of constitutional government." Hayashida does not record Itō's reactions to these three problems, but merely states that he left for Ōiso. Itō returned to Tokyo on June 22, the day the ceremonies marking the union of the Shimpotō and the Jiyūtō were held.[44]

Itō, according to Hayashida, had in mind three possible solutions to the challenge presented by the newly formed Kenseitō: one was to form a party with the other cabinet members and give battle to the Kenseitō in the general election; the second was to resign, form a party, and support the government; the third was to resign and hand over the reins of government to the Kenseitō. Of the three choices, Itō was said to have favored leaving the government and forming a party.[45]

Two days after returning to Tokyo, on June 24, Itō met with the other *genrō,* Yamagata, Inoue, Kuroda, Saigō, and Ōyama, to discuss

Itō's plan to organize a political party. Itō opened the meeting with the remark that the combining of the Jiyūtō and the Shimpotō left open no other course but the formation of a government party, led personally by himself. He intended, he said, to gather a group of "thinking men" and industrialists and give battle to the Kenseitō in the Lower House. Yamagata was first to respond. He prefaced his argument with the statement that no one denied that political parties were an integral part of a constitutional system. However, he continued, it was improper for a prime minister to organize a party. To do so, Yamagata asserted, would only serve to aggravate the contention between the government and the people. Yamagata, harking back to the principle of nonparty cabinets that Itō himself had endorsed and propounded in February 1889, insisted that the government must be impartial in its relationship with all parties. A party formed by a prime minister, Yamagata insisted, could not maintain an attitude of fairness and impartiality. Therefore it was undesirable and illogical for a prime minister to organize a political party.[46]

Itō replied that he had anticipated Yamagata's objections. Consequently, rather than expend more words he would resign his post without hesitation. He then said that this should amply satisfy Yamagata's objections about a prime minister forming a political party. Yamagata was quick with a rebuttal. He maintained that even if Itō left his present position, he was still a *genrō*. A *genrō,* Yamagata reminded Itō, never ceased to bear the responsibility of giving advice on crucial state matters. What Yamagata was saying, in effect, was that Itō could not resign from the status of *genrō*. At this point Itō's voice and countenance underwent a perceptible change. If Yamagata was going to oppose his plan to organize a party whether or not he remained prime minister, Yamagata left him no choice but to resign from all government positions, return all titles, and, as plain Itō Hirobumi, undertake the formation of a party. As a private citizen, he averred, there would be no need for him to sit in *genrō* meetings. Yamagata still did not yield. He came to the main point of his argument when he asked Itō whether his plan would not in practical effect pave the way for party cabinets. He further asked Itō if he did not think that the development of party cabinets was contrary to Japan's national polity and repugnant to the spirit of the imperially bestowed constitution.

Itō replied with his real reason for recommending the formation of a party under his own lead. He stated that the pros and cons of party cabinets were irrelevant. The heart of the matter was whether his action would contribute materially to the progress of the nation. In offering his plan, Itō said pointedly, he was only thinking of how to serve the best interest of his country. Since there seemed to be a fundamental difference in their views, he would have nothing more to say. Itō then made a stunning proposal.

He said that since he had already determined to resign, he would like to shift the discussion to the matter of a successor cabinet. He was thoroughly satisfied that it would not contravene the true intent of the constitution if he advised the throne to grant the mandate to organize the next cabinet to Ōkuma and Itagaki, the leaders of the new party which had an overwhelming majority in the Lower House. It is reported that Yamagata and the other *genrō* were "struck dumb with astonishment." Yamagata was first to recover. He reiterated his arguments for opposing party cabinets. The other *genrō* also opposed Itō's suggestion. Itō at this point pulled out his trump. He must have enjoyed it when he asked if anyone among those present would step up and assume the responsibility of forming the next cabinet. He took pains to point out to Yamagata that it was properly his task. Yamagata turned aside this thrust with the remark that he saw no reason why he should be singled out. Itō then laughed heartily. Since all the *genrō* washed their hands of the responsibility, there was no other course, he declared, but to ask the leaders of the political party. The meeting was adjourned on this note.[47]

Itō went directly to the Imperial Palace after this meeting, submitted his resignation as prime minister, and returned all his honors and titles. At the same time he recommended that Ōkuma and Itagaki be given the imperial mandate to form the succeeding cabinet. The *genrō,* summoned by the emperor, in his presence held another conference the following day, June 25, 1898. None of them expressed willingness to try to form the next cabinet, which in effect meant final approval of Itō's recommendation.

That evening Itō invited Ōkuma and Itagaki to the prime minister's residence to inform them of his action. Itagaki expressed great surprise at the sudden turn of events, but both he and Ōkuma promised to consult with the leaders of their respective "parties." This they did, and on June 26 they informed Itō of their willingness to form the next cabinet. The following day the emperor commanded Ōkuma and Itagaki to succeed Itō.[48]

There were still those who were unreconciled to Itō's action. Some called him a "rebellious subject [who was] leading the nation astray." Others called for the suspension of the constitution.[49] Chief of the General Staff Kawakami Sōroku suggested to Army Minister Katsura that Katsura and Navy Minister Saigō resign before Ōkuma and Itagaki formed their cabinet and then have the Army and Navy withhold recommendations for filling the service posts. However, the emperor commanded the two to remain in their positions, which meant that Itō had the emperor's ear at this time. On June 30, 1898, Japan's first party cabinet was formed.[50]

Itō's designation of Ōkuma and Itagaki as his successors has led to the suggestion that "Itō, anxious over the growing strength of the 'militarist' faction and prevented, by this very group, from establishing his own party, at last turned to the new party as a bulwark against Yamagata's power."[51] There is no question about the heat generated by Yamagata and his supporters in the cabinet against Itō's proposal to form a party. In the June 19 cabinet meeting, for instance, Army Minister Katsura and Home Minister Yoshikawa Kensei voiced strong disapproval.[52] It is also true that Itō himself has said that opposition within the cabinet prevented him from "speedily" accomplishing his plan.[53] However, there was another and probably more important reason for Itō's failure to form a party at this time: lack of support from business circles. Kaneko recalls that two powerful industrialists, Shibusawa and Iwasaki, did not go along with Itō's plan. This factor, Kaneko continues, led Itō to say that "the time was still premature" for the formation of his party.[54]

Itō, moreover, had very good and practical reasons for recommending Ōkuma and Itagaki to succeed him. By the time the *genrō* had met on June 24 to discuss Itō's plan to form a party the Kenseitō was an accomplished fact. This made it certain that Itō could not effect a compromise with one of the parties until the union broke apart. And cooperation with the Kenseitō as a whole would nullify the effect Itō wanted to create when he organized his own party: that of a government controlling for the first time a majority party. These political considerations added up to the fact that there was absolutely no hope that any government program could pass the Diet unless Itō could form his party and that party could capture a majority in the Lower House in the already scheduled special election. And by June 24 Itō was probably fully aware that he was not getting the support of the industrialists.[55]

Another reason may be suggested for Itō's recommendation of Ōkuma and Itagaki. Itō quite likely wanted to have more time to form his party, or to reassess the feasibility of trying to create a party without the participation of either the Jiyūtō or the Shimpotō.[56] The most compelling motive of all, however, is that Itō, by forcing Yamagata to accept an Ōkuma-Itagaki cabinet, helped set the precedent for a party cabinet, and paved the way for the day when he himself would establish a government party.

The formation of the Ōkuma-Itagaki cabinet, then, may be said to have been a defeat for Yamagata, not Itō. Such a party cabinet was hateful to Yamagata. Itō had struck at the very essence of Yamagata's political philosophy. *Jiji shimpō* at this time correctly observed: "His Imperial Majesty, by receiving Ōkuma and Itagaki in special audience and commanding them to form a cabinet, has determined that henceforth the cabinet will be formed by whatever party holds a majority in the Diet. It may be safely said, then, that the foundation of the party cabinet system has been established."[57] One can fully appreciate Yamagata's feelings when he wrote to a friend on June 26: "There has been a great political revolution in Japan. The Meiji government has finally capitulated, and we now have a party cabinet. There is no need for a defeated general to give further instructions to his troops. There is, I believe, no other recourse but to retire."[58]

Itō, however, could not have won this tactical victory had it not been for the fact that constitutional government in Japan had developed to a point where it was impossible to govern without a majority in the Lower House. And all the oligarchs were agreed that a smoothly functioning administration was an absolute necessity if Japan was to keep pace with the rest of the world. In his June 25 meeting with Ōkuma and Itagaki, Itō had placed heavy stress on this very point. "There is now hardly any doubt that [your party] easily controls a majority in the Diet and that the Diet, if it so wishes, is in a position to hinder the accomplishment of state affairs. It is consequently unquestionable that if you are given the responsibility of forming the next cabinet the conduct of state affairs will not be hindered by the Diet . . . I do not have the help of the lowliest member of a political party. And realizing that this makes it impossible to control a majority in the House, I handed in my resignation yesterday."[59]

The battle over whether Japan was to have a government party, then, was over for all practical purposes when Yamagata conceded in 1898. This leads to a final observation, which is a reiteration of a point made much earlier. The major political skirmishes during the Meiji period, like the one just discussed, were fought among and resolved by the oligarchs themselves. After 1890 the party men proved themselves more powerful, resourceful, realistic, and farsighted than they are usually credited with having been. But until the death of Yamagata in 1922 the oligarchs still played a vital role in politics on the national level.

The latent causes of faction are thus sown in the nature of man; and we see them everywhere brought into different degrees of activity, according to the different circumstances of civil society. A zeal for different opinions concerning religion, concerning government, and many other points, as well of speculation as of practice; an attachment to different leaders ambitiously contending for pre-eminence and power or to persons of other descriptions whose fortunes have been interesting to the human passions, have, in turn, divided mankind into parties, inflamed them with mutual animosity, and rendered them much more disposed to vex and oppress each other than to cooperate for their common good.

JAMES MADISON, THE FEDERALIST, NO. 10

X

ITŌ, YAMAGATA, AND THE KENSEITŌ: FORMATION OF THE SEIYŪKAI

A widely accepted explanation for Itō's creation of the Seiyūkai is that Itō, fearing the growing weight of Yamagata and the "militarist" faction, sought to use the party to counterbalance this threat.[1] It is undeniable that there was rivalry and jealousy between Itō and Yamagata; on the other hand, Itō was also probably motivated by other considerations. Even Yamagata had tacitly agreed that, under existing political conditions, a government party was necessary for the attainment of Japan's long-range aims. The only alternative was suspension of the constitution, of which he talked for a while. Itō, of course, felt even more strongly that national interests demanded the creation of a government party.

Although Yamagata's agreement was necessary before Itō could carry out his plan, Yamagata and his followers acquiesced only reluctantly to Itō's design, and they naturally sought to shore up the crumbling bureaucratic defenses against further anticipated encroachments by party men. Various measures were proposed and implemented. Among these were tightening the government's grip on the posts of service ministers in the cabinet, the revision of civil service regulations, and the redefinition of the role of the Privy Council. Such measures, however, should not be construed as evidence that the oligarchs as a whole were attempting to weigh down constitutionalism with impossible legal and administrative burdens. They were, rather, last-ditch efforts by the group around Yamagata to minimize the potential imbalance in the government foreshadowed by Itō's decision to organize his own party.

Many of these efforts, moreover, proved unsuccessful in practice. For one thing, the imminent final revision of treaties impelled the oligarchs to respect the constitutional structure they had created in part to impress the Western powers. For another, Yamagata did make exceptions to the ordinances, even if reluctantly, when he saw that the party men had to be placated in return for their cooperation. In essence, the same reasons that had compelled Yamagata to agree with Itō on the party issue forced him to compromise with the majority party in the Diet. Thus, Yamagata, during his second and last tenure as prime minister, showed himself prepared to come realistically to terms with the Kenseitō, for he had to have assurance that his budget program would pass in the Diet.

The party men were perfectly aware that the oligarchs tolerated them only because of the great number of members they could consistently elect to the Diet at each election. The members of the Kenseitō, in particular, were by this time confident of their bargaining strength. And rightly so, for they had been building up their bases of power in the provinces with single-minded determination and foresight. In fact, many of the concessions they had wrung from the government were specifically aimed at further strengthening of their hold in the provinces.

The Kenseitō's wisdom in concentrating on the provinces had been shown when Itō failed in his second attempt to organize a party without the support of the organized politicians.[2] This left him with only one course: he had to base his party on one of the major existing parties, namely the Kenseitō. However, there were three things Itō had to do before he could form his own party. He had to reshape the public image of the Kenseitō, making it seem to be a party not with narrow, selfish, and partisan interests, but one with broad, selfless, and national interests, and therefore eminently qualified to be a "national party." He also had to rationalize and popularize his decision to step down from the Olympian heights of a *genrō* into the mundane hurlyburly of party politics. This Itō did through a series of strenuous "campaign" talks that took him to all parts of Japan. And, most basic of all, he had to break up the Ōkuma-Itagaki coalition in order to free the Kenseitō for reorganization as a government party.

Many reasons have been given for the downfall of the short-lived Ōkuma-Itagaki cabinet (June 30, 1898–November 7, 1898).[3] Among them are lack of emphasis on basic principles, disagreement over legislative programs, inadequacy of anti-Sat-Chō sentiment, unwillingness to compromise on cabinet portfolios, and the backstage maneuverings of the Yamagata clique.[4] Certain contemporary observers, however, emphasized that Itō from the start wanted the cabinet to fail and, by his lukewarm attitude toward it brought about its failure. Miyake Setsurei, for example, offered the following interpretation. After Itō had helped to create the Ōkuma-Itagaki cabinet, he abruptly took a trip to China. Itō at this time had the cynical view that "what will split, will split." Miyake's basic argument is that if Itō had truly been sympathetic to the new cabinet he could have done much for it. He could have mediated between the two factions and seen to it that the cabinet's life was prolonged for at least a year. However, Itō wanted most of all to form his own party. Consequently, he was not averse to seeing the Kenseitō split into its original components.[5] The circumstances of Itō's transfer of power to the Kenseitō also appeared extremely suspicious to Ozaki Yukio.[6] Ozaki, therefore, maintained that Itō, instead of attacking the Kenseitō frontally, gave it responsibility before it had completed its organization, and in this manner brought about the failure of the Kenseitō-based Ōkuma-Itagaki cabinet.[7]

Furthermore, some three years after the collapse of the Ōkuma-Itagaki cabinet, Itō Miyoji recorded in his diary the following statements he made in a conversation with Itō:

Then the Kenseitō cabinet was formed. The Jiyūtō strongly urged me [to join the cabinet]. I firmly refused . . . Moreover, I decided to sacrifice myself in the battle to avenge the downfall of the Itō cabinet. I therefore went to the Mainichi nippō sha and undertook the vital responsibility of attacking the cabinet. I worked on Itagaki and others and finally brought about the breakup of the Kaishintō *[sic]* and caused the downfall of the Kenseitō cabinet . . . You were in China at that time, so you were unable to know personally of these facts. Not only this, the day before you left Japan for China you called on me, and on the grounds of prudence warned me that by no means must I attack the government. However, I saw things in a different light and did not obey your injunction. Regarding your absence as an excellent opportunity, I strongly assailed the misgovernment of the Kenseitō cabinet and finally caused its collapse. This was something in which the Itō faction secretly rejoiced.[8]

This entry, taken together with Miyake's analysis, provide some ground for thinking that Itō had not been saying what he actually felt about the Ōkuma-Itagaki cabinet. In other words, he was practicing what some have called *haragei*.[9] A later instance in which his conduct was strikingly similar may help clarify the point. Ozaki Yukio and Itō were the principals in this instance, and the time was three months after the formation of the first Katsura cabinet (June 2, 1901–January 6, 1906). In September 1901 Itō left for a visit to the United States, Europe, and Russia. According to Ozaki Yukio, Itō entrusted the reins of the Seiyū-kai to Matsuda Masahisa and himself. However, Ozaki continues, Itō did not leave any particular instructions on what the Seiyūkai's policy should be toward the Katsura cabinet. Ozaki says that after thinking about Itō's conduct he came to the conclusion that Itō had given both himself and Matsuda a blank check. Ozaki writes that his thoughts ran as follows: "Itō knows that I have been in opposition to every cabinet. If we are supposed to assist the Katsura cabinet, he would have given us explicit orders. Therefore, since he has left without saying anything, this means, 'topple the Katsura cabinet while I am gone' . . . What [Itō] actually wanted to say was, 'It would be awkward if this were done while I am present, so bring down the cabinet while I am gone.' "[10]

The "evidence," direct in the first instance and indirect in the second, is that Itō specifically cautioned his chief lieutenants against taking any hostile actions against the existing cabinets. Yet in both instances Itō's supporters flagrantly "disobeyed" his injunctions. The assumption is that they felt that this "disobedience" would not displease him. The difficulty in dealing with *haragei* is that, to assert that it was practiced at any given time one must contradict the record of events. But this is inevitable; it is the very nature of *haragei*. It enables a man to encourage surreptitiously a course of action which he desires but which is contrary to a "correct" and "acceptable" position that he is expected to maintain. *Haragei* not only spares embarrassment for its practitioners in their relationship with their contemporaries, but can serve as a painless way of manipulating the judgment of history in favor of the practitioners.

When Itō went to China it is more than likely that he had already decided that he could not form a party without relying on one of the established parties. This is not saying that concrete steps had already been taken to combine with the Jiyūtō, or even that an understanding had been reached between Itō and the Jiyūtō leaders. Itō, it may be argued, probably went to China for two reasons closely related to his second failure to form his own party. By recommending Itagaki and Ōkuma as his successors he had in effect created a party cabinet, which was anathema to Yamagata. It would have been pouring salt on the wound for Itō personally to start working immediately on his third attempt to create his own party. He had publicly to dissociate himself for a period from a project which Yamagata had so recently and so strongly condemned. In the second place, Itō had made the Ōkuma-Itagaki cabinet possible. The organization of the cabinet had saved him from the potential embarrassment of facing a hostile Diet. However, the very existence of the cabinet he had made possible in turn meant that he could not realize his aim of forming his own party based on the Jíyūtō. It would have been contrary to Itō's character to work overtly for the overthrow of the cabinet he had helped to create. Moreover, Itō must have realized that the public would react negatively to the type of political cynicism represented by a direct and immediate attack on the Ōkuma-Itagaki cabinet. Itō thus conveniently removed himself from the scene of conflict, leaving one of his leading field generals, Itō Miyoji, to serve as chief strategist.

As it turned out, Itō Miyoji's task was made easier because the Jiyūtō faction of the Kenseitō almost from the start acted as if it had reluctantly contracted the marriage with Ōkuma's party. There were many indications that the Jiyūtō was determined to battle its partner at every possible occasion and on any pretext. For example, right after the installation ceremony of the Ōkuma-Itagaki cabinet, Itagaki made the following comments to all the ministers gathered at the official residence of the prime minister: "I do not know when a fight among friends will arise over [the distribution] of influence and power . . . as well as for other reasons. However, Ōkuma and I will positively not take part in any fight. Even if we have to rid ourselves of all our followers, we promise that we will act in unison."[11] Itagaki clearly seemed to be protesting too much.[12]

The Shimpotō half of the Kenseitō also did not help matters by taking five cabinet posts to the Jiyūtō's three.[13] Katsura, in his autobiography, describes the inevitable result of what the Jiyūtō considered an inequitable distribution of cabinet seats. "The power of the cabinet lay mostly with the Shimpotō. Thus the Jiyūtō became more and more angry . . . and the situation between the two was practically like that between a dog and a monkey."[14]

This antagonism between the two parties was a situation that Itō Miyoji could easily exploit. Moreover, when Hoshi Tōru, possibly the most powerful man in the Jiyūtō at this time, returned from the United States in August 1898, he, too, quickly concluded that the Kenseitō had to split and the Jiyūtō combine with Itō.[15] Hoshi's unusual silence almost immediately after his return may very well be explained by his conviction that a split was inevitable. Kōno Hironaka writes that Hoshi told him: "On returning, I have discovered that the situation is much worse than I had expected. In fact, it is practically beyond repair. There is no choice as things stand but to have Itō become prime minister. However, we must not let old men lead us for long. Once the foundations have been laid, let us expel all the old men, beginning with Itō, and do as we please."[16]

It does not seem strange, then, that the Kanto faction of the Jiyūtō, Hoshi's main source of support, led the attack against Ozaki on the "Republic Speech" issue, and also that Ozaki reported that Itō Miyoji stood at the forefront of the attackers.[17] The conflicts between the Shimpotō and Jiyūtō, although partly motivated by the Jiyūtō's jealousy, may be said to have been purposely created by the Jiyūtō and Itō Miyoji to bring about the downfall of the Ōkuma-Itagaki cabinet.

The Yamagata faction, represented most actively by Katsura, also worked for the cabinet's downfall. The principal motive appears to have been their simple dislike of party cabinets.[18] Katsura was also the chief architect of the second Yamagata cabinet that succeeded the Ōkuma-Itagaki.cabinet. He rushed its formation through before Itō could return to Tokyo.[19] Katsura was afraid that if Itō returned Itō would be committed to help Ōkuma form an Ōkuma cabinet.[20] This discourtesy in excluding him from consultations on the successor cabinet angered Itō. It revealed a touch of pettiness on the part of Yamagata and Katsura.[21] However, the final result redounded to Itō's favor. He was spared the necessity of supporting Ōkuma's ambitions and was further dissociated in the public mind from the Jiyūtō and its attempts to bring down the Ōkuma-Itagaki cabinet. Furthermore, Itō would have found his later task of combining with the Jiyūtō immeasurably more difficult if he had supported Ōkuma and the Shimpotō at this juncture.[22] Itō's anger over the breach of *genrō* etiquette by Katsura and Yamagata should not be confused with his sentiments about the downfall of the cabinet.[23]

The thirteenth session of the Diet was convoked on November 7, 1898. The opening ceremonies were held nearly a month later, on December 3. This highly unusual state of affairs masked Yamagata's unwillingness to face the Diet without first coming to terms with the Kenseitō. Yamagata and Katsura both negotiated with the Kenseitō leaders, and the talks were carried out in Tokyo and Osaka.[24] The final price that Yamagata agreed to for Kenseitō support, on November 26, was the acceptance of a three-point platform:[25] the present cabinet would disavow the principle of nonparty cabinets; the cabinet would adopt the Kenseitō platform; and the government would exert every effort to afford the Kenseitō advantages and opportunities, in this way helping to enlarge the party's influence.[26]

It is evident that Itō had much to do with the final compromise reached by the Kenseitō and Yamagata. It would not even be surprising if Itō had had a hand in drawing up the conditions on which the compromise was based. Hara Kei has left the following record: "In the final analysis Hoshi . . . decided on the unconditional coalition because Itō, in Kobe, told Hoshi that the best policy was to support the government. This would enable [the Jiyūtō] to win the confidence of the public. Moreover, the Jiyūtō looks upon Itō as practically its future president."[27]

It would be a mistake to assume, merely because they did not receive any cabinet posts in return for cooperation, that Hoshi and the Kenseitō leaders were bargaining from a position of weakness. Hoshi was certain of the power of the parties. He assured the world, immediately after the Yamagata cabinet was formed, that a cabinet independent of political parties would collapse in three days.[28]

Hoshi's self-assurance was matched by an equally brave attitude on the part of Katsura. Katsura suggested successive dissolutions of the Diet and even the suspension of the constitution to compel the parties to act in a responsible manner.[29] If the government maintained a firm, determined posture, Katsura asserted, one of the parties would ally itself with the government. Katsura called his strategy of firmness "the policy of assaulting the center" *(chūō tokkan no saku)*.[30]

Furthermore, the Yamagata faction was quietly inaugurating a series of moves to complement the strong talk and to neutralize the potential gains in the administration that the parties were now in a better position to make. On May 15, 1900, Imperial Ordinances 193 and 194 were promulgated. These ordinances provided that only generals and lieutenant generals and admirals and vice-admirals on the active list could serve as army and navy ministers, respectively.[31] The traditional view of the meaning of these two ordinances is best summed up by the statement: "This procedure could completely throttle the real independence of any popular party from the demands of the military and naval men to block the completion of any cabinet until their terms were met."[32]

Yamagata, about a year before the promulgation of these ordinances, had also made other moves to make it more difficult for party men to poach on the bureaucratic preserve. In March 1899 Yamagata arranged for the issuing of three imperial ordinances. These were "Bunkan nin'yō rei" (Civil service appointment ordinance), "Bunkan bungen rei" (Civil service limitation ordinance), and "Bunkan chōkai rei" (Civil service discipline ordinance). The first provided that those of *chokunin* rank, the highest rank among civil servants, henceforth were subject to the same examination requirements as were *sōnin* (imperially appointed officials of the second rank) and *hannin* (third-rank civil servants, below imperially-appointed officials). The second defined the qualifications for each rank and guaranteed status and security. The third laid down rules governing the conduct of civil servants and provided punishment for the violation of these rules. These three ordinances, according to Hackett, were aimed at preventing "office hunting" by party members.[33]

Still another Yamagata effort in the direction of hampering party activities in the administration merits attention. In April 1899 Yamagata saw to it that the Privy Council's reviewing power was broadened to cover matters beyond those involving the interpretation of the constitution. The review of all imperial ordinances related to civil service regulations, for example, was brought within the Privy Council's scope. This changed the function of the Privy Council, as Hackett has observed, from one of advising to one of supervising.[34]

It is possible to interpret all of these moves not so much as forceful tactics to subdue further parties already demoralized by more than half a decade of battering by the oligarchs and by inter- and intraparty bickering, but rather as desperate efforts to prevent the administration from being completely overrun by the rapacious party men. For instance, Ordinances 193 and 194 may be seen as an attempt by Yamagata to preserve *at least* two ministries from the depredations of the party men.[35]

It can further be argued that the attempts to fortify the bureaucratic stronghold were not conspicuously successful. If, for example, Yamagata and Katsura were truly determined to carry out their threat to suspend the constitution, they had to be prepared for the stoppage of orderly governmental process. That both were not really willing to go this far is plainly indicated by their very serious efforts to come to terms with the Kenseitō before the thirteenth session began. And Tokutomi, in his analysis of Katsura's suggestion for suspending the constitution, also clearly saw that Katsura and Yamagata were actually not prepared to go as far as their strong talk hinted.

[I] believe that Katsura proposed his views merely to serve as a guide for the government's attitude toward the political parties. At the same time that Katsura was advocating the thesis of [repeated] Diet dissolutions, he was calling for a coalition with [one of] the parties. To form a coalition with a party is a pressing and practical matter. Even in a situation where the government and a party share the same ideologies and political principles, a party is not going to help the government without commensurate rewards. Sincerity and courtesy are empty gestures and not in the least bit effective. Although [he] was determined to resort to the ultimate step if by chance the situation demanded it. Katsura's basic intention was to adhere to as mild an attitude as possible. According to Katsura, Yamagata also agreed with him.[36]

There were at least two very good political reasons for Yamagata's and Katsura's moderation. The first was the need to halt the government's growing insolvency; the second was treaty revision. One problem that had plagued all the cabinets since the end of the Sino-Japanese War was a continually mounting fiscal deficit. This deficit was the result of ambitious postwar development projects, civil as well as military. The second Itō cabinet managed to pass several bills increasing taxes during the ninth session (1896), which increased revenues to 34,000,000 yen. However, the increase in revenues could not be applied to the budget for fiscal 1896, which, as a result, showed a deficit of 100,000,000 yen. The 1897 budget, notwithstanding the revenues from the tax increase, was 15,000,000 yen in the red. This deficit climbed to 26,000,000 yen by the time the 1898 budget was compiled. Matsukata, during his second tenure as prime minister, wanted to introduce a land-tax increase in the eleventh session of the Diet (1897). The anticipated income from this increase was 25,000,000 yen. However, the eleventh session was dissolved before this goal could be realized. The budget for fiscal 1899, compiled during the third Itō ministry, showed a deficit of 37,000,000 yen, which was expected to rise to 47,000,000 yen by the time the 1900 budget was compiled. The Itō cabinet introduced a land-tax increase during the twelfth session of the Diet (1898). This Diet session, too, was dissolved before any action could be taken. The Ōkuma-Itagaki cabinet decided against a land-tax increase. However, it planned to raise sake, income, and registration taxes, establish a new tax on sugar, and increase tobacco monopoly rates. This cabinet also fell before it could act.[37] By the time the Yamagata cabinet was formed, therefore, the problem of deficits was urgent, if not desperate. It is also easy to see why Itō, in discussing his plans to form his own party, told Kaneko that a government should be in existence for at least five years if it was to be able to get anything done. Suspending the constitution, as Katsura proposed, would not only have gravely hindered Japan's ambitious plans for postwar development; it would also have served to increase the deficit.

The dramatic and nearly unmanageable increases in the Japanese budget are an index of the accelerating changes Japan was experiencing at this time. Japan in 1898 was a different place from the Japan of, say, 1885. Japan in 1898 had taken the first steps as a colonial power and was on the verge of realizing the dream of treaty revision. Thanks to the indemnity from China, in itself an almost unbelievable development, Japan shifted to a gold standard, bringing herself in line with the major nations of the West. The foundations of a modern iron and steel industry were laid in 1896 and the first Japanese-made steel ships, small but service-able, heralded the modest beginnings of a shipbuilding industry. In domestic politics, the parties' interests had to be considered by the oli-garchs if the administration did not care to see its policies mauled in the Lower House. Itō had openly broken with Yamagata over the formation of party government and was busily engaged in the preliminary steps toward forming his own party. All of this was a far cry from the days in the mid-1880's when the politicians, not even formally organized as parties, were reduced to impotency and frustration whenever they sought to make their influence felt and accepted within the councils of the ad-ministration in Tokyo.

The difference in the positions of the parties is clearly illustrated by Yamagata's approach to the mounting national deficit. He proposed to raise the land-tax rate from 2.5 per cent to 4 per cent. The Kenseihontō led the opposition against the proposed tax increase, but in the Kenseitō itself opposition also mounted. The government then offered a com-promise. It proposed limiting the land-tax increase to 3.3 per cent, raising the residence tax to 5 per cent, and increasing the tobacco monopoly rates. When some in the Kenseitō still balked, the government finally agreed to place a five-year limit on the land-tax increase. The measure passed in this form in December 1898, and the deficit problem was solved, at least temporarily.[38]

The second reason why it would have been difficult to suspend the constitution was cogently stated by the *Kobe Weekly Chronicle* in an editorial: "Besides the popular excitement that would be engendered, such a course would almost certainly mean the indefinite postponement of Treaty Revision, and in the view of Japanese statesmen of all shades of opinion, everything must be subordinated to a consummation of Japan's ambition in this respect."[39]

Generally, the same arguments may be applied to the lack of immedi-ate effect on Japanese politics of Imperial Ordinances 193 and 194. The actions of the service ministers, who were controlled by the oligarchs, were also governed and delimited by the realities of Meiji political life.[40] The military commands, if they wished, could stop the administrative machinery by withholding personnel from the posts of service ministers. But this would have been like cutting off one's nose to spite one's face.

To the credit of the oligarchs, there is nothing to indicate that they were not realists of the first order.[41]

On the other hand, the members of the parties were more than aware of the aims and desires of the oligarchs and of their own role in the oligarchs' grand design for Japan. Hoshi was not indulging in wishful thinking when he assured all those who would listen that no cabinet could last without help from the parties, a proposition which, when re-stated, meant that the parties would exact their price for cooperation. The expression that follows takes on added interest because even the "clown" among the Meiji oligarchs was deadly serious about Japan's destiny and recognized one of the costs that had to be borne for its ful-fillment. Saigō Tsugumichi is speaking: "Under a constitutional system of government nothing can be achieved without the consent of the majority party. Consequently, at times, to bow to the orders of the [majority] party becomes unavoidable. Even though at times their de-mands are unreasonable, we must accept them. In order to achieve the great aims of the nation we must bear minor irritations. Looking at the larger picture, we must be willing to sacrifice a little in convenience and advantage."[42]

The exceptions to Yamagata's civil service ordinances inspired by the Kenseitō may very well represent the type of "minor" retreat the oli-garchs were compelled to make from time to time. Immediately after the ordinances were issued, Kenseitō leaders met with Yamagata and exacted a partial compensation for these ordinances, in the form of the dismissal of several officials who had been directly responsible for the drafting of the ordinances.[43] At the same time, the Kenseitō leaders com-pelled Yamagata to nullify to a certain extent the intent of the ordinances. Maeda writes:

When Yamagata was confronted by the Jiyūtō on the civil service reform, he tried to pacify the party by making exceptions. So he appointed Jiyūtō mem-bers to the posts of chief of the Metropolitan Police Board (Keishi sōkan), director of the Police Bureau of the Home Ministry (Keihō kyoku chō), and private secretaries. He also established a position of secretary in each ministry equivalent in rank to what was later a parliamentary vice-minister. He ap-pointed Jiyūtō members to these positions . . . The bureaucracy, hearing that vice-ministers and bureau chiefs were shifted because of party demands, were shocked and frightened. For the first time they realized the magnitude of party strength and influence. Their attitude consequently underwent a change, and they acceded to all Kenseitō requests without a murmur.[44]

Maeda, after describing the retreat of the bureaucrats, states that in the general election held in September 1899 to choose members of prefectural assemblies the Kenseitō captured about half of all the seats in the country.[45] This reference to the increase in party strength in the prefectural assemblies points to a major political benefit actively sought by the Kenseitō in return for cooperating with the government. Katsura, in his autobiography, shows that the Shimpotō was primarily interested in controlling power in the central government, whereas the Jiyūtō was basically interested in expanding its power in the provinces. Therefore, Katsura continues, the Jiyōtō laid immediate claims to the Home Ministry in the Ōkuma-Itagaki cabinet.[46] Later in his autobiography he complains that while Kenseitō support was extremely helpful in having the government's policies approved by the Lower House, there were many instances when the "coalition" with the Kenseitō caused the government "great inconvenience." And Katsura takes pains to point out that whenever provincial branches of the party and prefectural governors clashed, the government had to side with the party in twenty to thirty per cent of the cases. This meant that a party man or one sympathetic to the party was appointed governor. Katsura re-emphasizes that concessions on the party-prefectural issue were inevitable if the government hoped to carry out state measures.[47]

Concrete benefits gained by the Kenseitō in their stress on the provinces may be cited. When the prefectural governor was a party man or one friendly to the Kenseitō, he could see to it that party members were given protection and support on stumping tours. This factor was said to have helped increase the Kenseitō's influence, for example, in the Tōhoku area.[48] Success, according to one eye witness, was not limited to the Tōhoku area alone. Less than a year after the Kenseitō and the government agreed to cooperate, Hirata Tōsuke wrote to Yamagata:

It would not be wrong to regard the general election for the prefectural assemblies as a barometer of the fortunes of the government faction. According to our estimates the Jiyūtō will capture about five out of ten places and the Shimpo three out of ten. The Teikoku [Teikokutō, the former Kokumin kyōkai] will not take one place out of ten . . . The influence of the Shimpotō will take a precipitous drop. On the other hand, the power of the Jiyūtō will increase tremendously. I do not know whether this portends good or evil [for us].[49]

Ōkuma, whose party lost most through the Kenseitō's emphasis on strengthening its own local power and influence, clearly saw the wisdom of this policy and the realism of the arrangement between the Kenseitō and the Yamagata cabinet. He wrote:

The Yamagata cabinet was not based on the principle of nonparty cabinets in the strict meaning of the principle. [Members] of the Kenseitō were not taken into the cabinet. However, as compensation, the Kenseitō was given control over local administration . . . When a government party man [Kenseitō] became prefectural governor, he carried out the so-called positive policy. Wherever there were party faithfuls, railroad, harbor, bridge, dike and embankment projects were abundantly in evidence. Where the opposition parties held sway, no funds were available . . . Shizuoka, for example, resisted the encroachment of the Jiyūtō till the end. But when the Abe River overflowed, Shizuoka city was completely inundated.[50]

One last word must be added to the Kenseitō rationale for its rapprochement with and conduct toward the Yamagata cabinet. The party leaders were looking beyond Yamagata to Itō, their "future" president. Hence, if they were willing to swallow their pride and receive less for cooperating than they felt was their due, this was meant to prove their willingness to submerge party interests in the national interest.[51] They had to exhibit reasonableness and become "respectable" lest they antagonize Itō. The *Japan Weekly Mail*, an organ not too friendly to the Kenseitō, described thus the Kenseitō's growing success in making itself a respectable associate for Itō:

We cannot deny that the Liberals have shown considerable tact in [meeting the situation]. Had they advanced any grievance against the Yamagata cabinet; had they exhibited any signs of umbrage in suggesting a change in the situation, their proposal to Marquis Itō [that he take over the leadership of the Kenseitō] would have placed him in *the dilemma of having to choose between a political party and his old friends and colleagues*. But all complications of that kind have been prudently and adroitly avoided. [The Kenseitō] furnished the nation an object lesson illustrating the smooth and peaceful administrative potentialities created by their support, and . . . preserved such relations with Marquis Yamagata and his Ministers that no violent disruptions need result from the transfer of the Party's allegiance to Marquis Itō. (italics, mine).[52]

Closely related to the foregoing is the charge that the Kenseitō went "hat in hand" to Itō to ask him to become its leader and that the subsequent dissolution of the Kenseitō was "submission."[53] The Kenseitō did approach Itō humbly,[54] but the description still fails to do justice to the motivations of the Kenseitō leaders. The Kenseitō leaders were not working merely to place a foot in the door of the administration. This had already been accomplished right after the Sino-Japanese War. They were attempting to win their way into the administration itself, and this within the short period of a decade. The politicians were more than willing to balance superficial and short-term humiliations against the achievement of this overriding party goal. On August 27, 1900, two days after the inaugural committee of the soon-to-be-formed Seiyūkai met, Hoshi delivered a remarkably frank and arrogant speech, which was typical of the attitude of the party men toward their new role. In it he said: "The manifesto issued by Marquis Itō is full of things quite unsatisfactory to us, but the manly spirit, the characteristic of the true gentleman, does not allow us to contend these points in so far as their literary aspects are concerned. In short, everything depends upon substantial strength . . . We must give before we will be able to take."[55] And in practice it turned out precisely as Hoshi and the party men believed it would. Okazaki Kunisuke, a contemporary of Hoshi, recalls that from the very beginning Itō placed heavy emphasis on "the party" and listened to what Hoshi and others had to say.[56] Itō actually had very little choice, for the Seiyūkai was essentially the Kenseitō reconstituted. Of the 152 Diet members bearing the Seiyūkai label during the Diet's fifteenth session, only thirty could be counted as direct followers of Itō.[57] Looked at from another angle, the party men had helped, by their self-effacement and discipline, to split the oligarchy right down the middle. By smoothing the way for Itō to combine with them, they had proved that they, and not the oligarchs, were the successful practitioners of Katsura's grandiose "policy of assaulting the center."[58]

Still another measure of the Kenseitō's relative position of strength is that Itō himself, by this time, had fully realized that he could not form a party without Kenseitō help. *Jimmin,* an organ of the Kenseitō, expressed it this way: "The fact that the Jiyūtō and the Shimpotō have ten to twenty years of history behind them cannot be lightly dismissed. It should be remembered that a political party may be reorganized, but it can never be manufactured. At this stage, the only choice for Marquis Itō is to join with either the Jiyūtō or the Shimpotō . . . "[59] This factor explains Itō's frank efforts to try to reshape the image of the Kenseitō from that of a "partisan, selfish party" to that of a "national party."[60] Sometime in January 1899, for example, Itō stoutly defended the Kenseitō when the party was charged with the abuses with which he himself had often charged it:

Speaking to a visitor recently, Marquis Itō denied as unwarranted a report that the Liberals were demanding the reorganization of the Cabinet and hunting for offices in return for the assistance they rendered the Government in passing the tax-increase bills. He had heard nothing of the kind from the Liberal leaders, whom he had met lately. On the contrary, he had ascertained that the Liberals were working sincerely in the true interests of the Empire which they had at heart. Marquis Itō added that he had advised the Liberal leaders to collect able men, gifted with talent necessary for direction of national affairs, pointing out that suitable statesmen must be obtained if they were successfully to conduct the administration of the Empire.[61]

Even while Itō was doing his best to challenge the widely held view that the Kenseitō was not capable of statesmanship, he was embarking on a somewhat contradictory campaign of discrediting the political parties. He charged in Yamaguchi: "When I look upon the present parties I see parties that do not consider their primary object the administration, of the state. What I see is parties that merely aim at party benefits."[62] This speech was made during Itō's wide-ranging and taxing political tour to lay the groundwork for the party he planned to organize.[63] So while he was aware that he needed the Kenseitō as the base for his party and was thus compelled to utter kind words about it, he also had to justify publicly the necessity for forming an "entirely new" party. Hence his derogatory remarks about the existing parties.

The foregoing was not the only "contradiction" with which Itō had to deal. As mentioned in an earlier chapter, Itō, as the chief framer of the Meiji constitution, never conceded that anyone but the emperor possessed the prerogative of appointing and dismissing state ministers, who, therefore, were accountable only to him. Itō at this time suggested two ways in which the selection of party men as state ministers could be justified. The first was by using the principle of indivisible sovereignty as a cornerstone for the projected union of officialdom with the parties. He argued that to hold that those in the parties could not become officials was tantamount to saying that the emperor's prerogatives were restricted. It was the sovereign's prerogative to use whomever he wished. What was there to prevent the emperor from exercising his imperial judgment in selecting persons he felt to be suitable to run the government? Itō also reminded his audiences that it was a constitutional right of any Japanese subject to become an official, if he was qualified.[64] But once the emperor entrusted the government to a party, Itō concluded, the party had to remember its duty to conduct the government for all the people and not for selfish, partisan interests.[65]

The second way out of the dilemma was, in effect, to restrict the imperial prerogatives, which he had actually been advocating consistently over the years. Itō said that in practice imperial rights could be exercised by others by delegation. Thus, when a legislative branch was established it was partaking of the sovereign power of the emperor. Since this power was only delegated by the emperor to others, the emperor could take it back. Yet the constitution stipulated that this and other delegated powers could not be wrested away unreasonably. In this connection Itō attacked the beliefs of the students of the Chinese classics. These scholars, he charged, were convinced that absolutism alone reflected the national polity of Japan. They believed that all the land and subjects throughout the length and breadth of the nation belonged to the emperor. Itō insisted, however, that if land, for example, were bestowed and confiscated arbitrarily and without restraint, the subjects would be at the emperor's complete mercy. Constitutional government was different from absolutism in that it allowed a subject to retain what rightfully belonged to him. Constitutional government, in short, protected life and property through law. Without this guarantee, Itō said, there would in fact be tyranny rather than absolutism.[66] In other words, he was telling his fellow oligarchs that the political situation had developed to a point where the second half of the principle of nonparty cabinets could be applied: a responsible, national party was about to be born which could be entrusted with the affairs of state.

Itō also made one admitted shift in his ideas. This was that the English experience in constitutionalism was not to be ignored or derided. In fact, the words of Disraeli and Burke now served as inspiration for the model party Itō was seeking to organize. The party, according to Itō's reading of Disraeli, was to be a disciplined group owing unflinching and complete loyalty to a strong leader. The members of the Diet, who were to serve as the core of the party, were to be in the Burkeian tradition, representatives of the whole nation, and not the delegates of districts from which they were elected. Itō made it clear that while there was no need to repeat the errors made by the English, Japan would be wise to adopt "the good [points] of the English constitutional system."[67]

Itō finally realized his aim on September 15, 1900, the day the Seiyūkai came into being. Yamagata, in May of the same year, had already expressed his desire to resign.[68] On May 27 Itō was commanded to form a cabinet, but he declined. The siege of Peking by the Boxers in June 1900 stopped talk of Yamagata's resignation for the time being.[69] The siege was broken by the allied expeditionary force in mid-August 1900. Yamagata again indicated his desire to resign. Itō was in the midst of his activities in forming the Seiyūkai and was afraid that if he was compelled to succeed Yamagata at this point his plans and activities for the Seiyūkai would suffer. Itō made these thoughts clear to Yamagata in a letter dated September 9.[70] Yamagata nevertheless resigned on September 26, 1900.

Tokutomi suspects that Yamagata resigned before Itō had fully strengthened the organization of the Seiyūkai and thus forced Itō into the same position that Itō had placed Ōkuma and Itagaki in June 1898. Itō supports this point of view, for when he was asked to head his fourth ministry he told Hayashida, "It is a typical Yamagata military tactic to launch a surprise attack before the enemy has prepared his positions."[71] This jockeying between Itō and Yamagata over the timing for transferring the prime ministry leads to the question of why Itō formed the Seiyūkai. As stated at the opening of this chapter, a common explanation is that Itō was compelled to form a party in order to counter the expanding strength of Yamagata and his clique. It is also conceded that rivalry and jealousy did exist between these two. Suzuki Yasuzō, for one, says that the twenty years from 1887 to 1907 could be designated the period of the "Itō-Yamagata rivalry."[72] However, the thesis that Itō sought to create the Seiyūkai as a bulwark against Yamagata's growing strength runs counter to Itō's usual patterns of behavior.

Itō, if we are to accept the accounts of his contemporaries, cannot be accused of attempting to build an empire of personal followers. He was a rare political phenomenon in a land where political strength and fortunes are still measured by the number and loyalty of one's followers. Ozaki Yukio recalls, "Itō basically did not care whether [disciples] came or went. Consequently, his relations with them were extremely simple. It was his boast that he did not personally seek a single follower."[73]

The following quotations from the *Japan Weekly Mail*[74] indicate that there was no diminution in Itō's considerable self-confidence at the time he formed the Seiyūkai, for at this time he was the focus of almost wild public approbation, which he could have used to blunt any attacks by the Yamagata faction, had it been necessary: "Marquis Itō arrived at Nagano on the 10th instant, and received an ovation. Thousands of people turned out to welcome him, and there were illuminations [a lantern parade?] and other demonstrations of rejoicing. The Marquis undoubtedly possesses the confidence of the nation in an incomparably higher degree than any other living statesman."[75] And again, "It has seldom fallen to the lot of any statesman to occupy such a high position in the opinion of every section of a nation. There is absolutely no voice raised in Japan against the Marquis. The people are unanimous in regarding him as the most trustworthy publicist that the country possesses."[76]

Two motives may be attributed to Itō for forming the Seiyūkai. The first is that he felt that he had a tremendous personal stake in the success of constitutional government in Japan. As Itō himself said, "Since the establishment of constitutional government . . . I have felt a personal responsibility to see that it developed smoothly."[77] Itō, in a word, was firmly convinced that what he had wrought should be permanent and immutable and that constitutional government had to prove workable in Japan. "If it comes to the point . . . that [people] say that constitutional government is not suited for Japan and then conclude that we should suspend constitutional government, this will mean an unprecedented disaster in terms of Japan's future. The reason I have sacrificed everything to organize the Seiyūkai is that there exists the possibility [that constitutional government may be judged unworkable]. I do not in the least harbor any political ambitions."[78]

And the yardstick by which the failure or success of constitutional government would be measured was the ability of an administration under this form of government to last long enough to assure its success in carrying out national programs. Itō stressed this point repeatedly in his speeches prior to the formation of the Seiyūkai.[79] This was his second reason for creating the Seiyūkai. Itō's ideal party was a government party, disciplined and absolutely loyal to its leader. Such a party would solve the triple problems of administrative-legislative peace, uncontrolled and disruptive party demands for patronage, and the tendency of administration officials to ally themselves with Diet factions to the detriment of government plans and programs.

EPILOGUE

The founding of the Seiyūkai was the logical culmination of the political realities with which the oligarchs had been contending since 1890. It was a confident Itō who created the Seiyūkai. He was self-confident because of his acknowledged abilities and because he had imbibed the heady wine of "mass" adulation. He was further strongly convinced that he had finally established the correct balance of political forces to ensure stability, which in turn was the prerequisite for Japan's push toward greatness. He was almost immediately disappointed in his expectations, in somewhat the same fashion as the oligarchs in 1890, when the controls they had established in 1889 were found wanting.

Itō was beset with difficulties from two sources. One was Yamagata, the other the Seiyūkai. The *genrō,* as we have seen, were not united but contentious. Before 1890, when the oligarchs had full control of administrative power in Tokyo, this disunity did not weaken their hold on the government. After 1890, when the participation of the parties in the government was legalized, the *genro's* conflicting approaches to constitutional government enabled the parties to gain strength, slowly but consistently, at their expense. However, until 1898 the line held—a *genrō* was a recognizable, distinct, special political being. All the major decisions affecting them and their relationships with the parties were fought out and resolved within the inner councils of the *genrō*. In a word, the initiative remained largely, though not completely, in their hands. Then in 1898 Itō committed the unforgivable wrong and broke the *genrō* ranks by pushing for the formation of the Ōkuma-Itagaki cabinet. This was but a prelude to the even more abhorrent act of organizing a party and placing himself at its head. To Yamagata this final move was triply disturbing. Itō, with a callousness unbecoming a *genrō,* had sacrificed oligarchic "unity" and had deserted to the hated enemy—at least so it seemed to Yamagata. Moreover, to a Yamagata who had a penchant for precision and who tended to categorize others neatly as either friend or foe, Itō's new role as party leader with the right to visit the Imperial Palace presented a jarring anomaly. Most alarming of all, Itō's move threatened Yamagata's emperor-bureaucratic centered concept of government—an ideal he consistently and pertinaciously preached and served.

Yamagata therefore felt that Itō's divorce from the Seiyūkai was mandatory. Yamagata succeeded in three carefully considered moves. The first was an unmistakably clear lesson to Itō that control of the majority party in the Lower House did not necessarily assure smooth passage of his own policies. In 1901, during the fifteenth Diet session, Itō's tax increase measure was unceremoniously rejected by the House of Peers and was passed only when an imperial rescript was handed down. The second step was completed when Yamagata deprived Itō of the chance to succeed himself when he resigned the prime ministry in June 1901, he thought temporarily, to effect a cabinet shake-up. The third maneuver was consummated in 1903 when Itō gave up the leadership of the Seiyūkai and accepted the presidency of the Privy Council. In these confrontations with Yamagata, Itō was made painfully aware that he was nearly completely isolated from his former colleagues and from the center of compelling political power. Or, looked at from Yamagata's vantage point, the years immediately following 1900 were years when he gained mastery of the arena in which *genrō* politics was played.

Yamagata, Itō, and the other *genrō,* however, were all living on borrowed political time. For even in 1901 there were indications that they were losing the loyalty, if not the control, of their followers. Itō was the first to taste this bitter fruit. When Itō in 1901 failed to get *genrō* support for his fifth term as prime minister, Inoue Kaoru was given the opportunity to try. Inoue naïvely assumed that the Seiyūkai would automatically support him, but was quickly disabused of this notion by Hara Kei, Hoshi Tōru, and Saionji Kimmochi. The three in essence informed Inoue and Itō that Itō simply would not be able to throw Seiyūkai support behind Inoue if this meant that the party's interests would be sacrificed. This pronouncement was made less than a year after Itō had grandly and confidently taken over the presidency of the party. Yamagata would have found no comfort in Itō's predicament if he had known that at the very same time Katsura Tarō, his protégé, was nodding in agreement at a diatribe delivered by Itō Miyoji against the "arrogant *genrō* whose days were numbered." Katsura eight years later did more than agree. He declared his independence in a manner that must have cut Yamagata to the quick: he asserted that Itō, not Yamagata, was his patron saint.

In brief, the events in the few years following the formation of the Seiyūkai revealed that Yamagata was master of *genrō* politics and was therefore able to win a series of tactical victories over Itō. However, he was made to realize that there was one vital area over which he could not exercise control. He received hints of this when he saw that Itō could not promise Seiyūkai support to Inoue, and when in 1903 the transfer of the presidency of the party from Itō to Saionji was smoothly accomplished in spite of widespread fears that Itō's elevation to the Privy Council would mean the collapse of the Seiyūkai. This is not to say that Yamagata's powers were negligible. Political explanations do not permit the luxury of such simplistic conclusions. One of the key themes in Hara Kei's political life after he became a power in the Seiyūkai about 1905 or so, is that he had to take into consideration Yamagata's presence and power at every point, and was prevented by Yamagata from getting the ultimate prize, the prime ministry, until 1918. Still, the events of the two decades following the founding of the Seiyūkai may be explained, generally, as a continuation of the developments of the first decade of the constitutional experience. While the power of the *genrō* continued to be significant and had to be taken into account, the strength and influence of the parties continued to develop, tortuously, fitfully, gradually, but inexorably. One reason for this was the basic commitment of the *genrō* to constitutionalism. Another was that Yamagata was mortal and subject to the ravages of old age, whereas the parties were renewed constantly by new blood. Still another was that as Japan modernized and the government became increasingly huge and complex, government by a single clique became impossible. Even for a man like Yamagata, with a loyal and widespread following, the task was too great. A fourth was that the Japanese political animal—bureaucratic, plutocratic, or party—like those of the same species throughout the world, could unerringly sense even the slightest shift in the political balance and would avail himself of the new opportunities presented by the change. And for the reasons stated, the shifts tended to favor the parties over the *genrō,* which in turn had a cumulative effect on the development of the strength of the parties. The appointment of Hara as prime minister in part reflects the increasing power and fortune of the parties, for Yamagata, in the context of the times, had no other recourse.

What of Itō, who seemed to fade from active domestic politics after 1903? He discovered that for a person of his temperament and his life-long experience in *genrō* politics the demands of party politics were strange, difficult, and distasteful. He was more at home with a small group of men, sharing essentially the same background and goals. Moreover, he had thought that his active presence in the party would be enough to make of the Seiyūkai a disciplined body of troops. Instead, he found that he could not rid the Seiyūkai of the faults of parties he had been attacking in the preceding decade: undisciplined factionalism, self-seeking, crude-ness, rowdiness, and disrespect. He discovered also that party decisions made at the capital did not necessarily mean a forthcoming response in the provinces—a frustrating discovery for one who thought in terms of disciplined troops. So the important thing about Itō's elevation to the Privy Council is not so much that Yamagata and Katsura connived to bring it about, which they did, as that Itō did not fight it. Itō, no less than Yamagata, felt at home in the rarefied and comfortable atmosphere in which the *genrō* breathed and moved. Itō, however, left the great legacy. Despite the fact that he did not understand and could not cope with party politics, he *early* and *realistically* made the decision to combine with the parties and thus helped to shape the nature and style of Japanese pol-itics that has continued to this day—the combination of bureaucrats and politicians. But Yamagata must still be given an honored place beside Itō as a benefactor in the development of constitutional government in Japan. For his actions with respect to constitutional government in Japan were based on the tacit acceptance of two premises: that the Meiji con-stitution would provide the ground rules governing administration-party relations in carrying out state affairs, and that changing the rules of the game would be impracticable and dangerous in terms of achieving Ja-pan's major goals. Because he acted on the basis of these beliefs, Yama-gata made it inevitable that the parties would expand their small holdings to the point where the rise and fall of cabinets depended to a large extent on party support.

> *... the historian's view of the past is also conditioned*
> *constantly by the works of his predecessors ... the scope*
> *and point of view of his inquiry, his choice of sources*
> *and the questions he would ask of them, would all be*
> *influenced by the way in which these problems had been*
> *solved in the past.*
>
> WALLACE K. FERGUSON,
> THE RENAISSANCE IN HISTORICAL THOUGHT

CONCLUSIONS

The student of modern Japanese history finds the 1930's an extremely troublesome decade. A leading scholar speaks of it as "filled with complexities, contradictions, and confusion."[1] To most Western observers, the 1930's in Japan was also an era of the *fait accompli,* "government by assassination," the "rape of Nanking," "totalitarianism," "imperialism," and "militarism."[2] The Westerner might well think in these terms. To many Japanese intellectuals the 1930's was a period when Japan sunk into a dismal abyss *(kurai tanima).* It was a time that prompted the "liberal" Yoshino Sakuzō to state, "So Fascism has come to Japan ... "[3] It was this eventful decade that gave shape and content to the views on Meiji constitutional development generally held by Western scholars.[4] The judgment of many of these scholars is that democracy failed in Japan in the 1930's and that "the history of Japan after 1931 represented the logical culmination of previous trends ... "[5]

Western scholars searching for the causes of failure in the Meiji era almost invariably turned to works by prominent constitutional historians like Osatake Takeki, Suzuki Yasuzō, and Ōtsu Jun'ichirō. The pessimistic orientation of these historians has been discussed in earlier chapters; their conclusions fitted and strongly supported the failure thesis.[6] Even without recourse to works by Japanese constitutional historians there is sufficient material in English—the Meiji constitution and Itō's *Commentaries* are examples—to support the finding, if one is inclined to accept it, that Japan's political norm was despotism and absolutism.[7]

Modern Japan, however, has not always been viewed so negatively. Images of Japan have undergone changes, and so have judgments. In 1904, when Japan was an ally of Great Britain, a writer unequivocally asserted, " . . . the cause of Japan's greatness and of Japan's success can be summed up in one word—patriotism."[8] However, when patriotism was directed against one's own interests it became the "chauvinism" of McLaren in 1916 and the "militaristic expansionism" of Bisson in 1938.[9] It is not necessary, of course, for a long time to elapse before shifts in attitudes occur. A given individual may also have conflicting attitudes— for example, William Howard Taft, who in March 1905 was convinced that " 'the governing classes' of the Japanese had 'elevated the people,' and that he had 'no fear of a yellow peril through them.' " At the same time he remarked, " 'a Jap is first of all a Jap and would be glad to aggrandize himself at the expense of anybody.' "[10] Since the Russo-Japanese War, our image of Japan seems to have been greatly conditioned by her "aggressiveness," actual and potential, in foreign affairs.[11]

Today the pendulum has swung in the other direction. The relationship between the United States and Japan is generally friendly. Popular stereotypes of Japanese held by Americans undoubtedly reflect this change in relationship.[12] Scholarship, too, is beginning to enter a revisionist period. This is not to say that there is a one-to-one ratio between good relations and optimistic viewpoints; in fact two other reasons for revisionism will be discussed later, but certainly the historian should be aware that he, no less than his predecessors, is subject to what E. H. Carr calls a "natural human inclination to attach universal significance" to one's own experience.[13] The problem is to minimize the distorting effects of this predisposition on one's historical judgments.

Historians interpreting Japan's political and constitutional development emphasize the Meiji leaders' political efforts in solving the problems Japan faced. Political activities, naturally, are not carried out *in vacuo*. We must in part base our judgments upon an understanding of how these leaders saw their problems and articulated their hopes.[14] Three general conclusions emerge if we focus on how the Meiji leaders expressed their hopes for making a great Japan: (1) They drew on their Confucian background and their understanding of Confucianism to arrive at certain basic principles on which they planned to build the constitutional structure. (2) These Confucian concepts were doubly attractive because of certain striking similarities between the Confucian ideology and the ideals of "social monarchy" postulated by men like Lorenz von Stein and Hermann Roesler. (3) The appeal of Confucianism and of the theories of Stein and Roesler in turn lay in the fundamental premise accepted by the Meiji leaders that constitutionalism in Japan involved the sharing of power with the people, which would lead to a strong, modern, and acceptable Japan.

The Meiji leaders, as we have already seen, failed to create their Confucian-social monarchical state. The causes of their failure will be recapitulated to show that they, like politicians everywhere, were often confronted by the unbridgeable gap between political ideals and aspirations and political reality and unforeseeable contingencies. More importantly, the restatement of this failure will, I feel, paradoxically serve to underscore their enlightenment and greatness. How the Meiji oligarchs visualized, articulated, and attempted to solve the problems confronting Japan also has a special relevance today, because the question is frequently raised: Is Meiji Japan an appropriate model for the newly emerging nations? As will shortly become evident, it is my contention that the problems Meiji Japan faced and solved cannot really be equated with the experiences now being encountered by newly modernizing nations.

Whether the word "democracy" may be applied to Meiji Japan must be settled first. To speak of the failure of the democratic movement and of democracy in prewar Japan is to imply that democracy was attempted in Meiji Japan. Yet none of the Meiji leaders advocated the establishment of a democratic form of government. Ōkubo Toshimichi emphatically rejected democracy.[15] Itō did say, not with displeasure, that the adoption of a constitutional form of government perforce meant that some "democratic elements" would be introduced. Still, he did not appreciate the views of the Manchester school which gave rise to "ultra radical . . . ideas of freedom" among certain young intellectuals in Japan. Montesquieu, Rousseau, and Buckle also were singled out by Itō in unfavorable terms.[16] Even "the foremost liberal of the age," Fukuzawa Yukichi, never called for the creation of a democratic form of government, or the granting of the franchise to "the peasants and cart-pullers." He was as wary of the "tyranny of the masses" as he was of the "tyranny of a despot."[17] Yoshino Sakuzō, another "liberal" also shared with Fukuzawa and the Meiji oligarchs an elitist mentality and hoped that "the small enlightened intellectual class in the upper ranks of society" would "become conscious of their duty to guide the common people." But even more importantly, Yoshino manifested a skepticism about a democracy *(minshū shugi)* that merely emphasized the masses *(minshū)*, and he turned to the term with Confucian overtones, *mimponshugi* (democracy) to describe the "spiritual basis of constitutional government in Japan."[18]

It is perhaps appropriate that we should have noted the Confucian influence on Yoshino. For like Yoshino, the Meiji leaders phrased many of their modernization goals in Confucian terms. Recently there has been increasing emphasis put on "covert preparation" in the Tokugawa period which helped Japan to modernize. These developments included the rise of a literate, formally educated population and a professional, rationally structured bureaucracy.[19] The Confucianism of the Tokugawa period also helped to pave the road toward modernization by furnishing part of the rationale by which the Meiji leaders could find constitutionalism understandable and acceptable.[20]

The Confucian influence on the Meiji leaders is not surprising, for as Craig has pointed out, "It would be pointless to say that one area was more Confucian than another, for almost every school in every *han* was Confucian, and scholarship, if not otherwise designated, meant Confucian scholarship."[21] To be sure, others have stressed the all-prevading influence of Confucianism on the Meiji leaders, but they have seen it as having a negative effect on the history of modern Japan. "Perhaps the most basic—and most disastrous—error of appraisal in the past," says one interpreter, "has been the failure to recognize that the feudal and theocratic elements, rather than the democratic, have represented the determining motivation and source of authority for the total system."[22]

What then were the main Confucian themes which repeatedly appeared in the political thinking of the Meiji leaders? They believed first of all in a benevolent elitism which stemmed from their acceptance of a natural hierarchy based on ability. "Every country in the world has inhabitants of some sort," said Kido, "some of the people are wise and others foolish, some are rich and others poor. Those who are wise and able and competent to conduct affairs find their way to offices of state, while the wealthy preside over industry and give employment to the poor; all this is nothing more than the natural order of things everywhere."[23] We also see this emphasis on enlightened leadership in Itō's stress on an upper house whose members were "selected from mature statesmen, men of merit and erudite scholars."[24]

Like good Confucians, the Meiji leaders were fully aware that only a thin line divided enlightened from despotic elites. Yamagata pointed to the dangers of personal aggrandizement in the government, saying that the results would "affect the strength and cohesion of the entire people and become the cause of the decline of the nation."[25] Kido, Ōkubo, and Itō also warned against this threat implicit in government by an enlightened minority.[26] The aim of this selfless leadership was promotion of the welfare of the people. To Itō, the imperial house had "a single aim— the welfare and happiness of the nation," while to Kido it was "essential to nourish the people and having done this great results of the nation may calmly be awaited," and for Katō Hiroyuki this concern for the happiness of the people was based on "the great principle . . . that the government is made for the people, not the people for the government," while Yamagata predictably spoke of the elevation of the morals and the happiness of the people.[27]

The Meiji leaders felt that when the welfare and happiness of the people were secured, the nation would be peaceful, tranquil, orderly, wealthy, and strong. The people shared with the emperor the responsibility for achieving these goals—in the words of Itō: "Both ruler and ruled should apply their efforts smoothly and harmoniously to preserve tranquillity; to elevate the status of the people; to secure the rights and promote the welfare of each individual; and finally, by manifesting abroad the dignity and power of Japan, to secure and maintain her integrity and independence."[28]

If the sovereign and the governed were expected to exert efforts for the common good, the implication is that the masses could be educated and trained to rise up to the point where they could meaningfully participate in the government and share all the burdens in the development of a modern and strong Japan. The conscription system, the universal education system, the industrialization, the constitutional form of government were all predicated on this concept. In this important sense the Confucianism of the Meiji period differed from the Confucianism of the early period of borrowing from China (c.550 to c.850). In the earlier period, when the Japanese administrative system was reconstituted under Chinese influence, the result was further strengthening of the strongly aristocratic bent of the Japanese political system. Furthermore, as Sansom points out, "The Japanese failed, in borrowing the greatest of all Chinese institutions, to take over its essence, which was a respect for learning coupled with a desire for its spread."[29]

The fact that the Meiji leaders constantly reiterated these ideals does not in itself prove that they took them seriously. Moreover, they were capable, as in the Crisis of 1881 and in their confrontation with the Lower House in the 1890's, of saying one thing and meaning another. But reasons can be adduced to indicate that the Confucian tenets expounded at this time were meaningful and useful to the Meiji oligarchs. In the first place, it would be unrealistic and "unfair" to expect the Meiji oligarchs to be "revolutionaries" twice in a single lifetime. "It is not so easy as theoretically imagined," Itō was constrained to say, "to destroy that which has been existing and satisfactorily to construct something else to take its place. Rarely do destruction and construction proceed successfully together."[30] Thus it is not surprising that they reached back to an ideology that had served as the basis of their education in their most formative years. It is also natural that Itō would find comfort in the "crust of customs" that overlay Japanese society and would assert that what the Japanese lacked was not "mental or moral fiber, but the scientific, technical, and materialistic side of modern civilization."[31] Ōkubo's injunction that a constitution should be enacted that conformed to "our country's geography, the customs and sentiments of the people, and the spirit of the times," becomes understandable in this light.[32] This is not a reactionary position; rather this approach makes good psychological and sociological, as well as political sense.[33] Furthermore, the Meiji leaders at this time received support for their position from sources they considered highly reputable. When, for example, ex-President Grant visited Japan in the summer of 1878, he told the emperor that he hoped that the constitution would be based on and reflect the spirit of "over 2,000 years of Japanese history," and that constitutional government would be carried out in the same spirit. Kaneko, who reports this incident, says that those who were present, including Itō, were "inspired" by these words.[34] Kaneko also tells us that Herbert Spencer regarded it as nearly miraculous that "the new Constitution of Japan did no violence to the traditions and history of so ancient a race."[35]

In the second place, the Meiji oligarchs found solace in the Confucian emphasis on harmonious unity and in the mutual efforts of the ruler and the ruled. This was because their observation of developments in Europe led them to feel that the greatest threat to the political and social fabric of any nation was when the governors and the governed stood in confrontation with each other: the one stubbornly maintaining its prerogatives and the other seeking to enlarge its share of rights and privileges. This is the lesson Kido had learned from the Frenchman "Brook," who had said that many of his compatriots not only were deprived of more than half their legal rights but were eager to "wrongfully seize privileges never granted them."[36] This explains why the Meiji leaders took pride in the fact that the Meiji constitution was not wrested from the monarch as was Magna Carta in England, but was granted in the milieu "of the most cordial relations" prevailing between "the Throne and the people."[37] Itō's unceasing stress on the ideal of a "national" party free of factionalism and special interests, which would work with the administration in harmony and unity to achieve the goal of a strong Japan, can also be traced to these pre-Meiji influences.[38] The Seiyūkai, as we have noted, was also conceived by Itō in this image.

There was a third reason why the Confucian principles appealed to the Meiji leaders. Itō believed that these principles constituted in part the "moral and emotional factor" which had prevented Japanese laborers from degenerating into "spiritless machines and toiling beasts," and which would form "a healthy barrier against the threatening advance of socialistic ideas."[39] Here Itō was revealing not only his perspicacity by sensing the dangers of industrialization, but also the influence of his European tutors, and this leads to a fourth reason why Confucian ideas attracted the Meiji leaders.

The Meiji leaders believed that constitutional government was a major reason for the strength of advanced nations in Europe. In Prussia, a nation that attracted their particular attention at this time, they saw constitutionalism take the form of a "social monarchy." And the theoretical justifications for this system on important points coincided with their own Confucian values. This conclusion is also suggested by the economic historian Horie who says that he finds elements of the "organic theory of state" in Confucianism.[40] Moreover, Prussia was powerful, and the oligarchs undoubtedly saw a close connection between its "social monarchy" and its strength.[41]

An articulate exponent of "social monarchy" was Hermann Roesler, who in turn was influenced by Stein. Rudolf von Gneist was also a proponent of "social monarchy."[42] In June 1887 Roesler submitted a memorandum to Inoue Kowashi in connection with the drafting of the Japanese constitution. In this memorandum he explicitly laid down the guidelines for creating a "social monarchy" in Japan. The main ideas in his memorandum were that as Japan modernized and industrialized, the acquisitive bourgeois would become the dominant class, and their justifiable demands would have to be met. If the acquisitive drive of this class was left unchecked, the security of the other classes, including landowners and the propertiless, would be shaken. Therefore, it was the "most urgent task of the state to maintain impartially the welfare of the whole and a harmonious social balance by means of social legislation and an active administrative policy that works for the physical and spiritual welfare of the lower classes." To do away with class conflicts and to sustain an "ethical political attitude that places the welfare of the whole above class interests, the institution of hereditary monarchy is necessary. This monarchy, possessing the loyalty of the people, will be the procurer of the common welfare and the custodian of the weak."[43]

Siemes says that to Roesler the monarch was therefore a moderator in class conflicts and a maintainer of social order and balance. Furthermore, because parliaments were composed of political factions representing class interests, the monarch had to remain independent of parliament. Siemes, however, emphasizes that the "conception of a monarchical socialized state is not a negation of the liberal constitutional idea, but a complement to it. The monarch, standing above all class interests, can see to it that all members of society have an equal freedom of development, a freedom that in a class society is not sufficiently ensured by universal suffrage and the party system of parliament alone."[44] In short, Roesler, Stein, and Gneist attributed to the administration of the state "a creative function" independent of the legislature.[45] The ultimate purpose of this creative function was to meet the ever-changing requirements of modern life on the basis of "social law." This involved the conscious recognition of and working toward the realization of "true human freedom," that is, "the freedom to realize human and cultural values which cannot be realized without the collaboration of men; it is a freedom, therefore, that is closely connected with the cultural tasks of the community."[46]

How many of Roesler's ideas were acceptable to Itō we may gather from Itō's statement on the two great objectives of constitutional government: "In other words, the problem to be solved and the object to be attained by the Constitution of our country was not only the harmonizing and conciliating of conflicting tendencies of different interests within the state, as in the case of the majority of constitutional monarchies, but also the imparting of a new vitality to the public life and its citizens—a new and increased creative energy to the public functions of the state itself."[47]

Implicit also in this concept of social monarchy is enlightened elitism. For there must be those who assist the emperor in ruling, who, like the emperor, must stand above selfish and partisan struggles. This is the "transcendentalism" of Roesler, Inoue, Itō, and Yamagata, and inherent in it is acceptance of the idea of a natural or "real" aristocracy.[48]

This amalgamation of the traditional and the "modern" was not limited to the Meiji oligarchs. Kōno Hironaka, an early advocate of parliamentarism and later a prominent member of the Jiyūtō, described how the new was merged with the old in what seemed to be almost a religious experience. In March 1872, according to Kōno, while on horseback and reading a translation of John Stuart Mill's *On Liberty* he experienced in a flash a great revolution in his thinking. Though he had been nurtured in Chinese learning *(kangaku)* and Japanese learning *(kokugaku)* and was disposed toward anti-foreignism, he cast aside all his former views, except loyalty and filial piety, and became aware of the values of liberty and rights.[49]

Yoshino Sakuzō, too, shared this characteristic. He thought of democracy *(mimponshugi)* as a "functional process," and believed that "one could borrow its technique and attach it to a more indigenous ideology." This indigenous ideology was the Confucian tradition.[50]

All the emphasis on continuity in the Meiji leaders' thinking cannot obscure the new elements that they also added, though in the acceptance of the new, they were always heirs to tradition. As one student of Japan sensitively put it, " . . . there have been few periods in [Japanese] history when 'up-to-date' was not virtually the ultimate in praise."[51] The new was in the Meiji stress on the rights of the people. For Itō, a constitutional form of government was impossible "without full and extended protection of honour, liberty, property, and personal security of citizens, entailing necessarily many important restrictions of the powers of the crown," or without "virtues" such as "the love of freedom of speech, love of publicity of proceedings, the spirit of tolerance for opinions opposed to one's own, . . . " The new was also in Itō's concept of a limited monarchy, as seen in his complaint against the "survivors of former generations" who believed that any restriction of the imperial prerogative amounted to something like high treason.[52] He stated his view on limited monarchy even more clearly in a reply to Mori Arinori during one of the deliberative sessions of the Privy Council on the draft constitution.

What are the basic principles on which the constitution is based? The first is the limitation of the powers of the monarch, and the second is the guarantee of the rights of the subjects. Therefore, if in the constitution, only the responsibilities of the subjects, but not their rights, were enumerated, it would be meaningless to have the constitution. No matter what nation is involved, if the rights of the subjects are not guaranteed and the monarch's prerogatives are not limited, the result is that the subjects have to bear all the responsibility and the monarch has unrestricted power. We call this nation an absolutist monarchy. Therefore, when the monarchical prerogatives are limited and the duties and rights of the subjects are stated in a constitution, then and only then shall we possess the essence of a constitution.[53]

The emphasis on the emperor is in itself something new. Itō admitted in the Privy Council's deliberation on the draft constitution that Japan needed a "spiritual basis" for her drive toward modernization. Itō was convinced that a source of strength of European states lay in their religion and that the essence of European civilization was Christianity. He felt that Japan lacked a "central axis" for the people's sentiments such as Christianity provided in Europe. Buddhism, he felt, could not fulfill this role; he also dismissed Shintō. He believed that only the imperial institution could serve this purpose.[54]

The Meiji oligarchs were acting on sound psychological and political grounds in spotlighting the emperor. Alexander Gerschenkron, in unraveling the seeming conundrum of the appeal that the socialist Saint-Simon had for the greatest capitalist entrepreneurs in France, believes that "to break through the barriers of stagnation in a backward country, to ignite the imaginations of men, and to place their energies in the service of economic development, a stronger medicine is needed than the promise of better allocation of resources or even of the lower price of bread. Under such conditions even the businessman, even the classical daring and innovating entrepreneur, needs a more powerful stimulus than the prospects of high profits. What is needed to move the mountains of routine and the prejudice is faith—faith, in the words of Saint-Simon, that the golden age lies not behind but ahead of mankind. It was not for nothing that Saint-Simon devoted his last years to the formulation of a new creed, the 'New Christianity' . . . " He then adds that for Germany, which did not experience a political revolution or national unification, nationalism rather than the socialism of Saint-Simon was more appropriate as the ideology of industrialization.[55]

The synthesis of Confucian and "Western" political ideas hammered together by the Meiji oligarchs failed when put to the test of practical application. The political structure of the post-1890 period bore little resemblance to the ideal envisioned by the Meiji leaders. Itō's miserable failure to form a national party is evidence of this. Yoshino Sakuzō, on the eve of Japan's descent into the *kurai tanima,* made a judgment in which most interpreters probably shared. Yoshino stated that Itō and the bureaucrats under the influence of "Dr. Reusler" who praised the "Prussian monarchical autocracy" instituted the doctrine of direct and personal rule by the emperor. Under this concept the emperor and the people were considered "rival political forces and the affirmation of one involves the negation of the other." The Diet was created not to reflect popular opinion but to "furnish an organ of reference for the emperor in the practical policies of legislation." The people, after a long struggle against the "depotism of the government," finally "gained their point, and constitutional government in Japan today operates in a manner more or less similar to English usage. But this is not what the drafters of the constitution expected, nor is it compatible with the literal interpretation of the document. It might be said that in a sense the government is now conducted in a way quite contradictory to the spirit of the constitution."[56] Colgrove believes with Yoshino that the drafters' intent was to avoid "democratic rule and ministerial responsibility to an elected parliament," and this design is clearly evident in Itō's *Commentaries on the Constitution.*[57]

There are several reasons for the failure to realize the ideal body politic visualized by the oligarchs. For one thing, the structure was to be given life and vitality by men who were moved by Confucian/Japanese ideals of loyalty, selflessness, devotion, and sincerity. Itō said as much when he told Inoue Kowashi that all he had to do after 1890 was to approach the opposition with "sincerity" and no "malicious intent."[58] Inoue, however, correctly assessed the nature of the political animal when he said the only medium of exchange recognized and accepted by politicians in the opposition was power. *Chōya,* in the very first Diet session, noted that even those in the government, who were presumably more dedicated to Confucian ideals, were not immune to the lure of power.

The Meiji leaders also failed even while they were talking of "unity" because they were institutionalizing political fragmentation and giving legal rights to the potentially competitive parts of the body politic they were creating. The strongly elitist outlook of the oligarchs, traceable in part to their Confucian background, in part to their conviction that only they had the necessary qualifications to modernize Japan, and in part to their grave doubts about the selflessness and sense of responsibility of party men, made it certain that in the construction of a constitutional system they would retain a maximum of power. However, and this is equally important, the oligarchs recognized that other centers of power, including parties, existed, and they did grant to the House of Representatives, in which the parties would be prominent, certain powers and rights. Moreover, Itō and Inoue Kaoru believed that government by party would be possible, but sometime in the future. Itō's commitment to the acceptance of other organs in ideal polity can be seen in his adherence to the notion of *Rechtsstaat,* known as the "organ theory" in Japan. He explicitly stated that nine years were allotted for the preparation for constitutional government so that the administrative organs of the state might make ready to bring the central administration "in harmony with modern ideas of a constitutional 'Rechtsstaat.' "[59] Implicit in the notion of *Rechtsstaat* was that the oligarchs, as the emperor's advisers, could in the course of events be responsible to the other organs of the state, including the Diet.[60] If Itō was unable, or unwilling, because of pressure from other oligarchs, to see the dangers inherent in the "modern ideas of a constitutional *Rechtsstaat*," his closest followers were not. Kaneko, after hearing Itō's pronouncement in February 1889 told him: "To begin with, constitutional government is government by the majority. And to the extent that we have now adopted government by the majority, if the government does not also organize a party loyal to it, it cannot carry out effective government."[61]

Even more crucial, however, the opposition quickly saw matters in the same light. Shortly after the promulgation of the constitution Ōkuma aptly summarized its significance:

There appears to be dissatisfaction with our constitution and these views have been expressed in speeches and newspapers. Actually, the beauty of a constitution is that how it works in practice [is important]. It is not appropriate that one should be dissatisfied simply because the text is not satisfactory. It is especially pertinent to note that the principle of party cabinets should not be spelled out in a constitution. Naturally, therefore, you will not find a clear statement of this principle in the Meiji constitution. However, when the party members receive both the confidence of the emperor and the support of the people, the day of party cabinets will have arrived.[62]

It is in this light also that Itagaki's actions before and after the enactment of the Meiji constitution should be interpreted. Itagaki's realistic appraisal of his position before February 1889 convinced him that he and his supporters could not force the government to accept their views because of the preponderant political, economic, and military forces in the hands of the oligarchs. He did not have to be reminded that he could not succeed where the great Saigō had failed.[63] However, with equal perception, he was aware that the constitution and the oligarchs' commitment to constitutionalism provided precisely the entering wedge into the public power sector in Tokyo that he and his followers had long been seeking.[64]

It should also be recalled that Fukuzawa's *Jiji shimpō, Chōya shimbun,* and Brinkley's *Japan Weekly Mail* were not pessimistic about the parties' chances under the Meiji constitution. Indeed, before the Pacific War, a respectable body of non-Japanese opinion shared this view. Colgrove, for example, while maintaining that Itō's *Commentaries* was a "stumbling block" to a "liberal" interpretation of the constitution, also felt that the constitution itself did not prevent the development of party government.[65] "The language and spirit of this remarkable document," he said, "is sufficiently broad to admit of tremendous progress toward autocracy on one side or towards democracy and parliamentary government on the other side, without adding or subtracting a single clause."[66] The events after 1890 bore out the optimistic appraisal of Ōkuma and Fukuzawa and the correctness of the strategy of Itagaki and Hoshi, who were willing to work within the framework of the Meiji constitution. Again, the prewar interpreters were much more sanguine than some of the later scholars. Like Yoshino, they believed that Japan was moving toward the English parliamentary model. Quigley, for example, felt that the " . . . history of the Diet, with all the exceptions allowed for, is a history of increasing popular control."[67] Even during the Pacific War Embree anticipated the position now being taken by an increasing number of students on Japan.

As here outlined, the central government is by no means that of a free republic, nor does it approach the democracy of a monarchy like Britain. However, it is significant to note that there is provision for an elective body to pass on laws and to represent public interests in raising questions as to government policies. It is also worth noting, again, that the emperor is not an absolute emperor in the political sense and that new legislation comes about as a result of cabinet action, subject to criticism and advice by the privy council and other advisers, and only then is it promulgated by and in the name of the emperor. *Such an independent central government with a popularly elected lawmaking body exists nowhere else in Asia.*[68]

It is plain that the views of Colgrove, Quigley, and Embree contrast sharply with the interpretations of the wartime and immediately postwar scholars. And this points to an unintended parallelism with a touch of irony. Those who rigidly and literally interpret the constitution,[69] who conceive of the Japanese body politic as "one seamless whole," with all parts working together "in a single organism with its own special form of life," with the emperor, the keystone of the state structure, "not reigning, but ruling,"[70] who adjudge the constitutional and practical role of the Diet to be one of merely consenting to the acts of the government,[71] are interpreting the constitution and seeing the political structure in pretty much the same way as did the highly conservative Hozumi and Uesugi Shinkichi. We must, of course, grant the difference, that the Westerners were being critical of the situation and the Japanese legal scholars were not. Moreover, despite the final silencing of Minobe in the mid-1930's, Hozumi and Uesugi long maintained a losing position and were in a minority. This fact in turn, I feel, reflected the gradually shrinking circle of Yamagata's political power and influence. The obverse is Colgrove's perceptive statement that since "practice is the most profound justification of a doctrine . . . " therefore, " . . . it is not too much to say that the Ikki-Minobe theory of ministerial responsibility has been a rationalization of the actual tendency in Japanese practice over the course of half a century."[72]

Yet another reason may be suggested for the Meiji oligarchs' failure to achieve their constitutional state. Their very success in modernization created other centers of political power. These centers of power found it to their interest to maintain the fragmentation of the political structure that the Meiji constitution had itself aggravated. In this connection, the modern bureaucracy, the *zaibatsu*,[73] and the new military elite come to mind. Furthermore, modernization strengthened the hand of the party men as they made skillful use of the drives for better and more schools, the development of an ever-growing and complex communications and transportation network, the increasing demands for water conservancy, and flood-prevention projects to enlarge and solidify control over their constituencies.

In spite of the crumbling of the constitutional structure they had so assiduously put together, the Meiji oligarchs adjusted themselves to the unexpected and never wavered from their commitment to constitutionalism. In short, the Meiji oligarchs consciously and consistently chose to make constitutional government work despite the fact that in the course of its development they saw the idealized structure collapse and their control over the experiment gradually loosen. Some early writers, Yoshino among them, and to a lesser extent Colgrove, while maintaining that the oligarchs failed, implied that they were "defeated" by the people only after a long struggle. In a sense these scholars were saying that constitutionalism evolved on the English model while the oligarchs were "screaming and kicking" to prevent this from happening. Still others, in the pessimistic school, feel that constitutional government never quite got off the ground, since the demise of constitutionalism in the 1930's logically followed from the absolutist, autocratic system the Meiji leaders had established in 1890. Recently another approach has attracted the attention of scholars on modern Japan, based on the view that the "nondemocratic" or authoritarian nature of the Japanese state from 1868 to about 1890 is no longer particular cause for wonderment or censure. They maintain that in their historical context the Meiji oligarchs had to be authoritarian. They also maintain that the Japanese experience can be better understood and appreciated by comparing it with the experiences of the "late modernizers" today, and that what happened in Meiji Japan may be used to support certain general hypotheses about the modernization process. I share with this group the feeling that in the early stages of the Meiji period authoritarian control was present and necessary. But this statement demands qualification. The foreign and domestic factors with which the Meiji leaders had to deal, which in turn led to the formulation of their ideas and their approaches to problems, were unique—this is why some doubt can be cast on the thesis that the Meiji experience is applicable to the solution of problems faced by newly emerging nations.

The aim of the Meiji oligarchs was to create a strong, modern Japan capable of taking its place in the family of advanced, respected, civilized nations. They believed that constitutionalism was inextricably tied to success in this endeavor. From the beginning, the oligarchs never wavered in this conviction. Even while they exercised authoritarian control, the ralling cry was always "modernization *and* constitutionalism," and very early in the Meiji era they were beginning to act on this belief. To be sure, they favored gradualism, understandably, but there was never a major instance of backsliding to greater authoritarian control once a given step for loosening control had been taken. When there was the greatest need for tight and strong curbs in the first unsure years of destroying the old and building the new, and fighting off rebellions and bankruptcy, the Meiji leaders continued to advocate measures to loosen restraints. In a letter to Shinagawa Yajirō in December 1871 Kido suggested the establishment of a newspaper in the following terms: " . . . I should like to have it opened as if the government had nothing to do with it. I feel that it should be permitted to discuss the government's affairs to a certain degree—and even critically, if there is anything unreasonable about them."[74] Probably the best expression of the Meiji leaders' basic philosophy at this time was offered by Katō Hiroyuki: "In short it is my conviction that although for a time it is necessary that the government should exercise absolute authority, yet the great principle must not be forgotten that the government is made for the people, not the people for the government, and that it is needful to raise our country to the rank of a civilized nation by following implicitly the policy of Frederick in restricting the powers of the government, extending as far as possible the private rights of the people, encouraging liberty of speech, and promoting education."[75]

Four years after Katō's pronouncement and a mere ten years after the

Restoration, the Meiji government took the first major step in the *gradual*
"liberalization" of the regime and the encouragement of "liberty of
speech." This was the promulgation on July 22, 1878, of the "Regulations Concerning the Prefectural Assembly."[76] Like most of the steps
taken toward constitutional government, this one was carefully weighted
with controls. But the significance lay not so much in these controls as
in the fact that the step was taken, and taken at this time. This was less
than a year after the government had suppressed an exhausting, full-scale
rebellion. Japan also faced a grave financial crisis; she was fourteen years
away from laying the foundations of a modest indigenous iron and steel
industry and twenty-two years removed from any significant output of
ships. If anything, this was a most inauspicious time for experimenting
with elected assemblies. As Masumi Junnosuke has noted, the government in the beginning had a most difficult time getting candidates to
offer themselves for office and remain in office once elected. In other
words, the Meiji leaders were force-feeding "liberalization" to a citizenry
reluctant to accept the rights and duties of participation in government
affairs. When the results were not what had been expected and were
threatening the socio-political structure, the Meiji leaders continued to
take further steps calculated to relax their own hold. The provincial
assemblies, as we have seen, were regarded as extremely "troublesome
bodies" in the 1880's.[77] Still the government persisted in expanding the
people's role in government, and on April 14, 1888, promulgated the law
for the "Organization of the Government of Towns *(chō)* and Villages
(son)."[78] One sympathetic contemporary observer thus judged the consequence of this action: "Japan . . . has developed a good system of local
self-government and representative institutions, in the direction of greater
decentralization and broader popular prerogative."[79]

Three major difficulties therefore arise in using Japan as a model to
support the theory that authoritarian controls are effective in the early
stages of modernization: (1) Japan modernized by uneven stages. A conscription system that turned out peasant soldiers good enough to defeat
samurai in 1877 certainly would not have been a match for any contemporary Western army. The educational system limited compulsory education at first to only sixteen months, to four years in 1886, and only in
April 1908 to six years;[80] the university system did not turn out a steady
stream of bureaucrats until after the Russo-Japanese War. Industrialization, and the development of communication and transportation systems
also followed a staggered pattern as certain sectors matured earlier than
others. (2) In the meantime, the oligarchs were planning and conscien-

tiously implementing from very early days, schemes to "liberalize" political control. The Meiji constitution was only the last and greatest step in this continuing process. It may be stated that the Meiji oligarchs afford the classic case of rulers who persisted in laying the groundwork for "altruistic suicide." Of course, they did not look at the matter quite in this light, believing as they did that constitutionalism made Japan strong and modern. (3) The authoritarian nature of the Meiji regime is a subject that still can benefit from a dispassionate analysis. Let us take the example of the suppressive laws of the Meiji government. Much has been made of these laws in order to highlight the "authoritarian" nature of the Meiji regime. But considering the unstable, swiftly changing nature of the times, and the provocations, on occasion, of the antigovernment forces, the reactions of the oligarchs were truly mild.[81] The Meiji government also permitted relatively wide latitude to antigovernment movements: witness the activities and continued existence of the Jiyū minken undō, the attacks against the government over the issue of the Hokkaido Colonization Commission in 1881, and treaty revision in 1887. The thorough and open discussion of the role and powers of the emperor in the early 1880's would constitute a proud chapter in the history of any nation.[82] True, there was a major purge in 1881, newspapers were censored or publications suspended, editors were jailed, and opposition leaders sometimes hounded out of the capital or even out of the country. Still the true indications of the relatively light hand of the Meiji government are that the pressures were not unrelentingly and totally applied with bloody consequences, and on the whole the exiles and those purged returned to take an active and noisy part in politics, sometimes serving in the government with distinction. Furthermore, attacks against the government, often very vigorous, were a continuing phenomenon throughout the Meiji period.

When we shift our attention to the external world with which the Meiji oligarchs had to cope, we also see conditions radically different from those facing the leaders of the newly emerging nations of the mid-twentieth century. The Meiji era in the middle period paralleled the last great period in which the West sought to bear the white man's burden. This was a time of strong and confident imperialism, bolstered by unquestioned belief in its power and its righteousness. This was the period of extraterritoriality, unequal treaties, and what has been described as the neatest diplomatic device of the century, the principle of the most-favored-nation. It was also a period of optimism. It was, moreover, a time when "democracy" was considered the finest and ultimate form of government and it was thought that the Anglo-Saxon "races" alone were blessed with that special talent for making this form of government work. One writer, discussing Japan's attempt at it, and after allowing that "No other Oriental nation has ever yet shown itself capable of working parliamentary institutions; much less has it actually adopted them," continued by reminding his readers that "it must not be forgotten that the American Constitution was the work of the Anglo-Saxon race, who inherited the most glorious traditions, in whose bone was liberty, and in whose blood was independence. The task upon which they had entered was congenial to their nature."[83]

We can now understand why the Japanese of all political coloration were so defensive and loud in their protest that they could make constitutionalism work and would show the "white races" that they were not the only ones gifted with the talent to handle constitutionalism. We can now appreciate Itō's feelings as he sent Kaneko to America and Europe to determine whether the scholars of the advanced states of the West would find Japanese-style constitutionalism acceptable. This was nationalism, but it was not a completely blind, irrational, and violent type of nationalism. For the Meiji leaders were completely aware that full statehood was to be dispensed to Japan by self-assured, powerful states. Japan had to be on its best possible behavior and ready to present the necessary credentials, which included a "viable" constitutional form of government, in order to be admitted into the club of "civilized" nations. The Meiji leaders' commitment to constitutionalism was therefore doubly binding—on the one hand they believed that this form of government would make Japan strong; on the other they believed that this was one of the keys to acceptance by the West. One important consequence was the oligarchs' compromise with the opposition though they fully realized that each time they came to terms with the party men it meant still another step in the expansion of party power. Throughout the 1890's the oligarchs were willing to adjust their single-minded devotion to the building of a strong Japan in face of their distaste and mistrust of the party members. They did not permit themselves the luxury of impatience or reversion to "authoritarian" control.

The past three or four decades of the twentieth century have seen a gradual reversal of nineteenth-century optimism. An indication of this is that the very premises of democracy are being questioned. E. H. Carr puts it as follows: "Modern democracy is, in virtue of its origins, individualist, optimistic and rational. The three main propositions on which it is based have all been seriously challenged in the contemporary world."[84]

And in the place of *laissez-faire* and individualism, we have seen the rise of the "social security state" in the United States and the "welfare state" in Britain.[85] When Socialist Norman Thomas bemoans the adoption of his platform by the "other" parties in the United States, government participation in a wide array of activities has become not only respectable but expected.[86]

The acceptance of state planning and massive government action by the nations in the West has in a sense helped to make this approach to the problems faced by "late modernizers" acceptable. Heilbronner states the thesis that "the capacity for action of parliamentary governments is apt to prove inadequate to the heroic demands of rapid development. Parliamentary governments, even in those rare cases when they do not merely represent the privileged classes of peasant nations, naturally act to *slow down* the pace of social change by seeking to accommodate minority interests."[87]

These are the reasons, too, for the somewhat more optimistic judgments of Meiji constitutional developments by some scholars in the West. But the lesson of the previous pages is that the Meiji oligarchs were seeking to impose a constitutional form of government as Japan modernized. They did not justify authoritarian control as a means to modernize, except in the very early stage; it was always "modernization *and* constitutionalism," never "modernization *or* constitutionalism."

One final point must be made. The quality of Meiji leadership was unique. And it was this quality of leadership, perhaps as much as any other factor, that gave distinctive and incomparable tone and substance to the Meiji era.

BIBLIOGRAPHY · NOTES · GLOSSARY · INDEX

*There are, it is said, who
their spirits to cheer, slip
in a new title-page three
times a year . . .*

J. R. LOWELL, A FABLE FOR CRITICS
(Preliminary Note to the Second Edition)

BIBLIOGRAPHY

JAPANESE SOURCES

Ajiya 亞細亞, Vol. 1, No. 10 (Sept. 1, 1893).

Ariiso Itsurō 有磯逸郎. "Meiji ankoku shi: Jiyū minken ron no bokkō" 明治闇黒史自由民權論の勃興, *Chūō kōron* 中央公論, Vol. 20, No. 8 (1905).

———"Jiyūtō soshikigo no ichinen kan" 自由党組織後の一年間, *Chūō kōron*, Vol. 20, No. 9 (1905).

Asahi shimbun 朝日新聞.

Asahina Chisen 朝比奈知泉. *Rōkisha no omoide* 老記者の思出. Tokyo, 1938.

Asai Kiyoshi 浅井清. *Meiji rikken shisō ni okeru Eikoku gikai seido no eikyō* 明治立憲思想に於ける英国議会制度の影響. Tokyo, 1935.

Baba Tsunego 馬場恒吾. "Itō Miyoji ron" 伊東巳代治論, *Chūō kōron*, Vol. 45 (July 1930).

———*Dai shisō encyclopedia: Nihon seitō shi* 大思想エンサイクロペジア: 日本政党史. Tokyo, 1938.

Chōya shimbun 朝野新聞.

Dai ikkai teikoku Gikai yori dai kyūjūnikai teikoku Gikai ni itaru Shūgiin giin tōseki roku 自第一回帝国議会至第九十二回帝国議会衆議院議員党籍録, comp. Shūgiin jimukyoku 衆議院事務局. Tokyo, 1957.

Dai ikkai teikoku tōkei kan 第一回帝国統計巻. Tokyo, 1882.

Dai ikki kokkai shimatsu 第一期国会始末. Tokyo, 1891.

Dai ikki teikoku Gikai yōroku 第一期帝国議会要録, ed. Ueki Emori 植木枝盛. Tokyo, 1891.

Dai Nihon teikoku Gikai shi 第日本帝国議会誌. Tokyo, 1926.

Emori Yasukichi 江森泰吉. *Ōkuma haku hyaku wa* 大隈伯百話. Tokyo, 1909.

Eshū Daburyū (S. W.) 江洲枀撫流. "Kuroda Kiyotaka, Inoue Kaoru no ryōnin masa ni ninjō ni oyoban to shita koto" 黒田清隆井上馨の両人正に刃傷に及ばんとした事, *Meiji bunka kenkyū* 明治文化研究, Vol. 4 (Nov. 1928).

Fujii Jintarō 藤井甚太郎. "Nihon kempō seitei shi dan" 日本憲法制定史談, *Reki-*

shi chiri 歴史地理, Vol. 33, No. 4 (1919) to Vol. 34, No. 5 (1920). A series of eleven articles.

———*Nihon kempō seitei shi* 日本憲法制定史. Tokyo, 1922.

———and Moriya Hidesuke 森谷秀亮. *Sōgō Nihon shi taikei: Meiji jidai shi* 綜合日本史大系: 明治時代史. 2nd ed. rev.; Tokyo, 1940.

Fujii Shin'ichi 藤井新一. *Teikoku kempō to Kaneko haku* 帝国憲法と金子伯. Tokyo, 1942.

Fujita Tsuguo 藤田嗣雄. "Inoue Kowashi no kempō rippō e no kiyo" 井上毅 の憲法立法への寄與, *Nihon gakushiin kiyō* 日本學士院紀要, Vol. 12 (June 1954).

Fukaya Hiroji 深谷博治. *Shoki gikai: Jōyaku kaisei* 初期議会條約改正 (*Kindai Nilion rekishi kōza* 近代日本歴史講座, Vol. 4). Tokyo, 1940.

———"Dai ichiji Matsukata naikaku no Seimubu mondai no temmatsu" 第一次松方内閣の政務部問題の顛末, in *Meiji bunka no shin kenkyū* 明治文 化の新研究, ed. Osatake Takeki 尾佐竹猛. Tokyo, 1944.

Fukuchi Gen'ichirō 福地源一郎. "Shimbun shi jitsureki" 新聞紙實歴, in *Meiji bunka zenshū* 明治文化全集. Tokyo, 1928.

Fukuchi Shigetaka 福地重孝. "Kensei shoki no daigishi no seikaku" 憲政初期 の代議士の性格, *Nihon rekishi* 日本歴史, No. 79 (Dec. 1954).

———*Shizoku to samurai ishiki: Kindai Nihon wo okoseru mono—horobosu mono* 士族と士族意識: 近代日本を興せるもの—亡ぼすもの. Tokyo, 1956.

Fukuzawa zenshū 福沢全集. 10 vols.; Tokyo, 1925–1926.

Furushima Kazuo 古島一雄. "Rimpō kakumei wo ki ni: ichi rōseijika no kaisō" 隣邦革命を機に: 一老政治家の回想, *Chūō kōron,* Vol. 46, No. 1 (1951).

Gikai shi, see *Dai Nihon teikoku Gikai shi.*

"Gneist shi danwa" グナイスト氏談話, Pt. 1 of "Seitetsu yume monogatari" 西哲夢物語, in *Meiji bunka zenshū.*

Gotō Yasushi 後藤靖. "Nōmin minken no tenkai" 農民民權の展開, in *Rekishi to minshū: 1955 Nendo Rekishigakukenkyūkai taikai hōkoku* 歴史と民衆: 1955年度歴史學研究大会報告. Tokyo, 1955.

"Hakushi Roesler shi yuku" 博士ロエスレル氏逝く, *Taiyō* 太陽, Vol. 1 (Mar. 5, 1895).

Hara Kei nikki 原敬日記, ed. Hara Keiichirō 原奎一郎. 10 vols.; Tokyo, 1950– 1951.

Hattori Yukifusa (Shisō) 服部之總. "Meiji no dokusaisha" 明治の獨裁者, *Kaizō* 改造, Vol. 35, No. 10 (1954).

———and Irimajiri Yoshinaga 入交好脩. *Kindai Nihon jimbutsu seiji shi* 近代 日本人物政治史. 2 vols.; Tokyo, 1955–1956.

Hayashi Shigeru 林茂. "Dai san Gikai to dai ichiji Matsukata naikaku no gakai"

第三議会と第一次松方内閣の互解, *Kokka gakkai zasshi* 国家學会雑誌, Vol. 62 (Apr., May, Oct., Nov., 1948); *ibid.,* Vol. 63 (Mar. 1949).

Hayashida Kametarō 林田龜太郎. *Meiji Taishō seikai sokumen shi* 明治大正政界側面史. Tokyo, 1926.

───*Nihon seitō shi* 日本政党史. 2 vols.; Tokyo, 1927.

Hijikata Hisamoto 土方久元 and Itō Takumichi 伊東祐享. *Meiji tennō goseitoku* 明治天皇御聖徳. Tokyo, 1913.

Hirano Mineo 平野嶺夫. *Okazaki Kunisuke den* 岡崎邦輔傳. Tokyo, 1938.

Hori Makoto 堀真琴編, comp. *Gendai Nihon seiji kōza* 現代日本政治講座. Tokyo, 1941–1942.

Horie Eiichi 堀江英一. "Jiyū minken undō no tembō" 自由民權運動の展望, in *Rekishi to minshu: 1955 Nendo Rekishigakukenkyūkai taikai hōkoku.*

Ichijima Ken'ichi 市島謙一. *Ōkuma kō hachijūgonen shi* 大隈侯八十五年史. 3 vols.; Tokyo, 1926.

Ikeda Nagauma (Eima?) 池田永馬. *Kensei to Tosa* 憲政と土佐. Kōchi, 1941.

Imanaka Tsugimaro 今中次麿. "'Seitetsu yume monogatari' kaidai" 西哲夢物語解題, in *Meiji bunka zenshū,* rev. ed. (1955), Vol. 1.

Inada Masatsugu 稲田正次. "Kempō goshijun an no seiritsu katei" 憲法御諮詢案の成立過程, *Kokka gakkai zasshi,* Vol. 52, Nos. 8 and 9 (1938).

───"Kempō goshijun an no shūsei" 憲法御諮詢案の修正, *Kokka gakkai zasshi,* Vol. 53, Nos. 2–4 (1939).

───"Kempō kisō no keika ni tsuite" 憲法起草の経過, *Kokka gakkai zasshi,* Vol. 56, No. 11 (1942); *ibid.,* Vol. 57, No. 2 (1943).

───*Meiji kempō seiritsu shi* 明治憲法成立史. 2 vols.; Tokyo, 1960–1962.

Inada Shūnosuke 稲田周之助. "Nihon seitō ron" 日本政党論, *Hōgaku shimpō* 法學新報, Vol. 20 (Feb. 1910).

Inoue Kiyoshi 井上清. *Nihon seiji fuhai shi* 日本政治腐敗史. Tokyo, 1948.

───"Jiyū minken undō wo meguru rekishiteki hyōka ni tsuite" 自由民權運動をめぐる歴史的評価について, *Shisō* 思想, No. 379 (Jan. 1956).

Inukai Ken 犬養健. "Kokkai senkyo jishi" 国会選擧事始, *Chūō kōron,* Vol. 49, No. 6 (June 1934).

Isa Hideo 伊佐秀雄. *Ozaki Yukio den* 尾崎行雄傳. Tokyo, 1951.

Ishikawa Hanzan 石川半山. "Batsuzoku no dai bantō Itō shi" 閥族の大番頭伊東氏, *Chūō kōron,* Vol. 32, No. 7 (1917).

Ishikawa Mikiaki 石川幹明. *Fukuzawa Yukichi den* 福沢諭吉傳. 4 vols.; Tokyo, 1932.

Itagaki Taisuke 板垣退助. "Waga kuni kensei no yurai" 我国憲政の由來, in Takano Iwazaburō, comp., *Meiji kensei keizaishi ron.*

Itakura Takuzō 板倉卓造. "Seiji shisō shi jō kempō happu zen" 政治思想史上憲法発布前, *Hōgaku kenkyū* 法學研究, Vol. 3 (July 1924).

Itō Hirobumi 伊藤博文. "Hompō kempō seitei no yurai" 本邦憲法制定の由來, *Kokka gakkai zasshi,* No. 124 (June 15, 1897).

————Speech quoted in *Kokka gakkai zasshi,* Vol. 13, No. 154 (1899).

————"Kempō ritsuan no keika to sono riron to no gaisetsu" 憲法立案の経過 とその理論との概説, in *Itō kō zenshū,* Vol. 2.

————"Mokka no seijō to kempō seiji" 目下の政状と憲法政治, in *Itō kō zenshū,* Vol. 2.

————"Teikoku kempō no tokushoku to shinsei no kempō seiji" 帝国憲法の 特色と眞誠の憲法政治, in *Itō kō zenshū,* Vol. 2.

————*Hisho ruisan: Teikoku Gikai shiryō* 秘書類纂: 帝国議会資料. 2 vols.; Tokyo, 1934.

————*Kempō shiryō* 憲法資料. 3 vols.; Tokyo, 1936.

Itō Hirobumi hiroku 伊藤博文秘録, ed. Hiratsuka Atsushi 平塚篤. Tokyo, 1929.

Itō Hirobumi kō 伊藤博文公 (*Taiyō,* special issue; Nov. 1909).

Itō Jintarō 伊藤仁太郎. *Meiji rimenshi* 明治裏面史. 2 vols.; Tokyo, 1939.

"Itō ke monjo" 伊藤家文書. Manuscript; 91 vols.

"Itō kō no isshō" 伊藤公の一生; *Taiyō,* Vol. 15 (Oct. 1909).

Itō kō zenshū 伊藤公全集, ed. Komatsu Midori 小松緑. 3 vols.; Tokyo, 1928.

Itō Masanori 伊藤正徳. *Katō Takaaki* 加藤高明. 2 vols.; Tokyo, 1929.

"Itō nōshōmu daijin no jishoku" 伊東農商務大臣の辭職, *Taiyō,* Vol. 4 (May 5, 1898).

"Itō nyūtō mondai" 伊藤入党問題, *Chūō kōron,* Vol. 15 (July 1900).

Iwakura kō jikki 岩倉公實記. 3 vols.; Tokyo, 1928.

Jiji shimpō 時事新報.

Jimmin 人民.

Jiyū minken undō, see *Meiji shi kenkyū sōsho.*

Jiyūtō shi 自由党史, by Uda Tomoi 宇田友猪 and Wada Saburō 和田三郎, ed. Itagaki Taisuke 板垣退助. 2 vols.; Tokyo, 1910.

Kamishima Jirō 神島二郎. "Dai ikkai teikoku gikai shisei enzetsu no kankei shiryō" 第一回帝国議会施政演説の関係資料, *Kokka gakkai zasshi,* Vol. 66, Nos. 1–3 (1952).

————"Nihon no shisōka, kono hyakunen (21): Inoue Kowashi" 日本の思想 家この百年: 井上毅, *Asahi Journal* 朝日ジャーナル, Vol. 4 (Aug. 5, 1962).

Kamiya Takuo 神谷卓男. *Konoe Kazan kō* 近衞霞山公. Tokyo, 1924.

Kampō gōgai 9 Dec. 1892: Dai yonkai teikoku Gikai Shūgiin giji sokkiroku 官報 号外: 第四回帝国議会衆議院議事速記録, No. 7.

Kampō gōgai 31 May 1898: Dai jūnikai 第十二回 *teikoku Gikai Shūgiin giji sokkiroku,* No. 8.

Kampō gōgai 11 June 1898: Dai jūnikai teikoku Gikai Shūgiin giji sokkiroku, No. 16.

Kaneko Kentarō 金子堅太郎. "Itō kō to kempō seitei jigyō" 伊藤公と憲法制定 事業, *Kokka gakkai zasshi,* Vol. 24 (July 1910).

————"Nihon kempō seitei no yurai" 日本憲法制定の由来, *Shigaku zasshi* 史學雜誌, Vol. 22 (Oct. 1911).

——"Teikoku kempō seitei no yurai" 帝国憲法制定の由来, in *Meiji kensei keizaishi ron*.

——"Kempō seitei kaikyū dan" 憲法制定懐舊談, *Kokugakuin zasshi* 国學院雑誌, Vol. 25 (Apr. 1919).

——"Teikoku kempō no seishin kiso" 帝国憲法の精神基礎, *Nihon seishin kōza* 日本精神講座, Vol. 4 (Feb. 1934).

——"Naikaku seido sōshi tōji no tsuikai" 内閣制度創始当時の追懐, *Chūō kōron*, Vol. 51 (Feb. 1936).

——"Itō Hirobumi to watakushi" 伊藤博文と私, *Chūō kōron*, Vol. 51 (Aug. 1936).

——*Kempō seitei to Ōbeijin no hyōron* 憲法制定と歐米人の評論. Tokyo, 1938.

——*Itō kō wo kataru* 伊藤公を語る. Tokyo, 1939.

——*Itō Hirobumi den* 伊藤博文傳. 3 vols.; Tokyo, 1943.

Kawada Mizuho 川田瑞穂. *Kataoka Kenkichi sensei den* 片岡健吉先生傳. Tokyo, 1940.

Kawahara Jikichirō 川原次吉郎. "Nihon no seitō" 日本の政党, in *Seitō* 政党, ed. Rōyama Masamichi 蠟山政道. Tokyo, 1954.

Kazusa Takayoshi 上總天香. *Sekaiteki dai ijin: Itō kō* 世界的大偉人伊藤公. 2 vols.; Tokyo, 1909.

Kimura Tokio 木村時夫. "Fukuzawa Yukichi no Meiji kempō kan" 福沢諭吉の明治憲法觀, *Shikan* 史觀, No. 38 (June 1953).

"Ko Itō Miyoji haku no dampen: Kempō kisō tōji no kaiko" 故伊東巳代治伯の談片：憲法起草当時の回顧, *Meiji Taishō shi dan* 明治大正史談, Vol. 1 (Feb. 1937).

Kojima Tokumi 小島徳彌. "Meiji Taishō seitō hattatsu shi ron" 明治大正政党発達史論, *Taiyō*, Vol. 33 (Mar. 1927).

Kokkai 国会.

Kokumin no tomo 国民の友.

Kokumin shimbun 国民新聞.

Komatsu Midori 小松緑. *Itō kō to Yamagata kō* 伊藤公と山縣公. Tokyo, 1936.

Konishi Shirō 小西四郎. *Nihon zenshi: Kindai I* 日本全史：近代, Vol. 8. Tokyo, 1962.

Kudō Takeshige 工藤武重. *Meiji kensei shi* 明治憲政史. 2 vols.; Tokyo, 1922.

Kurihara Hirota 栗原廣太. *Hakushaku Itō Miyoji* 伯爵伊東巳代治. 2 vols.; Tokyo, 1937.

Kuroda Kiyotaka 黒田清隆. *Kan'yū nikki* 環游日記. 3 vols.; Tokyo, 1887.

Kurozukin 黒頭巾. "Hōi saretaru Itō kō" 包圍されたる伊藤公, *Chūō kōron*, Vol. 23, No. 9 (1908).

Maeda Renzan 前田蓮山. "Itō shi to Inukai shi" 伊東子と犬養氏, *Chūō kōron*, Vol. 32, No. 7 (1917).

——"Kempō no bannin, Itō Miyoji" 憲法の番人伊東巳代治, *Chūō kōron*, Vol. 49, No. 4 (1934).

————*Hara Kei den* 原敬傳. 2 vols.; Tokyo, 1943.

————*Hoshi Tōru den* 星亨傳. Tokyo, 1948.

Mainichi shimbun 每日新聞.

Maruyama Masao 丸山眞男. "Meiji kokka no shisō" 明治国家の思想, in *Nihon shakai no shiteki kyūmei.*

Masuda Tsuyoshi 増田毅. "Dai niji Itō naikaku: Hambatsu-seitō no teikei jidai" 第二次伊藤内閣藩閥: 政党の提携時代, *Kobe hōgaku zasshi* 神戸法學雜誌, Vol. 4 (Dec. 1954).

Masumi Junnosuke 升味準之輔. "Nihon seitō shi ni okeru chihō seiji no sho-mondai, Pt. 1: 1880 nendai no fu-ken kai" 日本政党史に於ける地方政治の諸問題: 一八八〇年代の府縣会, *Kokka gakkai zasshi,* Vol. 73, No. 4 (1959). Pt. 2: "Chihō minken kessha to sono shidōsha" 地方民權結社とその指導者, *ibid.,* No. 5. Pt. 3: "1890 nendai no seitō soshiki" 一八九〇年代の政党組織, *ibid.,* Nos. 5–6. Pt. 4: "Chihō ni okeru jitsugyō to seiji" 地方に於ける實業と政治, *ibid.,* Nos. 7–8.

Matsueda Yasuji 松枝保二. *Ōkuma kō sekijitsu dan* 大隈侯昔日譚. Tokyo, 1943.

Matsukage Sanjin 松影山人. "Yamagata kō to rikken seiji" 山縣公と立憲政治, *Kokka oyobi kokkagaku* 国家及國家學, Vol. 1 (Mar. 1913).

Meiji shi kenkyū sōsho: Jiyū minken undō 明治史研究叢書: 自由民權運動. Tokyo, 1956.

Meiji shiyō 明治史要, comp. Tokyo teikoku daigaku bungakubu shiryō hensanjo 東京帝国大學文學部史料編纂所. 2 vols.; Tokyo, 1933.

Minobe Tatsukichi 美濃部達吉. *Kempō seigi* 憲法精義. Tokyo, 1927.

Minoura Katsundo 箕浦勝人. "Zennendo no yosan wo shikō suru rigai" 前年度の豫算を施行する利害 in *Dai ikki kokkai shimatsu.*

Miyajima Seiichirō 宮島誠一郎. "Kokken hensan kigen" 国憲編纂起原, in *Meiji bunka zenshū* (1955), Vol. 1.

Miyake Setsurei (Yūjirō) 三宅雪嶺 (雄次郎). "Itō kō no kyōsōsha" 伊藤公の競争者, *Taiyō,* Vol. 15 (Oct. 1909).

————"Ōkuma haku" 大隈伯, *Chūō kōron,* Vol. 26, No. 1 (1911).

————"Inoue kōshaku" 井上公爵, *Chūō kōron,* Vol. 26, No. 2 (1911).

————*Dō jidai shi* 同時代史. 6 vols.; Tokyo, 1949–1954.

Miyazawa Toshiyoshi 宮澤俊義. "Genrō-in no kempō sōan ni tsuite" 元老院の憲法草案について, *Kokka gakkai zasshi,* Vol. 55, No. 4 (1941).

Mizuno Rentarō 水野錬太郎. "Rekidai naisō no omokage" 歴代内相の面影, *Chūō kōron,* Vol. 49, No. 11 (1934).

Mumeishi 無名氏. "Shin seitō no shuryōtaru Katsura kō no seijiteki keireki" 新政党の首領たる桂公の政治的経歴, *Chūō kōron,* Vol. 28, No. 5 (1913).

Nagata Shinnojō 永田新之允. *Ono Azusa* 小野梓. Tokyo, 1897.

Nakamura Kikuo 中村菊男. "Shoki Gikai to Hoshi Tōru" 初期議会と星亨, Pt. 1, *Hōgaku kenkyū,* Vol. 27 (Feb. 1954); Pt. 2, *ibid.* (May 1954); Pt. 3, *ibid.* (Oct. 1954).

Nakamura Yaroku 中村彌六. "Saionji kō no tokusei" 西園寺侯の特性, *Chūō kōron,* Vol. 26, No. 3 (1911).

Nakano Yoshio 中野好夫. "Chishikijin no tachiba" 知識人の立場, *Kaizō* (Dec. 1951).

Nakayama Yasumasa 中山泰昌, ed. *Shimbun shūsei Meiji hennen shi* 新聞集成明治編年史. 15 vols.; Tokyo, 1934–1936.

Nakayama Yoshisuke 中山義助. *Kōno Banshū [Hironaka] den* 河野磐州傳. 2 vols.; Tokyo, 1926.

Nichi nichi shimbun 日日新聞.

Nihon kokusei jiten 日本国政事典. 10 vols.; Tokyo, 1953–1958.

Nihon shakai no shiteki kyūmei 日本社会の史的究明編, comp. Rekishigakuken-kyūkai. Tokyo, 1949.

Nippon 日本.

Ōe Shinobu 大江志乃夫. "Gōnō minken no seiritsu" 豪農民權の成立, in *Rekishi to minshū: 1955 Nendo Rekishigakukenkyūkai taikai hōkoku.*

———"Gōnō minken undo no genryū" 豪農民權運動の源流, *Rekishigaku-kenkyū* 歴史學研究, No. 179 (Jan. 1955).

———"Minken undō seiritsu no gōnō to nōmin" 民權運動成立の豪農と農民, Pt. 1, *Rekishigakukenkyū,* No. 186 (Aug. 1955); Pt. 2, *ibid.,* No. 189 (Nov. 1955).

Ōe Taku 大江卓. "Seikai kaiko dan" 政界回顧談, *Taiyō,* Vol. 13 (Feb. 1907).

Ōishi Kiichirō 大石喜一郎. "Fukushima jiken" 福島事件, in *Rekishi to minshū: 1955 Nendo Rekishigakukenkyūkai taikai hōkoku.*

Oka Yoshitake 岡義武. "Teikoku Gikai no kaisetsu" 帝国議会の開設, *Kokka gakkai zasshi,* Vol. 58 (Jan. 1944).

———"Dai ichi gikai ni kansuru jakkan no kōsatsu" 第一議会に関する若干の考察, *Kokka gakkai zasshi,* Vol. 60 (Feb. 1946).

———*Kindai Nihon no keisei* 近代日本の形成. Tokyo, 1947.

———"Gaikanteki rikkensei ni okeru seitō: Seitō seijika to shite no Hara Kei" 外觀的立憲制に於ける政党: 政党政治家としての原敬, *Shisō,* No. 333 (Mar. 1953).

———*Gendai Nihon shōshi: Seiji shi* 現代日本小史: 政治史, ed. Yanaihara Tadao 矢内原忠雄. Misuzu Shobō ed.; Tokyo, 1953.

———*Yamagata Aritomo* 山縣有朋. Tokyo, 1958.

———"Shodai sōri: Itō Hirobumi" 初代總理: 伊藤博文, *Bungei shunjū* 文藝春秋, Vol. 37 (June 1959).

———*Kindai Nihon no seijika: Sono seikaku to ummei* 近代日本の政治家: その性格と運命. Tokyo, 1960.

Okazaki Kunisuke 岡崎邦輔. "Itō shishaku no dōraku" 伊東子爵の道楽, *Chūō kōron,* Vol. 32, No. 7 (July 1917).

Ōkubo Toshiaki 大久保利謙. "Meiji jūyonen no seihen to Inoue Kowashi" 明治十四年の政変と井上毅, in *Meiji bunka shi ronshū* 明治文化史論集. Tokyo, 1952.

————"Meiji jūyonen no seihen" 明治十四年の政変, in *Meiji shi kenkyū sōsho: Meiji seiken no kakuritsu katei* 明治史研究叢書: 明治政權の確立過程. Tokyo, 1957.

Ōkubo Toshikazu 大久保利和. *Ōkubo Toshimichi nikki* 大久保利通日記. 2 vols.; Tokyo, 1927.

————*Ōkubo Toshimichi monjo* 大久保利通文書. 10 vols.; Tokyo, 1927–1931.

Ōkuma Shigenobu 大隈重信. "Seikai no hen'ei" 政界の片影, *Taiyō*, Vol. 13, No. 3 (1907).

————"Seijika to shite no Itō kō" 政治家としての伊藤公, *Taiyō* 太陽, Vol. 15 (Nov. 1909).

————"Itō kō wo tsuitō suru" 伊藤公を追悼する, in *Ko Itō kōshaku tsuitōe enzetsu* 故伊藤公爵追悼会演説 (*Kokka gakkai zasshi*, No. 281; July 1910).

————"Nihon no seitō" 日本の政党, in Takano Iwazaburō, comp., *Meiji kensei keizaishi ron*.

Ōkuma Shigenobu kankei monjo 大隈重信関係文書. 6 vols.; Tokyo, 1934.

Okutani Matsuji 奥谷松治. *Shinagawa Yajirō den* 品川彌二郎傳. Tokyo, 1940.

Ōmachi Keigetsu 大町桂月. *Hakushaku Gotō Shōjirō* 伯爵後藤象二郎. Tokyo, 1914.

Ōmori Kingorō 大森金五郎 and Takahashi Shōzō 高橋昇造. *Saishin Nihon rekishi nempyō* 最新日本歴史年表. Tokyo, 1942.

Ono Hideo 小野秀雄. *Nihon shimbun hattatsu shi* 日本新聞発達史. Tokyo, 1922.

Osaka Mainichi shimbun 大阪毎日新聞.

Osatake Takeki 尾佐竹猛. "Teikoku gikai shi zenki" 帝国議会史前記, *Hōritsu oyobi seiji* 法律及政治, Vol. 1, No. 2 (June 1922) to Vol. 3, No. 5 (May 1924). A series of 21 articles.

————*Ishin zengo ni okeru rikken shisō* 維新前後に於ける立憲思想. 2 vols.; Tokyo, 1929.

————*Nihon kensei shi* 日本憲政史. Tokyo, 1930.

————*Ishin zengo ni okeru rikken shisō no kenkyū* 維新前後に於ける立憲思想の研究. Tokyo, 1934.

————"Kokken an ni tsuite" 国憲案に就いて, in *Meiji bunka kenkyū ronsō* 明治文化研究論叢. Tokyo, 1934.

————"Seinan eki ni kansuru ichi kōsatsu" 西南役に関する一考察, *Rekishi kyōiku* 歴史教育, Vol. 11 (Nov. 1936).

————"Gunjin seiji ni kan'yo subekarazu" 軍人政治に干與すべからず, *Hōritsu jihō* 法律時報, Vol. 9 (Jan. 1937).

————"Meiji jūhachinen: Shimbun zasshi ni arawareta shujusō" 明治十八年: 新聞雑誌に現れた種々相, *Meiji Taishō shi dan*, Vol. 1 (Feb. 1937).

————"Itagaki Taisuke yōkō mondai" 板垣退助洋行問題, in his *Meiji seiji shi tembyō*.

————*Meiji seiji shi tembyō* 明治政治史点描. Tokyo, 1938.

————*Nihon kensei shi taikō* 日本憲政史大綱. 2 vols.; Tokyo, 1938–1939.

————*Meiji Taishō seiji shi kōwa* 明治大正政治史講話. Tokyo, 1943.

————"Mutsu Munemitsu no nyūkaku jijō" 陸奥宗光の入閣事情, in his *Meiji Taishō seiji shi kōwa.*

————*Nihon kensei shi no kenkyū* 日本憲政史の研究. Tokyo, 1943.

————"Kempō seitei no ichi katei" 憲法制定の一過程, *Kokka gakkai zasshi,* Vol. 58, No. 1 (1944).

————and Hayashi Shigeru 林茂. *Gendai Nihon shi kenkyū: Seiji* 現代日本史研究: 政治. Tokyo, 1938.

Ōtsu Jun'ichirō 大津淳一郎. *Dai Nihon kensei shi* 大日本憲政史. 10 vols.; Tokyo, 1927–1928.

Ozaki Yukio 尾崎行雄. "Yosan iinkai no ryaku rekishi" 豫算委員会の略歴史, in *Dai ikki kokkai shimatsu.*

————"Seiyūkai ron" 政友会論, *Chūō kōron,* Vol. 24, No. 10 (1909).

————"Zōka no chōji" 造化の籠兒, *Taiyō,* Vol. 15 (Nov. 1909).

————"Itō, Ōkuma, Itagaki to watakushi" 伊藤, 大隈, 板垣と私, *Chūō kōron,* Vol. 53 (Mar. 1938).

————*Minken tōsō shichijūnen* 民權闘争七十年. Tokyo, 1952.

Rōyama Masamichi 蠟山政道. *Gendai Nihon bummei shi: Seiji shi* 現代日本文明史: 政治史. Tokyo, 1940.

Saiga Hakuai 雑賀博愛. *Ōe Ten'ya denki* 大江天也傳記. Tokyo, 1926.

Saitō Kumazō 斉藤熊藏. *Nihon seitō hattatsu shi* 日本政党発達史. Tokyo, 1917.

Sakata Yoshio 坂田吉雄. "Meiji zen hanki ni okeru seifu no kokkashugi" 明治前半期に於ける政府の国家主義, in Sakata Yoshio, comp., *Meiji zen hanki no nationalism* 明治前半期のナショナリズム. Tokyo, 1958.

Sakatani Yoshirō 阪谷芳郎. *Segai Inoue kō den* 世外井上公傳. 5 vols.; Tokyo, 1933–1934.

Sakuin seiji keizai dai nempyō: Nempyō hen 索引政治経済大年表: 年表篇. Tokyo, 1943.

Sasaki Sōichi 佐々木惣一. "Waga kempō to Stein" 我憲法とシュタイン, *Kyōto hōgakkai zasshi* 京都法學会雑誌, Vol. 8 (June 1913).

Sasuhara Yasuzō 指原安三. *Meiji seishi* 明治政史. 2 vols.; Tokyo, 1928–1929.

Satō Seirō 佐藤誠朗. "Meiji 17 nen 5 gatsu no Jiyūtōin meibo ni tsuite" 明治17年5月の自由党員名簿に就て, *Rekishigakukenkyū,* No. 178 (1954).

"Seikai no hyōmen ni noridashite kita Itō Miyoji shi" 政界の表面に乗り出して来た伊東己代治子, *Chūō kōron,* Vol. 32, No. 7 (July 1917).

Seikan Kyo Shujin 靜觀居主人. "Inoue kō ron" 井上侯論, *Chūō kōron,* Vol. 36, No. 2 (1911).

Seitō shi 政党史 (*Meiji shi* 明治史, Vol. 3). Taiyō, Feb. 1907.

Sekiyama Naotarō 関山直太郎. "Meiji nijūgonen goro no seitōin sōshi no kazu" 明治二十五年頃の政党員壯士の數, *Meiji bunka* 明治文化, Vol. 5 (Sept. 1929).

Shibuya Sasuke 澁谷作助. *Taketomi Tokitoshi* 武富時敏. Tokyo, 1934.

"Shigi kempō" 私擬憲法, *Kōjun zasshi* 交詢雑誌, No. 45:1–8 (Apr. 25, 1881).

Shimizu Shin 清水伸. *Doku-Ō ni okeru Itō Hirobumi no kempō torishirabe to Nihon kempō* 獨墺に於ける伊藤博文の憲法取調と日本憲法. Tokyo, 1939.

Shimoyama Saburō 下山三郎. "Meiji jūnendai no tochi shoyū kankei wo megutte" 明治十年代の土地所有関係をめぐつて, *Rekishigakukenkyū,* No. 176 (Oct. 1954).

———"Fukushima jiken shōron" 福島事件小論, Pt. 1, *Rekishigakukenkyū,* No. 186 (Aug. 1955); Pt. 2, *ibid.,* No. 187 (Sept. 1955).

Shinobu Seizaburō 信夫清三郎. *Mutsu Munemitsu* 陸奥宗光. Tokyo, 1938.

———*Meiji seiji shi* 明治政治史. 5th ed.; Tokyo, 1955.

Shinsen daijimmei jiten 新撰大人名辭典. 9 vols.; Tokyo, 1937–1941.

Soga Sukenori ō jijoden 曾我祐準翁自叙傳. Tokyo, 1931.

Suematsu Kenchō 末松謙澄. "Nijūsan nen no sō senkyo" 二十三年の總選擧, *Kokka gakkai zasshi,* Vol. 4, Nos. 44–45 (1890).

———"Itō kō no Ōshū ni okeru kempō torishirabe temmatsu" 伊藤公の欧州に於ける憲法取調顛末, *Kokka gakkai zasshi,* Vol. 26, No. 12 (1912).

———*Kōshi Itō kō* 孝子伊藤公. Tokyo, 1912.

Suzuki Yasuzō 鈴木安蔵. "Nihon kempō seitei ni taisuru Hermann Roesler no kiyo" 日本憲法制定に対するヘルメンロスレルの寄與, *Meiji bunka kenkyū,* Vol. 2 (May 1925).

———"Risshisha no 'Nihon kempō no mikomi an'" 立志社の「日本憲法の見込案, *Kokka gakkai zasshi,* Vol. 53 (Nov. 1939).

———*Gendai Nihon bummei shi: Kempō no rekishiteki kenkyū* 現代日本文明史：憲法の歴史的研究. Tokyo, 1940.

———"Kempō seiteiron no hassei" 憲法制定論の発生, *Chūō kōron,* Vol. 56, No. 3 (1941).

———"Rikken seiji eno kato" 立憲政治への過渡, *Chūō kōron,* Vol. 56 (May 1941).

———*Kempō seitei to Roesler* 憲法制定とロエスレル. Tokyo, 1942.

———*Meiji ishin seiji shi: Gendai Nihon no tanjō* 明治維新政治史：現代日本の誕生. Tokyo, 1942.

———*Seitō ron: Seitō to kokuminteki seiji soshiki* 政党論：政党と国民的政治組織. Tokyo, 1943.

———*Hyōden Itō Hirobumi* 評傳伊藤博文. Tokyo, 1944.

———*Jiyū minken undō shi* 自由民權運動史. Tokyo, 1947.

Tagawa Daikichirō 田川大吉郎. "Yamagata ni taishite omou tokoro" 山縣に対して思ふ所, *Chūō kōron,* Vol. 25, No. 10 (1910).

Takahashi Shingo 高橋清吾. "Meiji jūyonen no seihen ni tsuite" 明治十四年の政変について, *Waseda seiji keizaigaku zasshi* 早稲田政治経済學雑誌, No. 61 (Oct. 1938).

Takano Iwazaburō 高野岩三郎, comp. *Meiji kensei keizaishi ron* 明治憲政経済史論. Tokyo, 1919.

Tanaka Sōgorō 田中惣五郎. *Jūshin ron* 重臣論 (Hori Makoto, comp., *Gendai Nihon seiji kōza,* Vol. 4). Tokyo, 1941–1942.

Taruhito shinnō kōjitsu 熾仁親王行實. 2 vols.; Tokyo, 1929.

Taruhito shinnō nikki 熾仁親王日記. 6 vols.; Tokyo, 1935–1936.

"Terajima Munenori jijoden" 寺島宗則自叙傳, *Denki* 傳記, Vol. 3 (June 1936).

Tokutomi Iichirō 徳富猪一郎. *Kōshaku Katsura Tarō den* 公爵桂太郎傳. 2 vols.; Tokyo, 1917.

——*Kōshaku Yamagata Aritomo den* 公爵山縣有朋傳. 3 vols.; Tokyo, 1933.

——*Kōshaku Matsukata Masayoshi den* 公爵松方正義傳, 2 vols.; Tokyo, 1935.

——*Sohōjiden* 蘇峰自傳. Tokyo, 1935.

——"Chōshu sanson no hanashi: Itō, Yamagata, Inoue" 長州三尊の話: 伊藤, 山縣, 井上, *Chūō kōron,* Vol. 52 (Apr. 1937).

——"Itō, Ōkuma, Yamagata" 伊藤, 大隈, 山縣, *Chūō kōron,* Vol. 52, No. 5 (1937).

——"Sat-Chō jinshi" 薩長人士, *Chūō kōron,* Vol. 52, No. 6 (1937).

——"Itagaki Taisuke to Ōkuma Shigenobu: Nihon kensei no onjin" 板垣退助と大隈重信日本憲政の恩人, *Chūō kōron,* Vol. 52, No. 9 (Sept. 1937).

——"Happō yori nagametaru Ōkuma" 八方より眺めたる大隈, *Chūō kōron,* Vol. 52 (Oct. 1937).

——"Shōsetsu yori kinaru shōgai no Mutsu Munemitsu" 小説より奇なる生涯の陸奥宗光, *Chūō kōron,* Vol. 52 (Nov. 1937).

——"Shokan wo nobete Ōkuma kō wo kataru" 書翰を展べて大隈侯を語る, *Ōkuma kenkyū* 大隈研究, No. 3 (Oct. 1953).

Tokyo shimbun 東京新聞.

Tokyo teikoku daigaku ichiran 東京帝国大學一覽. Tokyo, 1943.

Toriumi Yasushi 鳥海靖. "Shoki gikai ni okeru Jiyūtō no kōzō to kinō" 初期議会における自由党の構造と機能, *Rekishigakukenkyū,* No. 255 (July 1961).

Tōyama Shigeki 遠山茂樹. "Nihon no shisō zasshi: Meiroku zasshi" 日本の思想雑誌: 明六雑誌, *Shisō,* No. 447 (1961).

——*et al. Nihon rekishi gaisetsu* 日本歴史概説. Tokyo, 1954.

Tsuda Shigemaro 津田茂麿. *Meiji seijō to shin Takayuki* 明治聖上と臣高行. Tokyo, 1928.

Tsuji Kiyoaki 辻清明. "Naikaku seido no juritsu: Tōji no yoron wo chūshin to shite" 内閣制度の樹立当時の輿論を中心として, *Kokka gakkai zasshi,* Vol. 58, No. 1 (1944).

Tsukada Masao 塚田昌夫. *Rikken minseitō shi* 立憲民政党史. 2 vols.; Tokyo, 1935.

Tsumaki Chūta 妻木忠太. *Kido Takayoshi monjo* 木戸孝允文書. 8 vols.; Tokyo, 1929–1931.

——*Kido Takayoshi nikki* 木戸孝允日記. 3 vols.; Tokyo, 1932–1933.

Uno Shun'ichi 宇野俊一. "Itō Hirobumi: Rikken seiyūkai kessei no zentei jōken wo chūshin ni" 伊藤博文: 立憲政友会結成の前提条件を中心に, *Rekishigakukenkyū,* No. 253 (May 1961).

Uyehara Etsujirō 植原悦二郎. "Katsura kō to Itō kō" 桂公と伊藤公, *Kokka oyobi kokkagaku,* Vol. 1 (Nov. 1913).

———*Nihon minken hattatsushi* 日本民權発達史. Tokyo, 1916.

Uzaki Kumakichi 鵜崎熊吉. *Inukai Tsuyoshi den* 犬養毅傳. Tokyo, 1932.

Uzaki Rojō 鵜崎鷺城. "Hyōmen ni noridashita Itō shi" 表面に乗出した伊東子, *Chūō kōron,* Vol. 32, No. 7 (July 1917).

Watanabe Ikujirō 渡辺幾治郎. "Meiji shi yori mitaru Ōkuma monjo" 明治史より見たる大隈文書, *Meiji bunka,* Vol. 6 (Mar. 1903).

———*Monjo yori mitaru Ōkuma Shigenobu kō* 文書より觀たる大隈重信侯. Tokyo, 1932.

———"Kempō seitei zengo" 憲法制定前後, *Rekishi kyōiku,* Vol. 11 (Nov. 1936).

———"Rikkenteki naikaku seido no sōshi ni tsuite" 立憲的内閣制度の創始に就いて, *Shikan,* Vol. 9 (Feb. 1936).

———*Meiji tennō to rikken seiji* 明治天皇と立憲政治. Tokyo, 1937.

———*Meiji tennō no seitoku: Jūshin* 明治天皇の聖徳: 重臣. Tokyo, 1941.

———*Mutsu Munemitsu den* 陸奥宗光傳. Tokyo, 1941.

———*Meiji tennō no seitoku: Seiji* 明治天皇の聖徳: 政治. Tokyo, 1942.

———*Meiji shi kenkyū* 明治史研究. Rev. ed.; Tokyo, 1944.

———*Ōkuma Shigenobu* 大隈重信. Rev. ed.; Tokyo, 1952.

———"Ōkuma Shigenobu no seikaku kenkyū: Jigyō wa seikaku no han'ei" 大隈重信の性格研究: 事業は性格の反映, *Ōkuma kenkyū,* No. 3 (Oct. 1953).

Yamada Tokazō 山田止戈三. "Shimbunshi yori mitaru Nihon ni okeru naikaku seiritsu no keishiki" 新聞紙より見たる日本に於ける内閣成立の形式, *Kokka gakkai zasshi,* Vol. 38, No. 4 (1924).

Yamazaki Rintarō 山崎林太郎. "Hoshi Tōru no hammen" 星亨の半面, *Chūō kōron,* Vol. 49 (Aug. 1934).

Yano Fumio 矢野文雄. "Yo ga seitō jidai" 予が政党時代, *Taiyō,* Vol. 13, No. 3 (1907).

———"Waga kuni rikken no taisei wo tsukutta sansei gun" 我国立憲の大勢を作つた三星群, *Shin kyū jidai* 新舊時代, Vol. 2 (Aug. 1926).

Yomiuri shimbun 讀賣新聞.

Yoshino Sakuzō 吉野作造. "Kempō happu izen ni okeru kempō shosōan" 憲法発布以前に於ける憲法諸草案, *Kokka gakkai zasshi,* Vol. 42 (July 1927).

———"Kempō to kensei no mujun" 憲法と憲制の矛盾, *Chūō kōron,* Vol. 44 (Dec. 1929).

———"Kosho chinchō" 古書珍重, *Tokyo Asahi shimbun* 東京朝日新聞 (Dec. 9, 1932).

———"Stein, Gneist to Itō Hirobumi" スタイン，グナイストと伊藤博文, *Kaizō,* Vol. 15 (Feb. 1933).

Yūbin hōchi shimbun 郵便報知新聞.

Zoku Fukuzawa zenshū 續福澤全集, ed. Iwanami Shigeo 岩波茂雄. 7 vols.; Tokyo, 1933.

Zoku Itō Hirobumi hiroku 續伊藤博文秘録, ed. Hiratsuka Atsushi 平塚篤. Tokyo, 1930.

WESTERN SOURCES

Anthony, David F. "The Administration of Hokkaido under Kuroda Kiyotaka, 1870–1882: An Early Example of Japanese-American Cooperation." Ph. D. thesis; Yale University, 1951.

Aubry, J. B. *The Chinese at Home,* quoted in Edward Eyre, ed., *European Civilization,* Vol. 3. New York, 1939.

Baelz,Toku, ed. *Awakening Japan: The Diary of a German Doctor,* tr. from the German by Eden and Cedar Paul. New York, 1932.

Beasley, W. G. "Councillors of Samurai Origin in the Early Meiji Government, 1868–1869," *Bulletin of the School of Oriental and African Studies,* Vol. 20. London, 1957.

Beckmann, George M. "Political Crises and the Crystallization of Japanese Constitutional Thought, 1871–1881," *Pacific Affairs,* Vol. 23 (Aug. 1954).

——*The Making of the Meiji Constitution: The Oligarchs and the Constitutional Development of Japan, 1868–1891.* Lawrence, 1957.

Billington, Ray Allen *et al.,* eds. *The Making of American Democracy: Readings and Documents,* Vol. 2. New York, 1962.

Bisson, T. A. *Japan in China.* New York, 1938.

——"Japan as a Political Organism," *Pacific Affairs,* Vol. 17 (Dec. 1944).

Borton, Hugh. *Japan's Modern Century.* New York, 1955.

——"Past Limitations and the Future of Democracy in Japan," *Political Science Quarterly,* Vol. 70 (Sept. 1955).

Brogan, D. W. and Douglas V. Verney. *Political Patterns in Today's World.* New York and Burlingame, 1963.

Brown, Sidney D. "Kido Takayoshi and the Meiji Restoration: A Political Biography, 1833–1877." Ph.D. thesis; University of Wisconsin, 1952.

——"Kido Takayoshi (1833–1877): Meiji Japan's Cautious Revolutionary," *Pacific Historical Review,* Vol. 25 (May 1956).

——"Ōkubo Toshimichi: His Political and Economic Policies in Early Meiji Japan," *Journal of Asian Studies,* Vol. 21 (Feb. 1962).

Buck, James H. "The Satsuma Rebellion of 1877: An Inquiry into Some of Its Military and Political Aspects." Ph.D. thesis; American University, 1959.

Burks, Ardath W. *The Government of Japan.* New York, 1961.

Burns, James MacGregor. "Two-Party Stalemate: The Crisis in Our Politics," *Atlantic* (Feb. 1960).

Butow, Robert J. C. *Japan's Decision to Surrender.* Stanford, 1954.

California State Senate, Special Committee on Chinese Immigration. *Report.* Sacramento, 1876.

Carr, Edward Hallet. *The New Society.* London, 1951.

Causton, E. E. N. *Militarism and Foreign Policy in Japan.* London, 1936.

Clement, Ernest W. "Local Self-Government in Japan," *Political Science Quarterly,* Vol. 7 (June 1892).

———and Uyehara Etsujirō, M.P. "Fifty Sessions of the Japanese Imperial Diet," *Transactions of the Asiatic Society of Japan,* 2nd ser., Vol. 2. Tokyo, 1925.

Clyde, Paul H. "Japan's March to Empire: Some Bibliographical Evaluations," *Journal of Modern History,* Vol. 21 (Dec. 1949).

Cody, Cecil E. "A Study of the Career of Itagaki Taisuke (1837–1919), A Leader of the Democratic Movement in Meiji Japan." Ph.D. thesis; University of Washington, 1955.

Colgrove, Kenneth. "Parliamentary Government in Japan," *American Political Science Review,* Vol. 21 (Nov. 1927).

———"Treaty-Making Power in Japan," *American Journal of International Law,* Vol. 35 (Apr. 1931).

———"The Japanese Privy Council," Pt. 1, *American Political Science Review,* Vol. 25 (Aug. 1931); Pt. 2, *ibid.* (Nov. 1931).

———"The Japanese Emperor," Pt. 1, *American Political Science Review,* Vol. 26 (Aug. 1932); Pt. 2, *ibid.* (Oct. 1932).

———"Powers and Functions of the Japanese Diet," Pt. 1, *American Political Science Review,* Vol. 27 (Dec. 1933); Pt. 2, *ibid.,* Vol. 28 (Feb. 1934).

———"The Japanese Cabinet," *American Political Science Review,* Vol. 30 (Oct. 1936).

———"The Japanese Constitution," *American Political Science Review,* Vol. 31 (Dec. 1937).

Craig, Albert. "The Restoration Movement in Chōshū," *Journal of Asian Studies,* Vol. 18 (Feb. 1959).

———*Chōshū in the Meiji Restoration.* Cambridge, Mass., 1961.

Crankshaw, Edward. *Khrushchev's Russia.* Baltimore, 1959.

Crowley, James B. "Japan's China Policy, 1931–1938: A Study of the Role of the Military in the Determination of Foreign Policy." Ph.D. thesis; University of Michigan, 1960.

———"A Reconsideration of the Marco Polo Incident," *Journal of Asian Studies,* Vol. 22 (May 1963).

Driver, Cecil. *Tory Radical: The Life of Richard Oastler.* New York, 1946.

Eltzbacher, O. "How Japan Reformed Herself," *Nineteenth Century and After,* Vol. 56 (July 1904).

Embree, John F. "Democracy in Postwar Japan," *American Journal of Sociology,* Vol. 50 (Nov. 1944).

Fagothey, Austin, S. J. *Right and Reason: Ethics in Theory and Practice*. Saint Louis, 1959.

Feldman, Horace Z. "The Meiji Political Novel: A Brief Survey," *Far Eastern Quarterly*, Vol. 9 (May 1950).

Fischer, George. *Russian Liberalism: From Gentry to Intelligentsia*. Cambridge, Mass., 1958.

Fukuzawa Yukichi. "The History of the Japanese Parliament," *Japan Weekly Mail* (Apr. 6, 1889).

——— *The Autobiography of Fukuzawa Yukichi*, tr. Eiichi Kyooka. Tokyo, 1934.

Gerschenkron, Alexander. "Economic Backwardness in Historical Perspective," in Bert F. Hoselitz, ed., *The Progress of Underdeveloped Areas*. Chicago, 1952.

Gorer, Geoffrey. "Themes in Japanese Culture," *Transactions of the New York Academy of Science*, Vol. 5 (Jan. 1943).

Griffis, William E. "The Constitution of Japan," *Chautauquan*, Vol. 12 (Feb. 1891).

——— "The Development of Political Parties in Japan," *North American Review*, Vol. 175 (1902).

——— "Ōkuma and the New Era in Japan," *North American Review*, Vol. 204 (Nov. 1916).

Hackett, Roger F. "Yamagata Aritomo: A Political Biography." Ph.D. thesis; Harvard University, 1955.

——— "Nishi Amane: A Tokugawa-Meiji Bureaucrat," *Journal of Asian Studies*, Vol. 18 (Feb. 1959).

Hall, John W. *Tanuma Okitsugu: Forerunner of Modern Japan*. Cambridge, Mass., 1955.

Hamada Kengi. *Prince Ito*. Tokyo, 1936.

Hane Mikiso. "English Liberalism and the Japanese Enlightenment, 1868–1890." Ph.D. thesis; Yale University, 1957.

Harootunian, Harry D. "The Economic Rehabilitation of the Samurai in the Early Meiji Period," *Journal of Asian Studies*, Vol. 19 (Aug. 1960).

Hayes, Samuel P., Jr. "Personality and Culture Problems of Point IV," in Bert F. Hoselitz, ed., *The Progress of Underdeveloped Areas*.

Heilbronner, Robert L. *The Future As History: The Historic Currents of Our Time and the Direction in Which They Are Taking America*. New York, 1959.

Horie Yasuzō. "Confucian Concept of State in Tokugawa Japan," *Kyoto University Economic Review*, Vol. 32 (Oct. 1962).

Hoshi Tōru. "The New Japan," *Harper's New Monthly Magazine*, No. 570 (Nov. 1897).

Humphreys, Mary G. "The Men of New Japan," *Century Illustrated Monthly Magazine,* Vol. 62 (Oct. 1901).

Idditti Smimasa. *The Life of Marquis Shigenobu Ōkuma.* Tokyo, 1940.

Ike Nobutaka. "Triumph of the Peace Party in Japan in 1873," *Far Eastern Quarterly,* Vol. 2 (May 1943).

———*The Beginnings of Political Democracy in Japan.* Baltimore, 1950.

———*Japanese Politics.* New York, 1957.

Isaacs, Harold R. *Scratches on Our Mind: American Images of China and India.* New York, 1958.

Itō Hirobumi. *Commentaries on the Constitution of the Empire of Japan,* tr. Itō Miyoji. Tokyo, 1889.

———"The Duties of Political Parties," in Alfred Stead, *Japan by the Japanese.* New York, 1904.

———*Marquis Itō's Experience,* tr. Kuramata Teizo. Nagasaki, 1904.

———"Some Reminiscences of the Grant of the New Constitution," in Ōkuma Shigenobu, ed., *Fifty Years of New Japan,* Vol. 1. London, 1909.

Iwata Masakazu. "Ōkubo Toshimichi: The Leading Protagonist on the Stage of the Restoration Drama." Ph.D. thesis; University of California, Los Angeles, 1960.

Iyenaga Toyokichi. "The Constitutional Development of Japan, 1853–1881," *Johns Hopkins University Studies in Historical and Political Science,* Vol. 9. Baltimore, 1891.

Jansen, Marius B. "Ōi Kentarō: Radicalism and Chauvinism," *Far Eastern Quarterly,* Vol. 11 (May 1952).

———*The Japanese and Sun Yat-sen.* Cambridge, Mass., 1954.

———*Sakamoto Ryōma and the Meiji Restoration.* Princeton, 1961.

"Japanese Constitutional Crisis and the War, The," by A Resident, *Contemporary Review,* Vol. 68 (Oct. 1895).

"Japanese Revolution, The," *Quarterly Review,* Vol. 200 (July 1904).

Kaneko, Baron Kentarō. "The Magna Charta of Japan," *Century Magazine,* Vol. 68 (July 1904).

Kawabe Kisaburō. *The Press and Politics in Japan: A Study of the Relations between the Newspaper and the Political Development of Modern Japan.* Chicago, 1921.

Kawai Kazuo. "Sovereignty and Democracy in the Japanese Constitution," *American Political Science Review,* Vol. 44 (Sept. 1955).

Kimura Motokazu. "Fiscal Policy and Industrialization in Japan, 1868–1895," *Annals of the Hitotsubashi Academy,* Vol. 6 (Apr. 1956).

Kōsaka Masaaki, ed. *Japanese Thought in the Meiji Era,* tr. and adapted by David Abosch. Tokyo, 1958.

Kuroda Kazuo. "Magazines Sold Out," *Japan Times* (Dec. 13, 1958).

La Barre, Weston. "Some Observations on Character Structure in the Orient: The Japanese," *Psychiatry,* Vol. 8 (Aug. 1945).

Lebra, Joyce C. "Japan's First Modern Popular Statesman: A Study of the Political Career of Ōkuma Shigenobu (1838–1922)." Ph.D. thesis; Radcliffe College, 1958.

———"Ōkuma Shigenobu and the 1881 Political Crisis," *Journal of Asian Studies,* Vol. 18 (Aug. 1959).

Linebarger, Paul, Chu Djang and Ardath W. Burks. *Far Eastern Governments and Politics: China and Japan.* New York, 1954.

Lockwood, William W. *The Economic Development of Japan: Growth and Structural Change, 1868–1938.* Princeton, 1954.

McGovern, William M. *Modern Japan: Its Political, Military, and Industrial Organization.* London, 1920.

McLaren, Walter W. *A Political History of Japan During the Meiji Era, 1867–1912.* London, 1916.

——— ed. *Japanese Government Documents* (*Transactions of the Asiatic Society of Japan,* Vol. 42), Pt. 1. Tokyo, 1914.

Maki, John M. "The Role of the Bureaucracy in Japan," *Pacific Affairs,* Vol. 20 (Dec. 1947).

———*Government and Politics in Japan: The Road to Democracy.* New York, 1962.

Mason, R. H. P. "The First Meiji Election." Ph.D. thesis; Australian National University, 1962.

Matsumoto Kaoru. "Development of Democracy in Japan Prior to 1945, and the Constitutional Controversy on the Nature of Monarchy," *Waseda Political Studies,* Vol. 1 (1957).

Mayo, Marlene J. "The Iwakura Embassy and the Unequal Treaties, 1871–1873." Ph.D. thesis; Columbia University, 1961.

Minger, Ralph E. "Taft's Missions to Japan: A Study in Personal Diplomacy," *Pacific Historical Review,* Vol. 30 (Aug. 1961).

Mitford, Algernon B. "Wanderings in Japan," *Littel's Living Age,* No. 113 (Apr. 1872).

Moore, H. M. "The First General Election in Japan," *New Review,* Vol. 3 (July 1890).

Murata Kiyoaki. "Cultivating the Constituency," *Japan Times* (Oct. 31, 1963).

Nagai Michio. "Herbert Spencer in Early Meiji Japan," *Far Eastern Quarterly,* Vol. 14 (Nov. 1954).

Neumann, William L. *America Encounters Japan: From Perry to MacArthur.* Baltimore, 1963.

Nishii Shii. *Kan-min no shōtotsu kyūchō,* quoted in *Japan Weekly Mail* (Feb. 28, 1903).

Norman, E. Herbert. *Japan's Emergence As a Modern State: Political and Economic Problems of the Meiji Period.* New York, 1940.

Olson, Lawrence A. "Hara Kei: A Political Biography." Ph.D. thesis; Harvard University, 1954.

Ozaki Yukio. "Constitutional Government in Japan," *Transactions and Proceedings of the Japan Society of London,* Vol. 29. London, 1932.

Perry, Walter S. "Yoshino Sakuzō, 1878–1933: Exponent of Democratic Ideals in Japan." Ph.D. thesis; Stanford University, 1956.

Piggot, Sir Francis. "The Itō Legend: Personal Recollections of Prince Itō," *Nineteenth Century and After,* Vol. 57 (Jan. 1910).

———"New Japan," *Fortnightly Review,* new ser., Vol. 52, No. 309.

Pittau, Joseph, S. J. "Ideology of a New Nation: Authoritarianism and Constitutionalism, Japan (1868–1890)." Ph.D. thesis; Harvard University, 1962.

———"The Meiji Political System: Different Interpretations," in Joseph Roggendorf, ed., *Studies in Japanese Culture.* Tokyo, 1963.

Potter, Henry C. "Impressions of Japan," *Century Illustrated Magazine,* Vol. 61 (Mar. 1901).

Quigley, Harold S. "Privy Council vs. Cabinet in Japan," *Foreign Affairs,* Vol. 9 (Apr. 1931).

———*Japanese Government and Politics.* New York, 1932.

———"Japan's Constitutions: 1890 and 1947," *American Political Science Review,* Vol. 41 (Oct. 1947).

———"How New is the New Japan?" *Virginia Quarterly Review,* Vol. 33 (Winter 1957).

———and John E. Turner. *The New Japan: Government and Politics.* Minneapolis, 1956.

Redman, H. Vere. "How the Cabinet is Controlled," *Contemporary Japan,* Vol. 1 (Dec. 1932).

Reischauer, Edwin O. "Our Asian Frontiers of Knowledge," *University of Arizona Bulletin Series,* Vol. 29 (Sept. 1958).

Reischauer, Robert K. *Japan: Government-Politics.* New York, 1939.

Roylance-Kent, C. B. "The New Japanese Constitution," *MacMillan's Magazine,* Vol. 70 (Oct. 1894).

Sansom, George B. *Japan: A Short Cultural History.* New York, 1943.

———*The Western World and Japan: A Study in the Interaction of European and Asiatic Cultures.* New York, 1950.

Sato Hiroshi. *Democracy and the Japanese Government.* New York, 1920.

Satow, Sir Ernest. *A Diplomat in Japan.* Philadelphia, 1921.

Scalapino, Robert A. "The Japanese Diet Today," *Parliamentary Affairs,* Vol. 5 (Summer 1952).

————*Democracy and the Party Movement in Prewar Japan: The Failure of the First Attempt.* Berkeley and Los Angeles, 1953.

————"Japan: Between Traditionalism and Democracy," in Sigmund Neumann, ed., *Modern Political Parties: Approaches to Comparative Politics.* Chicago, 1956.

————"The Left Wing in Japan," *Survey: A Journal of Soviet and East European Studies* (Aug. 1962).

————and Masumi Junnosuke. *Parties and Politics in Contemporary Japan.* Berkeley and Los Angeles, 1962.

Siemes, Johannes, S. J. "Hermann Roesler's Commentaries on the Meiji Constitution," *Monumenta Nipponica,* Vol. 17, Nos. 1–4 (1962).

Silberman, Bernard L. "The Political Theory and Program of Yoshino Sakuzō," *Journal of Modern History,* Vol. 31 (Dec. 1959).

Smith, Thomas C. "Landlords and Rural Capitalists in the Modernization of Japan," *Journal of Economic History,* Vol. 16 (June 1956).

Smith, Warren W., Jr. *Confucianism in Modern Japan: A Study in Japanese Intellectual History.* Tokyo, 1959.

Spitzer, Herman. "Psychoanalytic Approaches to the Japanese Character," in Geza Roheim, ed., *Psychoanalysis and the Social Sciences,* Vol. 1. New York, 1947.

Storry, Richard. *The Double Patriots: A Study of Japanese Nationalism.* New York, 1957.

————*A History of Modern Japan.* London, 1960.

Sutton, Joseph L. *A Political Biography of Inukai Tsuyoshi.* University Microfilms Publication 8421; Ann Arbor, 1954.

Ten Broek, J., W. Matson, and E. N. Barnhart. *Prejudice, War, and the Constitution.* Berkeley, 1954.

Teng Ssu-yu and John K. Fairbank. *China's Response to the West: A Documentary Survey, 1839–1923.* Cambridge, Mass., 1954.

Terry, Charles S. "Taking Exception," *Japan Society Forum* (Dec. 15, 1961).

Teters, Barbara J. "The Conservative Opposition in Japanese Politics, 1877–1894." Ph.D. thesis; University of Washington, 1955.

————"The Genrō-in and the National Essence Movement," *Pacific Historical Review,* Vol. 31 (Nov. 1962).

Thomas, Norman. "Rethinking Socialism," *Virginia Quarterly Review,* Vol. 34 (Winter 1958).

Tiedemann, Arthur E. "The Hamaguchi Cabinet, First Phase July 1929–February 1930: A Study in Japanese Parliamentary Government." Ph.D. thesis; Columbia University, 1959.

Tsunoda Ryūsaku, William Theodore de Bary, and Donald Keene, comps. *Sources of Japanese Tradition*. New York, 1958.

Utley, Freda. *Japan's Feet of Clay*. 2nd ed.; New York, 1937.
Uyehara Etsujirō. *The Political Development of Japan, 1867–1909*. London, 1910.

Vinacke, Harold M. *A History of the Far East in Modern Times*. 6th ed.; New York, 1959.
Voltaire. "A Conversation with a Chinese," in *Works of Voltaire*, Vol. 4. Ohio, 1905.

Wald, Royal J. "The Young Officers' Movement in Japan, ca. 1925–1935: Ideology and Actions." Ph.D. thesis; University of California, Berkeley, 1949.
Ward, Robert E. "Party Government in Japan: A Preliminary Survey of Its Development and Electoral Record, 1928–1937." Ph.D. thesis; Berkeley, 1948.
———"Political Modernization and Political Culture in Japan," *World Politics,* Vol. 15 (July 1963).
Wigmore, John H. "Parliamentary Days in Japan, with Illustrations," *Scribner's Magazine,* Vol. 10 (Aug. 1891).
———"Starting a Parliament in Japan," *Scribner's Magazine,* Vol. 10 (July–Dec. 1891).
Williams, Justin. "The Japanese Diet under the New Constitution," *American Political Science Review,* Vol. 42 (Oct. 1948).
Wilson, George M. "Politics and the People: Liang Ch'i-ch'ao's View of Constitutional Developments in Meiji Japan before 1890," *Papers on Japan,* Vol. 1. Harvard University, East Asian Research Center, 1961.
Wilson, Robert A. *Genesis of the Meiji Government in Japan, 1868–1871* (University of California Publications in History, Vol. 46). Berkeley and Los Angeles, 1957.

Yanaga Chitoshi. "Theory of the Japanese State." Ph.D. thesis; University of California, Berkeley, 1935.
———*Japan since Perry*. New York, 1949.
———*Japanese People and Politics*. New York, 1956.
———"Japanese Political Parties," *Parliamentary Affairs,* Vol. 10 (Summer 1957).
Yokoi Tokiwo. "New Japan and Her Constitutional Outlook," *Contemporary Review,* Vol. 74 (Sept. 1898).
Yoshino Sakuzō. "In the Name of the People," *Pacific Affairs,* Vol. 4 (Mar. 1931).
———"Fascism in Japan," *Contemporary Japan,* Vol. 1 (Sept. 1932).

NOTES

ABBREVIATIONS USED IN THE NOTES

CK   *Chūō kōron*
KGZ *Kokka gakkai zasshi*
RK   *Rekishigakukenkyū*

INTRODUCTION

1. Inada Shūnosuke, "Nihon seitō ron" (On Japanese political parties), *Hōgaku shimpō* (The law journal), 20:33 (Feb. 1910).

2. Nakano Yoshio, "Chishikijin no tachiba" (Where the intellectuals stand), *Kaizō* (Reconstruction; Dec. 1951), p. 92. Yoshida is cited as being an "outspoken foe of what he has frequently described as pale-faced intellectuals." *Japan Times* (Feb. 17, 1961).

3. *Asahi shimbun* (Dec. 18, 1958). For views on the Japanese intellectuals, see Yanaga Chitoshi, *Japanese People and Politics* (New York, 1956), pp. 19, 36–37; Ike Nobutaka, *Japanese Politics* (New York, 1957), Chap. 12, esp. pp. 247–250; Kuroda Kazuo, "Magazines Sold Out," *Japan Times* (Dec. 13, 1958); Robert A. Scalapino, "The Left Wing in Japan," *Survey: A Journal of Soviet and East European Studies* (Aug. 1962), pp. 102–111.

4. Yoshino Sakuzō was an exception. A biographer has written: "Overcoming the deep-seated hesitation of associating his name with 'dirty politics'—a hesitation shared by many of his scholarly colleagues, he set about bringing his professional knowledge to bear on the problems of the day to the end that political life might be purified and the Japanese nation be prepared to meet the challenge of its rapidly changing existence in the modern world." Walter S. Perry, "Yoshino Sakuzō, 1878–1933: Exponent of Democratic Ideals in Japan," Ph.D. thesis (Stanford, 1956), pp. 132–133.

5. The Japanese intellectuals do not, of course, form a unitary, cohesive body with a single, fixed view on constitutionalism and constitutional development. The refinements in interpretations are ably described by Joseph Pittau, S.J., "The Meiji Political System: Different Interpretations," in Joseph Roggendorf, ed., *Studies in Japanese Culture* (Tokyo, 1963), pp. 99–122. But basically our views coincide, for he concludes: "Japanese scholars in their interpretation of the Meiji political system often take for their point of reference the Western models of modernization. They tend to see Japanese political developments of the early Meiji period from a negative point of view." (p. 121)

CHAPTER I. ASSEMBLIES AND CONSTITUTIONS, EARLY MEIJI

1. Letter dated April 26, quoted in *Iwakura kō jikki* (The authentic documents of Prince Iwakura; Tokyo, 1928), II, 716. For detailed discussion of some of the reforms and revolutionary changes undertaken in the early years of the Meiji, see Iwata Masakazu, "Ōkubo Toshimichi: The Leading Protagonist on the Stage of the Restoration Drama," Ph.D. thesis (University of California, Los Angeles, 1960), pp. 229–294.

2. Albert Craig, "The Restoration Movement in Chōshū," *Journal of Asian Studies,* 18:187–197 (Feb. 1959), discusses the dangers in the lack of precise definitions when dealing with the roles of the samurai just before the Restoration. Note 4 of his article describes the distinctions in Meiji administrative categories of the former samurai.

3. Beasley notes that it was more than eighteen months before the country's governmental system "took anything like a stable shape." W. G. Beasley, "Councillors of Samurai Origin in the Early Meiji Government, 1868–9," *Bulletin of the School of Oriental and African Studies,* 20:89 (London, 1957). This is not to say that experimentation of sorts was not being carried out. The Seitaisho, called by some the Constitution of 1868 and by others the June Constitution, created a deliberative body that showed some Western influence. The careful constitutional historian, Inada Masatsugu, however, appears hesitant about stating unequivocally that the Seitaisho was a constitution. Inada Masatsugu, *Meiji kempō seiritsu shi* (A history of the Meiji constitution; Tokyo, 1960), I, 22–23. See also Minobe Tatsukichi, *Kempō seigi* (Commentary on the constitution of Japan; Tokyo, 1927), p. 2. For a full discussion of the Seitaisho, see Robert A. Wilson, *Genesis of the Meiji Government in Japan, 1868–1871* (University of California Publications in History, Vol. 56; Berkeley and Los Angeles, 1957), Chap. 3.

4. The Sa-in was created on July 29, 1871. For a description of its functions, see Osatake Takeki, *Ishin zengo ni okeru rikken shisō no kenkyū* (A study of constitutional thought at the time of the Restoration; Tokyo, 1934), pp. 622–639. This is the revised edition of Osatake's oft-cited *Ishin zengo ni okeru rikken shisō* (Constitutional thought at the time of the Restoration), 2 vols. (Tokyo, 1929).

5. Miyajima Seiichirō, "Kokken hensan kigen" (Origins of the compilations of our constitution), in *Meiji bunka zenshū* (Collected works on Meiji civilization), rev. ed. (Tokyo, 1955), I, 344. Itō Hirobumi himself recalled that the Meiji government's efforts in this field were hampered by the constant occurrence of intragovernmental splits and rebellions. Itō Hirobumi, "Hompō kempō seitei no yurai" (The beginnings of our constitutional system), *KGZ,* No. 124:531–536 (June 15, 1897).

6. Fukuzawa Yukichi, *The Autobiography of Fukuzawa Yukichi,* tr. Eiichi Kyooka (Tokyo, 1934), p. 143.

7. An early memorandum on the subject was introduced with the words that "practical difficulties" would result if the ideas contained in the addendum to the memorandum were put into effect immediately. Miyajima, pp. 346–347. See also Suzuki Yasuzō, "Kempō seiteiron no hassei" (The beginnings of the arguments for the enactment of a constitution), *CK,* 56.3:308 (1941). Part of the rationale for gradualism, of course, was the conviction in high places that the people were still much too immature for political responsibility. See, for example, the views of Kido and Ōkubo in Walter W. McLaren, ed., "Japanese Government Documents," *Transactions of the Asiatic Society of Japan,* Vol. 42, Pt. 1, pp. 572–573 (Tokyo, 1914); and George M. Beckmann, *The Making of the Meiji Constitution: The Oligarchs and the Constitutional Development of Japan, 1868–1891* (Lawrence, 1957), Appendix 2. See also Katō Hiroyuki, "Objections to the Establishment of a Deliberative Assembly Chosen by the People," in McLaren, "Documents," pp. 433–439.

8. Algernon B. Mitford, "Wanderings in Japan," *Littel's Living Age,* No. 113:38 (Apr. 1872). Kido himself recorded on September 7 and 8, 1869, that he had talked to an Englishman, "Mittohoru." Tsumaki Chūta, *Kido Takayoshi nikki* (The diaries of Kido Takayoshi; Tokyo, 1932–1933) I, 263. Another Englishman, Satow, also recorded a somewhat similar experience. He is writing of a time in 1867: "After dinner Gotō [Shōjirō] came on board to have a talk on politics. He spoke of his idea of establishing a parliament, and a constitution on the English model, and said that Saigō [Takamori] entertained similar notions." And again, "After this Yōdō [Toyoshige] and Gotō plied me with questions about the Luxemburg affair, the constitution and powers of parliament and the electoral system; it was evident that the idea of a constitution resembling that of Great Britain had

already taken deep root in their minds." Sir Ernest Satow, *A Diplomat in Japan* (Philadelphia, 1921), pp. 267, 270. For another indication of this interest, see Yanaga Chitoshi, "Theory of the Japanese State," Ph.D. thesis (University of California, Berkeley, 1935), Appendix 4: "Western Books Translated and Used in Japan During the Early Meiji Period."

9. Osatake Takeki, *Nihon kensei shi taikō* (An outline of Japanese constitutional history; Tokyo, 1938–1939), I, 279.

10. Miyajima, p. 346.

11. For a translation of the Charter Oath, see Nobutaka Ike, *The Beginnings of Political Democracy in Japan* (Baltimore, 1950), p. 36.

12. Quoted in Osatake, *Ishin zengo,* p. 719; see also Wilson, *Genesis,* p. 38.

13. McLaren, "Documents," p. xxxix. This is the group to which Osatake seems to be pointing when he speaks of the "popular mind." Osatake, *Ishin zengo,* Appendix 4, p. 67. Cf. E. Herbert Norman, *Japan's Emergence As a Modern State: Political and Economic Problems of the Meiji Period* (New York, 1940), p. 92.

14. E.g., see the views of Suzuki Yasuzō, in his *Meiji ishin seiji shi: Gendai Nihon no tanjō* (A political history of the Meiji Restoration: The birth of modern Japan; Tokyo, 1942), p. 426; and in his *Jiyū minken undō shi* (A history of the movement for parliamentary government, Tokyo, 1947), p. 16. See also Matsumoto Kaoru, "Development of Democracy in Japan Prior to 1945, and the Constitutional Controversy on the Nature of Monarchy," *Waseda Political Studies,* 1:63 (1957).

15. Osatake, *Nihon kensei shi taikō,* I, 256; Inada Masatsugu, *Meiji kempō,* I, 89–92. It should be pointed out that the term *kempō* as used in the very early days of the Meiji cannot always be rendered as "constitution," meaning the fundamental law of a nation. It was often used in the narrower sense of national laws, on the level, for example, of Imperial Household laws. *Kokken* and *seiki* (the latter term used by Kido in his petition of July, 1873) were some of the words used to denote "constitution" as we understand the term today. Osatake feels that the use of the term *kempō* as meaning "constitution" in the present-day sense, began in the 1880's. Itō Hirobumi, for one, is said to have chosen to use the word *kempō* to designate his constitution and to differentiate it from the Genrō-in draft constitution. See Osatake, *Ishin zengo,* Appendix 4, p. 81; Osatake, "Kokken an ni tsuite" (On the [Genrō-in] draft constitution), *Meiji bunka kenkyū ronsō* (Collection of studies on Meiji civilization; Tokyo, 1934), p. 167; Fujii Jintarō, *Nihon kempō seitei shi* (A history of the Japanese constitution; Tokyo, 1922), p. 103.

16. Other petitions and memoranda were presented in the meantime (Osatake, *Nihon kensei shi taikō,* I, 257, 281–282). Furthermore, interest in constitutions and assemblies antedated the Restoration. For example, Mizuno Echizen-no-kami, who occupied the highest administrative post in the Tokugawa government, ordered Sugita Seikei, aged 27, to translate the Dutch constitution. Sugita completed the translation in 1842. This was probably the first Japanese attempt to translate a Western constitution. Osatake, *Ishin zengo,* Appendix 4, pp. 64–65. The conciliar form of government suggested by the bakufu official Ōkubo Ichiō, who envisaged councils of major and minor lords, should also be mentioned. This idea was further developed by Sakamoto Ryōma and is part of his famous Eight-Point Plan. Marius B. Jansen, *Sakamoto Ryōma and the Meiji Restoration* (Princeton, 1961), pp. 168, 178, *et passim.* For material on constitutions and assemblies at the time of the Restoration, see Osatake Takeki's series of 21 articles, "Teikoku gikai shi zenki" (Early records on the history of the Imperial Diet), *Hōritsu oyobi seiji* (Law and politics), Vol. 1, No. 2 (June 1922) to Vol. 3, No. 5 (May 1924). The material in these articles served as the core of many of Osatake's later works. See also Fujii Jintarō's eleven articles, "Nihon kempō seitei shi dan" (Discourses on the history of the enactment of the Japanese constitution), *Rekishi chiri* (History and geography), Vol. 33, No. 4 (1919) to Vol. 34, No. 5 (1920). For discussions in English, see Robert Wilson, *Genesis,* pp. 35–36;

Yanaga, "Theory," pp. 250–255; Hane Mikiso, "English Liberalism and the Japanese Enlightenment, 1868–1890," Ph.D. thesis (Yale, 1957), pp. 253–256.

17. Miyajima, pp. 345–346. Etō Shimpei opposed Miyajima's petition because, in his view, Miyajima wanted to give the "people" too much leeway to interfere with state affairs, and because Miyajima's constitution was not what he considered an emperor-granted constitution. Miyajima, p. 346. Osatake, *Nihon kensei shi taikō*, I, 285–288; Inada Masatsugu, *Meiji kempō*, I, 105–107. It is fairly obvious that there was a wide range of views and proposals on constitutionalism among those in the government.

18. Miyajima, pp. 346–347; Osatake, *Nihon kensei shi taikō*, I, 289–292; Inada Masatsugu, *Meiji kempō*, I, 109–111.

19. Miyajima, p. 353; Osatake, *Nihon kensei shi taikō*, I, 293–294; Suzuki, *Meiji ishin*, pp. 428–429. Cf. Inada Masatsugu, *Meiji kempō*, I, 111–130.

20. Osatake, *Nihon kensei shi taikō*, I, 310; Inada, *Meiji kempō*, I, 195; Suzuki, *Meiji ishin*, p. 433. Suzuki states that the words *kokuhō kaigi* (assembly [for enacting] national laws), in Etō's October 1870 petition mean an assembly for drafting a constitution. Suzuki, *Meiji ishin*, pp. 424–425; cf. Inada Masatsugu, *Meiji kempō*, I, 90–91.

21. Sidney D. Brown, "Kido Takayoshi and the Meiji Restoration: A Political Biography, 1833–1877," Ph.D. thesis (University of Wisconsin, 1952), p. 309. Iwata arrives at a somewhat different conclusion. He states: "When they left Japan, Kido was much more imbued with a spirit of progress than Ōkubo; when they returned, Kido was more a conservative than Ōkubo. Impressed by the prosperity of the United States and Europe, Ōkubo became a stronger advocate of progressive reform while Kido, depressed by the plight of Ireland and the fate of Poland, was less enthusiastic for the Westernization of Japan." Iwata, p. 321. For one of the most readable accounts of the Iwakura Mission, see Brown "Kido Takayoshi," Chap. 3: "The Occident through Japanese Eyes, 1871–1873." See also Marlene June Mayo, "The Iwakura Embassy and the Unequal Treaties, 1871–1873," Ph.D. thesis (Columbia, 1961), which emphasizes Japan's attempt at treaty revision in 1872. As Dr. Mayo has stated: "I have elected to tell only the tale of the embassy's diplomacy." (p. 23; see also pp. 39–40)

22. For a detailed discussion, see Brown, "Kido Takayoshi," Chap. 7. See also Inada Masatsugu, *Meiji kempō*, I, 194–204; Suzuki, *Meiji ishin*, pp. 429–433; Osatake, *Ishin zengo*, Appendix 4, pp. 74–89; Beckmann, *Making of the Meiji Constitution*, pp. 28–33. Tsumaki Chūta, editor and compiler of Kido's diaries and papers and author of several biographies on Kido, dates the submission of Kido's petition in July 1873. This date has been accepted by most historians. See Tsumaki's annotation of Kido's petition in his *Kido Takayoshi monjo* (The Kido Takayoshi papers; Tokyo, 1929–1931), VIII, 127. See also Suzuki Yasuzō, *Gendai Nihon bummei shi: Kempō no rekishiteki kenkyū* (History of modern Japanese civilization: Studies of constitutions from a historical perspective; Tokyo, 1940), p. 157; Sidney D. Brown, "Kido Takayoshi (1833–1877): Meiji Japan's Cautious Revolutionary," *Pacific Historical Review*, 25:157 (May 1956). However, Osatake cites two dates, October 1873 and July 1873. Osatake, *Nihon kensei shi taikō*, I, 297, 310. See also Suzuki, *Meiji ishin*, pp. 429, 432. Kido returned to Japan from Europe on July 23, 1873. There is no mention in his diaries of any proposal or petition from the day of his return to the end of July. However, on September 15 he wrote that he had submitted "my proposal" to Sanjō Sanetomi, Itō, Ōkuma, and a ranking foreign affairs official named Ueno. Tsumaki, *Kido nikki*, V, 406, 425. In September 1873 Kido, after a brief exposition on "constitutionalism" and "gradualism," wrote, "This is what I earnestly desire. Hence, I submitted this memorandum to various officials in the government, and stressed the urgency of enacting a 'constitution.' Although it has not been accepted, I firmly believe in the ideas, and I have repeatedly drawn attention to them." Tsumaki's comment on this is that Kido was undaunted by the rejection of his petition submitted earlier in July and was diligently working on the officials to have his ideas accepted. Tsumaki, *Kido monjo*, VIII, 127–129.

23. Osatake, *Nihon kensei shi taikō*, I, 346; Sakata Yoshio, "Meiji zen hanki ni okeru seifu no kokkashugi" (The development of nationalism during the first half of the Meiji era), in Sakata Yoshio, comp., *Meiji zen hanki no nationalism* (Nationalism during the first half of the Meiji era; Tokyo, 1958), p. 20; Inada Masatsugu, *Meiji kempō*, I, 210–212. Ōkubo evinced an early interest in this subject and seemed rather sympathetic toward Miyajima's efforts. Miyajima, p. 346.

24. Suzuki and Osatake both feel that this final petition was the result of the Sa-in's reaction to the memorial submitted by Itagaki Taisuke and seven others on January 17, 1874. Suzuki, *Meiji ishin*, pp. 430–431; Osatake, *Nihon kensei shi taikō*, I, 294–295. See also Inada Masatsugu, *Meiji kempō*, I, 148–151.

25. Nagata Shinnojō, *Ono Azusa* (Tokyo, 1897), pp. 45–61.

26. Ōkuma Shigenobu, "Nihon no seitō" (Japan's political parties), in Takano Iwazaburō, comp., *Meiji kensei keizaishi ron* (Discourses on Meiji political and economic history; Tokyo, 1919), pp. 36–37. Kaneko Kentarō recalled that most of the members were bureaucrats and that "constitutionalism" was frequently the topic of study and discussion. Kaneko, "Teikoku kempō seitei no yurai" (Origins of our imperial constitution), *ibid.*, p. 10. Another association was the Ōmeisha (Society of Like Spirits), led by Numa Morikazu (Moriichi). Numa was at this time a senior secretary in the prime minister's office. Prince Arisugawa Taruhito was on hand frequently at the meetings of this group, and Kōno Togama, who later held posts on the ministerial level, was also a leading light. Hayashida Kametarō, *Nihon seitō shi* (A history of Japanese political parties; Tokyo, 1927), I, 169–170; Sasuhara Yasuzō, *Meiji seishi* (Political history of the Meiji; Tokyo, 1928–1929), I, 414. The translation for Ōmeisha was suggested by George M. Wilson, "Politics and the People: Liang Ch'i-ch'ao's View of Constitutional Developments in Meiji Japan before 1890," *Papers on Japan* (Harvard University East Asian Research Center) 1:223 (1961).

27. Of the ten, only Fukuzawa was not a bureaucrat after the Restoration, though he saw service under the Tokugawa bakufu.

28. For discussions of the Meirokusha, see Roger F. Hackett, "Nishi Amane: A Tokugawa-Meiji Bureaucrat," *Journal of Asian Studies*, 18:218–219 (Feb. 1959); Tōyama Shigeki, "Nihon no shisō zasshi: Meiroku zasshi" (Japan's ideological periodicals: The Meiji Six Association periodical), *Shisō*, No. 447:117–128 (1961); Kōsaka Masaaki, ed., *Japanese Thought in the Meiji Era*, tr. and adapted by David Abosch (Tokyo, 1958), pp. 61–133, 136; Hane, pp. 38–54.

29. Matsueda Yasuji, *Ōkuma kō sekijitsu dan* (Marquis Ōkuma reminisces about the past; Tokyo, 1943), Pt. 2, p. 17.

30. Osatake Takeki, *Meiji Taishō seiji shi kōwa* (Lectures on Meiji and Taishō political history; Tokyo, 1943), pp. 156–157; and Osatake, *Nihon kensei shi no kenkyū* (Studies in Japanese constitutional history; Tokyo, 1943), pp. 10–11.

31. *Taruhito shinnō nikki* (Diaries of Prince [Arisugawa] Taruhito; Tokyo, 1935–1936), II, 380; Osatake, *Nihon kensei shi taikō*, II, 460. A rather surprising phenomenon is the inexactness of certain prominent dates in reference works, as well as in standard secondary sources. This imperial order, for example, represents an important development in Meiji constitutional history. However, the *Meiji shiyō* (Meiji annals), comp. Tokyo teikoku daigaku bungakubu shiryō hensanjo (Institute for the Compilation of Historical Material, Faculty of Letters, Tokyo Imperial University; Tokyo, 1933), I, 454; *Sakuin seiji keizai dai nempyō: Nempyō hen* (A comprehensive chronological reference of politics and economics: Chronological table volume; Tokyo, 1943), p. 182; Sasuhara, I, 293–294, among others, give the date as September 6, 1876. In support of the September 7 date there is, besides the entry in Arisugawa's diaries, a letter written by Ōkubo to Iwakura on September 6. (See n. 34, this chapter.) See also Inada Masatsugu, *Meiji kempō*, I, 283–286.

32. Kaneko, "Teikoku kempō seitei," p. 5. See also Osatake, *Nihon kensei shi taikō*, II, 460.

33. Osatake, *Nihon kensei shi taikō*, II, 460–461; Itakura Takuzō, "Seiji shisō shi jō kempō happu zen" (A history of political thought before the promulgation of the constitution), *Hōgaku kenkyū* (Journal of law, politics, and sociology), 3:21 (July 1924); Asai Kiyoshi, *Meiji rikken shisō ni okeru Eikoku gikai seido no eikyō* (The influence of the English parliamentary system on Meiji constitutional thought; Tokyo, 1935), p. 285. Volume I of Todd's work was considered by the *Edinburgh Review* "one of the most useful and complete books which has ever appeared on the practical operation of the British constitution" *Edinburgh Review*, 125:578 (Apr. 1867). There is good reason for the interest of the oligarchs in this work because Todd in his Preface states: "the great and increasing defect in all parliamentary governments, whether provincial or imperial, is the weakness of executive authority." Quoted in *ibid.*, p. 579.

34. Ōkubo Toshikazu, *Ōkubo Toshimichi monjo* (The Ōkubo Toshimichi papers; Tokyo, 1927–1931), VII, 232÷233.

35. Osatake, *Nihon kensei shi taikō*, II, 461–464. Another source says that the first draft had made its appearance by October 14 of the same year. Watanabe Ikujirō, *Meiji tennō to rikken seiji* (The Meiji emperor and constitutional Government; Tokyo, 1937), p. 85. See also Inada Masatsugu, *Meiji kempō*, I, 292, 301–302.

36. Osatake, *Nihon kensei shi taikō*, II, 464–468. Cf. Inada Masatsugu, *Meiji kempō*, I, 304–305, 318–319.

37. Osatake, *Nihon kensei shi taikō*, II, 477. Cf. Inada, *Meiji kempō*, I, 319. When Prince Arisugawa first received the imperial commands, he wrote to Iwakura informing him that he would be shown the draft before it was presented to the throne. Letter dated September, 1876, quoted in *Iwakura jikki*, III, 327.

38. Quoted in *Iwakura jikki*, III, 652. See also Inada Masatsugu, *Meiji kempō*, I, 320. Some seem to feel that the drafters in this were following the emperor's desires as revealed by the sending of Todd's work to serve as a reference. See Itakura, p. 21; and Ike, *Political Democracy*, p. 93. Actually, the drafters consulted the constitutions of some fifteen nations and relied most heavily on the Belgian and Prussian constitutions as models. Miyazawa Toshiyoshi, "Genrō-in no kempō sōan ni tsuite" (On the Genrō-in draft constitution), *KGZ*, 55.4:32–33 (1941); Inada Masatsugu, *Meiji kempō*, I, 331–332; Itō Hirobumi, "Hompō kempō seitei," p. 535.

39. Letter from Itō to Iwakura, December 21, 1879, quoted in Kaneko Kentarō, *Itō Hirobumi den* (Biography of Itō Hirobumi; Tokyo, 1943), II, 188–189. Inada feels that this letter should be dated a year later, just prior to the final presentation of the draft to the emperor. Inada Masatsugu, *Meiji kempō*, I, 336–337. This is possible, as the letters under study, written during the Meiji, in many instances do not indicate the year, which must be ascertained by the contents. Osatake favors the 1879 date. Osatake, *Nihon kensei shi taikō*, II, 481.

40. Fujii Shin'ichi, *Teikoku kempō to Kaneko haku* (The imperial constitution and Count Kaneko; Tokyo, 1942), pp. 221–222. See also Osatake, *Nihon kensei shi taikō*, II, 468–477. Fujii points out that since this draft was the end product of consultations with many scholars, "it was a creditable job for that time." Fujii Shin'ichi, p. 221. Osatake describes it as being substantially similar to the Meiji constitution Itō himself drafted, except for such matters as the stipulations concerning the legislative power. Osatake, *Nihon kensei shi taikō*, II, 481.

41. *Ibid.*, II, 478–479; Asai, pp. 293–306.

42. Osatake, *Nihon kensei shi taikō*, II, 478–482; Inada Masatsugu, *Meiji kempō*, I, 320; Miyazawa, pp. 1–2. For a discussion of the Genrō-in attempt, including a comparison of the Genrō-in drafts and the Meiji constitution, see Barbara J. Teters, "The Conservative Opposition in Japanese Politics, 1877–1894," Ph.D. thesis (University of Washington,

1955), pp. 70–78; and her "The Genrō-in and the National Essence Movement," *Pacific Historical Review*, 31:359–366 (Nov. 1962).

43. Beckmann, *Making of the Meiji Constitution*, p. 111; Iwata, pp. 347–352. See also Inoue Kaoru's views, cited in Inada Masatsugu, *Meiji kempō*, I, 231; Maruyama Masao, "Meiji kokka no shisō" (The ideology of the Meiji state), in *Nihon shakai no shiteki kyūmei* (Historical studies of Japanese society), comp. Rekishigakukenkyūkai (Tokyo, 1949), p. 200.

44. McLaren, "Documents," pp. 568–569.

45. Brown, "Kido Takayoshi," p. 313; McLaren, "Documents," p. 570. Obviously, the sentiments expressed by the oligarchs were shared by other Japanese. Writing in 1891, a professor of political science at the Tokyo semmon gakkō (later known as Waseda) stated: "Experience has shown that representative government is the most efficient in securing the corporate action of the various members of the body politic against foreign enemies. When a country is threatened with foreign invasion, when the corporate action of its citizens against their enemy is needed, it becomes an imperative necessity to consult public opinion. In such a time centralization is needed. Hence the first move of Japan after the advent of foreigners was to bring the scattered parts of the country together and unite them under one head." Iyenaga Toyokichi, "The Constitutional Development of Japan, 1853–1881," *Johns Hopkins University Studies in Historical and Political Science*, 9:19 (Baltimore, 1891).

46. Beckmann, *Making of the Meiji Constitution*, p. 113.

47. McLaren, "Documents," p. 570.

48. Quoted in Kaneko, *Itō den*, II, 615.

49. Quoted in Osatake, *Nihon kensei shi no kenkyū*, p. 330. Ōkuma agrees. He says, "The impetus for the idea that some day Japan must have a constitutional government can be ultimately traced to foreign policy." Ōkuma, "Seikai no hen'ei" (On the political world), *Taiyō*, 13.3:161 (1907). The conservatives described by Teters also subscribed to this point of view. To them constitutionalism was not the end of national policy. Their ultimate goal was the unification and independence of Japan, and constitutionalism was to help achieve this end. These conservatives, however, were strong believers in a constitutional form of government based on a division of power equally among the executive, legislative, and judicial branches, and with the emperor serving as the ultimate authority. Teters, "Conservative Opposition," pp. 50, 11–12.

50. Speech quoted in *KGZ*, 13.154:6 (1899). See also *Japan Weekly Mail* (Dec. 29, 1900), p. 674.

51. Kaneko Kentarō, "Itō kō to kempō seitei jigyō" (Prince Itō and the writing of the constitution), *KGZ*, 24:999 (July 1910). Kaneko describes the views of the Westerners in full in his *Kempō seitei to Ōbeijin no hyōron* (The enactment of the constitution and the opinions of Europeans and Americans; Tokyo, 1938), pp. 177–351.

52. Letter to Matsukata Masayoshi, dated January 8, 1883, quoted in Kaneko, *Itō den*, II, 335–338.

53. It may also be argued that the Meiji leaders were fully aware of the problem of power-sharing from the beginning, and the low priority given to the introduction of constitutional government was in part a reflection of this awareness. In any case, Itagaki's petition and subsequent activities must have highlighted the problem for those in the Meiji administration.

54. It was a little after this time that Itō first made use of Inoue Kowashi. Itō recalled that he asked Inoue to draft the Imperial Rescript of April 1875, and that this was the first time he made such a request of Inoue. Osatake, *Meiji Taishō seiji shi*, pp. 156–157.

CHAPTER II. ITAGAKI AND THE MOVEMENT
FOR PARLIAMENTARY GOVERNMENT

1. The term has been translated as "democratic movement" (Ike, Beckmann); "popular rights movement" (Scalapino); "The Movement for People's Rights" (Norman, Jansen, Sansom); "The Free People's Rights Movement" (Craig); "Jiyū minken movement" *(Rekishigakukenkyū)*. "Movement for parliamentary government" is felt to be most descriptive of the activities of Itagaki and his supporters on the basis of the approach taken to the problem in this and the next chapter.

2. For an introduction to the ideas and works of this school, see Horie Eichi, "Jiyū minken undō no tembō" (A survey of the Jiyū Minken movement), *Rekishi to minshū: 1955 Nendo Rekishigakukenkyūkai taikai hōkoku* (History and the people: Reports of the 1955 conference of the Historical Studies Society; Tokyo, 1955), pp. 253–254; Ōe Shinobu, "Gōnō minken no seiritsu" (The formation of the Gōnō Minken), *ibid.*, pp. 255–256; Ōishi Kiichirō, "Fukushima jiken" (The Fukushima incident), *ibid.*, pp. 256–258; Gotō Yasushi, "Nōmin minken no tenkai" (The development of the Nōmin Minken), *ibid.*, pp. 258–260. Except in Horie's case, these are the resumés of the reports of the authors found in *ibid.*, pp. 83–106. The reports, in turn, are discussed in *ibid.*, pp. 107–131. See also Shimoyama Saburō, "Meiji jūnen dai no tochi shoyū kankei wo megutte" (On land ownership relations in the Meiji tens), *RK* No. 176:1–15 (Oct. 1954); Ōe Shinobu, "Gōnō minken undō no genryū" (The wellsprings of the Gōnō Minken movement), *RK*, No. 179:22–32 (Jan. 1955); Shimoyama Saburō, "Fukushima Jiken shoron" (A discussion of the Fukushima incident), Pt. 1, *RK*, No. 186:1–13 (Aug. 1955), Pt. 2, *RK*, No. 187:13–28 (Sept. 1955); Ōe Shinobu, "Minken undō seiritsu no gōnō to nōmin" (The peasant and the well-to-do farmer at the beginning of the Minken Undō), Pt. 1, *RK*, No. 186:14–23 (Aug. 1955), Pt. 2, *RK*, No. 189:23–34 (Nov. 1955). Even within this "school" there are, of course, differences in interpretation. See, for example, *Meiji shi kenkyū sōsho: Jiyū minken undō* (Studies in Meiji history series: Jiyū Minken movement; Tokyo, 1956), esp. "Commentary" by Tōyama Shigeki, pp. 11–26. Craig analyzes the views of the Bakumatsu period by scholars of similar persuasion in his *Chōshū in the Meiji Restoration* (Cambridge, Mass., 1961), pp. 269–270, 357.

3. Inoue Kiyoshi, who is no less leftist in inclination than the postwar theorists on the Jiyū Minken movement, has taken a different slant in his interpretation of the movement. He believes that the incidents that occurred during the movement led by the peasantry are insignificant, and that the postwar interpreters, by regarding only these incidents as revolutionary and historically meaningful, are guilty of misplaced and exaggerated emphasis. He asserts that the truly revolutionary aspect of the movement was the pronouncements and activities of Itagaki and his followers. Their assertions that people not only are to be ruled, but also have basic rights, that the people are sovereign, that government exists for the people, and finally their formation of a party on a national scale—these are historically more meaningful and important, Inoue says. Inoue insists that his birth in Tosa and the fact that he was raised with Itagaki's "greatness" dinned into his ears have nothing to do with his convictions. His long article, which traces the changes in the interpretations of the movement, starting with Yoshino Sakuzō and Osatake, presents his ideas regarding the movement and includes rebuttals of specific conclusions by the postwar school. See his "Jiyū minken undō wo meguru rekishiteki hyōka ni tsuite" (On the historical interpretations of the Movement for Parliamentary Government), *Shisō*, No. 379:47–63 (Jan. 1956).

4. For standard interpretations of this movement in English, see Ike, *Political Democracy*, Chaps. 5–14, 16, and Beckmann, *Making of the Meiji Constitution*. As Ike has stated, "The story of its formation in 1874, the spread of its influence all over the nation, and its eventual decline is the subject of the present study." Ike, *Political Democracy*, p. 55.

5. See, for example, Horie, p. 254.

6. For details of this split, see Ike, *Political Democracy*, Chap. 5, as well as his "Triumph

of the Peace Party in Japan in 1873," *Far Eastern Quarterly*, 2:286–295 (May 1943). The biographies of prominent political personalities usually contain helpful narratives of major occurrences such as this split. A long and documented account of the Korean question of 1873, for example, is found in Kaneko, *Itō den*, I, 729–770. Cody's account on the subject is also one of the most interesting. Cecil E. Cody, "A Study of the Career of Itagaki Taisuke (1837–1919), A Leader of the Democratic Movement in Meiji Japan," Ph.D. thesis (University of Washington, 1955), pp. 51–61.

7. Other important figures who resigned were Etō Shimpei and Soejima Taneomi, both of Saga.

8. For the views of the strong man of the peace faction, see Sidney D. Brown, "Ōkubo Toshimichi: His Political and Economic Policies in Early Meiji Japan," *Journal of Asian Studies*, 21:193 (Feb. 1962).

9. McLaren, "Documents," pp. 432–433; Ike, *Political Democracy*, pp. 56–59; *Jiyūtō shi* (History of the Liberal party), by Uda Tomoi and Wada Saburō, ed. Itagaki Taisuke (Tokyo, 1910), I, 85–92; Cody, pp. 64–68. For a translation of the petition, see McLaren, "Documents," pp. 426–433.

Ōmori Kingorō and Takahashi Shōzō, *Saishin Nihon rekishi nempyō* (A chronological table of modern Japanese history; Tokyo, 1942), p. 375; and Ōtsu Jun'ichirō, *Dai Nihon kensei shi* (A comprehensive constitutional history of Japan; Tokyo, 1927–1928), I, 786; and Itō, "Hompō kempō seitei," p. 532, give January 18 as the date of the presentation of the memorial. But Itagaki places the date as the seventeenth, and the petition, dated January 17, is quoted in full in Nakayama Yasumasa, ed. *Shimbun shūsei Meiji hen-nen shi* (A Meiji chronological history compiled from newspapers; Tokyo, 1934–1936), II, 117–118. See Itagaki Taisuke, "Waga kuni kensei no yurai" (Beginnings of Japan's constitutional system), *Meiji kensei keizaishi ron*, p. 188; Kaneko, *Itō den*, II, 823; Tsumaki, *Kido nikki*, II, 480–481.

10. Suzuki, *Jiyū minken*, p. 16. A view supported in part by Itō Hirobumi, who recalled that the memorial caused some excitement among "the people." Itō, "Hompō kempō seitei," p. 532. Of the signatories, Itagaki, Gotō, Etō, and Soejima were all former councilors; Yuri Kimimasa was a former governor of Tokyo-fu; Okamoto Kenzaburō was a high official in the Finance Ministry. Komuro Nobuo and Furuzawa Shigeru (the drafter), were recent returnees from England. Osatake, *Nihon kensei shi taikō*, II, 374.

11. Letter from Ōkubo to Zeisho Atsushi and Godai Tomoatsu, dated January 25, 1875, quoted in Suzuki, *Meiji ishin*, p. 444.

12. The eight signers first formed the Kōfuku anzen sha (Welfare and Security Society). After inviting others to join their group, it adopted the name Aikokukōtō. These activities seem to have taken place in January 1874, with the Aikokukōtō being formally organized on January 12. Itagaki, p. 186; *Jiyūtō shi*, I, 83. Cf. Robert A. Scalapino, *Democracy and the Party Movement in Prewar Japan: The Failure of the First Attempt* (Berkeley and Los Angeles, 1953), p. 45.

13. Itagaki, p. 189; Osatake, *Nihon kensei shi taikō*, II, 449; Sasuhara, I, 237.

14. *Jiyūtō shi*, I, 96–97, states that the attempt against Iwakura's life and the outbreak of the Saga Rebellion were the reasons for the government's refusal to act on the January 17 memorial. Actually, Kido in effect cleared Itagaki of any complicity in the Iwakura incident in a letter to Itō on January 18. While saying that Itagaki had expressed discontent in the talk they held the day before, Kido expressed doubt that Itagaki had anything to do with the attack. Tsumaki, *Kido nikki*, III, 184; Kaneko, *Itō den*, I, 824–825. Moreover, Kido met with Itagaki several times during January, February, and March to discuss assemblies and related subjects. Tsumaki, *Kido nikki*, II, 480–482, 485, 494, and III, 5. In view of the many discussions held between Kido and Itagaki, *Jiyūtō shi* (I, 94) wrongly concludes that Kido looked upon Itagaki with suspicion after the Iwakura attack and that this contributed to their estrangement.

15. Osatake, *Nihon kensei shi taikō*, II, 449; Osatake, *Nihon kensei shi no kenkyū*, p. 90.

16. "Risshisha" has been variously translated as "The Society to Establish One's Ambitions" (Scalapino, Cody); "Society of Free Thinkers" (Norman); "Society for Fixing One's Aim in Life" (Ike); "Achieving One's Aims Society" (Jansen).

17. See prospectus of the Risshisha, in *Jiyūtō shi*, I, 152–156; see also Cody, pp. 74–76; and Jansen, *Sakamoto Ryōma*, p. 373.

18. Suzuki, *Jiyū minken*, pp. 26–31. Suzuki (*ibid.*, p. 28) suggests that *Jiyūtō shi* overstresses the political aspects of the Risshisha. Cf. Norman, *Japan's Emergence*, p. 175.

19. Suzuki Yasuzō, "Rikken seiji e no kato" (Evolution toward constitutional government), *CK*, 56:306 (May, 1941). See also Jansen, *Sakamoto Ryōma*, pp. 372–374. The government's program for economic rehabilitation of the declassed samurai is discussed in Harry D. Harootunian, "The Economic Rehabilitation of the Samurai in the Early Meiji Period," *Journal of Asian Studies*, 19:433–444 (Aug. 1960).

20. Suzuki, *Jiyū minken*, p. 132; Rōyama Masamichi, *Gendai Nihon bummei shi: Seiji shi* (History of modern Japanese civilization: Political history; Tokyo, 1940), p. 132. Other ex-samurai organizations in Morioka, Yamagata, Kanazawa, Tottori, Takasaki, Mikawa, and Kagoshima also failed in their efforts to make good in the economic sphere. This failure caused them to shift their attention to political activities. Masumi Junnosuke, "Nihon seitō shi ni okeru chihō seiji no shomondai, II: Chihō minken kessha to sono shidōsha," (Problems in provincial politics in the history of Japanese political parties: Provincial political organizations and their leaders), *KGZ*, 73.5:2–3 (1959).

21. Rōyama, p. 132; Osatake, *Nihon kensei shi taikō*, II, 456; Ike, *Political Democracy*, p. 65.

22. The dearth of funds continually plagued the movement, even after the Jiyūtō was first organized in the early 1880's. Cody, pp. 110, 186–187.

23. Suzuki, *Jiyū minken*, p. 34; Itagaki, p. 190; Ike, *Political Democracy*, p. 65; Kawahara Jikichirō, "Nihon no seitō" (Political parties in Japan), in Rōyama Masamichi, ed., *Seitō* (Political parties; Tokyo, 1954), p. 115; Suzuki, "Rikken seiji e no kato," p. 307.

24. Sasuhara, I, 254; Osatake, *Nihon kensei shi taikō*, II, 458. Suzuki says that the Risshisha to the end was "essentially a *shizoku* political organization." Suzuki, *Jiyū minken*, p. 22.

25. Itagaki, p. 190.

26. See regulations of the Risshisha, Art. V, and Art. VII, clause 4; *Jiyūtō shi*, I, 157–158; Suzuki, "Rikken seiji e no kato," p. 307; Kawahara, pp. 115–116; Sasuhara, I, 254.

27. The following areas were represented in the Aikokusha. For our present purposes, no attempt is made to equate them exactly with present administrative boundaries. Kaga (Ishikawa), Chikuzen (Fukuoka), Buzen (Ōita), Satsuma (Kagoshima), Higo (Kumamoto), Inaba (Tottori), Aki (Hiroshima), Tosa (Kōchi), Iyo (Ehime), Sanuki (Kagawa), Awa (Tokushima). *Jiyūtō shi*, I, 178–179. It should be stressed again that all these areas, except Kaga, were west of Osaka. Cf. Scalapino, *Democracy*, pp. 58–59.

28. Quoted in Suzuki Yasuzō, "Risshisha no 'Nihon kempō no mikomi an'" (The Risshisha's draft constitution for Japan), *KGZ*, 53:77 (Nov. 1939). See also, Itō Hirobumi, "Hompō kempō seitei," pp. 532–533. There is no evidence, according to Cody, that before 1874 Itagaki himself had "developed his understanding of *jiyū-minken* ideas." Cody, pp. 106–107.

29. Ōkubo Kishichi, quoted in *Itō Hirobumi hiroku* (Private papers of Itō Hirobumi), ed. Hiratsuka Atsushi (Tokyo, 1929), p. 20. This work, together with a companion volume entitled *Zoku Itō Hirobumi hiroku* (Private papers of Itō Hirobumi, Second volume; Tokyo, 1930), are collections of Itō papers with comments by Itō's contemporaries on the subject touched upon in each document. Although at times the commentaries range far afield, they provide rich historical material. However, care must be used, for these reminiscences often contain errors of fact. Annotations by Hiratsuka are also not free from mistakes.

30. Osatake, *Nihon kensei shi taikō*, II, 458.

31. Tsumaki, *Kido nikki*, III, 139, 144, 151, 152.

32. Itagaki's tenure as councilor was short. On October 27, 1875, his resignation was accepted, after which he left for Tosa. For a chronicle of the running battle conducted by Itagaki against Kido and Itō over the interpretation of the Osaka agreements, see Kaneko, *Itō den*, I, 921–971. See also Inada Masatsugu, *Meiji kempō*, I, 239–276; Scalapino, *Democracy*, pp. 60–61.

33. In early February 1874 Etō Shimpei rose up in Saga at the head of some 2,500 men. He believed that Saigō in Satsuma and Itagaki in Tosa would also rise and that, in the general revolt that would follow, the government would be overthrown. His expectations were unfulfilled and the revolt was crushed within a month. He then went to Kagoshima to seek Saigō's protection, but was turned over to imperial authorities. Etō managed to escape to Tosa, where he sought Itagaki's help, but he was captured by government forces. He was convicted on April 13 and was executed on the same day in Saga Castle. Yanaga Chitoshi, *Japan since Perry* (New York, 1949), p. 63; Kaneko, *Itō den*, I, 832–845; Konishi Shirō, *Nihon zenshi: Kindai I* (A general history of Japan: The modern period, I; Tokyo, 1962), VIII, 344–346. For a detailed description of the revolt, see James H. Buck, "The Satsuma Rebellion of 1877: An Inquiry into Some of Its Military and Political Aspects," Ph.D. thesis (American University, 1959), pp. 82–91. See also Iwata, pp. 356–361.

34. Kaneko, *Itō den*, II, 51; Sasuhara, I, 294; Yanaga, *Japan since Perry*, pp. 63–65. In a coup planned closer to the seat of government, the samurai of the former Aizu han in northeastern Japan were to rise in Chiba on October 29, according to plans previously made with Maebara. However, the leaders were apprehended before the plot materialized. Kaneko, *Itō den*, II, 53.

35. Osatake, *Nihon kensei shi taikō*, II, 488–489; Kaneko, *Itō den*, II, 48–60. On the Shimpūren, Akizuki, and Hagi revolts, see also Buck, pp. 106–111.

36. Kaneko, *Itō den*, II, 61–91; Sasuhara, I, 296–298; Yanaga, *Japan since Perry*, pp. 66–67; Iwata, pp. 482–495; Buck, pp. 111–235. Buck's description is especially noteworthy for its knowledgeable attention to the military aspects of the rebellion.

37. Fujii Jintarō and Moriya Hidesuke, *Sōgō Nihon shi taikei: Meiji jidai shi* (Series on general Japanese history: History of the Meiji period), 2nd ed. rev. (Tokyo, 1940), XXV, 573; Tōyama Shigeki, "Kindai hen" (The modern period), in Tōyama Shigeki *et al.*, *Nihon rekishi gaisetsu* (An outline history of Japan; Tokyo, 1954), II, 76; Matsueda, pp. 41–42.

38. *Seitō shi* (History of political parties), Vol. 3 of *Meiji shi* (History of the Meiji era; Taiyō, Feb. 1907), pp. 21–22; Yanaga, *Japan since Perry*, p. 63. Itagaki had opposed the return of Etō and Soejima to their native Saga after the split over the Korean question in 1873, on the ground that such a move would provide the spark for an uprising. *Jiyūtō shi*, I, 95.

39. Fujii and Moriya, XXV, 569–571; Rōyama, p. 126; Ōtsu, II, 87–128; Osatake, *Nihon kensei shi taikō*, II, 497–502; Jansen, *Sakamoto Ryōma*, pp. 374–375. The differences of opinion among the advocates of parliamentarism over direct action or nonviolent political activities antedated this plot, and Hayashi was careful not to discuss the plans with Itagaki. *Jiyūtō shi*, I, 196, 255. See also Cody, pp. 71–72, 87–94. Cf. Saiga Hakuai, *Ōe Ten'ya denki* (Biography of Ōe Ten'ya; Tokyo, 1926), pp. 401–487.

40. On the pivotal issue of whether in 1877 Tosa should cast its lot with Satsuma or not, Cody admits the possibility that Itagaki may have secretly sided with the violence-inclined Tosa conspirators even while avowing peaceful intentions. However, Cody also reveals several reasons for Itagaki's reluctance to follow Saigō's path. Itagaki, according to Cody, believed that his principles for the establishment of a representative form of government through the force of public opinion were sound; that Saigō, who was not a skilled strategist, would make a costly and fruitless attempt to take the Kumamoto Castle which

would cause his ultimate failure; and that "it was not clever to fight against a government which was so strong." Cody, pp. 89–91.

41. *Seitō shi*, pp. 18, 21; Osatake, *Nihon kensei shi no kenkyū*, p. 91.

42. Suzuki, *Meiji ishin*, p. 438; Watanabe Ikujirō, "Kempō seitei zengo" (Before and after the enactment of the constitution), *Rekishi kyōiku* (Historical studies), 11:138 (Nov. 1936). Cf. Robert A. Scalapino, "Japan: Between Traditionalism and Democracy," in Sigmund Neumann, ed., *Modern Political Parties: Approaches to Comparative Politics* (Chicago, 1956), p. 310.

43. Sasuhara, I, 305; Hayashida, *Seitō shi*, I, 94–95. Sugita Teiichi, a wealthy landlord, attended. *Jiyūtō shi*, I, 297.

44. To the March 1879 meeting came some 80 delegates representing 21 local societies in 18 prefectures. However, the Kantō and Ōhoku (north-central Japan) areas were still virtually unrepresented. Almost the same group attended the November meeting. Itagaki, pp. 194–195; *Jiyūtō shi*, I, 321–325.

45. *Jiyūtō shi*, I, 331–332; Sasuhara, I, 336–337. Cf. account in Ike, *Political Democracy*, p. 88. The backgrounds of the participants became an issue between the government and *Chōya shimbun* at this time. The government chose to belittle the movement by saying that it was merely made up of disgruntled ex-samurai. *Chōya* on July 9, 1880, in a heated rebuttal, flatly stated that the *shizoku* were no longer leaders of the movement. It is true that more and more those calling themselves commoners were found on the rolls of the organizations participating in the movement. In the March 1880 petition of the Kokkai kisei dōmei kai, 28 of the 95 signatories designated themselves as commoners *(heimin)*. (There were actually 97 signatures, but two signed twice. Four called themselves neither commoners nor *shizoku*. One said that he was a farmer.) In fact, this trend was a continuous one. From October 1881 to November 1882, 80 per cent of those who joined the Jiyūtō were commoners. Satō Seirō, "Meiji 17 nen 5 gatsu no Jiyūtōin meibo ni tsuite" (On the May 1884 party list of Jiyūtō members), *RK*, No. 178: 31–38 (1954). See also Osatake, *Meiji Taishō seiji shi*, pp. 155–156. However, before generalizing about the participants, a more precise definition of the term commoner must be made. For example, even a tentative check of those who signed the March 1880 petition as commoners shows that at least two were *shi* (samurai) and another a *gōshi* (country samurai). See *Shinsen daijimmei jiten* (The new biographical dictionary; Tokyo, 1937–1941), I, 318; II, 553; V, 24–25; and Ōtsu, I, 5. It appears, then, that some of the signers at least were not thinking of themselves as commoners in the sense of the administrative category created by the Meiji government and the han. The point is that a careful study of the so-called commoners would probably show that, *Chōya*'s statement notwithstanding, the *shizoku* were still the moving force in the movement at this time. It is not implausible that those who would participate in movements such as this one would deliberately reject symbols of their special status for designations connoting a greater measure of egalitarianism. A case in point is Ono Azusa, who, though not a member of the movement, in November 1869 "on his own accord left the ranks of the samurai and became a commoner." Nagata, pp. 3, 24–25.

46. *Jiyūtō shi*, I, 332. It is clear that the participants still came predominantly from western Japan. Of the 87,000 members of the societies said to be represented in the petition of March/April 1880, Kōchi accounted for 48,431 and Hiroshima for 20,252. *Jiyūtō shi*, I, 356–357. If the above figure for Kōchi is correct, that area can boast of being one of the most politically conscious in Japan, then and now. The male population of all ages (assuming that few, if any, females participated) of Tosa in 1880 was 287,604. *Dai ikkai teikoku tōkei kan* (Imperial Japan statistical tables, No. 1; Tokyo, 1882), p. 60. There are indications that Tosa was vibrantly alive politically. See Osatake, *Nihon kensei shi taikō*, II, 504. See also, Ariiso Itsurō, "Meiji ankoku shi: Jiyū minken ron no bokkō" (A behind-the-scenes history of the Meiji: The spread of the movement for parliamentary government), *CK*, 20.8:35–36 (1905).

47. *Jiyūtō shi*, I, 345, 377.

48. Osatake, *Nihon kensei shi taikō*, II, 527–531.

49. *Jiyūtō shi*, I, 437–438, 455–458; Ike, *Political Democracy*, p. 101.

50. *Ibid.*, p. 90; Scalapino, *Democracy*, pp. 59, 64, 88; Norman, pp. 177–179; Walter W. McLaren, *A Political History of Japan during the Meiji Era, 1867–1912* (London, 1916), p. 131; Beckmann, *Making of the Meiji Constitution*, pp. 39–46, 53, 60; Bernard L. Silberman, "The Political Theory and Program of Yoshino Sakuzō," *Journal of Modern History*, 31:311 (Dec. 1959); *ibid.*, p. 312; Emori Yasukichi, *Ōkuma haku hyaku wa* (Count Okuma speaks on a hundred topics; Tokyo, 1909), p. 418. Liang Ch'i-ch'ao also believed that "popular agitation" caused the government to make concessions at the Osaka kaigi and finally to establish a constitutional system. George Wilson, pp. 198–201, 216.

51. For a detailed account of the conference, see Kaneko, *Itō den*, I, 887–920. See also Brown, "Kido Takayoshi," Chap. 5; Cody, pp. 78–83; Iwata, pp. 443–452; Ōtsu, I, 848–858; Sakatani Yoshirō, *Segai Inoue kō den* (Biography of Inoue Segai [Kaoru]; Tokyo, 1933–1934), II, 612–627; Inada Masatsugu, *Meiji kempō*, I, 229–239.

52. Iwata delineates the Formosan Expedition and the diplomatic problems involved in interesting detail. Iwata, pp. 366–443. See also Buck, pp. 91–100.

53. Actually, Itō had been to Shimonoseki early in November to urge Kido to return to Tokyo. Kido refused, even after an imperial order had been given. Inada Masatsugu, *Meiji kempō*, I, 229.

54. Quoted in *Itō Hirobumi hiroku*, p. 23.

55. Quoted in Ōkubo, *Okubo monjo*, VI, 255–256. It is possible that Ōkubo is referring to the activities preceding the formation of the Aikokusha.

56. Kaneko, *Itō den*, I, 907–909. Kido consented to return to Tokyo on January 27. *Ibid.*, I, 908. See also Itō's recollections, in *Itō Hirobumi kō* (Prince Itō Hirobumi), special issue of *Taiyō* (Nov. 1909), 15:44. Inada Masatsugu, *Meiji kempō*, I, 233–235. In a similar vein, Ōkubo wrote on February 4: "This morning, Itō called. He told me about his talk with Kido and Itagaki. I replied that I could find no objections." Ōkubo Toshikazu, *Ōkubo Toshimichi nikki* (Diaries of Ōkubo Toshimichi; Tokyo, 1927), II, 374.

57. Tsumaki, *Kido nikki*, III, 152; Ōkubo, *Ōkubo nikki*, II, 376; *Jiyūtō shi*, I, 184. Ōkubo and Kido met in Kobe on January 5, 1875. Kido did not meet Itagaki until January 22. Inada Masatsugu, *Meiji kempō*, I, 231–232.

58. Tsumaki, *Kido nikki*, III, 151. See entry for February 9 in Ōkubo, *Ōkubo nikki*, III, 375–376. See Itō's recollections in *Itō kō zenshū* (The collected works of Prince Itō), ed. Komatsu Midori (Tokyo, 1928), III, 19–22; also, Inada Masatsugu, *Meiji kempō*, I, 233–234, 236–238.

59. Maruyama p. 200. Fujii Jintarō, a pioneer in the study of Meiji constitutional history, very early reached the same conclusion. Fujii, *Nihon kempō*, p. 115. See also *Seitō shi*, p. 22; Inada Masatsugu, *Meiji kempō*, I, 238–239. Discussing the ins and the outs, William E. Griffis, a long-time resident of Japan, had also grasped this point. He wrote: "In reality, there are no conservatives; all are progressives and, in certain phases, radical." Griffis, "The Development of Political Parties in Japan," *North American Review*, 175:678 (1902), a position also maintained by Cody who states, "A study of Itagaki's career proves that both he and other top party men were far closer to the aims of the government leaders than is generally admitted." Cody, p. 4. It must be pointed out, however, that important members of the opposition held much more liberal views than did Itagaki and Gotō. Where Itagaki at this time did not support a free franchise, Ōi Kentarō advocated a free ballot. Marius B. Jansen, "Ōi Kentarō: Radicalism and Chauvinism," *Far Eastern Quarterly*, 11:308 (May 1952).

60. Osatake, *Nihon kensei shi taikō*, I, 256–257; Osatake, *Ishin zengo*, pp. 631–632. Etō also submitted his "Kokuhō kaigi no gian" (Proposal for a legislative assembly) in 1870.

One section is titled "Chihō giin no koto" (On local assemblies). Osatake, *Nihon kensei shi taikō*, I, 281–282.

61. Tsumaki, *Kido nikki*, II, 485; Inada Masatsugu, *Meiji kempō*, I, 207.

62. The date of passage was May 3. Ōkubo was assassinated on May 17. See Sasuhara, I, 306, 308; Kaneko, *Itō den*, II, 96; Osatake, *Nihon kensei shi taikō*, II, 511. At the time of the establishment of the assemblies, the motive given was that the existence of the assemblies would make it easier for the government to collect taxes. Moreover, the elections for the first assemblies were very calm, almost sleepy affairs, and there was difficulty finding candidates willing to serve. See Masumi Junnosuke, "Nihon seitō shi ni okeru chihō seiji no shomondai, I: 1880 nendai no fu-ken kai" (Problems in provincial politics in the history of Japanese political parties, Part 1: The prefectural assemblies in the 1880's), *KGZ*, 73.4:2, 4 (1959). This supports Thomas C. Smith's contention that the *gōnō* (wealthy peasants) who were "politically potent" did not support broadening the base of government, since this development would threaten their control. Smith, "Landlords and Rural Capitalists in the Modernization of Japan," *Journal of Economic History*, 16:181 (June 1956). Cf. account in Scalapino, *Democracy*, p. 64. Ōkubo's assassins also charged that he was pursuing an economic policy that neglected the ex-samurai. However, in this area too, the killing may have caused only a "slight modification" of the government's economic program. Brown, "Ōkubo Toshimichi," p. 197.

63. Ōkuma Shigenobu, "Nihon no seitō," p. 36.

64. Letter from Yamagata to Itō, dated July 4, 1879, quoted in Osatake, *Nihon kensei shi taikō*, II, 521–522. Translation is from Ike, *Political Democracy*, p. 93; see also Beckmann, *Making of the Meiji Constitution*, p. 50. This letter may provide a hint to Yamagata's character. Yamagata was known as one of the most careful and prudent of the leaders of the Meiji period. Ozaki Yukio said of him: "Yamagata went over a problem repeatedly, so he never made a major error in his life." Quoted in Isa Hideo, *Ozaki Yukio den* (A biography of Ozaki Yukio; Tokyo, 1951), p. 580. Hackett, in his biography of Yamagata, states that Yamagata conducted his political activities as if he were engaged in a military campaign and that he dreaded defeat, like any good military man. Hackett then concludes that this caution was rewarded because Yamagata never suffered a major political defeat. Roger F. Hackett, "Yamagata Aritomo: A Political Biography," Ph.D. thesis (Harvard University, 1955), p. 190.

65. Quoted in Tokutomi Iichirō, *Kōshaku Yamagata Aritomo den* (The biography of Prince Yamagata Aritomo; Tokyo, 1933), II, 839. As Hackett puts it, "He did recognize, however, that after a gradual evolution a representative assembly under a constitution would be desirable." Hackett, "Yamagata," p. 143.

66. One of the more fascinating personalities of his time, perhaps because he has left so many detailed and penetrating comments about his contemporaries, their actions, and ideas. (See, for example, Jansen, *Sakamoto Ryōma*, pp. 97, 105–106.) He opposed Itagaki and the movement for parliamentary government, but he was a believer in constitutional government. On his return to Japan after having been abroad with the Iwakura mission, he told Prime Minister Sanjō Sanetomi that the first step Japan should take was to draft a constitution. He considered that the politics and customs of the United States had a great deal of merit. That he was a gradualist, however, there is no question. Tsuda Shigemaro, *Meiji seijō to shin Takayuki* (The Meiji emperor and his subject Takayuki; Tokyo, 1928), pp. 275–276, 286.

67. Quoted in *Iwakura jikki*, III, 745–746. The problem of properly weighing expressions of concern is also encountered by a historian discussing another era in modern Japanese history. He writes: "The references of the October Incident in the Saionji-Harada *Memoirs* convey a deep concern over the 'political' behavior of the army officers but do not imply a plot of serious dimensions." James B. Crowley, "Japan's China Policy, 1931–

1938: A Study of the Role of the Military in the Determination of Foreign Policy," Ph.D. thesis (University of Michigan, 1960), p. 81n17.

68. Tsuda, pp. 500–501.

69. *Ibid.*, p. 500. See also Teters, "Conservative Opposition," p. 32.

70. Quoted in Osatake, *Nihon kensei shi taikō,* II, 577.

71. Nagata, p. 96. For a brief biography of Ono, see Hane, pp. 56–58.

72. Fukuzawa is regarded by many as perhaps the most influential single person in the Meiji period. See, for example, the description of Fukuzawa in *ibid.*, pp. 26–38.

73. *Fukuzawa zenshū* (The collected works of Fukuzawa [Yukichi]; Tokyo, 1925–1926), VIII, 217–218. See also recollection of Uchida Roan, quoted in Osatake Takeki, *Nihon kensei shi* (Japanese constitutional history; Tokyo, 1930), p. 308.

74. Beckmann, *Making of the Meiji Constitution,* p. 112. See also June 16, 1899, speech by Itō, quoted in *Itō zenshū,* II, 318. Some Japanese see themselves as being extremely sensitive to history. "It may be said that there are no people who respect history more than the Japanese and that there is no nation that emphasizes the study of history as does Japan." Fukuchi Shigetaka, *Shizoku to samurai ishiki: Kindai Nihon wo okoseru mono-horobosu mono* (The samurai class and the samurai spirit: Causes of the rise and fall of modern Japan; Tokyo, 1956), p. i.

75. McLaren, "Documents," pp. 568–569.

76. *Ibid.*, p. 574. Cody points to another contribution of the movement when he states, "Because of the effectiveness with which aims were publicized and members gained, these organizations contributed to an awakening of political consciousness among a people disciplined to accept without question the decisions of a ruling oligarchy." Cody, p. 2. This, of course, is not the same thing as saying that the movement was politically powerful.

77. Ono in this petition also called for the establishment of a national assembly by 1881. Nagata, pp. 102–103.

78. Memorial submitted by Itō Hirobumi on December 14, 1880, quoted in Kaneko, *Itō den,* II, 192–201. Translated in full in Beckmann, *Making of the Meiji Constitution,* Appendix v. This and other translations form a useful part of Beckmann's work. It should be noted that leaders of the movement, too, did not want the bloody experiences in Europe to be repeated in Japan. Cody, p. 215. The idea that a constitutional form of government must inevitably be established in Japan is expressed in a somewhat different, but interesting, manner in Iyenaga (p. 20): "I believe with Guizot, that the germ of representative government was not necessarily 'in the woods of Germany' as Montesquieu asserts, or in the Witenagemot of England; that the glory of having a free government is not necessarily confined to the Aryan family or to its more favored branch, the Anglo-Saxons. I believe that the seed of representative government is implanted in the very nature of human society and of the human mind. When the human mind and the social organism reach a certain stage of development, when they are placed in such an environment as to call forth a united and harmonious action of the body politic, when education is diffused among the masses and every member of the community attains a certain degree of his individuality and importance, when the military form of society transforms itself into the industrial, then the representative idea of government springs forth naturally and irresistibly. And no tyrant, no despot, can obstruct the triumphal march of liberty." Iyenaga is not speaking from an antioligarchy, promovement for parliamentary government point of view in his short work (see pp. 42–43, 49–52, 55). Although there is some danger of overemphasis, one can find an amazing similarity in the reasons the oligarchy cited for establishing constitutional government and those stated by Yoshino Sakuzō. As his biographer has stated: "In many respects Yoshino was spiritual kin of the men who founded the Meiji regime . . . " (see Perry, pp. 131, 135–137, 152–153).

79. See Rōyama, pp. 140–144, for a brief commentary on these laws. See also Osatake,

Nihon kensei shi taikō, II, 509; Scalapino, *Democracy,* pp. 60, 60n49, 64–65; McLaren, "Documents," sections on "Public Meetings and Associations," and "Press and Publication Regulations."

80. Osatake, *Nihon kensei shi taikō,* II, 602–603. Osatake is speaking of the years 1882–1883. Scalapino, describing an earlier period, writes: "Actually, until about 1875 Meiji Japan had experienced an extraordinary period of political freedom, but thereafter the government felt obliged to retreat via a series of edicts on press, assemblage, and general political activities. Although these authoritarian moves were rather moderate when compared with actions in modern totalitarian states, they hampered political activities and shaped them to some degree." Scalapino, "Japan: Between Traditionalism and Democracy," p. 311.

81. The government had other troubles to keep it occupied. At this time the Meiji government faced a grave financial crisis. In most of the accounts of Meiji developments by prominent Meiji political personages, it would be possible to find mention of this financial crisis, which threatened to wreck the government. Both Itō and Ōkuma, for example, recall that the years immediately after the Satsuma Rebellion were extremely difficult years because of this "grave" financial crisis. Itō Hirobumi, "Hompō kempō seitei," p. 536; Matsueda, p. 43. Two men who were close to the throne also emphasize that the national finances after the Satsuma Rebellion were in an extremely perilous state, and that there was good reason for "extreme concern for the future." Hijikata Hisamoto and Itō Takumichi, *Meiji tennō goseitoku* (The imperial virtues of the Meiji emperor; Tokyo, 1913), pp. 158, 167. The Satsuma Rebellion was financed by the printing of inconvertible notes. The government printed 27 million yen, and the Fifteenth National Bank also issued another 15 million. This contributed to a runaway inflation, which was aggravated by the distribution of capitalized pension bonds with the valuation of the then unbelievable 173 million yen. See Kimura Motokazu, "Fiscal Policy and Industrialization in Japan, 1868–1895," *Annals of the Hitotsubashi Academy,* 6:19–20 (Apr. 1956); Yanaga, *Japan since Perry,* pp. 138–139. There is no question but that the Meiji leaders considered the fiscal problem the most serious facing the government at this time. The activities of proponents of parliamentary government must have paled in comparison to the magnitude of this problem.

CHAPTER III. ITŌ AND ŌKUMA: THE CRISIS OF 1881

1. Ironically, Ōkubo, on the morning of his assassination, gave this appraisal of the accomplishments of the Meiji government. He began with the assumption that thirty years would be necessary to achieve the goals set up by the government. He considered the first ten years the beginning of the development of the new Japan. He felt that the second stage would see the "establishment of internal order and the completion of the program of strengthening the nation." He believed that Japan was moving into this stage. Iwata, p. 497.

2. The *Japan Weekly Mail* (Sept. 10, 1870), p. 422. See also descriptions in Idditti Smimasa, *The Life of Marquis Shigenobu Ōkuma* (Tokyo, 1940), pp. 130, 144–145.

3. Gotō Shōjirō is also rated highly as a politician. Jansen, *Sakamoto Ryōma,* p. 356.

4. Cody, p. 267. The importance of the part a person performed in the Restoration drama is, of course, relative. Itō's role was greater than Ōkuma's, but less significant than that of the giants of the period, Kido Takayoshi, Ōkubo Toshimichi, Saigō Takamori. Craig touches on Itō's activities prior to the Restoration in his *Chōshū in the Meiji Restoration,* pp. 232–233, 236, 249, *et passim.* Cf. Beasley, pp. 100, 102.

5. Ōkuma had cut himself off even from his home prefecture when he had failed to take a stand one way or the other during Etō's abortive rebellion. Joyce C. Lebra, "Japan's

First Modern Popular Statesman: A Study of the Political Career of Ōkuma Shigenobu (1838–1922)," Ph.D. thesis (Radcliffe, 1958), p. 480.

6. A lengthy definitive work in Japanese on the crisis is Ōkubo Toshiaki's "Meiji jūyonen no seihen" (The crisis of 1881), in *Meiji shi kenkyū sōsho: Meiji seiken no kakuritsu katei* (Studies in Meiji history series: The sources of the establishment of Meiji political power; Tokyo, 1957). This is a revision and expansion of his earlier contribution, "Meiji jūyonen no seihen to Inoue Kowashi" (Inoue Kowashi and the crisis of 1881), *Meiji bunka shi ronshū* (Essays on the history of Meiji civilization; Tokyo, 1952), pp. 613–652. See also Joyce C. Lebra, "Ōkuma Shigenobu and the 1881 Political Crisis," *Journal of Asian Studies*, 18:475–487 (Aug. 1959).

7. Matsueda, p. 256.

8. Ichijima Ken'ichi, *Ōkuma kō hachijūgonen shi* (The life of Marquis Ōkuma; Tokyo, 1926), I, 864–865; Ōkubo Toshiaki, "Seihen," quoting from Kabayama Sukenori's diary, pp. 146–148.

9. *Iwakura jikki*, III, 652–653. Ōkubo says that the reason for requiring these memoranda was that the three state ministers felt the need to solidify the government's position and to re-emphasize gradualism in the face of the "surging" movement for parliamentarism. Ōkubo, "Seihen," p. 48. Arisugawa was appointed minister of the Left on February 28, 1880. On February 29 (1880 was a leap year), he met with Iwakura and Sanjō and they pledged to "stabilize and strengthen the foundations of the state by enacting a constitution." *Taruhito nikki*, III, 305; *Taruhito shinnō kōjitsu* (Activities of Prince [Arisugawa] Taruhito; Tokyo, 1929), B, 86. See also Takahashi Shingo, "Meiji jūyonen no seihen ni tsuite" (On the crisis of 1881), *Waseda seiji keizaigaku zasshi* (Waseda journal of politics and economics), No. 61:13–14 (Oct. 1938); Osatake, *Nihon kensei shi taikō*, II, 483.

10. Prince Arisugawa had asked Yamagata to submit his memorandum on June 6, 1879. Tokutomi, *Yamagata*, II, 841; *Iwakura jikki*, III, 656–698. All memoranda except Ōkuma's are reproduced in these pages. Ōkuma's petition is reproduced in *ibid.*, III, 702–714. See also Inada Masatsugu, *Meiji kempō*, I, 426–433. For translations of the petitions of Yamagata, Itō, and Ōkuma, see Beckmann, *Making of the Meiji Constitution*, Appendixes 4, 5, and 6; for Kuroda's opinion, see David F. Anthony, "The Administration of Hokkaido under Kuroda Kiyotaka, 1870–1882: An Early Example of Japanese-American Cooperation," Ph.D. thesis (Yale, 1951), pp. 147–148. The submission of these petitions over such a protracted period of time certainly raises questions about the premise that government concern about the "surging" movement prompted them. The authorities were moving at a pace of their own making. It must be emphasized that the constitutional problem, though important, was but one of the many problems with which the Meiji leaders had to deal. On the other hand, the fact that they were occupied with other business does not mean that they were not interested in the constitutional question.

11. Kaneko, *Itō den*, II, 202. This indicates that the practice of coming to an imperial conference with a unanimous decision apparently was not rigidly followed during the Meiji era. See Robert J. C. Butow, *Japan's Decision to Surrender* (Stanford, 1954), pp. 166–177, esp. p. 167n1, for a description of the conditions obtaining in the 1930's.

12. Kaneko, *Itō den*, II, 202; Inada Masatsugu, *Meiji kempō*, I, 454–455; Sakatani, *Inoue kō*, III, 209–210.

13. Ichijima, I, 824–826; Watanabe Ikujirō, *Ōkuma Shigenobu*, rev. ed. (Tokyo, 1952), pp. 129–130. Ōkubo does not give any definite answer on the reasons for and the accomplishments of the Atami talks. Ōkubo Toshiaki, "Seihen," pp. 52, 64n1. See also Sakatani, *Inoue kō*, III, 211–212.

14. See letter from Itō to Iwakura, dated May 29, 1881, quoted in *Ōkuma Shigenobu kankei monjo* (Ōkuma Shigenobu documents; Tokyo, 1934), IV, 269.

15. *Iwakura jikki*, III, 698. There is no record as to when Arisugawa asked Ōkuma to submit his views. Prince Arisugawa writes that on March 11, 1881, Ōkuma called on him.

Taruhito nikki, III, 416. A letter from Iwakura to Ōkuma, dated March 31, 1881 refers to Ōkuma's petition. *Ōkuma monjo*, IV, 229. So it may be assumed that Ōkuma was asked on or about March 11.

16. This is further substantiation of the suggestion that it was possible to go before the emperor without previous consultation among leading officials and without unanimity of views.

17. *Iwakura jikki*, III, 698; Inada Masatsugu, *Meiji kempō*, I, 456–458. Itō told Sasaki Takayuki that Ōkuma submitted his memorandum in March. Quoted in Kaneko, *Itō den*, II, 994. There is some question as to the authorship of Ōkuma's petition. The standard Ōkuma biography (Ichijima, I, 794) credits both Yano Fumio and Ono Azusa. See also Beckmann, *Making of the Meiji Constitution*, p. 54n3; Ike, *Political Democracy*, p. 94; Idditti, p. 211. Yano Fumio, however, says, "I wrote the entire document." Quoted in *Itō Hirobumi hiroku*, p. 216. See also Ōkubo Toshiaki, "Seihen," 113. Ōkubo points out that there is no documentary evidence at present to show that Ono had anything to do even with revisions, although Ono would have been a logical person for that task. *Ibid.*, pp. 115, 119. Cf. Osatake, *Nihon kensei shi taikō*, II, 567.

18. Ichijima, I, 795; *Iwakura jikki*, III, 567.

19. *Ibid.*, III, 698. It is not certain when Iwakura and Sanjō were shown Ōkuma's memorandum. Inada feels that the letter from Itō to Iwakura dated May 29, and quoted earlier, is probably an answer to Iwakura's inquiry as to whether Itō had shown the memoranda of the other councilors to Ōkuma. Inada believes that Iwakura was trying to determine from Itō whether Ōkuma had submitted his memorandum even though he knew of the views of the others. Inada therefore feels that this exchange between Itō and Iwakura indicates that Iwakura and Sanjō were shown Ōkuma's memorandum before the end of May at the latest. Inada Masatsugu, *Meiji kempō*, I, 466.

20. Kaneko, *Itō den*, II, 204. Yamagata and Itō were the only two who presented their opinions to the emperor. Inada Masatsugu, *Meiji kempō*, I, 465–466.

21. There was an understanding among those concerned that the Genrō-in draft constitution would go through Iwakura's hands before presentation to the throne. Osatake believes that Arisugawa was following the earlier example when he showed Ōkuma's petition to Iwakura. Osatake, *Nihon kensei shi taikō*, II, 569.

22. *Iwakura jikki*, III, 699; Ichijima, I, 809. The similarity with Ono's 1878 writings should be noted.

23. *Iwakura jikki*, III, 699; Kaneko, *Itō den*, II, 208. Inada feels that it was Inoue Kowashi's idea to have Iwakura see Ōkuma, and to have Ōkuma say that his views did not differ greatly from Itō's. This would then enable Iwakura to tell Sanjō to show Ōkuma's memorandum to Itō. In this way, Itō would be moved to take over the responsibility for the constitutional question. Inada Masatsugu, *Meiji kempō*, I, 492.

24. According to Itō's recollection, he was the one who demanded to see Ōkuma's memorandum. He told Sasaki Takayuki that Sanjō and Arisugawa hesitated, so he threatened to go directly to the emperor. Arisugawa therefore had no choice but to show Itō the memorandum. Itō does not say when he first heard of Ōkuma's memorandum or when he demanded to see it. Sasaki recorded his conversation with Itō on October 4, 1881. Quoted in Kaneko, *Itō den*, II, 995.

25. *Iwakura jikki*, III, 699; *Itō Hirobumi hiroku*, p. 216. *Ibid.*, p. 219, has a photocopy of Itō's comment saying that he asked Sanjō for Ōkuma's memorandum. The copying of this extremely long petition was typical of Itō. A biographer of Ōkuma has aptly characterized this aspect of the Itō personality. "One cannot imagine Itō without pen and ink; he was indefatigable in preparing minutes or writing letters." Idditti, p. 413. Itō is therefore an extremely rich source for any historian of the Meiji period. On the other hand, it is said that there is no specimen of Ōkuma's handwriting extant. Lebra, "Ōkuma Shigenobu and the 1881 Political Crisis," p. 480.

26. The historian Hattori Korefusa (Shisō) raised this point early in 1948. Ōkubo Toshiaki, "Seihen," p. 65. Actually, the chances are that Itō found out earlier than June 27, the day he had copied Ōkuma's memorandum. For one thing, Inoue Kowashi, as we shall see, had been working with Itō on many state matters and can hardly be expected to have kept quiet once Iwakura showed Ōkuma's memorandum to him. Inada also believes that Itō, Inoue, and Itō Mĭyoji were working "closely together" from early or mid-June. Inada Masatsugu, *Meiji kempō*, I, 491. Moreover, Motoda Eifu was given the task of commenting on all the memoranda submitted by the councilors, including Ōkuma's. He submitted his views sometime in June 1881. *Ibid.*, I, 441–446. It is hard to believe that there was no leakage sometime prior to June 27. It should be recalled that Ōkuma feared that this would happen when he told Arisugawa that he preferred not to put his ideas down in writing.

27. Sanjō was also absent from the capital for about three weeks when he went to Atami from April 24 to May 12. *Ibid.*, I, 465. So this accounts for three weeks.

28. One councilor said that the national assembly did not have to be established for "a hundred years," while another said "thirty years." *Ibid.*, I, 453, 455.

29. For a discussion, see *ibid.*, I, 431–452.

30. *Ibid.*, I, 497; *Iwakura jikki*, III, 699; letter from Itō to Sanjō, dated July 1, quoted in Kaneko, *Itō den*, III, 206–207. In the letter Itō complained of the state ministers' failure to decide on a "fundamental policy."

31. Letter dated July 2, 1881, quoted in Kaneko, *Itō den*, II, 207–208. This was in reply to a letter Iwakura had written to him on the same day. Quoted in Inada Masatsugu, *Meiji kempō*, I, 496.

32. *Iwakura jikki*, III, 700–701; Kaneko, *Itō den*, II, 208; Inada Masatsugu, *Meiji kempō*, I, 498.

33. Iwakura wrote to Itō the same day to report on his talk with Ōkuma. Iwakura said that he discovered *for the first time* that Ōkuma had submitted his memorandum at Arisugawa's request. He was therefore convinced, he said, that Ōkuma was not trying to do something out of the ordinary. Letter quoted in *ibid.*, I, 498. It seems strange that Arisugawa never mentioned this fact to Iwakura, or Iwakura never thought to ask Ōkuma when they met in June. It appears that Iwakura was seeking all means to ameliorate the deteriorating relationship between Itō and Ōkuma.

·34. *Iwakura jikki*, III, 701; Kaneko, *Itō den*, II, 208–209.

35. *Ibid.*, II, 209.

36. *Ibid.*, II, 210.

37. *Ibid.* This exchange between Itō and Ōkuma is based on the writings of Sasaki Takayuki cited earlier. See *ibid.*, II, 994–996.

38. *Ibid.*, II, 212; *Taruhito nikki*, III, 459; see letter from Sanjō and Arisugawa to Iwakura, dated July 12, 1881, quoted in Kaneko, *Itō den*, II, 212–213. Iwakura was recuperating from an illness at this time at the Arima hotsprings in the Kobe area. He had left Tokyo on July 6. *Iwakura jikki*, III, 715; Inada Masatsugu, *Meiji kempō*, I, 500.

39. Ōkubo Toshiaki, "Seihen," pp. 67–68. See letter from Iwakura to Inoue Kowashi, dated June 19, 1881, quoted in Itō Hirobumi, *Kempō shiryō* (Documents related to the constitution; Tokyo, 1936), I, 58. Inada thinks that this letter indicates that Iwakura had shown Ōkuma's memorandum to Inoue and had asked Inoue to write memos on the subject. Inada, however, takes pains to point out that he has no corroborative evidence for his conjecture. Inada Masatsugu, *Meiji kempō*, I, 467.

40. Ōkubo Toshiaki, "Seihen," pp. 68–69. Inoue suggested two alternatives: make Arisugawa responsible for drafting the constitution, and submitting the draft to the cabinet. The cabinet (or the state ministers and the councilors) in the presence of the emperor would then debate the draft; or create an organ in the Imperial Household Ministry, put

Arisugawa in charge of the drafting and have the cabinet debate the draft. Quoted in Inada Masatsugu, *Meiji kempō*, I, 488–489.

41. On June 21 and 22 Iwakura wrote to Sanjō and Arisugawa urging the two to discuss discreetly with Itō the creation of an organ for drafting the constitution. *Ibid.,* I, 492–493.

42. Ōkubo Toshiaki, "Seihen," pp. 68–71, 75. See also Inada Masatsugu, *Meiji kempō*, I, Preface, p. 6. On July 1 Inoue Kowashi wrote to Iwakura reporting that he had talked with Itō the day before. Inada believes that Inoue at that time had urged Itō to take responsibility for drafting the constitution. Inoue also followed up with a letter to Itō on July 2. In this letter Inoue appears to patronize the state ministers. "Can there be one among the state ministers who can be responsible [for drafting the constitution]? [Therefore] I would like to have you assume the great task of drafting the constitution." He also said that if Itō did not take over the job, he would resign and return to his native Kumamoto. Quoted in *ibid.,* I, 495, 497–498.

43. Letter quoted in Kaneko, *Itō den,* II, 210–212. Ōkubo says that Iwakura's suggestion was obviously based on proposals submitted by Inoue Kowashi on June 22. Ōkubo Toshiaki, "Seihen," p. 70; also, Inada Masatsugu, *Meiji kempō,* I, 493.

44. The "General Principles," "Principles," and "Opinions" are quoted in *Iwakura jikki*, III, 717–729. Cf. Inada Masatsugu, *Meiji kempō,* I, 484. The "Opinions" are translated by Beckmann, in *Making of the Meiji Constitution,* Appendix 7. A letter from Iwakura to Inoue Kowashi, dated June 28, is believed to indicate that Inoue had sent "Opinions No. 2 and 3" to Iwakura. Quoted in Inada Masatsugu, *Meiji kempō,* I, 471; see also, *ibid.,* p. 472. Sometime very late in June Inoue also sent to Itō the three "Opinions," a memorandum, and copies of the June 19 and 28 letters from Iwakura. Itō Hirobumi, *Kempō shiryō,* I, 49–60.

45. Ōkubo Toshiaki, "Seihen," p. 86. Other authorities voice a similar view. See, for example, Suzuki Yasuzō, *Kempō seitei to Roesler* (Roesler and the Japanese constitution; Tokyo, 1942), pp. 141–144; Ōtsu, II, 787.

46. *Iwakura jikki,* III, 717–721; Suzuki, *Roesler,* p. 144. All the materials submitted by Iwakura at this time were written by Inoue Kowashi. Ōkubo Toshiaki, "Seihen," pp. 86–87; Suzuki, *Roesler,* p. 95; *Iwakura jikki,* III, 737.

47. When Ōkubo Toshimichi was assassinated, Inoue Kaoru was in London. He hurried back and was appointed a councilor on July 29, 1878. His appointment was opposed by imperial attendants like Motoda Eifu and Sasaki Takayuki, as well as by councilors from Satsuma, Kuroda Kiyotaka and Kawamura Sumiyoshi. However, when Ōkuma threatened to resign Iwakura and Sanjō "had to go along" and approve of Inoue's appointment. Tsuda, p. 415.

48. Ike (*Political Democracy,* p. 92) designates it as the "Takahashi Disturbance."

49. Kaneko, *Itō den,* II, 113–116. See also Tsuda, p. 420.

50. Tsuda, p. 524. Sasaki and Motoda had good reason to feel antagonistic toward the councilors in general and Itō in particular. A few days after Ōkubo was cut down in May 1878, they raised the issue of "direct or personal rule" by the emperor. This in their eyes meant that they would participate in political and administrative affairs at the same time that they were attending to the needs of the emperor. In this way they hoped to undercut the "arbitrary rule" of the few councilors. Iwakura was unhappy about this development but seemed unable to do anything about it. Itō resolved the issue in October 1879, when he abolished the system of imperial attendants. Professor Ōkubo's judgment of Itō's role at this time is significant: "Itō, as representative of the cabinet, met head-on [the anti-Sat-Chō challenge of the imperial attendants]. He masterfully overcame them and decisively carried out the abolition of the system of imperial attendants." Kaneko, *Itō den,* II, 140–145; Ōkubo Toshiaki, "Seihen," p. 48.

51. Idditti, p. 128.

52. Tokutomi Iichirō (Sohō), "Shokan wo nobete Ōkuma kō wo kataru" (To discuss

Marquis Ōkuma by delving into [Ōkuma's] papers), *Ōkuma kenkyū* (Studies on Ōkuma), No. 3:150 (Oct. 1953). Behind Inoue stood the German scholar Roesler, and Inada points out that without his help Inoue would have found it impossible to present his views when requested by Iwakura. Inada Masatsugu, *Meiji kempō*, I, 467.

53. Ozaki Yukio, "Itō, Ōkuma, Itagaki to watakushi" (Itō, Ōkuma, Itagaki, and I), *CK*, 53:353 (Mar. 1938). There is truth in his statement, but Ozaki, who was one of the secretaries at this time, may be exaggerating their power.

54. Ōkubo Toshiaki, "Seihen," p. 90n1; see also Inada Masatsugu, *Meiji kempō*, I, 491.

55. See McLaren, "Documents," pp. 41–42, for text. It should be pointed out that Iwakura opposed the promulgation of the April 14 rescript. Inada believes that while Iwakura was not against the enactment of a constitution, he was not for the establishment of a constitutional system. Inada, *Meiji kempō*, I, 286–287. The fact that the rescript was promulgated, and the added fact that in his December 1880 memorandum Itō clearly called for the establishment of a constitutional system, are hints of the realities of the power relationship between Iwakura and Itō.

56. Letter from Itō to Inoue, dated November 22, 1880, quoted in Inada Masatsugu, *Meiji kempō*, I, 430–431; see also Ōkubo Toshiaki, "Seihen," pp. 60–61.

57. Ōkubo, "Seihen," p. 91n1; Kaneko, *Itō den*, II, 146–154.

58. This distinction is clearly evident in Butow's description (pp. 80–83) of the power that the "eleven military and civilian aides known as secretaries and assistant secretaries" exercised in the meetings of the Supreme Council between August 1944 to May 1945. The point is, however, that they could be and finally *were* excluded from the meetings. We shall also see in Chapter V that Itō's public position on the principle of nonparty cabinets produced considerable consternation among his secretaries, Inoue, Itō Miyoji, and Kaneko, because it differed, they said, from the position taken and "agreed upon" in private.

59. See, for example, views of Kamishima Jirō, in his "Nihon no shisōka, kono hyakunen (21): Inoue Kowashi" (Japanese thinkers of the past century (21): Inoue Kowashi), *Asahi Journal*, 4:93 (Aug. 5, 1962). We shall see later that while Itō appreciated talent and would unstintingly make use of it, he was also known for his coolness toward those whom he felt had outlived their usefulness. One wonders why, in the last years of his life, Inoue with obvious bitterness told his friend, "I wasted my whole life for Itō." Quoted in Ōkubo, "Seihen," p. 87.

60. Wang Mang became emperor of China in A.D. 8. Before he assumed the position, it is said that he received hundreds of thousands of petitions urging him to become emperor, although he was already exercising imperial powers. He acceded, but only after a show of great reluctance.

61. Quoted by Iwabashi Tetsusuke in a letter to Ōkuma, in *Ōkuma monjo*, IV, 365–368. Letter dated October 6, 1881.

62. Itō Miyoji adds that the draft of the Rescript of October 11 was written by Inoue. Itō, Inoue, and he then discussed the draft and revised it. Kurihara Hirota, *Hakushaku Itō Miyoji* (Count Itō Miyoji; Tokyo, 1937), I, 64. See also Tsuda, pp. 503–504.

63. Quoted in Ōkubo, "Seihen," p. 121. This memorandum is also found in *Ōkuma monjo*, IV, 336–345. Tokutomi says of Iwakura, "Actually by this time [the 1881 crisis], Iwakura was already old and lacked vigor." Tokutomi, "Shokan wo nobete Ōkuma kō wo kataru," p. 150.

64. Americans working for the Japanese government in Hokkaido at this time called the Kaitakushi the "Colonial Department." A definitive work in English on the development of Hokkaido is Anthony's "The Administration of Hokkaido under Kuroda Kiyotaka, 1870–1882: An Early Example of Japanese-American Cooperation." As the title suggests, Anthony does not concern himself too much with politics in Tokyo.

65. Anthony, pp. 20, 22–24.

66. Tokutomi Iichirō, *Kōshaku Matsukata Masayoshi den* (Biography of Prince Matsukata Masayoshi; Tokyo, 1935), I, 795–797. See also Sasuhara, I, 363.

67. Kaneko, *Itō den*, II, 214–215; Sasuhara, I, 363. This proposal, after it was approved, because of the above conditions has been described as a "great scandal." Scalapino, *Democracy*, p. 76; see also Ike, *Political Democracy*, p. 95. It should be noted, however, that the decision to abolish the commission was in keeping with the government policy announced on November 5, 1880. This policy called for the disposal by the government to private ownership of unprofitable enterprises which were imposing a financial burden on the state. There is some evidence that the whole project of colonizing Hokkaido was unprofitable. For example, Iwasaki Yatarō, representing interests opposing Godai Tomoatsu, who headed the group desiring to purchase the properties, candidly declared that the sale to Godai would be helpful to them, because it would entail heavy financial burdens for the purchaser, thus contributing to the downfall of a commercial rival. Ōkuma also later admitted that because of the inflation at this time, the value of the properties may not have been as great as the public believed. See memorandum from Kuroda to Sanjō, quoted in Sasuhara, I, 365–366; Watanabe Ikujirō, *Meiji shi kenkyū* (Studies in Meiji history), rev. ed. (Tokyo, 1944), pp. 132–133; Tsuda, pp. 548–549; Matsueda, p. 254. Cf. Ōkubo Toshiaki, "Seihen," pp. 121–128.

68. *Taruhito nikki*, III, 464; *Chōya shimbun* (Aug. 5, 1881); letter from Sanjō to Iwakura, dated July 31, 1881, quoted in *Iwakura jikki*, III, 737–739; Ōkubo Toshiaki, "Seihen," p. 95; Inada Masatsugu, *Meiji kempō*, I, 508–509; Kaneko, *Itō den*, II, 215. If a basic cause for the downswing of Satsuma influence in the government after the death of Ōkubo can be stated, it is the instability of Kuroda Kiyotaka, Ōkubo's logical heir-apparent. Kuroda was a dipsomaniac who became violent under the influence of liquor. Perhaps the anger directed against Ōkuma by the Satsuma faction is in part a reflection of the awareness of the weakness of the leadership. Besides the candlestick-throwing incident, other acts of violence ascribed to Kuroda are: murdering his wife; grappling with Kido Takayoshi; threatening Sano Tsunetami and Inoue Kaoru with pistols on different occasions; an attempted slashing of Inoue with a sword; still another instance of bodily assault on the volatile Inoue. See Komatsu Midori, *Itō kō to Yamagata kō* (Prince Itō and Prince Yamagata; Tokyo, 1936), pp. 51–60; Nakayama Yoshisuke, *Kōno Banshū den* (Biography of Kōno Banshū [Hironaka]; Tokyo, 1926), I, 213; Itō Jintarō, *Meiji rimenshi* (An inside history of the Meiji; Tokyo 1939), II, 147; Eshū Daburyū (S.W.), "Kuroda Kiyotaka, Inoue Kaoru no ryōnin masa ni ninjō ni oyoban to shita koto" (The incident in which Kuroda Kiyotaka and Inoue Kaoru both sought to slash each other), *Meiji bunka kenkyū*, (Studies on Meiji civilization), 4:61–62 (Nov. 1928); Komatsu, pp. 62–64; *Itō Hirobumi hiroku*, p. 84; Kaneko, *Itō den*, II, 466; Watanabe, *Meiji shi*, p. 169. There is evidence that Kuroda's disability started very early and plagued him throughout his life. Kaneko, *Itō den*, I, 900; Tsumaki, *Kido nikki*, III, 140; letter from Inoue to Itō, dated September 11, 1889, in "Itō ke monjo" (The Itō letters; unpub.), 34:1032a–b. See Anthony, Chap. 2, for a biographical sketch of Kuroda.

69. Ōkubo Toshiaki, "Seihen," p. 95.

70. One of the developments most commonly mentioned in connection with the uproar over the proposed sale is the participation of Fukuchi Gen'ichirō, editor of the pro-government *Nichi nichi*, in the attack against the government. This fact is usually cited to show that public opinion was almost completely against the government. Matsueda, pp. 254–255; Ōkubo Toshiaki, "Seihen," pp. 95–96; Osatake, *Nihon kensei shi taikō*, II, 573; Isa, *Ozaki*, p. 97; Suzuki, *Jiyū minken*, p. 56. One historian attributes Fukuchi's defection to personal pique. He says that Fukuchi was angered because he learned of the plan by Itō, Inoue, and Ōkuma to have Fukuzawa publish a paper to disseminate government views. Ono Hideo, *Nihon shimbun hattatsu shi* (A history of the development of the press in Japan; Tokyo, 1922), p. 119. Inoue, writing to Itō on January 16, 1881, indicates that

Inoue talked to Fukuchi about the newspaper on that date. "Itō monjo," XIV, 123b. Fukuchi switched back to supporting the government a little more than a half year later.

71. Ōkubo Toshiaki, "Seihen," p. 96; Osatake, *Nihon kensei shi taikō*, II, 573; Sasuhara, I, 368–370; Watanabe, *Meiji shi*, p. 133; Inada Masatsugu, *Meiji kempō*, I, 509. Rallies were also held in Yokohama, Shizuoka, Osaka, Wakayama, and the Asakusa district in Tokyo. Ōkubo Toshiaki, "Seihen," p. 96. Ōkuma's recollection is that Itagaki and Gotō attended the Shin tomi za rally. However, Itagaki left Tosa late in August and did not arrive in Tokyo till September 16. Matsueda, p. 255; Ōkubo, "Seihen," p. 96; Itagaki, p. 200.

72. Quoted in *Iwakura jikki*, III, 744–750.

73. *Ibid.*, III, 750–752, quotes the petition in full. See also *Soga Sukenori ō jijoden* (Autobiography of Soga Sukenori; Tokyo, 1931), p. 319. The political role of these men, particularly of Tani, is fully and clearly analyzed in Teters, "Conservative Opposition," pp. 1–38, 62–69. The conservatives are described as "a rather ill-defined, yet cohesive, body of conservative men who were constantly critical of the actions and policies of those entrenched in power in the government, but who were reluctant to accept *in toto* the new parties and their programs."

74. Watanabe, *Meiji shi*, p. 131; Kaneko, *Itō den*, II, 216; Fukuzawa, *Autobiography*, p. 339.

75. Osatake, *Nihon kensei shi taikō*, II, 576–577; Kaneko, *Itō den*, II, 216–217.

76. Quoted in *Iwakura jikki*, III, 753; see also Ōkubo Toshiaki, "Seihen," p. 99; letter from Sanjō to Iwakura, dated August 29, quoted in Inada Masatsugu, *Meiji kempō*, I, 510. According to this letter Itō was already busily moving to reverse the sale decision. On September 6 Iwakura wrote to Sanjō saying that it would be regrettable if the government reversed itself because of the "popular commotion." Quoted in *ibid.*, I, 510.

77. There must have been more than a little suspicion on the part of those in Tokyo that Iwakura did not want to return to Tokyo to participate in a decision on Ōkuma. On September 1 Iwakura asked that he be given a six-week extension of his "vacation" on the ground that he had not completely recovered from illness. *Iwakura jikki*, III, 752. Sanjō, in his September 6 letter, said that Iwakura would be permitted a three-week extension. It should be noted that if Iwakura stayed away for three weeks, he would return after the end of the imperial tour. Cf. Inada, *Meiji kempō*, I, 512.

78. *Iwakura jikki*, III, 754–756; Inada, *Meiji kempō*, I, 512–514. About a month after the August 29 letter from Sanjō to Iwakura, Inoue wrote to Itō, urging the reversal of the sale decision on generally the same ground. He said that while the government might consider it a minor question, the people regarded it as a great one. The government, he continued, should not let this matter distract it from the primary issue of constitutionalism. Cited in Kamishima, "Inoue Kowashi," p. 95; Ōkubo Toshiaki, "Seihen," pp. 140–141.

79. *Iwakura jikki*, III, 756; Tokutomi, *Matsukata*, I, 803–805.

80. This was late in August 1881. *Taruhito nikki*, III, 477–478; Tokutomi, *Matsukata*, I, 801–802. Kuroda had left Yokohama by ship on August 9. Inada, *Meiji kempō*, I, 511. This is another reason to doubt Kuroda's presence in the imperial party.

81. This was on October 5. See letter from Itō to Sanjō, dated October 5, quoted in Kaneko, *Itō den*, II, 221–222. See also, Ōkubo, "Seihen," p. 136.

82. This step may have been taken because on September 26 Iwakura telegraphed Sanjō saying that he desired to remain in Kyoto for three more weeks because of the grave illness of Princess Katsura and because he himself was not fully recovered. *Iwakura jikki*, III, 760–761.

83. *Ibid.*, III, 761–762.

84. *Ibid.*, III, 762. Princess Katsura died on October 3, thus depriving Iwakura of one of his excuses to remain in Kyoto. *Ibid.*, III, 762.

85. *Ibid.*, III, 762–764. See also Ōkubo, "Seihen," pp. 143–144, and letter from Itō to

Iwakura, dated October 8, quoted in Kaneko, *Itō den,* II, 223–224, and letter from Inoue to Iwakura, dated the same day, quoted in *Iwakura jikki,* III, 766–767; Inada, *Meiji kempō,* I, 519–520.

86. *Taruhito nikki,* III, 500. Note that Kabayama's diary places the arrival at 2:40 p.m. Quoted in Ōkubo, "Seihen," p. 146.

87. *Iwakura jikki,* III, 774–775; Ōkubo, "Seihen," p. 146. Councilors Ōkuma and Ōki Takatō did not attend. Inada, *Meiji kempō,* I, 525.

88. *Iwakura jikki,* III, 775–776; Kaneko, *Itō den,* II, 727–732.

89. Tsuda, pp. 531–534. This account is based on what the emperor told Sasaki on October 13, 1881.

90. Matsueda, pp. 257–258. Among those who followed Ōkuma out were Yano Fumio, Ono Azusa, Inukai Tsuyoshi, Ozaki Yukio and Shimada Saburō. Ōkubo, "Seihen," pp. 37, 42n1; Lebra, "Ōkuma Shigenobu and the 1881 Political Crisis," pp. 486, 486n39.

91. The imperial conference broke up at 12:30 a.m. on the twelfth. Itō and Saigō informed Ōkuma about 1:00 a.m. that he was out. *Taruhito nikki,* III, 500; Matsueda, p. 257.

92. The rescript was made public on October 13. See Ōkubo, "Seihen," p. 145; Tsuda, p. 530. For a translation, see Beckmann, *Making of the Meiji Constitution,* Appendix 8. Ike is in error in saying (*Political Democracy,* p. 171) that "the government solemnly promised to adopt a written constitution with the promulgation of this Rescript." It seems that the 1890 date for the establishment of the national assembly was definitely fixed just one day before the fateful meeting held on Ōkuma's ouster. Inoue wrote to Itō on October 10: "On the matter of the date [for establishing the national assembly], I met with Kuroda this morning, and we reached an agreement on 1890." Quoted in "Itō monjo," 14:134. Itō, in an October 7 letter to Iwakura, had suggested 1890. Quoted in Inada, *Meiji kempō,* I, 524. When Yamada showed the draft of the rescript to Iwakura on September 18, the date for the establishment was set at 1888. *Ibid.,* I, 521–522; see also discussion in *ibid.,* pp. 526–527.

93. Idditti, pp. 29–30.

94. Even earlier, he had impressed Guido F. Verbeck in Nagasaki as one of his most promising pupils. William E. Griffis, "Ōkuma and the New Era in Japan," *North American Review,* 204:663 (Nov. 1916).

95. Idditti, pp. 111–112, 115–116, 120; Ichijima, III, 790–792. Ōkuma, in April 1869, was taken off his position in the Foreign Affairs Ministry. Watanabe, *Ōkuma Shigenobu,* p. 397. The importance of the rank of vice-minister becomes apparent when it is seen that the ministers were usually daimyō or *kuge,* who were usually figureheads.

96. During most of this period he also headed the Finance Ministry. *Ibid.,* pp. 61–62.

97. Idditti, pp. 188–189. See also Miyake Yujirō (Setsurei), "Itō kō no kyōsōsha" (Prince Itō's rivals), *Taiyō,* 15:209 (Oct. 1909); and "Itō kō no isshō" (The life of Prince Itō), *ibid.,* p. 46. Ōkuma himself has said that he was the "leading councilor" at this time. Matsueda, pp. 256, 285.

98. See, for example, Idditti, pp. 412–413; Watanabe, *Meiji shi,* pp. 285–298.

99. Miyake, "Itō kō no kyōsōsha," p. 211. See also, Miyake's "Ōkuma haku" (Count Ōkuma), *CK,* 26.1:122–127 (1911).

100. *Nippon* (Aug. 20, 1896). For characterizations of Ōkuma, see Tokutomi Iichirō, "Happō yori nagametaru Ōkuma" (Ōkuma as seen from all angles), *CK,* 52:256–269 (Oct. 1937); "Ōkuma Shigenobu no seikaku kenkyū: Jigyō wa seikaku no han'ei" (Studies in the personality of Ōkuma Shigenobu: Deeds are the index to character), by the leading biographer and apologist for Ōkuma, Watanabe Ikujirō, in *Ōkuma kenkyū,* No. 3:46–96 (Oct. 1953); and Oka Yoshitake, *Kindai Nihon no seijika: Sono seikaku to ummei* (Statesmen of modern Japan: Lives and characteristics; Tokyo, 1960), a somewhat expanded version of a series of essays he wrote for *Bungei shunjū* (Literary miscellany) in 1959 and 1960.

101. Henry C. Potter, "Impressions of Japan," *Century Illustrated Magazine,* 61:668

(Mar. 1901). See also views expressed by "A Resident," in "The Japanese Constitutional Crisis and the War," *Contemporary Review,* 68:462 (Oct. 1895); "The Sage of Waseda," *Kobe Weekly Chronicle* (May 9, 1900), pp. 379–380.

102. Tokutomi Iichirō knew both Itō and Ōkuma. While he is speaking of a much later time, he feels that Itō had and showed respect for Ōkuma. Tokutomi, "Happō yori naga-metaru Ōkuma," p. 266.

103. Takahashi, p. 22; Yano Fumio attributes Ōkuma's paramount position in the government to Ōkuma's control of the Finance Ministry. As Yano says, "Without Ōkuma's consent, the other ministries could do nothing." Matsueda, p. 37 (Pt. 2); Ichi-jima, I, 702.

104. Matsueda, pp. 276–277; Ichijima, I, 733–735.

105. Takahashi, p. 23; Ichijima, I, 700–701; Isa, p. 100.

106. Quoted in Takahashi, pp. 23–24; cf. account in Ichijima, I, 704.

107. Idditti, p. 189.

108. This was Ōkuma's position when Iwakura questioned him about the memoranda submitted by both him and Itō. Itō also was led to believe that Ōkuma would not deviate from "gradualism" Kaneko, *Itō den,* II, 205.

109. Quoted in *Itō Hirobumi hiroku,* p. 217.

110. See, for example, Watanabe Ikujirō's *Monjo yori mitaru Ōkuma Shigenobu kō* (Marquis Ōkuma Shigenobu as seen through documents; Tokyo, 1932), p. 94. There is no question but that the three were close. This is indicated by the friendly, light-veined letter Itō sent to Ōkuma and Inoue discussing Ōkuma's and Inoue's contemplated trip to Atami. Letter dated January 5, 1881, *Ōkuma monjo,* IV, 195. Inoue was Itō's closest and life-long friend. He was of bold and daring temperament, and in this respect found a kindred spirit in Ōkuma. Throughout his life Inoue seems to have felt that it was his ap-pointed duty to perform unpleasant tasks for Itō, his more prudent, not too brave junior colleague from Chōshū. For characterizations of Inoue, see *Mainichi shimbun* (Aug. 11, 1892); *Kokkai* (Aug. 21, 1892); Mary G. Humphreys, "The Men of New Japan," *Century Illustrated Monthly Magazine,* 62:826–828 (Oct. 1901); Toku Baelz, ed., *Awakening Japan: The Diary of a German Doctor,* tr. from the German by Eden and Cedar Paul (New York, 1932), pp. 65–66, 102; Miyake Setsurei, *Dō jidai shi* (A history of my times), Vol. 2 (Tokyo, 1951), pp. 76–78; Tokutomi Iichirō, "Chōshū sanson no hanashi: Itō, Yamagata, Inoue" (Recollections of the big three of Chōshū: Itō, Yamagata, Inoue), *CK,* 52:267 (Apr. 1937); ten men write their impressions of Inoue in *CK,* 26:65–96 (Feb. 1911). This is one of a series of articles printed by *CK* at this time on major Meiji personalities by men who knew them. Of uneven quality, they are nevertheless valuable for the sidelights they cast on these figures.

111. See letter from Fukuzawa to Itō and Inoue, dated October 14, 1881, quoted in Ishikawa Mikiaki, *Fukuzawa Yukichi den* (Biography of Fukuzawa Yukichi; Tokyo, 1932), III, 71–74. About this time too, Fukuzawa asked Inoue whether the three would not fight over the prime ministry once constitutional government was established. Inoue laughingly replied that there was absolutely no danger of them ever falling out. Quoted in Ishikawa Mikiaki, III, 76–76; see also Inada Masatsugu, *Meiji kempō,* I, 463. The news-paper envisioned by the foursome was not published, but Fukuzawa went on to found the respected *Jiji shimpō* (Current affairs daily). Ōkubo Toshiaki, "Seihen," p. 55.

112. Baba Tsunego, *Dai shisō encyclopedia: Nihon seitō shi* (The comprehensive ency-clopedia: A history of Japanese political parties; Tokyo, 1938), p. 147; *Seitō shi,* p. 37. Hayashida Kametarō does not believe that Ōkuma was motivated by desire to get the better of his colleagues but feels that it was natural for Ōkuma to try to curb Sat-Chō power in the government. Hayashida, *Meiji Taishō seikai sokumen shi* (A sidelight history of the Meiji Taishō political world; Tokyo, 1926), I, 51–52. (Hayashida apparently died after completing only one volume.) Hayashida knew many of the major political per-

sonalities of the Meiji period and took part in some of the events he describes.

113. Ōkubo, "Seihen," p. 111, Inada, *Meiji kempō*, I, 457. Cf. Ōtsu, II, 469–470.

114. Ōkubo, "Seihen," p. 111. Professor Ōkubo emphasized this point in a conversation with me in August 1957, at the Kensei shiryō shitsu (Constitutional government documents room) in the Diet Building. Hane ("English Liberalism," p. 261) believes that Ōkuma knew that these views were not similar to those held by the others.

115. See, for example, Inada *Meiji kempō*, I, 514–518.

116. See Oka Yoshitake, *Gendai Nihon shōshi: Seiji shi* (A short history of modern Japan: Political history), ed. Yanaihara Tadao, Misuzu Shobō edition (Tokyo, 1953), p. 83; Ōkuma, "Seikai no han'ei," p. 164; Suzuki, *Jiyū minken*, pp. 55–56; Watanabe Ikujirō, "Meiji shi yori mitaru Ōkuma monjo" (Ōkuma papers as interpreted through Meiji history), *Meiji bunka*, 6:9–10 (Mar. 1903); Tōyama, "Kindai hen," II, 83–84; Saitō Kumazō, *Nihon seitō hattatsu shi* (A History of the Development of Political Parties in Japan; Tokyo, 1917), pp. 65–67; Osatake Takeki and Hayashi Shigeru, *Gendai Nihon shi kenkyū: Seiji* (Studies in modern Japanese history: Politics; Tokyo, 1938), pp. 113–114; Scalapino, *Democracy*, pp. 66–67; Ike, *Political Democracy*, pp. 95–96; Beckmann, *Making of the Meiji Constitution*, pp. 56–57, 60.

117. It has been suggested by some that Ōkuma and Kuroda were sent on this tour to rid the capital of two of the principals in the incident, so that those remaining in Tokyo could discuss freely means to bring about a solution. Suzuki, *Jiyū minken*, p. 56; *Seitō shi*, p. 38. Ōkubo and Baba also say that Kuroda accompanied the emperor on the tour. Ōkubo, "Seihen," p. 95, and Baba, *Nihon seitō shi*, p. 147. This explanation for the absence of Ōkuma and Kuroda is difficult to believe. In the first place, the outcry did not become clamorous until after the tour had started. Moreover, Kuroda went to Hokkaido on official business and *met* the imperial party in Hokkaido. *Taruhito nikki*, III, 477–478; letter from Itō to Ōkuma, dated August 2, 1881, in *Ōkuma monjo*, IV, 287–289; Inada, *Meiji kempō*, I, 511. A letter from Kitabatake Harufusa to Ōkuma, dated October 3, 1881, speaks of Kuroda's return to Tokyo (*Ōkuma monjo*, IV, 350–354). Kuroda returned to Yokohama on September 10. Inada, *Meiji kempō*, I, 513. The imperial tour ended on October 11.

118. For a biographical sketch of Yano, see Hane, "English Liberalism," pp. 55–56.

119. Yano Fumio, "Yo ga seitō jidai" (My political party period), *Taiyō*, 13.3:167 (1907). Osatake, *Nihon kensei shi taikō*, II, 576; Suzuki Yasuzō, *Hyōden Itō Hirobumi* (A critical biography of Itō Hirobumi; Tokyo, 1944), p. 145. Suzuki, however, errs in making Yano Fumio a leader in the attack against the government on this issue.

120. The letters written to Ōkuma at this time are illustrative of the confusion among Ōkuma's supporters and sympathizers. Even those in very high government positions, like those on the outside, depended on rumors for their enlightenment. See, for example, letter from Yamazaki Naotane to Ōkuma, dated August 25, 1881, quoted in *Ōkuma monjo*, IV, 314–315; and from Kitabatake Harufusa to Ōkuma, dated October 3, 1881, in *ibid.*, IV, 350–354.

121. Ōkuma has been described as "audacious," "headstrong," "marked with courage and heroic daring," and having "utmost confidence in his own ability to handle any situation." Watanabe, *Meiji shi*, p. 290; *Kokumin no tomo* (Friends of the people; July 3, 1891); Nishii Shii, *Kan-min no shōtotsu kyūchō* (The critical state of the friction between officials and the people), quoted in *Japan Weekly Mail* (Feb. 28, 1903), p. 229; Idditti, p. 413.

122. Yano, "Yo ga seitō jidai," p. 167. See also Yano Fumio, "Waga kuni rikken no taisei wo tsukkutta sansei gun" (The three leading lights in the creation of constitutionalism in Japan), *Shin kyū jidai* (The old and the new age), 2:5 (Aug. 1926). Letters written at this time support Yano's contentions. The Ōkuma forces certainly did not think that they were in a fight to a finish at this point. Ono warned Ōkuma, for example, that "evil men" were trying to cause a split between him and Itō. Letter from Ono to Ōkuma, dated September 29, 1881, quoted in *Ōkuma monjo*, IV, 332–336. Komatsu Akira, on September 25, also

asked Ōkuma to "cooperate" with Itō, and coupled this request with the prediction that should there be a split between the two it would be a "tragedy for the nation." *Ibid.*, IV, 329–332.

123. Watanabe, *Meiji shi*, p. 144. Ōkubo agrees in essence with Watanabe's conclusion. Ōkubo, "Seihen," p. 107.

124. See *Ōkuma monjo*, IV, 287–319, for the August letters.

125. The letter quoted in *ibid.*, IV, 326–329.

126. Quoted in Watanabe, *Ōkuma Shigenobu*, p. 137.

127. Quoted in Osatake, *Nihon kensei shi taikō*, II, 576. Itō had already linked Ōkuma to Fukuzawa in June 1881. Inada, *Meiji kempō*, I, 500, 503–504.

128. Ōkubo, "Seihen," p. 133.

129. Inada, *Meiji kempō*, I, 507, 512–514. In late July Sanjō dispatched Inoue Kowashi to the south, where he met both Iwakura and Inoue Kaoru. It can be surmised that the subject of the conversations was the type of constitution Japan was going to enact. Inoue Kowashi returned to Tokyo early in August. Ōkubo, "Seihen," pp. 88–90, esp. the letters from Inoue Kaoru to Itō, dated July 27, 1881, and Matsukata to Inoue Kowashi, dated August 2, 1881. Inada says that Itō sent Inoue to see Iwakura and that the purpose was to discuss a problem concerning the Ryukyus. He believes that constitutionalism was also discussed. Inada, *Meiji kempō*, I, 503. On August 6 Itō wrote to Inoue Kaoru indicating that plans were laid for ridding the government of Ōkuma's plans for an English-modeled constitutional system. Quoted in *ibid.*, I, 506.

130. In January 1933 Yada Isa, onetime disciple of Fukuzawa, in a speech in Nagoya, disclosed that in the summer of 1881 he was told to go to northern Japan to make speeches opposing the proposed sale. The reason was, Yada explained, that Mitsubishi had navigational rights in Hokkaido, and if the proposed sale was actually consummated Mitsubishi rights would be endangered. Yada also spoke on the need to hasten establishment of a national assembly. See Ōkubo, "Seihen," pp. 125–126, 129n12. It must have been obvious to everyone that those associated with the Ōkuma camp were the principals in the assault against the government on the sale issue. Ōkubo ("Seihen," p. 96), after listing the names most prominently connected with the uproar concludes: "I would like to point out that those who led the attack were mostly those who were later connected with the Kaishintō or were from Mita [Keiō gijuku] and the Kōjunsha.

131. Quoted in Ishikawa, III, 59–60. Fukuzawa and Itō were estranged after the crisis. They met only once before Fukuzawa died in 1901. This was in May 1898 at a garden party given by Fukuzawa. Ōkubo, "Seihen," p. 55. Yano Fumio seems to say in one article that they were the victims of the machinations of those in the government. "The fact that the Ōkuma faction was ousted can be blamed," he says, "on our naïveté. We paid no attention to the fact that there were devious means and methods used in the political world and that there was much to learn in this world of politics." Yano is more to the point in another work when he charges that to accuse the Ōkuma clique of working together with the attackers of the government was just an excuse for those who sought to topple Ōkuma and that the fact that these rumors were believed was a "victory for the propaganda of the other side." Yano, "Yo ga seitō jidai," p. 167, and Matsueda, p. 40 (Pt. 2). Osatake also suggests the possibility that these rumors were manufactured by those in the government. Osatake, *Nihon kensei shi taikō*, II, 577. Inada believes that Itō and Inoue Kaoru were behind the decisions on the ouster of Ōkuma and on constitutionalism. Inada, *Meiji kempō*, I, 514, 517–518, 530. See also Ōkubo, "Seihen," pp. 131–132.

132. Watanabe maintains, for example, that the split between Itō and Ōkuma was in the making sometime before 1881. He cites a visit by the emperor to Ōkuma's residence on April 8, 1878, as the beginning of the cleavage between the two men. Itō apparently was jealous about the visit. Watanabe, *Meiji shi*, p. 298. See also Ōkubo, "Seihen," pp. 41, 48–49. One source, however, comparing Itō and Ōkuma, stated that Itō did not grasp for

power and that he was willing to let others exercise it. *Ajiya,* Vol. 1, No. 10 (Sept. 1, 1893). Yano Fumio paid Itō this tribute: "Itō always subordinated personal affairs to state affairs. He never used his position for personal gain." Matsueda, p. 62 (Pt. 2).

133. Ishikawa, III, 77–78. See also Yano Fumio's recollection in *Itō Hirobumi hiroku,* p. 216.

134. The rescript of April 1875 and Itō's memorandum of December 1880 also contain strong statements on gradualism. Kaneko, *Itō den,* II, 196–197, 200.

135. Yoshino Sakuzō maintained that Ōkuma's proposals were not as radical as painted by Itō and the three state ministers. Ōkubo, "Seihen," p. 112.

136. Inada, *Meiji kempō,* I, 428–429.

137. A measure of the seriousness of Itō's belief that Ōkuma was trying to do him one better on the matter of writing a constitution is that Ōkuma's memorandum was called *shigi kempō.* Both Itō and Itō Miyoji designated it as such and Yano Fumio says that this is the name that was given to Ōkuma's document. Quoted in *Itō Hirobumi hiroku,* p. 216. This fact gave rise for a time to the belief that Ōkuma had submitted something else besides his memorandum. See, for example, Yoshino Sakuzō, "Kempō happu izen ni okeru kempō shosōan" (Draft constitutions written before the Meiji Constitution), *KGZ,* 42:59 (July 1927); and Ichijima, I, 794. Osatake doubts that Ōkuma submitted another document and feels that the confusion stemmed from Ōkuma's close association with members of the Kōjunsha who produced a *shigi kempō* at this time. Osatake, *Nihon kensei shi taikō,* II, 569. I am inclined to believe that there was no confusion and that in Itō's eyes Ōkuma did submit what amounted to a "draft constitution."

138. Quoted in Tokutomi Iichirō, "Itō, Ōkuma, Yamagata," *CK,* 52.5:280 (1937). See also Inada, *Meiji kempō,* I, 454.

139. Matsueda, p. 38 (Pt. 2). Ōkuma himself recalls: "I gathered a lot of men of talent and proceeded with reform. However, because I proceeded too swiftly, when gradualism would have been wiser, I made enemies over and above the many that I already had. The number [of enemies] increased, and about 1879–1880 the Sat-Chō group gradually started to oppose me." Matsueda, p. 247.

140. Ōkubo later became Ōkuma's champion in the government. However, Tokutomi suggests that Ōkubo did not trust Ōkuma implicitly. Therefore, Ōkubo had Matsukata work under Ōkuma and serve as a sort of *metsuke* (censor). Tokutomi, "Itō, Ōkuma, Yamagata," p. 278.

141. In early 1880 a change in the government structure was instituted. Under this reorganization councilors no longer were to serve concurrently as heads of ministries. Consequently, Councilor Ōkuma relinquished his post as finance minister. In another major shift Itō was succeeded by Matsukata in the Home Ministry. Ōkuma's biographers see this as an attempt by anti-Ōkuma forces in the government to lessen his influence by removing him from the control of the powerful Finance Ministry. See Idditti, p. 205; Ichijima, I, 702–703. See also Tsuji Kiyoaki, "Naikaku seido no juritsu: Tōji no yoron wo chūshin to shite" (On the establishment of the cabinet system: As seen from the point of view of contemporary opinion), *KGZ,* 58.1:108–109 (1944); cf. Sakatani, III, 128–131.

142. Ichijima, I, 573. Tokutomi asserts that Ōkuma actually became loquacious after he lost his leg in the bombing attempt on his life in 1889 and began his career at Waseda University. Tokutomi, "Happō yori nagametaru Ōkuma," p. 258. One foreigner, describing Ōkuma, wrote: "What one does not learn from Count Ōkuma is that among the foreigners, he has the reputation of being the frankest man in Japan, where frankness is not the trait most cultivated." Humphreys, "Men of New Japan," p. 830. One begins to suspect that the traits that made Ōkuma so attractive to foreigners were the very ones that went against the grain with his contemporaries in the government, for the simple reason that they were so un-Japanese.

143. Ichijima, I, 573.

144. *Ibid.*, I, 816–817; Tsuda, pp. 500–502. Sasaki indicated belief in the rumors about Ōkuma and said that Ōkuma's actions were "not proper." Tsuda, p. 508.

145. Quoted in Ichijima, I, 823.

146. Osatake believes that while the Satsuma Rebellion proved to be an "agonizing experience of the first order" for those from Satsuma who remained loyal to the government, the power of the Satsuma faction remained undiminished because the rebellion swept away the dissidents within the ranks. Osatake Takeki, "Seinan eki ni kansuru ichi kōsatsu" (A thought on the Satsuma Rebellion), *Rekishi kyōiku*, 11:114 (Nov. 1936). See also Matsueda, p. 239.

147. In the memorandum to Ōkuma, cited earlier, Ono said that the Satsuma clique could be written off as possible supporters because their anxiety over their deteriorating strength would make them unite against the Ōkuma group. In this same memorandum Ono said, "Itō is vacillating and appears to dream of [creating] a Sat-Chō alliance . . . " This memo was written, as stated earlier, sometime in September or October. We have also seen that as late as September 29 Ono and other Ōkuma supporters were hoping that a split between Itō and Ōkuma would not occur. Ono's attributing "vacillation" to Itō undoubtedly stems from his annoyance with Itō's seeming disinterest in Ōkuma's fate; he did not know, of course, that Itō had already created a Sat-Chō alliance. Ono's view is interesting for another reason. It is representative of the impatience often expressed by subordinates of the Ono, Ozaki, Inoue rank toward their superiors. Inoue was also sometimes dissatisfied with what he considered Itō's overly cautious attitude. Inada, *Meiji kempō*, I, 503. Itō, however, usually had his way, because he had to deal with other proud, sensitive, independently-minded councilors as well as state ministers. He knew that without their concurrence and support he could not carry out his plans against Ōkuma and implement his own ideas.

148. Yano, recalling the period just prior to the crisis, writes that Ōkuma "aroused jealousy" because he was the center of power in the government without the advantage of coming either from Satsuma or Chōshū. Yano, "Yo ga seitō jidai," pp. 166–167.

149. *Ibid.*, p. 167. Yano's recollection about the lack of ill-feeling toward Ōkuma among the top layer of bureaucrats does not square with the contemporary records left by people like Ono, Iwabashi Tetsusuke, Fukuzawa Yukichi, Ōkuma, or even with Yano's other recollections.

150. Matsueda, p. 63 (Pt. 2).

151. *Ibid.*, p. 319.

152. Quoted in Tokutomi, "Itō, Ōkuma, Yamagata," p. 279; see also Matsueda, p. 248; and Ishikawa, III, 58–59. Fukuzawa also quotes a "rumor" which echoes Ōkuma's charges. Ishikawa, III, p. 60. Yano's recollections are quoted in Matsueda, pp. 42, 52–53, 57 (Pt. 2).

153. Inada, *Meiji kempō*, I, 427.

154. Quoted in Watanabe, *Ōkuma*, pp. 146–147.

155. Matsueda, pp. 36–37 (Pt. 2). The reason Ōkuma gives for his defeat is also pertinent. He says: "The situation changed suddenly, and as a stone falls down from the mountain top, popular attention focused on me. My big mistake was my overconfidence which led me to believe that the *hambatsu* and the military could be ignored." Matsueda, p. 248.

156. *Ōkuma monjo*, IV, 341.

157. Ishikawa, III, p. 59. In the letter to Inoue and Itō quoted earlier, Fukuzawa wrote that the most "fantastic aspect of the whole business was that there were those who actually suggested that it was not beyond possibility that he, by acting in concert with the Risshisha of Tosa, would become a revolutionary." *Ibid.*, III, 79. See also Inada, *Meiji kempō*, I, 521.

158. Fukuzawa was also unfriendly to the Itagaki group, according to Hane: "He frowned upon the more radical wing of the political party movement and called them

'vulgar advocates of popular rights.' " Hane, "English Liberalism," p. 242.

159. Itagaki, pp. 200–202. Cf. Cody, pp. 111–115. Itagaki thus agrees with Fukuzawa that the issue was one between those in the government. "It was really a temporary insanity among the men in office," Fukuzawa says (*Autobiography*, p. 339).

160. The widespread popularity of England in Japan at this time is discussed in Hane, "English Liberalism," pp. 9–25. Inoue Kowashi must have believed that this factor compounded the threat posed by the eloquent champions of English liberal philosophy. See also *ibid.*, pp. 218–252, for a useful discussion of the ideas on constitutionalism held by Fukuzawa and his adherents.

161. Letter dated July 12, quoted in Kaneko, *Itō den*, II, 248–249. See also Inada, *Meiji kempō*, I, 501–505. Sanjō's remark to Iwakura that Ōkuma's "defection" to the Fukuzawa camp had angered "everyone" in the government should be recalled.

162. *Iwakura jikki*, III, 721–725; Inada, *Meiji kempō*, I, 471, 474–477; Beckmann, *Making of the Meiji Constitution*, pp. 143–146.

163. *Iwakura jikki*, III, 725–727; Inada, *Meiji kempō*, I, 477–478; Beckmann, *Making of the Meiji Constitution*, pp. 146–147.

164. *Iwakura jikki*, III, 727–729; Inada, *Meiji kempō*, I, 478–480. Beckmann, *Making of the Meiji Constitution*, pp. 147–148. The "Shigi kempō" appeared in *Kōjun zasshi*, No. 45:1–8 (Apr. 25, 1881).

165. Tokutomi, "Shokan wo nobete Ōkuma kō wo kataru," p. 147. See also Inada, *Meiji kempō*, I, 468.

166. Sasaki, in his petition, made direct reference to the movement for parliamentarism. Kawada and Nakamura, in their petitions, while mentioning the "popular outcry," made no direct mention of the movement. Sasaki and Hijikata Hisamoto favored expelling Ōkuma from the government. Inada, *Meiji kempō*, I, 520. Of the four generals, Torio Koyata and Miura Gorō were from Chōshū, Tani Kanjō from Tosa, and Soga Sukenori from Chikuzen (Fukuoka). Their petition is believed to have been the direct cause for the promulgation of the Soldiers' Rescript on January 4, 1882, admonishing the military to eschew participation in politics. Osatake Takeki, "Gunjin seiji ni kan'yō subekarazu" (Soldiers ought not to participate in politics), *Hōritsu jihō* (The law review), 9:4 (Jan. 1937). See also *Soga jijoden*, pp. 319–320; and Teters, "Conservative Opposition," pp. 24, 32, 52–53, 56–58.

167. Ōkubo, "Seihen," pp. 99–103, 132. See also, Inada, *Meiji kempō*, I, 520–521. *Nichi nichi* (Oct. 8, 1881) said that the government was split into at least four groups over the sale issue, with one group advocating a "change in the present government." It is entirely possible to downgrade the constitutional issue a bit and to emphasize the conflict between cliques in the government and to come up with a somewhat different version of the crisis.

168. There were, it is true, several incidents involving members of the government in the years 1882 and 1884 (Norman, *Japan's Emergence*, p. 182). However, Fukuzawa's analysis of the movement places its "effectiveness" in perspective. His first point is that the movement was by no means widespread. The second factor to remember, he says, is that "the government treated the movement with a great deal of indifference, and in time it gradually subsided." Fukuzawa then lists the reasons for the government's attitude: the movement lacked funds; its only weapons were the tongue and the pen; the government was backed by military power and funds; the government also controlled a "highly disciplined and effective" police force. *Fukuzawa zenshū*, VIII, 217–219. The *Japan Weekly Mail* published a translation of this position: "The History of the Japanese Parliament" *ibid.* (Apr. 6, 1889), p. 336. See also Kimura Tokio, "Fukuzawa Yukichi no Meiji kempō kan" (Fukuzawa Yukichi's views on the Meiji Constitution), *Shikan* (Historical perspectives), No. 38:48–53 (June 1953). In the letter from Iwakura to Sanjō, dated September 6, 1881, quoted earlier, Iwakura stated: "Granting that the government is facing its greatest difficulty since the Restoration, we still control the armed forces and the police. There is there-

fore nothing we cannot do." Quoted in Inada, *Meiji kempō*, I, 510–511. Harold M. Vinacke, *A History of the Far East in Modern Times*, 6th ed. (New York, 1959), p. 109, writes perceptively about the crisis and its effects: "This action may be interpreted in two ways. It may be considered as forced by the party agitation and particularly by Count Okuma's somewhat spectacular action, or it may be construed as being the next considered step in the reorganization movement, which merely happened to coincide with the other event. During the two decades following the Restoration the government seemed to pursue alternately a policy of advance and one of restraint. Thus it may be considered to have had in mind the taking of certain steps, regardless of public opinion, but only as the time for them appeared to be ripe."

169. Two outstanding exceptions are the executions of Oguri Tadamasa, who favored fighting the anti-shogunate forces to the end with French help (Jansen, *Sakamoto Ryōma*, p. 66n18), and Kondō Isami, who headed the Shinsengumi, a bakufu band of *rōnin* assassins. Both were killed in the early months of 1868.

CHAPTER IV. ITŌ AND THE DRAFTING OF THE MEIJI CONSTITUTION

1. Plenty of works on the Meiji constitution in English are available. See Itō Hirobumi, *Commentaries on the Constitution of the Empire of Japan*, tr. Itō Miyoji (Tokyo, 1889); Harold S. Quigley, *Japanese Government and Politics* (New York, 1932), Chaps. 3–8, 10, 11, 14; and Kenneth Colgrove's series of articles in *American Political Science Review*: "The Japanese Privy Council," 25: 589–614, 881–905 (1931); "Powers and Functions of the Japanese Diet," 27:885–889 (1933), and 28:23–29 (1934); "The Japanese Emperor," 26:642–659, 828–845 (1932); "The Japanese Cabinet," 30:903–922 (1936); "The Japanese Constitution," 31:1027–49 (1937). Quigley and Colgrove are still quite useful. For more recent works, see Paul Linebarger, Chu Djang and Ardath W. Burks, *Far Eastern Governments and Politics: China and Japan* (New York, 1954), Chap. 16; Ike, *Political Democracy*, Chap. 15; Beckmann, *Making of the Meiji Constitution*, Chap. 7; Joseph Pittau, S.J., "Ideology of a New Nation: Authoritarianism and Constitutionalism, Japan (1868–1890)," Ph.D. thesis (Harvard, 1962). Pittau does not limit himself to the Meiji constitution but traces the development of the various streams of constitutional thought before 1890. His was adjudged the outstanding thesis in political science at Harvard in 1962 and awarded the Toppan Prize (Harvard University Press, in press).

2. See Watanabe, "Kempō seitei zengo," p. 149; Watanabe, *Meiji shi*, pp. 291–292; Oka Yoshitake, *Yamagata Aritomo* (Tokyo, 1958), pp. 37–38; Kaneko, *Itō den*, II, 257. Some non-Sat-Chō people conceded in part the validity of the Sat-Chō claims. "Of course," said Yano Fumio, "the main achievements of the Restoration can be credited to the Sat-Chō. Consequently, there is no escaping the Sat-Chō wielding power." Yano, "Yo ga seitō jidai," p. 167. See also Tokutomi, "Itō, Ōkuma, Yamagata," p. 273; and Kawai Kazuo, "Sovereignty and Democracy in the Japanese Constitution," *American Political Science Review*, 49:669 (Sept. 1955).

3. *Dai Nihon teikoku Gikai shi* (Records of the Imperial Diet; Tokyo, 1926), I, 1492. Kawahara Shigesuke, a member of the House of Representatives at which Kabayama directed this outburst recalls that Kabayama was "deadly serious" and was "truly determined to die [for his beliefs]." Quoted in *Itō Hirobumi hiroku*, p. 17. A foreigner who worked as a legal adviser to the Japanese government writes: "And he [Itō] spoke as one who believed in the high destiny of his country, and in himself as the appointed agent to carry it to its fulfillment." Sir Francis Piggot, "The Itō Legend: Personal Recollections of Prince Itō," *Nineteenth Century and After*, 57:175 (Jan. 1910).

4. Itō Hirobumi, "Teikoku kempō no tokushoku to shinsei no kempō seiji" (The uniqueness of our constitution and true constitutional government), quoted in *Itō kō zenshū*, ed. Komatsu Midori (Tokyo, 1928), II, 178; and Itō Hirobumi, "The Duties of

Political Parties" (a translation of the Seiyūkai "Manifesto"), in Alfred Stead, *Japan by the Japanese* (New York, 1904), p. 73.

5. Letter to Inoue Kaoru, dated October 30, 1900, quoted in Kaneko, *Itō den*, III, 472. See also Itō Hirobumi, "Mokka no seijō to kempō seiji" (The present political situation and constitutional government), quoted *Itō zenshū*, II, 280. Yamagata's feelings toward the parties may be gauged by his designation of party members as "those despicable men of the parties." Paraphrased in Kaneko, *Itō den*, III, 379.

6. Osatake, *Nihon kensei shi taikō*, III, 592–594; Shimizu Shin, *Doku-Ō ni okeru Itō Hirobumi no kempō torishirabe to Nihon kempō* (Itō Hirobumi's constitutional studies in Germany and Austria and the Japanese constitution; Tokyo, 1939), p. 164. A variation of this theme is Sansom's belief that the Meiji constitution was "surprisingly" similar to the constitution that would have been enacted without reference to foreign examples had the government "logically pursued the line of development that it had already taken during its conflict with opposition parties." George B. Sansom, *The Western World and Japan: A Study in the Interaction of European and Asiatic Cultures* (New York, 1950), p. 358. See also Linebarger *et al.*, p. 359n21.

7. Suzuki, *Hyōden Itō*, p. 172.

8. Itō Hirobumi, "Hompō kempō seitei," p. 538. Itō in this instance is obviously being overly modest. Fukuchi Gen'ichirō once lamented that his inability to read German prevented him from rebutting effectively the arguments of those who were asserting that sovereignty resided in the people. Fukuchi Gen'ichirō, "Shimbun shi jitsureki" (My newspaper career), in *Meiji bunka zenshū*, XVII, 18–19.

9. In a conversation with Osatake in the early 1930's, quoted in Osatake, *Nihon kensei shi no kenkyū*, p. 356.

10. Letter from Inoue Kowashi to Iwakura, dated July 1, 1881, quoted in Osatake, *Nihon kensei shi taikō*, II, 726; Asai, pp. 415–416.

11. For discussions of this controversy, see Osatake, *Nihon kensei shi taikō*, II, 595–603; Asai, pp. 390–400. See also Hayashida, *Seitō shi*, I, 37.

12. *Awakening Japan*, p. 62. Baelz believes (*ibid.*, pp. 115–116) that the victory by Japan over China in 1895 was the turning point in the people's attitude toward the emperor.

13. Letter dated August 21, 1882, quoted in Kaneko, *Itō den*, II, 297. Yoshino Sakuzō dates this letter August 11. Yoshino, "Stein, Gneist to Itō Hirobumi" (Stein, Gneist, and Itō Hirobumi), *Kaizō*, 15:72 (Feb. 1933). In letters to Inoue Kaoru, Itō repeats the above sentiments. "There are few scholars in the world like Stein," he wrote on October 22, 1882, "who expound the 'monarchical principle.' Most advocate popular 'democracy.' To invite the latter will not benefit Japan at all." And on November 22, 1882, he again wrote: "[Stein] is a teacher who advocates the very principles [we need] for rebutting the pernicious tendencies in Japan. There is no doubt that for both theory and practical [application] he will be of benefit to us." Quoted in Kaneko, *Itō den*, II, 320, 322. Itō later recalled that after the lectures in Europe he finally came to understand "what European constitutional government was and what constitutions were." Itō, "Hompō kempō seitei," p. 540.

14. Kaneko, *Itō den*, II, 342. For a discussion of the background of the European trip, see Osatake Takeki, "Itagaki Taisuke yōkō mondai" (On Itagaki Taisuke's trip to Europe), in his *Meiji seiji shi tembyō* (Sketches in Meiji political history; Tokyo, 1938), pp. 152–179; Cody, pp. 159–168.

15. See letter from Saionji to Iwakura, dated May 10, 1883, quoted in Kaneko, *Itō den*, II, 342–343. In this letter Saionji makes the following remarks: "In short, I believe that we cannot see a change of heart [in Itagaki]. There is no question about his extreme fear and hatred of the Satsuma people and his displeasure at the Kaishintō. I do not know how the talks between Gotō and Itō turned out, but here again I believe that Gotō is disappointed . . . Actually, there is much discord between Gotō and Itagaki."

16. Inada, "Nihon seitō ron," p. 41.

17. *Japan Weekly Mail* (Jan. 2, 1891), p. 12. See also Cody, pp. 126, 128–129.

18. Letter to Matsukata, dated September 6, 1882, quoted in Kaneko, *Itō den*, II, 308–316.

19. See, for example, Seikan Kyo Shujin, "Inoue kō ron" (On Marquis Inoue), *CK*, 26.2:70 (1911); Nakamura Yaroku, "Saionji kō no tokusei" (Distinctive characteristics of Marquis Saionji), *CK*, 26.3:75 (1911); Kurozukin, "Hōisaretaru Itō kō" (The beleaguered Marquis Itō), *CK*, 23.9:77–78 (1908); Ozaki Yukio, "Zōka no chōji" (A natural child of fortune), *Taiyō*, 15:170 (Nov. 1909).

20. Itō was born in a peasant household and was probably the lowest born among the major Meiji figures. Kengi Hamada, *Prince Itō* (Tokyo, 1936), p. 5. Itō's rise to the highest post in the government, the prime ministry, has often been compared to the accomplishment of the one-time farmer from Owari, Hideyoshi, who became prime minister in 1586. See Osatake Takeki, "Meiji jūhachinen: Shimbun zasshi ni arawareta shujusō" (1885: Various aspects revealed in newspapers and magazines), *Meiji Taishō shi dan* (Journal of discourses on Meiji and Taishō history), 1:10 (Feb. 1937); Watanabe, *Meiji shi*, pp. 159–160.

21. Oka Yoshitake, "Shodai sōri: Itō Hirobumi" (The first prime minister: Itō Hirobumi), *Bungei shunjū*, 37:76–99 (June 1959).

22. Itō and his suite left Yokohama on March 14, 1882. Within a few days of his arrival in Berlin, on May 16, he had met his tutor, Rudolf von Gneist. (Letter from Itō to Matsukata, dated May 24, 1882, in Kaneko, *Itō den*, II, 270–272.) Except for the time off to visit Prince Arisugawa in Paris, a short Christmas vacation, traveling to institutions where he studied, and a trip to Russia for the coronation of Czar Alexander III, Itō conscientiously applied himself to his studies. For descriptions of his activities in Europe, see Suematsu Kenchō, "Itō kō no Ōshu ni okeru kempō torishirabe temmatsu" (Details of Prince Itō's constitutional studies in Europe), *KGZ*, 26.12:1869–80 (1912); Yoshino, "Stein, Gneist, to Itō Hirobumi," pp. 60–67; Kaneko, *Itō den*, II, 263–360; Inada Masatsugu, *Meiji kempō*, I, 568–598.

23. One of the basic guidelines for drafting the constitution that Itō laid down to his assistants was that all possible openings for amending the constitution should be eliminated. For example, he ruled that Japan's territorial boundaries would not be mentioned in the constitution, because boundaries change, and the constitution, Itō stated, should not be revised with every change of national boundaries. For Kaneko's recollections on Itō's desire for an unchanging constitution, see the following articles by him: "Itō kō to kempō seitei jigyō," pp. 986–989; "Kempō seitei kaikyū dan" (Reminiscences of the enactment of the constitution), *Kokugakuin zasshi*, 25:13–14 (Apr. 1919); "Teikoku kempō no seishin kiso" (The spiritual foundations of the imperial constitution), *Nihon seishin kōza* (Lectures on the Japanese spirit), 4:4–5 (Feb. 1934). Piggot's recollections of Itō, cited earlier, should be recalled in this connection.

24. Kaneko, "Itō kō to kempō seitei jigyō," pp. 985–986. Kaneko also remembered that Itō "fervently stressed that even if [the constitutions] of other nations were composed of seven parts people's rights and three parts sovereign's rights, and Japan's [constitution] contains the inverse ratio, there was no question but that Japan was a constitutional state." Kaneko Kentarō, "Nihon kempō seitei no yurai" (History of the enactment of the Japanese constitution), *Shigaku zasshi* 22:14–15 (Oct. 1911). See also Itō, "Hompō kempō seitei," p. 538.

25. Letter dated May 24, 1882, quoted in Kaneko, *Itō den*, II, 271. See also Suzuki, *Hyōden Itō*, p. 208; Inada Masatsugu, *Meiji kempō*, I, 196. In fairness to Gneist it should be pointed out that he emphasized the principle of power-sharing and believed in political mobility. He told Itō that control over fiscal powers was a key to determining the eventual balance of power between the executive and legislative branches of government, and took pains to point out that the powers to levy new taxes and to float public loans should be granted to the national assembly. To withhold these powers from the assembly, he asserted,

would make the establishment of a legislature meaningless. Gneist also believed that fixed expenditures should be determined by law. For Gneist's views, see "Gneist shi danwa" (Lectures by Mr. Gneist), Pt. 1 of "Seitetsu yume monogatari" (A dream account of Western philosophy), in *Meiji bunka zenshū*, I, 432–477. Lorenz von Stein, Itō's Austrian tutor, on his part, did not conceive of the powers of the executive as being absolute. In fact, he advocated separation of powers to prevent the executive from overwhelming the legislature and suggested that "those who organize the government must be those who possess the confidence of the majority of the legislature." See letter from Stein to Kuroda Kiyotaka, dated January 6, 1889, quoted in Itō, *Kempō shiryō*, III, 252–286. Kuroda had met Stein in Vienna in 1887 while on a world tour. Kuroda Kiyotaka, *Kan'yū nikki* (Diary of a world tour; Tokyo, 1887), II, 480–481. See also Sasaki Sōichi, "Waga kempō to Stein" (Our constitution and Stein), *Kyoto hōgakkai zasshi* (Journal of the Law Department of Kyoto Imperial University), 8:185–189 (June 1913).

26. Kaneko, *Itō den*, II, 357–360. Yoshino estimates that Itō studied in Berlin for a period of about five months and in Vienna for two. He compares this with approximately one and a half months spent in London and concludes that Itō did not get much studying done in London, Paris, or Belgium. Itō was in Paris and Belgium for a total of approximately three weeks. Yoshino, "Stein, Gneist, to Itō Hirobumi," pp. 62–63; Suzuki, *Hyōden Itō*, pp. 214, 217–218; letter from Itō to his wife and daughter, dated February 28, 1883, quoted in Suematsu Kenchō, *Kōshi Itō kō* (The dutiful Prince Itō; Tokyo, 1912), p. 271; Kaneko, *Itō den*, II, 307; letter from Saionji to Iwakura, dated May 10, 1883, in *ibid.*, II, 342; Inada, *Meiji kempō*, I, 568.

27. Suzuki, *Roesler*, p. 153; Kaneko, *Itō den*, II, 372–373; Fujii Shin'ichi, *Teikoku kempō*, p. 257; Inada, *Meiji kempō*, I, 691–692; Kudō Takeshige, *Meiji kensei shi* (A constitutional history of the Meiji; Tokyo, 1922), I, 271.

28. Kaneko, *Itō den*, II, 413; Yanaga, *Japan since Perry*, pp. 188–189.

29. In March 1884 he was appointed head of the Imperial Household Ministry. He was already a councilor and because he was the leading councilor was, for all practical purposes, "prime minister."

30. Kaneko, *Itō den*, II, 383–386; Itō Hirobumi, "Kempō ritsuan no keika to sono riron to no gaisetsu" (General remarks on the evolution of and the theories involved in drafting the constitution), in *Itō zenshū*, III, 184–185; Hattori Yukifusa (Shisō) and Irimajiri Yoshinaga, *Kindai Nihon jimbutsu seiji shi* (A political history of modern Japan as seen through the major personalities; Tokyo, 1955–1956), I, 152; Osatake, *Nihon kensei shi taikō*, II, 712–717; Kaneko Kentarō, "Naikaku seido sōshi tōji no tsuikai" (Recollections of the time when the cabinet system was established), *CK*, 51:116 (Feb. 1936).

31. Kaneko, "Nihon kempō seitei no yurai," p. 13.

32. *Ibid.*, pp. 15, 20. Kaneko's recollection is that most of 1886 was also spent in trying to work out measures to cope with the mass unemployment of bureaucrats from Satsuma and Chōshū which resulted from the establishment of the cabinet system. Kaneko, "Naikaku seido sōshi tōji no tsuikai," pp. 117, 120–122.

33. See the following articles by Inada Masatsugu: "Kempō goshijun an no seiritsu katei" (On the formation of His Majesty's draft constitution submitted to deliberation), *KGZ*, 52.8:62–83 and 52.9:56–84; "Kempō goshijun an no shūsei" (Revision of His Majesty's draft constitution submitted for deliberation), *KGZ*, 53.2:43–83 (1939), 53.3: 44–81, 53.4:102–125; "Kempō kisō no keika ni tsuite" (On the process of drafting the Japanese constitution), *KGZ*, 56.11:66–85 (1942), 57.2:35–69 (1943). Extremely detailed, and using basic sources usually unexploited by the non-Japanese, these articles are definitive. Inada has since published the second volume of his *Meiji kempō seiritsu shi* (Tokyo, 1962) which includes some of the material in these articles. Kaneko Kentarō's articles serve as a basic and full source. However, the repetition of material, errors of fact, and contradictions detract somewhat from their usefulness. See also description in Kaneko, *Itō den*, II,

569–631; Suzuki, *Roesler*. For descriptions in English, see Ike, *Political Democracy*, Chap. 15, and Beckmann, *Making of the Meiji Constitution*, Chap. 6; Pittau, "Ideology," Chap. 8.

34. Many major political accomplishments in Japan, credited to well-known figures, are usually traceable to some minor and subordinate bureaucrat. Itō's direction of and participation in the drafting process, however, was substantive and important. See, for example, comment by Suzuki, in *Hyōden Itō*, pp. 263–264. See also Inada, *Meiji kempō*, II, 1.

35. It is rather unfortunate that Inoue Kowashi, one of the most important and outstanding personalities in Meiji political life, has been deprived of credit in two major Western works on Meiji political history. Ike and Scalapino both mistake Inoue Kaoru, Itō's closest friend, for Inoue Kowashi, Itō's most respected brain-truster. Ike, *Political Democracy*, pp. 171, 176–178; and Scalapino, *Democracy*, pp. 67n69, 163. For a fairly detailed description of Inoue Kowashi's contribution to the Meiji constitution, see Fujita Tsuguo, "Inoue Kowashi no kempō rippō e no kiyō" (Inoue Kowashi's contributions to constitutional law), *Nihon gakushiin kiyo* (Proceedings of the Japan Academy), 12:75–131 (June 1954). See also Kamishima, "Inoue Kowashi," pp. 91–97.

36. Brilliant, dynamic, highly controversial, and certainly one of the handsomest men in Meiji public life, Itō Miyoji served Itō long and well. Like Inoue Kowashi, Itō Miyoji eventually drifted away from Itō, but, in one of those political behavioral patterns somewhat confusing to a neophyte student of Japanese politics, continued his loyal support. Itō Miyoji is discussed in a series of nine articles in *CK*, Vol. 32, No. 7 (July 1917), under the general title, "Seikai no hyōmen ni noridashite kita Itō Miyoji shi" (Count Itō Miyoji's "reappearance" on the political scene).

37. Kaneko studied at Harvard Law School from October 1876 to November 1878. A promising young bureaucrat, he was working for Terajima Munenori in the Genrō-in when he first came to Itō's attention. Kaneko drew up a long list of questions on specific constitutional problems, probably designed to embarrass Itō, who was in Europe. The fact that Itō did not let this deter him from appointing talent where he found it is typical of him. The choice of these three indicates another facet of Itō's character. In an age when han loyalty was important, Itō selected as his closest supporters three men from three different han. Inoue Kowashi was from what is now Kumamoto, Kaneko Kentarō was from Fukuoka, and Itō Miyoji was from Nagasaki. See Kamishima Jirō, "Dai ikkai teikoku gikai shisei enzetsu no kankei shiryō" (Materials on administrative policy addresses of the first Imperial Diet), *KGZ*, 66.1–3:93 (1952); Kurihara, I, 1; Fujii Shin'ichi, pp. 1, 227–233; Baba Tsunegō, "Itō Miyoji ron" (On Itō Miyoji), *CK*, 45:205 (July 1930). See also Kaneko, "Teikoku kempō seitei," pp. 19–21.

38. Osatake's evaluation of Roesler's contributions is pointed: "Inoue sounded out Roesler's views on every conceivable matter. It would thus not be an exaggeration to say that our constitution was really drafted with Inoue listening with one ear to Roesler." Osatake, *Nihon kensei shi taikō*, II, 728. See also Suzuki Yasuzō, "Nihon kempō seitei ni taisuru Hermann Roesler no kiyo" (Hermann Roesler's contributions to the enactment of the Japanese constitution), *Meiji bunka kenkyū*, 2:46–71 (May 1935); "Hakushi Roesler shi yuku" (The late Dr. Roesler), *Taiyō*, 1:148–149 (Mar. 5, 1895); Fujita, p. 87. The best work in English on Roesler and the Meiji constitution is Johannes Siemes, S.J., "Hermann Roesler's Commentaries on the Meiji Constitution," *Monumenta Nipponica*, 17.1–4:1–66 (1962). Albert Mosse, under whom Itō studied in Berlin and who came to Japan in the spring of 1887, also contributed. Although his replies to questions put to him by the Japanese were first rate, he was somewhat overshadowed by the brilliant Roesler. See Osatake, *Nihon kensei shi taikō*, II, 728; Yoshino, "Gneist, Stein to Itō Hirobumi," p. 66; "Hakushi Roesler shi yuku," p. 148. Other foreigners also participated. One of them, Sir Francis Piggot, describes his experience in his "The Itō Legend," pp. 174–176.

39. In the letter to Matsukata quoted earlier, Itō also wrote: "Because there are still

eight more years before the convoking of the national assembly, I cannot but believe that some disturbances are inevitable, stemming from the impatience of the outs . . . It is human nature to champ at the bit and to want to do something when one is frustrated." Kaneko, *Itō den,* II, 271.

40. Fourteen men in all were appointed to the Bureau for the Study of Administrative Reforms. However, soon after its creation Itō had Inoue, Kaneko, and Itō Miyoji meet separately and secretly after official hours, either at his home or at his official residence. Kaneko recalls that the demand for secrecy made it impossible for them to consult friends and to use clerks for assistants, making their work all the more difficult. Kaneko, "Naikaku seido sōshi tōji no tsuikai," p. 116, and "Nihon kempō seitei no yurai," pp. 18–19. Much of the drafting was done on Natsushima, where Itō had a summer residence. Although escape from Tokyo's humid summer weather was one reason for moving to Natsushima, the island's isolated position off Yokosuka, in Kanagawa, made it ideal from a security standpoint. Kaneko, *Itō den,* II, 577–578; Kaneko Kentarō, *Itō kō wo kataru* (We remember Prince Itō; Tokyo, 1939), pp. 70–71; Kurihara, I, 110–111; Isa, p. 246; "Ko Itō Miyoji haku no dampen: Kempō kisō tōji no kaiko" (A little reminiscing by the late Count Itō Miyoji: Recollections of the time when the constitution was drafted), *Meiji Taishō shi dan,* 1:15 (Feb. 1937). For security measures taken during the Privy Council deliberations, see Kaneko, "Itō kō to kempō seitei jigyō," p. 994, and "Nihon kempō seitei no yurai," pp. 27–28.

41. *Seitetsu yume monogatari* was published in 1887 in this manner and distributed. *Jiyūtō shi,* II, 629; Kaneko, "Teikoku kempō seitei," pp. 25–26; Osatake, *Nihon kensei shi taikō,* II, 684, 750. For a discussion of this "work," which has been of some interest to Japanese historians, see Oka Yoshitake, *Kindai Nihon no keisei* (The building of modern Japan; Tokyo, 1947), pp. 270–271n3; Imanaka Tsugimaro, "*Seitetsu yume monogatari* kaidai" (Explanatory notes on *A dream account of Western philosophy*), in *Meiji bunka zenshū,* rev. ed. (1955), I, 21–26; Yoshino Sakuzō, "Kosho chinchō" (Valuable old works), *Asahi shimbun* (Tokyo, Dec. 9, 1932).

42. Itō may justifiably be designated as the "Great Mediator" of the Meiji era. Pro- and anti-Itō periodicals have frequently pointed to his ability to mediate and to bring together in relative harmony the Meiji oligarchs. See, for example, *Chōya shimbun* (Oct. 15, 1889); *Nichi nichi shimbun* (Jan. 5, 1890); *Nippon* (Sept. 25, 1892); *Ajiya,* Vol. 1, No. 10 (Sept. 1, 1893).

43. Hayashida, *Seikai sokumen shi,* I, 118. (This work is based chiefly on the recollections of Kaneko.) See also Kaneko, *Itō den,* II, 258–262. Cf. Inada, *Meiji kempō,* I, 565–567. The terms "left" and "conservative" are being used advisedly. It is foolhardy to try to pin labels on any major participant or group in the Meiji period. In this instance, Teters suggests the dangers inherent in loosely applying labels when she writes: "What is remarkable is that its [the Genrō-in's] members, for the most part men who not only never participated in the party movement but were deeply opposed to it, tried, not once but twice, to secure a constitution providing for genuine legislative powers for a Diet which would be in part representative of the people and wholly independent of the executive . . . Conservative they were, but, as the story of their activities in and around the Genrō-in discloses, their very conservatism compelled many of the *kokusuishugisha* [participants in the Movement for the Preservation of the National Essence] to develop a constitutional theory which was, in its context, surprisingly liberal." Teters, "The Genrō-in and the National Essence Movement," p. 378.

44. This clash, as we have seen earlier, was reflected even in the use of the Japanese term for constitution. See also Osatake, *Nihon kensei shi,* pp. 318–322. Personal antagonism between Itō and Terajima may also have entered the picture. Ōkuma says that even from the earliest days of the Meiji era, Terajima had constant arguments with Itō and Inoue Kaoru and was always on the receiving end of their teasing. Matsueda, p. 193.

45. Fujii Shin'ichi, p. 227; see also Osatake, *Nihon kensei shi taikō*, II, 667–668.

46. *Ibid.*, II, 668, 758. Terajima himself writes that the Genrō-in had a reputation for being peopled by radical advocates of parliamentarism. And Ōkuma remembers that Terajima, at least after 1881, read the work of the nihilist Mikhail Bakunin. "Terajima Munenori jijoden" (Autobiography of Terajima Munenori), *Denki* (Biography), 3:128 (June 1936); and Matsueda, p. 192. The "conservatives" in government in 1881 also urged that the Genrō-in be given genuine legislative power, and that the elected representatives of this body be permitted to deliberate on the draft constitution. Teters, "Conservative Opposition," pp. 67, 79–84.

47. Kaneko, "Teikoku kempō seitei no yurai," pp. 26–27; Kaneko, *Itō den*, II, 363.

48. Kaneko, "Teikoku kempō seitei no yurai," pp. 27–28. In the August 3, 1882, issue of the Tokyo-Yokohama *Mainichi shimbun*, Kaneko Kentarō, at this time a senior secretary in the Genrō-in, is reported as saying that he believed Japan should not adopt the policies of Bismark. Quoted in Osatake, *Meiji seiji shi tembyō*, p. 289. It seems that anti-Prussian sentiments existed even in Itō's own suite when he went to Europe. He recalls that those in his party who favored the English system were unimpressed by the ideas of Gneist and Stein and made appropriate comments, such as, "this is trite," "there is no use in considering such a point." Itō Hirobumi, "Hompō kempō seitei," p. 540.

49. Osatake, *Nihon kensei shi no kenkyū*, pp. 322–325. On Motoda, see Sansom, *Western World and Japan*, pp. 368, 375.

50. Quoted in Kaneko, *Itō den*, II, 629. See also Suzuki, *Hyōden Itō*, pp. 237–238, 250. Motoda found an ally in the able conservative from Tosa, Sasaki Takayuki, who constantly sought to reduce *hambatsu* power. Teters, "Conservative Opposition," pp. 54–56. Osatake believes that the conflict extended even to the Education Rescript of 1890. He feels that Motoda wanted to enact one great code embracing the constitution and the Education Rescript. Itō naturally opposed this. Although Inoue Kowashi participated in the drafting of the rescript, Osatake suggests that Inoue was an unhappy participant. He feels that the Itō faction not only opposed the plan to include the Education Rescript in the constitution, but was against the rescript itself. Osatake Takeki, "Kempō seitei no ichi katei" (Drafting the imperial constitution), *KGZ*, 58.1:2–13 (1944). Itō told Tokutomi Iichirō that when he realized how influential Motoda was he arrived at an "understanding" with him. Tokutomi, "Sat-Chō jinshi" (The men of Sat-Chō), *CK*, 52.6:310 (1937).

51. Itō Hirobumi: "Teikoku kempō no tokushoku to shinsei no kempō seiji," p. 170; and "Kempō ritsuan no keika to sono riron to no gaisetsu," pp. 194–195. See also Kaneko, *Itō den*, II, 629; Suzuki, *Hyōden Itō*, pp. 237–238, 250.

52. Kaneko does not disclose what the precedent was. He only says that it was found in the Senate Laws of Italy. *Itō Hirobumi hiroku*, p. 149. This preoccupation with finding precedents also lay behind Kaneko's search for precedents for holding Privy Council sessions in secret. See Kaneko, "Nihon kempō seitei no yurai," pp. 25–27; and Ike, *Political Democracy*, p. 179.

53. There were apparently many conflicts of opinion during the Privy Council deliberations. One description reads: "The fiery arguments and the heated debates . . . the extremely intense give and take [in the presence of the emperor] was probably unprecedented and perhaps will never again be repeated." Hijikata and Itō, p. 210. Changes were made in the draft, but, as Osatake says, "the aims of the drafters were fully realized in spite of the few revisions." Kaneko, *Itō den*, II, 625–628; Osatake, *Nihon kensei shi no kenkyū*, pp. 333–335. Kaneko, "Teikoku kempō no seishin kiso," pp. 14–17; Osatake, *Nihon kensei taikō*, II, 782.

54. Although Liang Ch'i-ch'ao belongs to the orthodox school of interpreters of Meiji constitutional history, he anticipated this question. "Although the standard of people's rights in the Japanese constitution does not equal that of the Western constitutions, you can certainly see that the people have accomplished rather a lot in getting them into actual

operation. Some people may doubt this and ask how such an imperially-granted constitution received from above could be that way. But they do not know that its motivation actually came from the people and not from the government." Quoted in George Wilson, p. 201.

55. Teters ("Conservative Opposition," pp. 85–102) discusses the constant opposition to Itō's ideas by the "conservative" members of the Privy Council. They were especially vocal in their attempts to broaden the Diet's powers.

56. The one major effort against the government in this period, as we have seen, was centered around the question of treaty revision. For a description, see Oka, *Kindai Nihon no keisei*, pp. 265–278; Teters, "The Genrō-in and the National Essence Movement," pp. 368, 371–376.

57. Toriumi Yasushi, "Shoki gikai ni okeru Jiyūtō no kōzō to kinō" (The structure and function of the Jiyūtō [Liberal party] in the early Japanese parliament), *RK*, No. 255:7 (July 1961).

58. Ōkuma could have attended either as the foreign minister or as a privy councilor.

59. Kaneko, "Teikoku kempō seitei," p. 38. Osatake has an interesting interpretation of Ōkuma's "dereliction" of duty. He feels that Ōkuma was silent for fear of losing, if he argued with Itō, for he was fully aware that Itō had made a special study of constitutions. Ōkuma, according to Osatake, did not want to lose "prestige." Osatake, *Nihon kensei shi taikō*, II, 784.

CHAPTER V. PREPARING FOR "PARLIAMENTARY" GOVERNMENT

1. See Beasley, p. 91.

2. Dajōkan Orders No. 68–71 established the position of Keeper of the Privy Seal, abolished the Dajōkan, and established the cabinet system. Orders are quoted in Kaneko, *Itō den*, II, 484–486. It should be pointed out that there were several changes in the administrative structure prior to 1885 and that the Dajōkan system described here represents a simplified montage of the system as it existed from 1869.

3. The ubiquitous Dr. Baelz (p. 124) again leaves a revealing glimpse of Meiji political realities: "Yesterday," begins Dr. Baelz's record for May 9, 1909, "we had another meeting at Prince Arisugawa's . . . Itō made a remark which struck me by its extraordinary frankness. Addressing himself to Prince Arisugawa, he said: 'It is really very hard luck to be born a crown prince. Directly he comes into the world he is swaddled in etiquette, and when he gets a little bigger he has to dance to the fiddling of his tutors and advisers.' Thereupon Itō made a movement with his fingers as if he were pulling the strings of a marionette."

4. Sanjō, the *dajōdaijin*, was appointed Lord Keeper of the Privy Seal, and Itō saw to it that he received a life annuity of 5,000 yen to soften the blow of his demotion. Prince Arisugawa, the minister of the Left, was given the rank of chief of the General Staff, an honorary post. Kaneko, *Itō den*, II, 493; *Taruhito nikki*, IV, 343.

5. For discussions of this reform, see Watanabe Ikujirō, "Rikkenteki naikaku seido no sōshi ni tsuite" (On the establishment of the constitutional cabinet system), *Shikan*, 9:82–99 (Feb. 1936); Tsuji, pp. 78–126; Kaneko, *Itō den*, II, 441–486; Inada, *Meiji kempō*, I, 732–761; Beckmann, *Making of the Meiji Constitution*, pp. 75–76.

6. Letter dated January 15, 1886, quoted in Kaneko, *Itō den*, II, 491.

7. There are others who also see in the appointments of Ōkuma in 1888 as foreign minister in Itō's cabinet and Gotō in 1889 as communications minister in Kuroda's cabinet preparatory moves toward the same end. Still others see in these appointments attempts by the oligarchy to split and weaken the opposition. See Shinobu Seizaburō, *Meiji seiji shi* (Meiji political history), 5th ed. (Tokyo, 1955), pp. 8–9; Fukaya Hiroji, "Shoki gikai: Jōyaku kaisei" (The early sessions of the Diet: Treaty revision), Vol. 4 of *Kindai Nihon*

rekishi kōza (Modern Japanese history series; Tokyo, 1940), pp. 98, 175; Oka, *Kindai Nihon no keisei*, pp. 296–297; Hayashida, *Seikai sokumen shi*, I, 146; Ike, *Political Democracy*, pp. 186–187; Scalapino, *Democracy*, pp. 141–142. These conclusions are plausible but still largely conjectural. In Ōkuma's case, the primary aim was to use his talents to handle the thorny treaty-revision problem. See Kaneko, *Itō den*, II, 547–586; Watanabe, *Monjo yori mitaru Ōkuma Shigenobu*, pp. 136–146; Ichijima, II, 77–82. The reasons for offering Gotō a cabinet post, in spite of the many guesses, are still not clear. See, for example, Osatake's views in his *Nihon kensei shi taikō*, II, 813–814, and Ōmachi Keigetsu, *Hakushaku Gotō Shōjirō* (Count Gotō Shōjirō; Tokyo, 1914), pp. 639–640.

8. For a brief sketch of Mutsu in English, see *Far East*, 2:424–428 (Sept. 20, 1897). See also Watanabe Ikujirō, *Mutsu Munemitsu den* (Biography of Mutsu Munemitsu; Tokyo, 1941); and Shinobu Seizaburō, *Mutsu Munemitsu* (Tokyo, 1938).

9. Osatake Takeki, "Mutsu Munemitsu no nyūkaku jijō" (Circumstances surrounding Mutsu Munemitsu's entry into the [Yamagata] cabinet), in his *Meiji Taishō seiji shi kōwa*, pp. 185–186. Some of the dates Osatake gives are erroneous and may prove confusing. The same material by Osatake, in an article in *Meiji bunka*, 16:1–10 (Apr. 1943), contains the same errors.

10. Osatake, "Mutsu Munemitsu no nyūkaku jijō," pp. 186–188; Watanabe, *Mutsu*, pp. 221–222; Shinobu, *Mutsu*, pp. 190–191.

11. Letter from Aoki Shūzō, quoted in Watanabe, *Mutsu*, p. 222.

12. Osatake, "Mutsu Munemitsu no nyūkaku jijō," pp. 190–196; Watanabe, *Mutsu*, pp. 226–229. Cf. *Hara Kei nikki* (Diaries of Hara Kei), ed. Hara Keiichirō (Tokyo, 1950–51), I, 473. Mutsu was also elected a representative from Wakayama in the first general election held in July 1891.

13. Yamagata, according to Tokutomi, was said to have been truly afraid of losing Mutsu to the opposition at this critical time. Tokutomi Iichirō, "Shōsetsu yori kinaru shōgai no Mutsu Munemitsu" (The stranger-than-fiction life of Mutsu Munemitsu), *CK*, 52:283 (Nov. 1937).

14. One of the reasons that Mutsu's predecessor, Iwamura Michitoshi, was selected for the post was that as the elder brother of Hayashi Yūzō, a prominent figure in the defunct Jiyūtō circles, he was in a good position to deal with that "party." Miyake, *Jidai shi*, II, 398.

15. Osatake, "Mutsu Munemitsu no nyūkaku jijō," pp. 185–186. See also Hackett, "Yamagata," p. 210.

16. Kaneko, *Itō den*, II, 707–732.

17. *Ibid.*, II, 731. See also letter from Itō to Kuroda Kiyotaka, dated October 21, 1890, quoted in *Zoku Itō Hirobumi hiroku*, pp. 63–64.

18. Letter dated October 23, 1890, quoted in Kaneko, *Itō den*, II, 731.

19. Kurihara, I, 141; Watanabe Ikujirō, *Meiji tennō no seitoku: Jūshin* (The virtues of the Meiji emperor: His advisers; Tokyo, 1941), p. 264.

20. Usually rendered as "transcendental cabinets."

21. Quoted in Sasuhara, II, 36–37.

22. Quoted in *ibid.*, II, 37–42.

23. This would have Itō speaking on February 13. There is no record of an Itō speech for that date. Kaneko is most likely referring to Itō's speech of February 15.

24. Quoted in Hayashida, *Seikai sokumen shi*, I, 213–214.

25. Kaneko, *Itō wo kataru*, pp. 100–104.

26. Ernest W. Clement and Uyehara Etsujirō, M.P., "Fifty Sessions of the Japanese Imperial Diet," *Transactions of the Asiatic Society of Japan*, 2nd ser., 2:21 (Tokyo, 1925).

27. Osatake, *Nihon kensei shi taikō*, II, 810.

28. Suzuki Yasuzō, for example, writes: "Neither Inoue Kowashi nor Iwakura had any doubts that parties would inevitably emerge under a constitutional system. Their problem was whether or not immediately to make political party power the basis for creating or

dismissing a government administration." Suzuki, *Seitō ron: Seitō to kokuminteki seiji soshiki* (A discourse on political parties: Political parties and their popular political basis; Tokyo, 1943), p. 72. Yamagata, too, never denied the right of parties to exist in a parliamentary system. See Kaneko, *Itō den,* II, 304, and III, 379; Hackett, "Yamagata," pp. 276–278; Inada, *Meiji kempō,* I, 454. See also, views of Toriumi, in his "Shoki gikai ni okeru Jiyūtō kōzō to kinō," pp. 16–17. Scalapino, *Democracy,* p. 88, and n. 131.

29. Inoue Kaoru's conversations with Fukuzawa Yukichi in January 1881 should be recalled, for they show that the three leading figures in the government at that time did not overlook the possibility of such a development.

30. Teter's conservatives, however, disagreed with the oligarchs' view of their role and importance. She writes: "Moreover, the same conservative doctrine of the nature of the nation also provided good reason for opposition to the oligarchy, which was by definition also rule by faction, and for the interests of a single narrow group, rather than the whole nation. The conservative opposition also believed that *hambatsu* role was irresponsible, arbitrary and heedless of the interests of the individual on which national unity also depended on good part." Teters, "Conservative Opposition," p. 3.

31. Speech by Itō before the presidents of the prefectural assemblies, February 15, 1889, quoted in Sasuhara, II, 41. Cf. Scalapino, *Democracy,* p. 153. Inoue Kowashi's remarks on the inevitability of party governments should be recalled.

32. "Inoue is talented, cultured, and has shown himself one of the most capable men in modern Japan . . . He has adapted himself to Western civilization and habits more perfectly than any of his compatriots." Baelz, pp. 65–66. See also Watanabe, *Meiji shi,* p. 137.

33. Quoted in the *Japan Weekly Mail* (Apr. 27, 1889), p. 397.

34. See Osaka *Mainichi shimbun* (Nov. 4 and 5, 1889).

35. See Hackett, "Yamagata," pp. 194, 226.

36. Hara Kei once wrote of Yamagata: "On these points Yamagata greatly differed from Itō. Yamagata had no profound thoughts about the nation or the Imperial House." *Hara nikki,* VI, 307. See also comment by another contemporary, Torio Koyata, quoted in Hayashi Shigeru, "Dai san gikai to dai ichiji Matsukata naikaku no gakai" (The Third Diet and the collapse of the Matsukata cabinet), *KGZ,* 62:30n67 (May 1948).

37. It is very possible that Yamagata clearly foresaw the practical dangers of giving an inch on this vital issue. In a letter written by Yamagata, who was in Europe, to Yoshikawa Kensei and Tanaka Kōken, he observed, "Administrative power is centralized but in practice authority shifts to the legislature." Quoted in Hackett, "Yamagata," p. 177.

38. Speech delivered on June 16, 1899, in Nagoya. Quoted in *Itō zenshū,* II, 305. Hiratsuka reports that when Itō spoke he hardly ever depended on notes. Consequently, most of his speeches contained repetitions of his basic ideas. *Zoku Itō Hirobumi hiroku,* Preface.

39. Quoted in *Itō zenshū,* II, 130.

40. Itō, "Hompō kempō seitei," pp. 542–543.

41. There was a good, but not necessarily controlling reason, for advocating the principle of nonparty cabinets. If the oligarchs at this time maintained connections with an official party, as Inoue Kowashi suggested, this would in effect be admitting that party cabinets were possible then and there. This would have been foolhardy, as there was no guarantee that a government party would be in control after the first election. Moreover, there was also an excellent reason for the government's attitude toward party cabinets. Fukuchi Gen'ichirō, recalling the organization of the Teiseitō, said: "Although the present cabinet does not openly subscribe to the principle of party cabinets, to the extent that it adheres to the same philosophy as does the Rikken teiseitō, it is to all intents and purposes the Rikken teiseitō cabinet." Quoted in Ōtsu, II, 552. The Rikken teiseitō was formed on March 18, 1882 by Fukuchi, Maruyama Masakura of the *Meiji nippō,* and Mizuno Torajirō of the *Tokyo shimpō.* It was an open secret that Itō, Inoue Kaoru, and Yamada Aki-

yoshi were supporters of the party. The Teiseitō was dissolved on September 24, 1883. See Hayashida, *Seitō shi,* I, 175–178, 236; Ōtsu, II, 549–567; Ariiso Itsurō, "Jiyūtō soshikigo no ichinen kan" (The one year after the formation of the Jiyūtō), *CK,* 20.9:50 (1905). Cf. Sakatani, III, 261–263.

42. In 1878 a bureaucrat in the Genrō-in, in justifying the limitation of powers in the prefectural assemblies, wrote: "Naturally, the *fu-ken kai* will frequently [attempt to] discuss matters pertaining to the [central] government. For example, the metropolitan areas or prefectures are responsible for provincial taxes. However, the discussion of provincial taxes [in the provincial assemblies] will inevitably involve questioning the merits or fairness of the taxes. From [this questioning] will arise inquiries about the military system and the census, which is but the first step in meddling in [central] government affairs by the [provincial assemblies]." Quoted in Masumi Junnosuke, Pt. 4: "Chihō ni okeru jitsugyō to seiji" (Provincial economic enterprises and politics), *KGZ,* 73.7–8:3 (1959).

CHAPTER VI. THE CONSTITUTION IN PRACTICE: THE FIRST DIET

1. Hara Kei (Takashi) believed that this was the result of the limited franchise and public apathy. *Hara nikki,* I, 489. For contemporary accounts of the first election in English, see John H. Wigmore, "Starting a Parliament in Japan," *Scribner's Magazine,* 10:33–51 (Jul.–Dec. 1891); H. M. Moore, "The First General Election in Japan," *New Review,* 3:67–75 (Jul. 1890); William E. Griffis, "The Constitution of Japan," *Chautauquan,* 12:591–596 (Feb. 1891). For a comprehensive account of the results of the election, see Suematsu Kenchō, "Nijūsan nen no sō senkyo" (The general election of 1890), *KGZ,* 4.44:555–571 (1890), and 4.45:618–635 (1890). Fukuchi Shigetaka, "Kensei shoki no daigishi no seikaku" (Characteristics of the representatives of the first phase of constitutional government), *Nihon rekishi,* No. 79: 28–33 (Dec. 1954), is in the main a refutation of some of the findings in Suematsu's articles. R. H. P. Mason, "The First Meiji Election," Ph.D. thesis (Australian National University, 1962), is not presently available, but is expected to be published, and should cast much light on this election.

2. Ōtsu Jun'ichirō, the author of the classic *Dai Nihon kensei shi,* was elected from Ibaraki. He divides the "quasi-government party" votes as follows: Taiseikai, 79, and Kokumin Jiyūtō, 5. There were 45 Independents. Ōtsu, III, 542. An extremely helpful source for determining party affiliations is the *Dai ikkai teikoku Gikai yori dai kyūjūnikai teikoku Gikai ni itaru Shūgiin giin tōseki roku* (A record of the party affiliations of members of the House of Representatives from the first to the ninety-second Diets), comp. Shūgiin jimukyoku (Tokyo, 1957).

3. Hackett, "Yamagata," p. 209.

4. Confusion may arise from two different dates which may be given as the beginning of the Diet session. Clement, in his "Table of Sessions of the Diet," in Clement and Uyehara, gives the date as November 29, 1890. See also Yanaga, *Japan since Perry,* p. 216. Uyehara Etsujirō in the "Chronology" in his *The Political Development of Japan, 1867–1909* (London, 1910), cites November 25. See also Scalapino, *Democracy,* p. 154. Uyehara arrives at the earlier date by dating the beginning from the time the Diet is convoked *(shōshū),* while Clement considers the beginning of a session the formal opening ceremony with the emperor in attendance *(kaiin shiki).* Uyehara's practice in his "Chronology" is recommended, since important Diet business, such as the election of officers, is dealt with immediately after the convoking of the Diet. See, for example, *Gikai shi,* I, 417–429; cf. "Gikai shichijūnen no ayumi" (The Diet's seventy years), *Asahi* (Dec. 20, 1960).

5. *Taruhito nikki,* V, 408. Wigmore, "Starting a Parliament," p. 107. Wigmore's article is valuable, not only because he was an eyewitness, but because he was a reporter with a strong sense of history and of the dramatic.

6. Oka Yoshitake, "Teikoku Gikai no kaisetsu" (Inauguration of the Imperial Diet),

KGZ, 58:46 (Jan. 1944); Oka cites one good reason for equating the budget question with the first session. Only six other bills were passed during this session. *Ibid.,* pp. 74–76. See also Tokutomi, *Matsukata,* II, 353; and Ozaki Yukio, "Yosan iinkai no ryaku rekishi" (A short history of the Budget Committee), in *Dai ikki kokkai shimatsu* (The first session of the Diet; Tokyo, 1891), p. 23. This thin volume is one of the richest sources on the first session, with articles by Kaishintō members who participated in it.

7. Oka, *Gikai,* pp. 46–49; Tokutomi, *Matsukata,* II, 355. See also Nakamura Kikuo, "Shoki Gikai to Hoshi Tōru" (Hoshi Tōru and the early sessions of the Diet), *Hōgaku kenkyū,* 27:13–14 (Feb. 1954). A series of three, Nakamura's articles present a readable background of the first through the fifth sessions of the Diet. The Jiyūtō supported the government's program to expand the army and navy, so the cuts were in administrative costs. Cody, p. 232.

8. *Gikai shi,* I, 645; Oka, *Gikai,* p. 51.

9. Quoted in Harold S. Quigley and John E. Turner, *The New Japan: Government and Politics* (Minneapolis, 1956), app. 2: "The Old Constitution of the Empire of Japan," p. 420.

10. Oka, *Gikai,* p. 50. See also "Dai ichi Gikai ni kansuru jakkan no kōsatsu" (Some reflections on the first Diet), *KGZ,* 60:63–78 (Feb. 1946), by the same author, for a discussion of this constitutional problem.

11. Matsukata had, in the meantime, spoken again on February 5. *Dai ikki teikoku Gikai yōroku.* (A record of essential matters in the first Imperial Diet), ed. Ueki Emori (Tokyo, 1891), p. 280—a useful work which classifies events of the first session by subject matter. See also *Gikai shi,* I, 835; Oka, *Gikai,* pp. 52–53. On January 20 the Diet building burned to the ground. The cause was apparently defective wiring. On January 29 the House of Peers began to meet at the Imperial Hotel and the House of Representatives at the former Engineering College (Kōbu daigakkō). Oka, *Gikai,* p. 52; Kaneko, *Itō den,* II, 737; John H. Wigmore, "Parliamentary Days in Japan, with Illustrations," *Scribner's Magazine,* 10:244 (Aug. 1891).

12. *Gikai shi,* I, 879–881; Oka, *Gikai,* p. 54.

13. Letter from Itō Miyoji to Itō, dated February 13, 1891, in Itō Hirobumi, *Hisho ruisan: Teikoku Gikai shiryō* (Classified collection of private papers: Materials on the Imperial Diet; Tokyo, 1934), I, 180. In this letter Itō Miyoji is repeating to Itō what he reported to Yamagata as Itō's original outburst. Hara Kei supports Itō's views. "Of late, the government's attitude toward the Diet has been extremely confused, and its policy pronouncements have always been ill-timed. There is much room for concern about the future. Mutsu [Munemitsu] got up from his sick bed to visit Yamagata to discuss problems, but he still doesn't know what the government's policies are." *Hara nikki,* I, 522.

14. *Gikai shi,* I, 927–928; Oka, *Gikai,* pp. 55–56; Ōtsu, III, 583–587. In an extremely long footnote Oka discusses Yamagata's speech. Oka says that the speech was based on a draft written by Itō Miyoji, and that it must have been written early in February because Yamagata showed the draft to Inoue Kowashi on February 4. In the meantime Yamagata had made his February 10th speech. On February 11 and 12 Itō saw Itō Miyoji and the former had some harsh words about Yamagata. Said Itō: "Recently, I advised the prime minister that to prevent [the nation's] headlong plunge into danger he should unequivocally state what have been the government's fixed and unchanging national policies for the past twenty years. I did so, believing that this would have a most salutary effect. The prime minister did not avail himself of the golden opportunity. Rather, when he did speak, he gave a short, meaningless, valueless, ineffectual speech. He does not make use of the proper medicine at the right time as prescribed by the doctor. The first stage of the illness has passed, and the second stage is rapidly passing, and still he hesitates and doubts the orders of the doctor . . . When opportunity is lost, wrong methods are used, and the patient is on the verge of death, it is then too late." Oka, *Gikai,* pp. 57–62; Itō, *Hisho: Teikoku Gikai,* I, 181–182.

15. *Gikai shi*, I, 928.

16. Itō, *Hisho: Teikoku Gikai*, I, 180–181; Oka, *Gikai*, p. 63; Tokutomi, *Yamagata*, III, 13; Asahina Chisen, *Rōkisha no omoide* (Reminiscences of a veteran newspaperman; Tokyo, 1938), p. 27.

17. Kaneko, *Itō den*, II, 270; Oka, *Gikai*, pp. 65–66.

18. Oka, *Gikai*, pp. 64–77; Ikeda Nagauma (Eima?), *Kensei to Tosa* (Tosa and constitutional government; Kōchi, 1941), pp. 30–31; Nakayama Yoshisuke, II, 139–142, 151. As early as 1884 Itagaki pledged that if in 1890 the rough and radical members of the Jiyūtō were to attack the government without any thought of compromise he would control them and make their behavior conform to the demands of constitutional government. Masumi, Pt. 2, p. 7.

19. *Nichi nichi shimbun* (Feb. 20, 1891).

20. Oka, *Gikai*, pp. 67–68; Ōtsu, III, 589–590; Itō, *Hisho: Teikoku Gikai*, I, 121–123; *Gikai shi*, I, 972–976.

21. See, for example, Kojima Tokumi, "Meiji Taishō seitō hattatsu shi ron" (A discourse on the development of political parties in the Meiji and Taishō eras), *Taiyō*, 33:86 (Mar. 1927); Ōtsu, III, 597; Kudō I, 355–356; Scalapino, *Democracy*, p. 157 and n. 23.

22. Oka, *Gikai*, p. 68. See also Saiga, pp. 572–576; Cody, p. 232. There seems to be one piece of indirect evidence that bribery may have been used sometime during the first session. In a letter to Itō, dated December 12 (probably in 1891), Mutsu spoke of "the customary method of corruption" with which the government hopes to inveigle the Diet members, and he expressed fears that this method would prove effective "in this session." Quoted in "Itō monjo," 52:190.

23. See letter from Mutsu to Matsukata, dated February 24, 1891, quoted in Tokutomi, *Matsukata*, II, 370; Shinobu, *Mutsu*, p. 195. See also Ōtsu, III, 596.

24. *Gikai shi*, I, 1072; Oka, *Gikai*, p. 73; Tokutomi, *Yamagata*, III, 17–18. For an excellent account of factionalism in the Jiyūtō, see Masumi Junnosuke, Pt. 3: "1890 nendai no seitō soshiki" (Party organizations in the 1890's), *KGZ*, 74.5–6:59–65 (1959).

25. Griffis provides perspective on the matter of corruption when he states that Hoshi Tōru learned his lessons in the United States. Griffis, "Development of Political Parties," p. 685.

26. Linebarger, Djang, and Burks, p. 407.

27. Article LXIV, quoted in Quigley and Turner, p. 420.

28. Itō appears to have contradicted himself when he ordered the consecutive dissolutions of the fifth and the sixth sessions of the Diet. These dissolutions were only indirectly related to constitutional questions. The reason for Itō's actions is discussed in Chap. VIII.

29. Letter dated December 14, 1890, quoted in Hackett, "Yamagata," pp. 220–221.

30. "Mainly as a result of the Sino-Japanese War and the growing armament and colonial enterprises which followed in its wake, the expenditures of the national government tripled from 1893 to 1903." William W. Lockwood, *The Economic Development of Japan: Growth and Structural Change, 1868–1938* (Princeton, 1954), p. 35. Compare the problem of the Tokugawa rulers, as described by John W. Hall, with the budget problem faced by the Meiji oligarchs. Hall, *Tanuma Okitsugu: Forerunner of Modern Japan* (Cambridge, Mass. 1955), pp. 5–6. Even without an expanding budget the government would suffer if a budget was not passed by the Diet and the previous year's budget had to be used. This argument was presented by Minoura Katsundo, another participant in the first session. His reasoning was: The Finance Law strictly stipulated that the respective ministries could not spend money for any other purpose than that for which the money was specifically appropriated. The aims and structure of each year's budget differed from year to year, and what was considered important one year might not seem so in another year. Hence the government, when it chose or was forced to use the previous year's budget, would often find that it would have money to spare for activities it considered not vital, while it faced

fiscal starvation for critical projects. See his "Zennendo no yosan wo shikō suru rigai" (The pros and cons of carrying over the previous year's budget), in *Dai ikki kokkai shimatsu,* pp. 89–98.

31. See, for example, McLaren, *Political History,* p. 212; Robert K. Reischauer, *Japan: Government-Politics* (New York, 1939), p. 112; Hayashida, *Seitō shi,* I, 383.

32. Ike, *Political Democracy,* p. 188. See also Hugh Borton, *Japan's Modern Century* (New York, 1955), p. 143. Scalapino tends toward this point of view, though less positively. For example, he cites Suzuki Yasuzō's view that the nine years between the announcement that a constitution would be granted and its actual promulgation gave the government nine vital years "to mold the interpretation of the document so as to freeze the status quo." Scalapino, *Democracy,* pp. 86–87n129; see also his comments on pp. 86–87, 149–151. Cf. Robert A. Scalapino and Masumi Junnosuke, *Parties and Politics in Contemporary Japan* (Berkeley and Los Angeles, 1962), p. 13.

33. *Japan Weekly Mail* (Apr. 20, 1889), p. 380. Fukuzawa Yukichi also was of the opinion that party cabinets were inevitable, particularly after "second generation" statesmen who could not boast of meritorious services to their country took over from the oligarchs. See *Zoku Fukuzawa zenshū* (Collected works of Fukuzawa, second series), ed. Iwanami Shigeo (Tokyo, 1933), II, 617–619. See also *Jiji shimpō* (May 28, 1890 and Apr. 26, 1891).

34. *Yūbin hōchi shimbun* (Jan. 9, 1891). Inoue is said to have made the statement in the spring of 1888. A little over a year later he stated: "When the Diet is inaugurated its members will deliver their opinions in the halls of the Diet. It is clear that the government will be forced to adopt policies which do not run counter to public opinion. Public opinion is basically the opinion of a political party which holds a numerical majority in the Diet. It was for this reason that I said that it would be impossible for the cabinet to stand entirely aloof from political parties. On the other hand, insofar as one faces the Diet in one's capacity as state minister, it may not be impossible for one's views to be passed whether or not one is a leader of a political party." *Osaka mainichi* (Nov. 5, 1889). See also Teters, "Conservative Opposition," p. 110.

35. On the other hand, government supporters were nearly always in an unenviable position. Katō Seinosuke, describing a period slightly later than the time under consideration, recalled: "Those who belonged to government parties were extremely unpopular. There were incredible stories to the effect that [members of government parties] would wait for dark and cover their heads with hoods when they visited a state minister's residence. Even those who were disinterested felt sorry for the way government party men were rejected by the people." Quoted in *Itō Hirobumi hiroku,* p. 122. On June 25, 1892, Hara Kei was asked to join the Kokumin kyōkai, a quasi-government party. Hara refused on the ground that, "these parties never succeed." *Hara nikki,* II (a), 45. For other comments on the status of government parties in the eyes of the public, see Ōkuma, "Nihon no seitō," p. 140; Suzuki, *Jiyū minken,* p. 90.

36. *Chōya shimbun* (Jan. 13, 1892). See also editorial in *Japan Weekly Mail* (Feb. 4, 1893), p. 136; Ōkuma, "Nihon no seitō," pp. 140–141; Masumi, "1890 nendai no seitō soshiki," p. 72n4; Kaneko, *Kempō seitei to Ōbei no hyōron,* pp. 173–174.

37. Joseph L. Sutton, *A Political Biography of Inukai Tsuyoshi,* University Microfilms Publication 8421 (Ann Arbor, 1954).

38. *Ibid.,* pp. 252–256. For a description of the time, effort, and money present-day Japanese politicians expend to win elections, see Kiyoaki Murata, "Cultivating the Constituency," *Japan Times* (Oct. 31, 1963).

39. Sutton, p. 59. Uyehara says that this is the most effective method in Japan because "Japanese are easily moved by sentiment." Uyehara, *Political Development,* p. 272.

40. Sutton, pp. 61–62 *et passim.*

41. The *eta* served as bodyguards, and later, with universal suffrage, as a source of votes. *Ibid.*, p. 119.

42. *Ibid.*, p. 121.

43. Reading the *Gikai shi* would bear out this point. One source gives the following figures for those in the first Diet who had previously served in the prefectural assemblies. Of the 300 representatives, 134 were former members; of this number, 28 were presidents, and 12 served as vice-presidents. Wigmore, "Parliamentary Days," p. 246. See also Scalapino and Masumi, p. 11. The assemblymen mixed business with pleasure. In Saitama, many an assemblyman, finding things dull in Urawa city after assembly hours, would rush off to the Yoshiwara district of Tokyo. When the provincial officials wanted their bills passed, they would round up the representatives from their favorite brothels, take them to a "teahouse," and ply them with women and sake. But this tactic notwithstanding, the representatives "firmly maintained their integrity (!)" and either revised or rejected most of the bills. Masumi, "1880 nendai no fu-ken kai," p. 7.

44. Hackett, "Yamagata," pp. 171–172. See also McLaren, *Political History,* pp. 132 and 147; Linebarger, Djang, and Burks, p. 356.

45. McLaren, *Political History,* pp. 130–131. Osatake Takeki cites the example of Nagasaki where no one opposed the prefectural governor when he decided that Matsuda Masahisa was to be president of the assembly. However, once Matsuda assumed office, the Nagasaki Prefectural Assembly ceased being simply an organ of inquiry, and even the governor was "treated as a child" by Matsuda. Osatake, *Nihon kensei shi taikō,* II, 513. See also "The Japanese Constitutional Crisis and the War," p. 460; *Japan Weekly Mail* (Dec. 22, 1900), p. 645; and the Tokyo *Nichi nichi* (Jan. 14, 1887). Masumi states that the roots of the antagonism displayed by the assemblies lay in the reason for establishing them—which was to make it easier for the government to collect taxes. Masumi also divides the 1880's into two periods. The first half was characterized by general antipathy toward the prefectural authorities by the assembly members. In the second half, while antigovernment sentiment persisted, there was a trend toward a split among the assembly members along pro- and antiprefectural government lines. Masumi, "1880 nendai no fu-ken kai," pp. 2–4.

46. "Since this was the first constitutional regime not conducted by the white race, and because this [was destined] to destroy the proud boast that only the white race was capable of carrying out constitutional government, a seriousness [about making the experiment succeed] permeated the entire nation, so as to prevent [Japan's] being laughed at by foreigners." Osatake, *Meiji Taishō seiji shi,* p. 90. The concern over "face" was also evident in the years immediately preceding the Restoration. In point 6 of an 1867 agreement between Tosa and Satsuma are the words: "We should establish national principles for which we will not need to feel shame in the light of customs elsewhere in the world." Quoted in Jansen, *Sakamoto Ryōma,* p. 301. Jansen perceptively points out that "many of the values and some of the language, of the later Meiji government," were expressed by both the last shōgun, Keiki, and the men who opposed him. See *ibid.,* p. 228n40 and p. 302.

47. *Hōchi shimbun's* statement on the subject (Nov. 29, 1890) is representative: "Is not this a happy event of which we in this country may well be proud before all the countries in the world? . . . This is a memorable day, for we have received the light of constitutional government before hundreds of millions of people in the many countries in the Orient. This is a memorable day, because we can prove to Europe and America that constitutional government is not a product peculiar to the West and that it can be established without bloody conflicts." See also Itō's speech in the House of Peers, 1891, quoted in Kaneko, *Itō den,* II, 741–742; Itō's speech at Ōtsu, 1898, quoted in *Japan Weekly Mail* (May 4, 1898), p. 432.

48. Quoted in Uyehara, *Political Development,* pp. 220–221. Matsukata's February 16 speech, quoted earlier, should be recalled. See also Asahina, pp. 24–25 and Saiga, p. 570. National pride, of course, was also expressed in a more virulent manner. Sir Francis

Piggot remembered: "And here is a curious illustration of this nationalist spirit. If this unfortunate translation [into English] of the Constitution is criticized, the ready answer of youthful officials today is . . . 'Well, it does not much matter. What has been done for the foreigner is quite sufficient. Japan is for the Japanese.'" Piggot, "New Japan," *Fortnightly Review,* LII (New series), 52.309:337.

49. Quoted in *KGZ,* 13.154:6 (1899).

50. Cody, pp. 173–174; see also pp. 176, 221, 224, 230–231, 250–251. See also Jansen, *Sakamoto Ryōma,* p. 368, Perry, pp. 163–164.

51. In a letter to Itō, Inoue Kaoru cautioned him against carelessly mentioning Yamagata's "weak points" in "light banter with followers and others," because there was a possibility of misunderstanding when this got back to Yamagata. Letter dated June 13, 1892, in "Itō monjo," 16:388b.

52. Ozaki Yukio had this to say about the relationship between the two men: "They constantly fought each other, and there was unending friction. Friends on the surface, bitter enemies below the surface . . . [One day] Yamagata and I were reminiscing. Yamagata was using extremely honorific terminology with a great deal of feeling. I thought that he was speaking about the former emperor. However, on listening closely, I was surprised to note that Yamagata was talking about a clash with Itō. He must have used honorific language on purpose to convey a sense of ridicule." Ozaki Yukio, *Minken tōsō shichijūnen* (My seventy-year struggle for democracy; Tokyo, 1952), pp. 33–34.

53. Scalapino, *Democracy,* p. 117. The following remarks on the state of contemporary American politics may be relevant. "Who, then, does run American politics? Not party leaders, but office holders and office seekers who achieve power through their personal followings rather than their party power . . . They are far more dedicated to their leader than to their party, for they will advance as their leader advances, even though the party as a whole declines . . . We lack popular control of the policy-making process. Our splintered parties set up barriers between the people and their governments rather than simplifying the alternatives, clarifying competing doctrines, and allowing the victorious majority to govern." James MacGregor Burns, "Two-Party Stalemate: The Crisis in Our Politics," *Atlantic* (Feb. 1960), pp. 40–41.

54. "The friction within the Meiji government stemmed from the propensity of cabinet members to adhere feudalistically to their own spheres of influence. This had been the situation since the Restoration. The aim of the cabinet system created by Itō was to unify and strengthen the cabinet and to eliminate these conflicts. However, because [Itō] created it merely to give the government a modern appearance without infusing it with a democratic foundation, he was unable to root out this deeply entrenched tendency toward factionalism." Hattori and Irimajiri, I, 180.

55. Oka states that the fact that Yamagata asked Itō Miyoji to soften the text of the February 16 speech indicates that Yamagata was hopeful of an amicable solution. Oka, *Gikai,* p. 66. Tokutomi says that Matsukata from the beginning wanted to compromise. Tokutomi, *Matsukata,* II, 368. And, as stated earlier, Itō encouraged compromise on the budget issue.

56. Suzuki, *Jiyū minken,* pp. 233–235; see also Ōe Taku, "Seikai kaiko dan" (Recollections of the political world), *Taiyō,* 13:175–176 (Feb. 1907). Mutsu Munemitsu, always close to those in this group, and Hara Kei also gave the same rationale for joining the government. Maeda Renzan, *Hoshi Tōru den* (A biography of Hoshi Tōru; Tokyo, 1948), pp. 201–202, 230; Fukuchi Shigetaka, *Shizoku to samurai ishiki,* pp. 194–202, esp. p. 199.

57. "Ōkuma always said that Itō was a coward. I do not know whether Itō was a coward, but he was extremely prudent, thorough and conciliatory. He hated to do things by fighting with people . . . He tried to accomplish everything with as much harmony as possible." Watanabe, *Meiji shi,* p. 165.

58. Hackett, "Yamagata," p. 316, also p. 208.

59. *Japan Weekly Mail* (Apr. 20, 1889), p. 381.

60. *Chōya shimbun* (Nov. 28, 1890). That *Chōya* could be so positive in its views may be traced to the fact that the leaders of the opposition parties, after all, were themselves members of the government in the decade 1871–1881.

CHAPTER VII. ITŌ AND YAMAGATA: THE NATURE AND ROLE OF PARTIES

1. For reasons for Yamagata's action, see Tokutomi, *Yamagata,* III, 34–37; Rōyama, p. 275; Yamada Tokazō, "Shimbunshi yori mitaru Nihon ni okeru naikaku seiritsu no keishiki" (The formation of the cabinet in Japan as seen through the newspapers), *KGZ,* 38.4:52 (1924).

2. Kaneko, *Itō den,* II, 747, 752.

3. *Ibid.,* II, 752–753. Saigō can justly lay claim to the title "Jester of the Meiji oligarchy." He went to exhaustive lengths to play practical jokes on his colleagues. His carefree and irresponsible attitude extended to his official life, preventing him, for extended periods of time, from performing even the nominal duties of his offices. Hence, it is possible that the offer of the prime ministry at this time was not a real offer. Tokutomi says that the emperor never considered Saigō for the position of prime minister, a euphemism for rejection by the top advisers to the emperor. Saigō's lighthearted approach to his official and nonofficial duties may be another reason for the decline in Satsuma fortunes. Tokutomi, "Sat-Chō jinshi," p. 304; Kurihara, I, 112–113; Komatsu, pp. 134–140; Mizuno Rentarō, "Rekidai naisō no omokage" (Images of several home ministers), *CK,* 49.11:152–157 (1934).

4. Kaneko, *Itō den,* II, 752–754; Hayashida, *Seitō shi,* I, 477; Tokutomi, *Matsukata,* II, 375–376. The formation of the Matsukata cabinet also marked the beginning in a publicly recognizable form of the "Conference of Elder Statesmen" (Genrō kaigi). The participants at this time were usually Itō, Yamagata, Kuroda, Inoue Kaoru, Saigō, Ōyama Iwao, and Yamada Akiyoshi. They met whenever a cabinet appeared to need "advice and guidance," as well as when a new cabinet had to be formed. The Matsukata cabinet was dubbed the "Behind-the-Scenes Cabinet" *(Kuromaku naikaku)* because of the support it received from the elder statesmen. Tanaka Sōgorō, *Jūshin ron* (On the elder statesmen), Vol. 4 of Hori Makoto, comp., *Gendai Nihon seiji kōza* (Lectures on recent Japanese politics; Tokyo, 1941–1942), p. 70; Kaneko, *Itō den,* II, 774; Ōkuma, "Nihon seitō ron," p. 143.

5. With the ouster of Ōkuma from the government in 1881, only members of two of the four major han that played crucial roles in the Meiji Restoration remained to monopolize all the key positions. The Sat-Chō clique was for all practical purposes the Meiji government, and members from these two competing and highly jealous han worked out a *modus vivendi* which may be described as "maintaining the Sat-Chō balance." Simply stated, this involved a distribution of political power between Satsuma and Chōshu that was as equitable, practical, and face-saving as possible. The pressures compelling this political balancing act were manifold. In part they were: the conviction, as voiced by Kabayama, that the Sat-Chō were primarily responsible for the Meiji Restoration and alone capable of directing Japan's destiny; the subordination of their jealousy of each other to their greater jealousy of the other han; the watchfulness of the lower echelon Sat-Chō bureaucrats, who realized that the breakdown of the "balance" would seriously affect their own positions.

6. *Jiji shimpō* (Nov. 1, 1889).

7. This incident also raises doubts about the fairly widely held belief that it was only after the promulgation by Yamagata of Imperial Ordinances 193 and 194 in 1900 that the military was given the weapons to prevent any cabinet from being formed.

8. For example, in the draft constitution, a clause of Article XII read, "The composition *(hensei)* of the Army and Navy will be fixed by imperial ordinance." Ōyama opposed

this clause on the ground that imperial ordinances were drafted by the cabinet and then presented to the emperor for sanction. He further reasoned that if the time came when party cabinets were formed, this would permit the party in power to determine the composition of the armed forces. Consequently, the wording was changed to "The composition of the Army and Navy will be fixed by imperial decision." Itō later suggested adding the words "as well as the number of permanent personnel in the armed forces." In this manner the cabinet was bypassed on matters affecting the composition of the armed forces. Kaneko, "Teikoku kempō no seishin kiso," pp. 14–17.

9. Kaneko, *Itō den*, II, 788–790; see also Hattori and Irimajiri, I, 180–181.

10. Tokyo *Nichi nichi* (May 6, 1891), quoted in Yamada, pp. 53–54. See also Fukaya Hiroji, "Dai ichiji Matsukata naikaku no Seimubu mondai no temmatsu" (An account of the question of the Political Affairs Bureau of the first Matsukata cabinet), in Osatake Takeki, ed., *Meiji bunka no shin kenkyū* (New studies in Meiji civilization; Tokyo, 1944), pp. 421–423.

11. *Ibid.*, pp. 440, 447.

12. *Ibid.*, p. 423; Kaneko, *Itō den*, II, 778. See *ibid.*, II, 1048–1054 for a reproduction of the document in full.

13. *Ibid.*, II, 779; *ibid.*, II, 1055–59 has the text in full. One of the primary aims of the "Covenant" was to stop cabinet ministers from attacking each other in newspapers and magazines. Itō Miyoji, for example, in a letter to Itō, mentions bitter attacks against Mutsu by a newspaper supporting Shinagawa Yajirō, the home minister. "Itō monjo," 26:168.

14. Shinagawa, of Chōshū, represented Yamagata's influence in the Matsukata cabinet, just as Mutsu served as Itō's representative. See Hackett, "Yamagata," pp. 224, 220–231; Isa, pp. 440–441.

15. Letter quoted in Watanabe, *Mutsu*, pp. 243–245.

16. Letter from Itō Miyoji to Itō, dated August 13, 1891, quoted in *ibid.*, pp. 243–245. Mutsu had earlier been handpicked for the post by Itō himself. The fact that Shinagawa was given the "privilege" of explaining the document and recommending Mutsu indicates the lengths to which the Meiji oligarchs went to maintain each others' political "face."

17. Kaneko, *Itō den*, II, 780; *Hara nikki*, II(a), 16.

18. Quoted in Kaneko, *Itō den*, II, 785–788. Hara records three reasons for Mutsu's resignation: (1) cabinet ministers did not comply with the agreements; (2) any attempt to enforce the agreements strictly would have meant splitting the cabinet; (3) the cabinet ministers refused to disclose the expenditures of their secret funds. *Hara nikki*, II(a), 17.

19. Letter dated November 3, 1891, paraphrased in Watanabe, *Mutsu*, pp. 250–251.

20. Watanabe, *Meiji shi*, pp. 183–184. Itō went to Yamaguchi ostensibly to participate in commemorative activities for the former lord of the Chōshū han. He left Yamaguchi on November 14. Kaneko, *Itō den*, II, 795–796.

21. Quoted in *ibid.*, II, 822–823. Some have seen in Itō's plan to form a party a radical departure in thinking. Isa, for example, writes: "For a person who formerly hated parties as something abhorrent, and who could only conceive of those who espoused people's rights as dissatisfied ruffians, it was an amazing step to take." Isa, p. 455.

22. Letter to Tokudaiji Sanenori, quoted in Kaneko, *Itō den*, II, 809–811.

23. Itō's remarks were in reply to a letter from Tokudaiji dated December 26, 1892, and are quoted in *ibid.*, II, 820–821. Ōkuma substantiates Itō's diagnosis of the weakness of the government's position: "The reason the cabinets were unsettled and unstable in the past was the lack of unity among the cabinet members. Therefore, the weakness of the cabinet, was rooted, not in attacks from without, but in internal disunity." Quoted in Ichijima II, 219.

24. Kaneko, *Itō den*, II, 823. However, he was not completely alone. Mutsu, Minister of Justice Tanaka Fujimaro and Privy Councilor Kōno Togama supported Itō. *Ibid.*, II, 831.

25. Quoted in *ibid.*, II, 823–825.

26. Quoted in *ibid.*, II, 825.

27. *Ibid.*, II, 826.

28. *Ibid.*, II, 827–830. In the meantime, the second session of the Diet had been convoked on November 21, 1891. The Lower House was dissolved on December 25, 1891, over the issue of budget reductions.

29. The emperor himself also purportedly expressed hopes that "good subjects" would be elected. See letter from Tokudaiji to Itō, dated December 26, 1891, quoted in *ibid.*, II, 818–819. Certain leftist interpreters believe, as does Inoue Kiyoshi, that "It was definitely not a suggestion from below, and was something the emperor himself thought up." Inoue Kiyoshi, *Nihon seiji fuhai shi* (A history of the corruption in Japanese political life; Tokyo, 1948), p. 52; see also Hattori and Irimajiri, I, 182. Inoue, Hattori, and Irimajiri put much too great an emphasis on the emperor's role in decision-making. Baelz reveals an incident which indicates that the emperor, at least in this instance, could not even make a decision affecting his personal relationship with the empress. "The Emperor," writes Baelz (p. 97), "could not endure that the Empress' throne should be as lofty as his. He wanted a higher one, but Inoue protested. When Inoue, paying a casual visit to the palace, found that a thick silken mat had been smuggled beneath the emperor's throne, he dragged it out and flung it into the corner of the room, which naturally led to a great row." (Tokyo, June 6, 1891).

30. Yanaga, *Japan since Perry*, p. 218. For eyewitness accounts of the interference in Okayama, see Inukai Ken, "Kokkai senkyo jishi" (The early elections for the National Diet), *CK*, 49.6:139–151 (June 1934); see also Shibuya Sasuke, *Taketomi Tokitoshi* (Tokyo, 1934), pp. 132–134. Apart from the positive opposition of the government, Ozaki Yukio remembers that he ran under the added handicap of being a Diet member who had been "admonised by the emperor" *(chokkan giin)*. Ozaki, *Minken tōsō*, p. 81. Furthermore, balloting was open and the name of the candidate had to be written out in the presence of a government official. Sutton, pp. 84–85; Wigmore, "Starting a Parliament," p. 106.

31. Quoted in Tokutomi, *Matsukata*, II, 432. Shinagawa's prediction was fully borne out by the final casualty figures compiled by the government. Twenty-five were reported killed and 388 injured. It is said that many did not report deaths or injuries because they feared possible government action against them. Hayashida believes that if the real figures were compiled, they would be "shockingly high." Hayashida, *Seitō shi*, I, 337; see also Hattori and Irimajiri, I, 182.

32. Letter to Matsukata, dated February 15, 1891, quoted in Tokutomi, *Matsukata*, II, 434. Hara Kei recorded that when the election results were known the number of representatives from the opposition parties reportedly was unexpectedly large. *Hara nikki*, II(a), 33.

33. Ōtsu, III, 683–684. See also Sekiyama Naotarō, "Meiji nijūgonen goro no seitōin sōshi no kazu" (The number of strong-armed men and party members around 1892), *Meiji bunka*, 5:52 (Sept. 1929).

34. For example, *Kokkai* (Feb. 17, 1892), after the results of the election were finally known, declared that it knew positively of two cases in Tokyo alone where election interference by officials prejudiced the cause of "moderate" candidates.

35. Even when the debate over Itō's plan to form a party was most intense, mention was made of "compromise with Ōkuma's party and others." Letter from Inoue Kaoru to Itō, January 26, 1892, quoted in Kaneko, *Itō den*, II, 824. Though this possibility was expressed with some distaste by Inoue, it is of interest that he made the statement at all.

36. The *Japan Weekly Mail* (Nov. 26, 1892), p. 649, commenting on the Kokumin kyōkai, organized by Shinagawa with Yamagata's blessing, pointed out: "A Cabinet relying on the support of an openly organized political party is as much a party Cabinet

as a Cabinet which acknowledges itself liable to be driven out of office by the vote of a hostile majority in the House of Representatives."

37. Hackett, "Yamagata," p. 226.

38. Yamagata is credited with the following prediction: "The origin of the new regime and the spirit of the Constitution are all against the introduction of party politics; if ever a party Government is formed, our country will, I am sure, go the way of Spain or Greece." Idditti, p. 323.

39. This was at a meeting of the elder statesmen at Matsukata's official residence on February 23, 1892. Kaneko, Itō den, II, 831–832.

40. Mutsu, writing to Itō on June 5, 1892, said: "I believe that the time is not too far removed when 'great ability' will be required." "Itō monjo," 51:69b; see also Kaneko, Itō den, II, 841.

41. Shinagawa's biographer says that prior to the election Shinagawa issued secret orders to the prefectural authorities ordering them to take measures so that "representatives loyal to the nation are elected, and that destructive people are not." The biographer adds, however, that he personally has not seen these instructions. Okutani Matsuji, Shinagawa Yajirō den (Biography of Shinagawa Yajirō; Tokyo, 1940), p. 282. See also Tagawa Daikichirō, "Yamagata ni taishite omou tokoro" (In thinking about Yamagata), CK, 25.10:66 (1910); and Hackett, "Yamagata," pp. 229–231; Kaneko, Itō den, II, 832; Tokutomi, Matsukata, II, 437–438; Kurihara, I, 162.

42. Tokutomi, Matsukata, II, 438–443, 447; Kaneko, Itō den, II, 834.

43. Hara Kei records that the reasons for Mutsu's resignation were his opposition to election interference and conflicts with Shinagawa over how to deal with the Diet. Hara nikki, I, 36. Itō Miyoji reported to Itō that Mutsu's determination to fix blame for the interference was so strong that he was causing Matsukata some anxiety. Letter dated February 29, 1892 in "Itō monjo," 26:138b. Itō Miyoji himself disapproved of election interference. The sentiments of these two clearly reflect the strong position Itō took on this matter. Ibid., 31:740.

44. Soejima was close to Itagaki as well as to Ōkuma. Kōno was an old and trusted friend of Ōkuma. Isa, pp. 456–457, 467; see also, Hayashida, Seitō shi, I, 351.

45. Gikai shi, I, 1797, 1564–68, 1831–57, 1891–99; Kaneko, Itō den, II, 838–839; Tokutomi, Matsukata, II, 452–454.

46. Hayashi, KGZ, 62:16–22 LXII (Apr. 1948). This is the first of a series of five articles, which constitute the most exhaustive study of the subject.

47. Inoue Kaoru, writing at a slightly later date, pointed out to Itō that the Jiyūtō and Kaishintō both suffered from intimidation by non-Diet members. Letter dated February 16 (1893), "Itō monjo," 16:399. For a discussion of the non-Diet member group in the Jiyūtō, see Masumi, "1890 nendai no seitō soshiki," pp. 49–59.

48. Itagaki was elected party president at this meeting, but his elevation actually was a victory for the rising Hoshi Tōru. One of the most colorful, complex, and important politicians in modern Japan, Hoshi has actually received little critical attention from either Japanese or Westerners, granted the existence of several biographies and articles in Japanese. This represents a serious gap in our understanding and appreciation of the beginnings of the party system in Japan. Masumi sheds some needed light on Hoshi in ibid., pp. 66–71.

49. It is worth repeating, however, that Itagaki also wanted to see the constitutional experiment succeed because "Confusion, disorder and dissolution of the Diet would bring discredit to Japan . . . " Cody, p. 224. Masumi analyzes the Hoshi-Ōi rivalry in "1890 nendai no seitō soshiki," pp. 62–63. For a good sketch of the background, ideas, and activities of Ōi, see, Marius B. Jansen, The Japanese and Sun Yat-sen (Cambridge, Mass., 1954), pp. 41–48; also Jansen's "Ōi Kentarō," pp. 307–316.

50. Nakamura Kikuo, "Shoki gikai to Hoshi Tōru," Pt. I, pp. 16–17. See letter from Suematsu to Itō, dated May 15, 1892, in "Itō monjo," 47:85–89b.

51. Letters from Suematsu to Itō, dated May 17 and 20, 1892, in *ibid.*, 47:77–79b, and 48:134.

52. The editorial, however, voiced the "hard" line. This, according to Hayashi, indicated a policy split in the Jiyūtō. For a full discussion of the efforts of the moderate faction in the Jiyūtō, see Hayashi, *KGZ*, 62:22–30 (Apr. 1948). On May 21 Itō Miyoji wrote Itō that the Jiyūtō members did not forcefully seek to carry out the resolution they had voted for "the other day." "Itō monjo," 29:524–525b. See also Cody, pp. 239–243.

53. Letter from Yamagata to Itō, dated May 18, 1892, quoted in Hayashi, *KGZ*, 62:20n5 (Apr. 1948). See also *ibid.*, Pt. 2, in *KGZ*, 62:29 (May 1948).

54. Itō also believed that the opposition parties were in a mood to compromise. *Ibid.*, Pt. 2, pp. 29–30, 34–35.

55. Letter from Itō Miyoji to Itō, dated May 21, 1892, in "Itō monjo," 2:524b. See also Kamiya Takuo, *Konoe Kazan kō* (Prince Konoe Kazan; Tokyo, 1924), pp. 51–55.

56. Hayashi, Pt. 3, in *KGZ*, 62:23–39 (Oct. 1948). Tokutomi, *Matsukata*, II, 455–478. Shirane Sen'ichi, vice-home minister and closely linked with Yamagata and Shinagawa, was angered by the rapprochement between the government and the Jiyūtō. He threatened to resign because of it. Government supporters in the Diet also were disturbed and considered withdrawing support. The resignation of Home Minister Soejima Taneomi, one of the key figures in the government-Jiyūtō negotiations, apparently appeased government supporters. Hayashi, Pt. 3, pp. 23–39; *Hara nikki*, II(a), 44.

57. Kaneko, *Itō den*, II, 847–852. One suspects that Yamagata was reciprocating Itō's reluctance to serve as president of the House of Peers during the first Yamagata ministry. Hayashi believes that Yamagata finally consented to join the cabinet because a split between Itō and himself would only invite public comment and expose them to ridicule. Hayashi, Pt. 4, in *KGZ*, 62:39 (Nov. 1948). Hayashi discusses the abortive plan to have Itō succeed Matsukata, (*ibid.*, pp. 31–51).

58. Kaneko, *Itō den*, II, 858–859. Hayashi is not too clear in explaining why Takashima, Kabayama, and Ōki opposed the inclusion of Inoue Kaoru in the proposed Itō cabinet, which was one concrete reason for Itō's troubles. See letter from Itō Miyoji to Itō, dated July 10, 1892, in Hayashi, Pt. 4, p. 51n177. See also Sakatani, IV, 193.

59. Kōno attached certain conditions before he accepted. One was that the Kokumin kyōkai be recognized as a political party and be subject to the same controls as the opposition parties. Another was the transfer of the troublesome vice-home minister, Shirane. Still another was a free hand to deal severely with the prefectural governors who had "instilled bad feelings" among the people under their jurisdiction. Hayashi, Pt. 5, in *KGZ*, 63:79 (Mar. 1949). See also the *Japan Weekly Mail* (June 11, 1892), p. 779; *Kokumin shimbun* (June 8, 1892).

60. Gotō Shōjirō worked for Kōno's appointment as home minister. Gotō's hand may also be seen in the conditions Kōno attached before accepting. Hayashi, Pt. 5, p. 79.

61. *Ibid.*, pp. 86–87; Kaneko, *Itō den*, II, 859; *Japan Weekly Mail* (July 30, 1892), pp. 139–140.

62. Kaneko, *Itō den*, II, 859–860; Hayashi, Pt. 5, pp. 80, 87–88. Tokyo *Nichi nichi* (July 31, 1892); Tsuda, p. 75.

63. Kaneko, *Itō den*, II, 860.

64. *Ibid.*, II, 860; Hayashi, Pt. 5, pp. 91–92. According to Itō Miyoji, the move by Ōyama, Kawakami, and Nirei was planned by Shinagawa. Letter to Itō, dated July 30, 1892, in "Itō monjo," 27:233–235b.

65. Scalapino is perhaps overly hasty when he places Matsukata in the "militarist" faction. Scalapino, *Democracy*, p. 159. Ōkuma's characterization of Matsukata is probably closer to the truth. "Generally," says Ōkuma, "Matsukata can be regarded as having belonged to the 'civil' faction. He was an extremely mild person and he definitely was not one who would resort to violence." Ōkuma, "Nihon no seitō," p. 144. Actually, the dis-

tinction made between the "civil" and "military" factions in the government is artificial and unrealistic. See, for example, the views of Cody, p. 61.

66. Scalapino, *Democracy*, p. 138.

67. Fukaya, "Seimubu mondai," p. 426.

68. The centripetal pull of Chōshū ties may have been stronger than the centrifugal force of political animosity. The offspring of Itō, Katsura, and Shirane have intermarried.

69. See Osatake, *Meiji seiji shi tembyō*, pp. 214–218, esp. p. 214. Hoshi probably had clashes in the Diet in mind when he wrote the following words, but they may justifiably be applied to the second election as well. "In any case it can now be truthfully stated that parliamentary government in Japan has passed the experimental stage, and is established among the permanent institutions of the land. Of course this has not been accomplished without friction between the executive and legislative branches of the government . . . Every such struggle has been carried on scrupulously within the limits defined by the Constitution, and every disputed question has been settled in accordance with its provisions." Hoshi Tōru, "The New Japan," *Harper's New Monthly Magazine*, No. 570:894 (Nov. 1897). Talk of a "strong party" in the government desiring to maintain power at bayonet point was widespread in the capital at this time. However, the *Japan Weekly Mail* (July 23, 1892), p. 98, brushed such talk aside: "We entirely agree with the *Nichi Nichi Shimbun* in thinking that there is not the slightest ground for apprehending a serious attempt to carry out such a programme." See also *Nichi nichi shimbun* editorials for July 9 and 10, 1892.

70. On July 17, for example, Itō Miyoji wrote to both Itō and Inoue Kaoru predicting that the Matsukata cabinet had only a short life ahead and therefore should be toppled as quickly as possible. "Itō monjo," 26:211. And the *Japan Weekly Mail* (June 13, 1891), p. 677, summarized press views with the statement, "All the newspapers unite in recommending him to openly assume the supreme direction of the State."

CHAPTER VIII. THE SECOND ITŌ MINISTRY: ITŌ AS A CONSTITUTIONAL STATESMAN

1. Itō became the first prime minister when the cabinet system was created in 1885. He was succeeded by Kuroda Kiyotaka of Satsuma in 1888. Yamagata was appointed prime minister in 1889.

2. Yamagata held the portfolio of justice, Inoue Kaoru was home minister, Ōyama Iwao war minister, Kuroda communications minister, and Gotō agriculture and commerce minister. Since these men, along with the prime minister, were the most prominent men in the government, the cabinet was popularly known as the Cabinet of Elder Statesmen (Genkun naikaku). Kaneko, *Itō den*, II, 864. Mutsu Munemitsu was foreign minister, and Kōno Togama education minister. The cabinet was also distinctive in that a person from a minor clan was appointed to a major cabinet position for the first time since the Restoration. Watanabe Kunitake, the finance minister, was from the petty Takashima han of Shinshū (Nagano). All previous cabinet ministers had been former retainers of the Satsuma, Chōshū, Tosa, and Hizen clans, the Tokugawa government, or the Three Houses of the Tokugawa. *Chōya* (Aug. 9, 1892). Years later this cabinet was still remembered by Ozaki Yukio as "perhaps one of the best that has ever existed in Japan." Ozaki Yukio, "Constitutional Government in Japan," *Transactions and Proceedings of the Japan Society of London*, 29:37 (London, 1932).

3. There were six (fourth through ninth) sessions during Itō's tenure as prime minister. The fourth, seventh, eighth, and ninth did not end in dissolution. But the seventh and eighth were special cases since they were convened during the Sino-Japanese War and the opposition wholeheartedly supported the government. The fifth and sixth sessions were dissolved.

4. *Gikai shi*, II, 359; Kaneko, *Itō den*, II, 865; *Zoku Itō Hirobumi hiroku*, pp. 76–77. To his dying day Itō was bothered by the loss of his teeth, particularly when he made speeches *Ibid.*, p. 77.

5. Kaneko, *Itō den*, II, 865.

6. *Ibid.*, II, 871–872. Cf. account in *Gikai shi*, II, 591–592.

7. Letter dated January 7, 1893, quoted in Kaneko, *Itō den*, II, 872–874.

8. Letter dated January 8, 1893, quoted in *ibid.*, II, 874–876.

9. Letter from Suematsu to Itō, dated May 17, 1892, in "Itō monjo," 47:77b. In a letter from Itō Miyoji to Itō, dated June 22, 1892, Itō Miyoji reported that "some in the government, some in the Diet, and some in the parties . . . hoped that Itō would become prime minister." Quoted in Hayashi, Pt. 4, pp. 40–41n141.

10. Letter from Inoue Kaoru to Itō, dated August 21, 1892, in "Itō monjo," 17:401a–b. All of this did not escape the Kaishintō's notice. Itō Miyoji informed Itō that the Kaishintō newspapers were pointedly raising the question of the "relationship" between the government and the Jiyūtō. Letters dated August 21, 1892, in *ibid.*, 25:27a–b; August 29, 1892, *ibid.*, 25:41. On November 21, 1892, Shimada Saburō of the Kaishintō leveled an attack in public against the Jiyūtō. This volley was returned by Hoshi, and the rift between the two parties widened. See Nakamura Kikuo, Pt. 3, pp. 29–30, 36–37n2. See also Uyehara Etsujirō, *Nihon minken hattatsushi* (A history of Japanese liberalism; Tokyo, 1916), pp. 272–273, and Ōtsu, III, 768.

11. Letter dated November 26, 1892, in "Itō monjo," 17:489–490b.

12. *Gikai shi*, II, 708, 854, 856, 873. For a detailed exposition of the budget question after the Diet reconvened, see Kaneko, *Itō den*, II, 885–903.

13. *Ibid.*, II, 901–903; *Gikai shi*, II, 1105.

14. Scalapino, *Democracy*, 165–166, also n. 47. The term *mintō*, or "popular parties," was used to designate the antigovernment parties, the most prominent being the Kaishintō and the Jiyūtō. See Ōtsu, III, 542.

15. From about this time, to the Hoshi-Ōi confrontation was added the Hoshi-Kōno rivalry. Nakamura, Pt. 3, p. 26, describes this rivalry. See also Masumi, "1890 nendai no seitō soshiki," p. 62.

16. Ozaki Yukio, "Seiyūkai ron" (On the Seiyūkai), *CK*, 24.10:84 (1909).

17. This was not the first time since 1891 that the emperor had "intervened" in Diet affairs. During the third session a constitutional problem arose over the budget powers of the two houses. The problem was resolved by the handing down of a *chokusai* (imperial decision). See Kaneko, *Itō den*, II, 843–847. The term *shōchoku* (imperial edict) is used to describe the rescript handed down during the fourth session. However, when the cabinet asked for "intervention," it had used the term *chokusai*. *Ibid.*, II, 898–899.

18. Letter to Itō, dated January 19, 1893, in "Itō monjo," 16:395b. A little later Inoue wrote an extremely fascinating letter to Itō. In it he reported: "As I understand it, here is the actual state of affairs revealed in the secret report. The minister of the Imperial Household Hijikata yesterday morning was visited first by three, then later by five non-Diet members of the Jiyūtō. They told him that the clash between the government and the Diet had troublesome implications for the state. Hence, they said, the minister of the Imperial Household should now give serious consideration to this matter and exert efforts so that *His Imperial Majesty would hand down an August mandate* commanding the government to work in a harmonious and cooperative manner with the Diet and reduce the sufferings of the people by alleviating the burden of taxation. However, [Hijikata] unequivocally refused. He asked them to leave, saying that from the point of view of his official duties as minister of the Imperial Household interference into state matters was not permitted." (Italics mine.) Letter dated February 1, 1893, in *ibid.*, 16:397b. It is possible that those who visited Hijikata were disgruntled members of the Ōi faction who were seeking every possible means to dissolve the Diet. It is significant that the idea of using a mandate from

the emperor to end the deadlock over the budget was the one ultimately followed by the government.

19. This is besides the administrative and naval reforms Itō promised and later carried out. Uyehara considers these reforms "great and courageous." Uyehara, *Political Development*, p. 225.

20. Hara Kei was very unhappy about the rescript, but Mutsu told him to keep his comments to himself because it was Itō's idea. Hara cites three reasons for opposing the rescript: There were those who asserted that if the cabinet had really assumed its responsibilities, it would not have taken this step; to demand by fiat payment from salaries was unconstitutional; the aim of the House of Representatives was not to deny funds for naval expansion, but to reform the Navy Ministry. The cuts were not motivated by a lack of funds. So, to make the emperor and civil servants pay was contrary to the aim of the House of Representatives. *Hara nikki*, II (a), 81.

21. The Kokumin kyōkai was formed on June 22, 1892, by Shinagawa Yajirō and Saigō Tsugumichi. It served as the rallying point for progovernment politicians and during most of its existence was anti-Itō. A study of the causes of its formation and ultimate failure would lead to a fuller understanding of Meiji political realities.

22. Adding fuel to the fire, Hoshi's faction, through Mutsu, had pledged support to the government on foreign policy.

23. *Gikai shi*, II, 1182. The motion was based on the charge that Hoshi received bribes in connection with the establishment of the National Stock Exchange. Hoshi sued *Kaishin shimbun*, the organ of the Kaishintō, which made the allegations. He won the case, but he could not dispel the suspicion that he had received bribes. Kaneko, *Itō den*, II, 926; Uyehara, *Nihon minken*, pp. 296–297; Hayashida, *Seitō shi*, I, 403.

24. *Gikai shi*, II, 1182–98; Hayashida, *Seitō shi*, I, 404–405; Kaneko, *Itō den*, II, 926. Uyehara asserts that the Lower House was willing to stop at depriving Hoshi of the presidency. However, his stubbornness turned most of the members of the House against him. Uyehara, *Nihon minken*, p. 299. See letters from Itō Miyoji and Suematsu Kenchō to Itō. Both report that the Jiyūtō was split into pro- and anti-Hoshi supporters. Letter from Itō Miyoji, dated November 30, 1893, in "Itō monjo," 27:288–291b. Letter from Suematsu, undated, but probably sent on or about the same day, in *ibid.*, 47:12–13. See also Cody, pp. 243–245.

25. Kaneko, *Itō den*, II, 927–929.

26. In the nonconfidence memorial were the following words: "Your humble subjects earlier . . . nominated Hoshi [as president of the House of Representatives]. We are ashamed of having asked for this imperial appointment. This was the result of our lack of sagacity." *Gikai shi*, II, 1191, 1198–99.

27. Uyehara, *Political Development*, pp. 154–155.

28. For Scalapino's analysis of the use of the memorial, see his *Democracy*, pp. 168–169.

29. Hayashida, *Seitō shi*, I, 406–408; Kaneko, *Itō den*, II, 929; *Gikai shi*, II, 1204–05, 1228.

30. Kaneko, *Itō den*, II, 923, 938; *Gikai shi*, II, 1288–92, 1306. The antigovernment conservatives like Tani Kanjō, Torio Koyata, and Soga Sukenori also joined Ōi Kentarō and his faction in attacking the government at this time. See Teters, "Conservative Opposition," pp. 116–126.

31. Kaneko, *Itō den*, II, 938–951; Watanabe, *Mutsu*, pp. 287–298.

32. The Jiyūtō gained 38 seats in this election and raised its membership in the Lower House from 81 to 119. The Kokumin kyōkai, on the other hand, lost some 54 seats, its strength being reduced from 80 to 26. Ōtsu, IV, 68–69. A letter from Itō Miyoji to Itō indicates that Ōi and Hoshi were making every effort to weaken each other's position, including sending strong-arm men from one area to another. Itō Miyoji also reports that

he received a call for support from Takeuchi Tsuna, a Jiyūtō leader. Letter dated February 23, 1894, in "Itō monjo," 27:285a–b.

33. Kaneko, *Itō den,* II, 964–969; *Gikai shi,* II, 1501–02. The Diet was convoked on May 12. *Ibid.,* II, 1497.

34. *Ibid.,* II, 1513–27; Kaneko, *Itō den,* II, 970; Ōtsu, IV, 88.

35. Kaneko, *Itō den,* II, 971; Watanabe, *Mutsu,* p. 302. Kōno Hironaka was at this time cooperating with Itō through Itō Miyoji. Masumi, "1890 nendai no seitō soshiki," p. 64. Itō Miyoji's experience served him well when he brought about the Itō–Itagaki rapprochement after the Sino-Japanese War.

36. *Gikai shi,* II, 1535–44, 1546–52, 1561–67, 1755–60; Kaneko, *Itō den,* II, 971–973.

37. *Ibid.,* II, 974–976; *Gikai shi,* II, 1796. Yamagata was one of the strongest advocates of dissolution. See Yamagata's letters to Itō, dated May 17 and June 1, 1894, quoted in Hackett, "Yamagata," pp. 240–241.

38. These steps have been widely criticized, then as now, as being "unconstitutional." See Watanabe, *Mutsu,* p. 304.

39. The desire for treaty revision, of course, cut across political boundaries. A specialist in the ideas of Fukuzawa Yukichi, for example, writes: "Japan had only recently opened its door to the outside world. Moreover, Japan was under the threat of the eastward movement of the Western powers. Hence Japan's pressing goal was the expansion of national power. Anything that would work harm to the independence of the nation, no matter how minor the internal conflict, had by all means to be avoided. The growth of parliamentarism naturally was vital. But [Fukuzawa's] fundamental premise was that if in the process [the evolution toward parliamentarism] aggravated the conflict between the government and the people, [parliamentarism] had to be sacrificed in favor of the expansion of national rights and power." Kimura, p. 48. Inoue Kaoru disclosed to Itō an informant's report declaring that the Jiyūtō did not want the Itō cabinet to fall because it would then be replaced by a cabinet of the "so-called military faction." The Jiyūtō was afraid, the report continued, that this would in turn kill hopes for a quick treaty revision. "Itō monjo," 7:420a–b.

40. Letter dated December 5, 1893, in *ibid.,* 52:120–121b. A month earlier Mutsu wrote about a visit by the minister from Britain, who also asked what the Japanese Government intended to do about the "serious problem." Letter to Itō, dated October 12, 1893, in *ibid.,* 52:108a–b.

41. Letter dated November 25, 1893, in *ibid.,* 52:151a–b.

42. Quoted in Watanabe, *Mutsu,* pp. 298–299.

43. *Ibid.,* pp. 298–299.

44. Mutsu reported that Ōi Kentarō and two or three other strong-arm followers physically assaulted a missionary and his wife on a train and then tossed them out. Letter to Itō, dated March 8, 1894, in "Itō monjo," 52:131a–b.

45. Watanabe, for example, writes that "many" in the opposition did not care to press for votes against the government on foreign policy issues. Watanabe, *Mutsu,* pp. 300–301. Also, as mentioned earlier, the Jiyūtō antigovernment actions could in part be explained on the basis of the Jiyūtō's attempts to maintain its appearance as an opposition party.

46. *Hara nikki,* II(a), 103. Uyehara's judgment on the reasons given for the dissolution is that they were "vague abstractions and it is hardly possible to put one's finger on them." Uyehara, *Nihon minken,* p. 317.

47. Paraphrased in Kaneko, *Itō den,* III, 43. The incident that prompted Lord Kimberley's outburst was the demand made of the Korean government by the Japanese minister, Ōtori Keisuke, that a British employee of the Korean government be expelled from the country. Mutsu's reaction on hearing this was predictable. He wrote: "On balance, no matter what the circumstances [and how serious the provocation] in Korea, it is unreasonable [for Ōtori] to demand the expulsion of this single Englishman, since [this demand]

may cause the great achievement which is on the verge of being consummated in London to collapse in one instant." Quoted in Watanabe, *Mutsu*, p. 307.

48. Quoted in Teters, "Conservative Opposition," p. 121.

49. One of the most widely held beliefs on the cause of the war is that Itō, distracted beyond endurance by his difficulties with the Diet, brought about the war to shift the nation's attention abroad and away from internal affairs. A typical expression of this belief is the following by a contemporary resident of Japan: "This war has, for the time, averted the utter breakdown of Japan's new constitutional machinery . . . And so it came to pass that at the very time when men boded, if not actual civil war, at least serious intestine commotions, from Kiushiu to Hokkaido there was but one mind and will and purpose in the nation . . . Itō had again played a trump card, the strongest that could possibly be played. There is little doubt that for some time he had looked to a war with China as a possible solution for the Japanese constitutional difficulty, for Itō is a man who sees a long way ahead. "Japanese Constitutional Crisis and the War," p. 475. See also McLaren, *Political History*, p. 229; *Japan Chronicle* (Nov. 18, 1909), p. 923, quoting *Tōyō keizai* (Oriental economist); William M. McGovern, *Modern Japan: Its Political, Military, and Industrial Organization* (London, 1920), pp. 71–73; Clement and Uyehara, p. 11; E. E. N. Causton, *Militarism and Foreign Policy in Japan* (London, 1936), pp. 105–106; Freda Utley, *Japan's Feet of Clay*, 2nd ed. (New York, 1937), p. 255. If, however, one accepts the reason for the double dissolution given in the text, one must seek other causes for the war. It should be repeated that long before the outbreak of the Sino-Japanese War, the Jiyūtō was much closer to the government positions on defense and foreign policy than is generally assumed. See Cody, pp. 235, 246.

50. Itō Miyoji, in a long letter to Itō, suggested plans for the government's role in the election. He began with the assumption that election interference was impossible, but that this did not prevent the government from giving legal and moral support to those the government hoped to see elected. Some of the steps he suggested were the transfer of those prefectural governors who had clear connections with the Kokumin kyōkai, speech-making by cabinet ministers, and control of the opposition press. Letter dated June 5, 1894, in "Itō monjo," 31:686–689b. However, Hara Kei's verdict on the election was that the government did not interfere and assumed a "completely neutral position." *Hara nikki*, II(a), 100.

51. Kaneko, *Itō den*, III, 120–126. The Lower House held only four sessions, October 15, 19, 20, and 21. *Gikai shi*, II, 1811–23.

52. *Japan Weekly Mail* (Oct. 27, 1895), p. 470; see also *ibid.* (Oct. 6, 1894), p. 382. A typical expression of the sentiments at this time appeared in the antigovernment *Yomiuri shimbun*: "We propose that at the very beginning of the Seventh Diet session members of both Houses, as representatives of the entire nation, unanimously pass the following resolution: 'The House of Peers (the House of Representatives), in obedience to the imperial declaration of war, is resolved that it will approve all the measures taken by those in power for the prosecution of the Sino-Japanese War, and will give undivided support to those in power, so that a glorious triumph may be achieved and the situation in the Far East completely changed.' " *Yomiuri shimbun* (Aug. 28, 1894).

53. Kaneko, *Itō den*, III, 129–130; *Gikai shi*, III, 1. Cf. Yanaga, *Japan since Perry*, p. 245.

54. Kaneko, *Itō den*, III, 131.

55. *Ibid.*, III, 254. For aims and policies of the association, see Hayashida, *Seitō shi*, I, 434–435.

56. The term "postwar development (or construction)" *(sengo keiei)* is frequently encountered after the Sino-Japanese War. The foundations for "postwar development," however, were being laid before the war. The term is often applied to Japan's efforts at expanding its military establishment, particularly to the addition of six more army divisions and a seven-year naval expansion program. However, nonmilitary development was

also included in the program of "postwar development." See, for example, Masuda Tsuyoshi, "Dai niji Itō naikaku: Hambatsu-seitō no teikei jidai" (The second Itō ministry: The era of oligarchy-party rapprochement), *Kobe hōgaku zasshi,* 4:483 (Dec. 1954).

57. Kurihara, I, 197–190. For other accounts, see Baba, "Itō Miyoji ron," pp. 206–208; Maeda, *Hoshi Tōru,* pp. 271– 272; Kazusa Takayoshi, *Sekaiteki dai ijin: Itō kō* (Prince Itō: A great man by world standards; Tokyo, 1909), II, 151–153; Cody, pp. 248–253.

58. Hayashida, *Seitō shi,* I, 436. Following the axiom that in politics no one gives anything without return or expectation of benefit, the Jiyūtō attached certain conditions. One was that the government would first show the Jiyūtō the drafts of the budget, all important bills, and new policies before submission to the Diet. Maeda, *Hoshi Tōru,* p. 272.

59. Kaneko, *Itō den,* III, 258–259; *Mainichi shimbun* (Dec. 1, 1895). According to letters from Itō Miyoji to Itō, three leaders of the Jiyūtō—Hayashi Yūzō, Kōno Hironaka, and Matsuda Masahisa—demanded that Itagaki be given a cabinet post if the government went through the forthcoming ninth Diet session with little trouble. Itō Miyoji, however, warned them that to push too hard on this matter would cause six months of effort to end in failure. He himself opposed Itagaki's entry; Itō favored "waiting for the right moment." Both letters dated November 6, 1895, in "Itō monjo," 28:388a–b and 411–412b.

60. Kaneko, *Itō den,* III, 277.

61. *Hara nikki,* II(a), 134.

62. Yamagata himself is described as being "displeased but resigned" to Itō's alliance with the Jiyūtō. Hackett, "Yamagata," p. 270. Ozaki Yukio says that Yamagata called Itō a "traitor" for combining with the Jiyūtō. Isa, p. 552.

63. Hara has left a record of the situation immediately preceding Nomura's resignation. He reports that a group from the Jiyūtō, led by Hoshi, pressed Itō one day to make specific concessions, such as the appointment of Jiyūtō members as prefectural governors. Itō is said to have agreed to these demands up to a certain specified point. On the way back from the prime minister's residence the group called on Nomura and asked if the previous instructions he had given to the prefectural governors were still in effect. These instructions had assured the governors that the coalition between the government and the Jiyūtō was merely a "meeting of minds." This, and the fact that the government still adhered to the principle of nonparty cabinets, according to Nomura, made it unwise to make definite concessions to the Jiyūtō. Nomura and the Jiyūtō representatives had a violent argument which remained unsettled when they parted. *Hara nikki,* II(a), 132. Itō Miyoji also reported this incident and complained that Nomura should exercise more caution when talking with Jiyūtō leaders, for "from a trivial incident can result great complications." It is obvious that Itō Miyoji was definitely pro-Jiyūtō by this time. Letter to Itō, dated January 19, 1896, in "Itō monjo," 28:429a–b. See also letter from Mutsu to Itō in *ibid.,* 51:55.

64. Quoted in Kaneko, *Itō den,* III, 288.

65. Hoshi was appointed envoy extraordinary and minister plenipotentiary to the United States.

66. Itagaki was unhappy about the announcement that his name had been stricken from the Jiyūtō rolls. He had preferred to keep this matter secret. To assuage the hurt, the Political Affairs Committee of the Jiyūtō passed a secret resolution assuring Itagaki that his "spiritual" connection with the Jiyūtō was the thing that mattered, not the formality of having his name off the party lists. Letter from Itō Miyoji to Itō in "Itō monjo," 28: 385–387b. Ōkuma Shigenobu, on the other hand, believed that having Itagaki remove himself from the Jiyūtō was a face-saving act made in behalf of the government. He is said to have described it trenchantly and succinctly as a pretext that "recalls an old proverb of stopping one's ears to steal a bell." Quoted in the *Japan Weekly Mail* (May 9, 1896), p. 525. See also Masuda, pp. 498, 502n1; *Nichi nichi shimbun* (Apr. 15, 1896).

67. Quoted in the *Japan Weekly Mail* (Apr. 18, 1896), p. 445. See also *ibid.* (Apr. 18, 1896), p. 446.

68. Kaneko, *Itō den,* III, 293. He died a year later, on August 24, 1897, at the age of fifty-four. Another prominent figure preceded him by a few weeks. On August 4 Gotō Shōjirō died at the age of sixty.

69. Matsukata was appointed finance minister on March 17, 1895. He resigned on August 25, 1895, because of differences over postwar fiscal problems. Tokutomi, *Matsukata,* II, 537, 626. According to Tokutomi, Matsukata's political friends, including Tokutomi, had urged his resignation. The basic reason was that even at this early date a Matsukata-Ōkuma combination was being discussed, and they did not want Matsukata to "fall" with the Itō cabinet. Tokutomi, "Happō yori nagametaru Ōkuma," pp. 259–260.

70. Among the leaders of the Jiyūtō, only Kōno favored Ōkuma's entry. His reason was that Itagaki and Ōkuma should cooperate with each other against the oligarchs. Masuda, p. 502.

71. Kaneko, *Itō den,* III, 294–295; Tokutomi, *Matsukata,* II, 638; Ōtsu, IV, 675–677. Ōishi Masami and Inukai Tsuyoshi, who were very active promoters of the Matsukata-Ōkuma alliance, were afraid that Matsukata might just possibly accept Itō's offer. They persuaded Matsukata to go to the Kyoto-Osaka region about this time. Ichijima, II, 217; Uzaki Kumakichi, *Inukai Tsuyoshi den* (Biography of Inukai Tsuyoshi; Tokyo, 1932), pp. 151–153.

72. Kaneko, *Itō den,* III, 296–297; Tokutomi, *Matsukata,* II, 638–639; Cody, pp. 260–263. Itō resigned without formally consulting the Jiyūtō. He had earlier said that he would "act together" with the Jiyūtō on all matters. Masuda, p. 502.

73. *Nippon* was of similar conviction. It asserted that the problem was simply one of choosing between Ōkuma and Itagaki. It charged that Itō had neither the courage nor the sense of responsibility to make the choice, and that "it was an easy problem having no direct bearing upon great affairs of state." *Nippon* (Aug. 30, 1896). See also comments in *Nichi nichi shimbun* (Sept. 3, 1896).

74. Itō later remarked in a speech: "The prime minister during the first Diet session was the same prime minister we have today, Marquis Yamagata. He fully discharged his responsibilities and did not dissolve the Diet at that time . . . As things stand now, there are no prospects that there will be a need to dissolve the Diet. We must say that Yamagata has performed his tasks to perfection. I have been prime minister twice. Unfortunately, I have always had to resort to dissolutions." Quoted in *Itō zenshū,* II, 136. See also Itō's remarks in *ibid.,* III, 180 (Pt. 3).

75. Hayashida, *Seitō shi,* I, 441. See also Kurihara, I, 197.

76. Komatsu Midori, who knew Itō Miyoji, says of him: "Although his own rank was low, he wielded power as if he were Itō's intendant *(daikan).* And there was many an occasion when he called out state ministers and himself undertook to solve difficult problems with them." Komatsu, *Itō to Yamagata,* p. 87. Okazaki Kunisuke says he personally heard Itō Miyoji give a state minister a loud and vigorous tongue lashing. Okazaki, "Itō shishaku no dōraku" (What Count Itō does for relaxation), *CK,* 32.7:45–46 (July 1917). See also Uzaki Rojō, "Hyōmen ni noridashita Itō shi" (Count Itō's "reappearance"), *CK,* 32.7:42 (July 1917); Suzuki, *Hyōden Itō,* p. 39.

77. As Itō Miyoji himself said: "At present the relationship between [Jiyūtō] head-quarters and Itagaki is not very smooth. I am doing my best to improve this relationship. Itagaki and I get along quite well." Quoted in Cody, p. 263.

78. The *Japan Weekly Mail* (July 9, 1892), p. 48.

79. Suematsu Kenchō, prominent bureaucrat and Itō's son-in-law, joined the Jiyūtō in November 1898, just prior to the breakup of the Ōkuma-Itagaki cabinet. Hirano Mineo, *Okazaki Kunisuke den* (Biography of Okazaki Kunisuke; Tokyo, 1938), pp. 232–235. Masumi Junnosuke, in a conversation at Tokyo Metropolitan University in August 1962, suggested that the number of former bureaucrats with Tokyo Imperial University back-

grounds who joined or maintained close ties with the parties rapidly increased after the Russo-Japanese War.

CHAPTER IX. ITŌ AND HIS "NATIONAL PARTY"

1. The second Matsukata ministry is discussed in some detail in Lebra, "Ōkuma, Modern Statesman," chap. 4; "Party Development and the Second Matsukata Cabinet."
2. Ōishi Masami, quoted in Ichijima, II, 221–222; cf. accounts in Tokyo *Nichi nichi shimbun* (Sept. 25, 1896), quoted in *Nihon kokusei jiten* (Dictionary of Japanese politics; Tokyo, 1953–1958), II, 687; Ichijima, II, 217–220; Scalapino, *Democracy*, pp. 171–172. See also, the seven-point platform based on Ōkuma's draft submitted by Matsukata to the prefectural governors on September 12, 1896. Ichijima, II, 227–228; Tokutomi, *Matsukata,* II, 664. See also Lebra, "Ōkuma, Modern Statesman," pp. 179–180.
3. The Shimpotō was inaugurated on March 1, 1896. It could claim 103 Diet members, of whom fifty-one came from the Kaishintō and thirty-three from the Rikken kakushintō (Constitutional reformists). See *ibid.,* p. 173.
4. Ichijima, II, 220–221; Isa, pp. 555–556; Ozaki, *Minken tōsō,* p. 95. Ōkuma's relationship with his wife was apparently very close and atypical of the prevailing Japanese pattern. See Ichijima, II, 209–211; Tokutomi, "Happō yori nagametaru Ōkuma," pp. 263–264. It may be of some historical and sociological interest to note that three extremely powerful personalities of the Meiji period, Ōkuma, Inoue Kaoru, and Mutsu Munemitsu, all were reported to have been fearful of their wives. Tokutomi, "Happō yori nagametaru Ōkuma," p. 265, and "Shōsetsu yori kinaru shōgai no Mutsu Munemitsu," p. 283.
5. As stated in the previous chap. Ōishi Masami and Inukai Tsuyoshi were actively working for a Matsukata-Ōkuma entente. See also Lebra, "Ōkuma, Modern Statesman," p. 177.
6. The government actually could count on some 160 votes, of which 94 came from the Shimpotō. The Jiyūtō could muster 88 votes. See Tsukada Masao, *Rikken minseitō shi* (History of the Constitutional Democratic Party; Tokyo, 1935), I, 87.
7. Tokutomi, *Matsukata,* II, 645–650. Kaneko, *Itō den,* III, 300. The budget was the major item of business. The Jiyūtō, though not necessarily sharing the Shimpotō's enthusiasm for the Matsukata government, was obliged to back the budget because Matsukata's spending program was similar to the one the Jiyūtō had strongly supported under Itō's ministry. Itō Miyoji's biography gives another reason for the quiet session. On January 11, 1897, the empress dowager died. Out of respect to her memory, the Diet "restrained" itself. Kurihara, I, 277.
8. In May 1897 several members of the Audit Bureau who had complained of irregularities on the part of the chief of the bureau were dismissed. In another incident, the head of the Judiciary Department of the Government-General of Taiwan was relieved for being overly conscientious in pointing out corruption in the government-general. These dismissals, in turn, served as one of the reasons for the resignations of Shimpotō men from two rather important government posts. Takahashi Kenzō was chief cabinet secretary and Kōmuchi Tomotsune was director of the Legislative Bureau when they submitted their resignations in October 1897. Because these two men were among those chiefly responsible for the coalition between Matsukata and the Shimpotō, their resignations heralded the imminent split of the coalition. Ichijima, II, 276–277; Ōtsu, IV, 730–731. Cf. Kaneko, *Itō den,* III, 320, and Tokutomi, *Matsukata,* II, 654. Lebra states that Takahashi clashed with Army Minister Takashima on several occasions. Lebra, "Ōkuma, Modern Statesman," p. 185.
9. Kaneko, *Itō den,* III, 321; Tokutomi, *Matsukata,* II, 655; Ichijima, II, 279–280; Maeda, *Hoshi Tōru,* pp. 293–294.
10. Kaneko, *Itō den,* III, 323–324; Tokutomi, *Matsukata,* II, 659–660. According to

Matsuda Masahisa, however, the concessions he was able to squeeze out of Matsukata were: Hoshi as minister of justice; appointment of another party man to an unspecified ministry; five bureau chiefs' posts; six or seven prefectural governorships; election campaign funds; and the adoption of the Jiyūtō platform. The Jiyūtō rejected this arrangement because the Tosa faction was looking ahead to a tie-up with the anticipated third Itō ministry (Masumi, "1890 nendai no seitō soshiki," p. 64).

11. Kaneko, Itō den, III, 324; Tokutomi, Matsukata, II, 661–664.

12. Quoted in Tokutomi Iichirō, Kōshaku Katsura Tarō den (Biography of Prince Katsura Tarō; Tokyo, 1917), I, 758.

13. Lebra, "Ōkuma, Modern Statesman," p. 179.

14. Kaneko, Itō den, III, 331. See also Lebra, "Ōkuma, Modern Statesman," pp. 181–182, 184.

15. Yokoi Tokiwo, "New Japan and Her Constitutional Outlook," Contemporary Review, 74:456 (Sept. 1898). When the Shimpotō and the Jiyūtō amalgamated and formed the Kenseitō in 1898, Tokutomi says, "The faction known as the Satsuma clique rushed to join forces with it. And there were even civil and military bureaucrats in the government who quickly set up liaison with [the new party]." Tokutomi, Katsura, I, 784.

16. Ōkuma is credited with making the proposal on October 16. Kaneko, Itō den, III, 320; see also Hara nikki, II (a), 229.

17. Kaneko, Itō den, III, 326; Ōtsu, IV, 744; Watanabe, Ōkuma Shigenobu, pp. 211–212. See also Hara nikki, II(a), 232, and Idditti, p. 303. Scalapino, quoting Ōtsu, IV, 744, writes: "Gotō sought for an alliance between Itō and Ōkuma, but that the Premier hesitated when Ōkuma asked for three cabinet seats." Scalapino, Democracy, p. 173. There is no mention of Gotō in Ōtsu's account. If Gotō Shōjirō is meant, he had been dead for nearly a year and a half when Itō met with Ōkuma.

18. The fifth general election, scheduled for March 15.

19. Kaneko, Itō den, III, 326–327. Itō Miyoji and Hayashi Yūzō were principal mediators in these talks. Sakatani, IV, 557. Ōkuma and Itagaki had very good cause for wanting the home ministry. The home minister's role during an election was a crucial one. He controlled the prefectural governors and the police. By enforcing the law strictly against political opponents, and leniently toward sympathizers, he could shift the balance to those he favored. This advantage, combined with the already existing party organizational strength, could almost assure victory at the polls for the party that controlled this ministry. This is what A. Morgan Young probably had in mind when he declared, "Governments always win elections." Japan Weekly Chronicle (May 19, 1932), p. 636. See also Idditti, p. 304. Actually, Ward is more to the point when he states that " . . . a party government never loses an election. Non-party governments have suffered defeats on several occasions." Robert E. Ward, "Party Government in Japan: A Preliminary Survey of Its Development and Electoral Record, 1928–1937," Ph.D. thesis (University of California, 1948), p. 524; see also pp. 524–526.

20. Kaneko, Itō den, III, 331, 353; Kurihara, I, 286–287; Tokutomi, Katsura, I, 768–770. See also Kazusa, II, 181–182; Kawada Mizuho, Kataoka Kenkichi sensei den (The biography of Kataoka Kenkichi; Tokyo, 1940), pp. 718–719; Cody, pp. 263–265.

21. Ōtsu, IV, 749. The other seats were divided as follows: Kokumin kyōkai, 26; Yamashita kurabu, 48; Dōshi kurabu, 14; Independents, 23.

22. Kaneko, Itō den, III, 353–354.

23. Scalapino takes the position that Itō promised Itagaki a cabinet post. Scalapino, Democracy, 172n64. See also Baba, "Nihon seitō shi," p. 157. Taiyō believes that Itō Miyoji reached the agreement with the Jiyūtō without Itō's prior knowledge. "Itō nōshōmu daijin no jishoku" (The resignation of Agriculture Minister Itō), Taiyō, 4:246 (May 5, 1898). See also Maeda, Hoshi Tōru, p. 296.

24. Tokutomi, *Katsura*, I, 771–772; Sakatani, IV, 596; Ōtsu, IV, 746. Idditti, p. 305, writes that no one in the cabinet took the Jiyūtō demand seriously.

25. Kaneko, *Itō den*, III, 354. See also Masumi, "1890 nendai no seitō soshiki," p. 65. Katsura takes credit for Itō's rejection of the Jiyūtō demand. See letter from Katsura to Yamagata, dated April 17, 1898, quoted in Tokutomi, *Katsura*, I, 773–775.

26. Ōtsu, IV, 747. It is also said that Itō Miyoji resigned because of rumors involving him in the Dojima scandal. These rumors said that he abused his position as agriculture and commerce minister and leaked secrets which benefitted his business friends. Itō Miyoji, as a consequence, faced violent attacks. Ishikawa Hanzan, "Batsuzoku no dai bantō Itō shi" (Count Itō the leading manager of the clan faction), *CK*, 32.7:49 (1917).

27. "Itō nōshōmu daijin no jishoku," p. 246. Maeda Renzan traces the unfriendliness between the two to the time of the first Itō ministry (December 22, 1885 to April 29, 1888). Itō Miyoji at this time is said to have attacked Foreign Minister Inoue's treaty revision plan. Maeda Renzan, "Kempō no bannin, Itō Miyoji" (Itō Miyoji, the Constitution's guardian), *CK*, 49.4:193 (1934). Itō Miyoji apparently did not get along with most of Itō's followers, including Mutsu and Inoue Kowashi. See Maeda Renzan, "Itō shi to Inukai shi" (Count Itō and Mr. Inukai), *CK*, 32.7:61 (1917); Baba, "Itō Miyoji ron," p. 208; Tokutomi, "Itō, Ōkuma, Yamagata," p. 284.

28. Inoue at this time had the reputation of being antiparty. This reputation is probably undeserved. It was common knowledge at this time that Inoue hated the Jiyūtō. During the fourth session of the Diet, a Jiyūtō member criticized Inoue, specifically pointing out all of his "misconducts" since the Restoration. Miyake writes that even the usually courageous Inoue was put out by the attacks during this session. Maeda says that Inoue's hostility toward the Jiyūtō after this session was deep and abiding. Miyake Yūjirō (Setsurei), "Inoue kōshaku" (Marquis Inoue), *CK*, 26.2:68 (1911); Maeda, *Hoshi Tōru*, p. 297; Sakatani, IV, 556, 596–597; Komatsu, *Itō to Yamagata*, p. 92; Baba, "Itō Miyoji ron," p. 208. Arai Shōgo delivered the speech in question on December 8, 1892. Ironically, at this time, he was not a member of the Jiyūtō, but of the four-man Tōyō jiyūtō (Eastern Liberal Party) which had broken off from the Jiyūtō in November 1892. *Kampō gōgai 9 Dec. 1892: Dai yonkai teikoku Gikai Shūgiin giji sokkiroku* (Official gazette extra, 9 Dec. 1892: Shorthand record of proceedings, House of Representatives, fourth Imperial Diet session), No. 7: 116–118; "Dai ikkai teikoku Gikai yori dai kyūjūnikai teikoku Gikai ni itaru Shūgiin giin tōseki roku," p. 12, 15, 18.

29. Hayashida, *Seitō shi*, II, 1–2; Idditti, p. 305; Isa, p. 573; Tokutomi, *Katsura*, I, 782.

30. Kurihara, I, 394–407; Komatsu, *Itō to Yamagata*, pp. 93–94; Uzaki Rojō, p. 43.

31. This is the basic theme of Olson's thesis on Hara Kei. See esp. chap. 15, "Summary and Conclusions." Lawrence A. Olson, "Hara Kei: A Political Biography," Ph.d. thesis (Havard, 1954). There apparently was some jealousy between these two rising politicians. Hara noted that Itō Miyoji was speaking ill of him to Itō. Hara also wrote that he discussed Seiyūkai organizational plans with Itō Miyoji to avoid the latter's jealousy in their relationship with Itō. *Hara nikki*, II(a), 323, 287.

32. Kaneko, *Itō den*, III, 356. The *Kampō gōgai* of 31 May, 1898, reports the vote as follows: 116 for the motion, 171 against, 2 votes invalid. *Kampō gōgai 31 May 1898: Dai jūnikai teikoku Gikai Shūgiin giji sokkiroku*, No. 8:113–130. Itō Miyoji, after his failure to win a cabinet post for Itagaki, called on the latter and apologized for not being able to deliver on his promise. Itagaki in appreciation pledged that the Jiyūtō would not oppose the government in the twelfth session. Matsuda Masahisa, however, interposed the condition that this promise held good only so long as the government refrained from introducing a tax increase measure, which was then being discussed. Kurihara, I, 298; Ichijima, II, 285. Cf. Kawada, pp. 732–733.

33. Kaneko, *Itō den*, III, 356–357.

34. Uyehara, *Political Development*, p. 175. See also Satō Hiroshi, *Democracy and the Japanese Government* (New York, 1920), p. 34.

35. Kaneko, *Itō den*, III, 358; Yanaga, *Japan since Perry*, pp. 215, 265; Norman, *Japan's Emergence*, p. 189; speech by Itō before the Lower House, May 25, 1898, quoted in Kaneko, *Itō den*, III, 361. See especially Ward, "Party Government," pp. 9–18: "Survey of National Election Laws to 1925."

36. Maeda, *Hoshi Tōru*, p. 398; Kaneko, *Itō den*, III, 367–368. The twenty-four votes were mostly from the Kokumin kyōkai. Cf. *Kampō gōgai* 11 June 1898 which records the vote as follows: for the government measure, 27; against, 247; invalid votes, 3. *Kampō gōgai 11 June 1898: Dai jūnikai teikoku Gikai Shūgiin giji sokkiroku*, No. 16:313–316.

37. Suzuki Yasuzō feels that Itō finally decided to form his party on this date. Suzuki, *Hyōden Itō*, p. 309.

38. *Yomiuri* reported that after the vote (on the land tax measure) necessitated a dissolution, Itō decided to form a "powerful political party." Quoted in the *Kobe Weekly Chronicle* (June 18, 1898), p. 534.

39. Kaneko, *Itō den*, III, 369–379.

40. Watanabe Kōki was the first president of the Imperial University in Tokyo. *Tokyo teikoku daigaku ichiran* (Catalog of the Tokyo Imperial University; Tokyo, 1943), p. 510; *Shinsen daijimmei jiten*, VI, 571.

41. Lebra, "Ōkuma, Modern Statesman," p. 191; Furushima Kazuo, "Rimpō kakumei wo ki ni: ichi rōseijika no kaisō" (Recollections of an old politician on the occasion of the revolution in a neighboring country), *CK*, 46.1:160 (1951); Kaneko, *Itō den*, III, pp. 369–370; *Hara nikki*, II(a), 244.

42. Kaneko, *Itō den*, III, 373; Hayashida, *Seitō shi*, II, 3–4. Hayashida, the source of much of the narration on Itō's efforts, was closely associated with Itō at this time and worked diligently to help consummate Itō's plan.

43. Kaneko, *Itō den*, III, 374–376. Iwasaki was governor of the Bank of Japan at this time. Hackett is of the view that prominent industrialists freely contributed money. Hackett, "Yamagata," p. 275. Magoshi Kyōhei, a prominent industrialist, did donate a princely sum of 300,000 yen. Hayashida, *Seitō shi*, II, 4. It is to be noted that Magoshi was closely related to the Mitsui interests. See *Shinsen daijimmei jiten*, V, 576.

44. Hayashida, *Seitō shi*, II, 4–5.

45. *Ibid.*, II, 5–6. Hamada, p. 122; *Hara nikki*, II(a), 244.

46. On June 18 Yamagata had written to Matsukata on the same subject. The gist of his opinion was that since the two parties were planning to unite, for the government to form a party (Kinnōtō, or Loyalist Party) was unavoidable. But the Loyalist Party differed from the existing "popular parties" in that the former would reject the principle of party cabinets. Accordingly, the person who would form the Loyalist Party must stand outside the government. If a member of the government assumed leadership of the Loyalist Party, he should leave the government and support the government from without. Kaneko, *Itō den*, III, 377–378.

47. *Ibid.*, III, 377–380. Hackett, "Yamagata," pp. 278–279. Hara Kei duly recorded that there were violent arguments in the imperial conference on June 24. *Hara nikki*, II(a), 244.

48. Kaneko, *Itō den*, III, 380–391; a transcript of the meeting between Itō, Ōkuma, and Itagaki, taken down by Itō Miyoji, appears in *ibid.*, III, 383–390; Ichijima, II, 293. See also Cody, pp. 266–270.

49. Kaneko, *Itō den*, III, 390–391. *Keika nippō* described the resignation of Itō as "the ruin of the Meiji government." Quoted in the *Kobe Weekly Chronicle* (July 2, 1898), p. 580. Ninomiya Kumajirō of *Keika nippō* was one of Yamagata's closest followers. See Tokutomi Iichirō, *Sohōjiden* (Autobiography; Tokyo, 1935), p. 357.

50. Tokutomi, *Katsura*, I, 789–790; Mumeishi, "Shin seitō no shuryōtaru Katsura kō no seijiteki keireki" (The political career of Prince Katsura, the leader of the new party), *CK*,

28.5:34 (1913); Suzuki, *Seitō ron,* p. 98. Katsura, describing the Ōkuma-Itagaki cabinet, wrote: "This cabinet . . . is designated by party politicians as a party cabinet. However, in my opinion, it is more to the point to call it a cabinet based on a political party. The reason is that the service ministries are filled by nonparty members. [Thus] it is proper to characterize it as a half-paralyzed cabinet, for while it is based on a party, it lacks freedom of complete movement." Quoted in Tokutomi, *Katsura,* I, 769.

51. Scalapino, *Democracy,* p. 174. This is also the interpretation offered by McLaren, *Political History,* p. 253. The *Kobe Weekly Chronicle* saw in Itō's action a sagacious move to temper the irresponsibility of the opposition with a taste of responsibility (Aug. 20, 1898), p. 134; (Dec. 3, 1898), pp. 457–458.

52. Kaneko, *Itō den,* III, 376. Hayashida is wrong when he states that no one voiced dissent. Hayashida, *Seitō shi,* II, 4. Itō, when he met with Itagaki and Ōkuma on June 25, told them: "I cannot say that there is no concern [about my actions] in the cabinet." Quoted in Kaneko, *Itō den,* III, 385.

53. *Ibid.,* III, 384.

54. Kaneko Kentarō, "Itō Hirobumi to watakushi" (Itō Hirobumi and I), *CK,* 51:118 (Aug. 1936).

55. *Nippon* (June 27, 1898) editorialized that the *genrō* realized that a *hambatsu* party could not be quickly formed and that they entertained doubts about victory in the election. This is why, *Nippon* continued, Ōkuma and Itagaki were given the job of taking over from Itō.

56. Kaneko, *Itō den,* III, 376.

57. *Jiji shimpō* (June 29, 1898). Uyehara wrote of this development: *"For its real importance lies in the fact that it had completely disposed of the prejudice that a person directly connected with a political party could not become a Cabinet Minister."* Uyehara, *Political Development,* p. 241. Cf. McLaren, *Political History,* pp. 256–257.

58. Quoted in Suzuki, *Seitō ron,* p. 98. Hackett, "Yamagata," pp. 280–281.

59. Kaneko, *Itō den,* III, 384. According to Kaneko, Itō believed that a cabinet should have a tenure of at least four to five years to be effective. Kaneko, "Itō Hirobumi to watakushi," p. 118.

CHAPTER X. ITŌ, YAMAGATA, AND THE KENSEITŌ: FORMATION OF THE SEIYŪKAI

1. McLaren is one of the earliest proponents of this theme. He writes that everyone attending the inaugural ceremony of the Seiyūkai knew that "Itō was there for the purpose of joining hands with the Opposition in an attempt to overthrow his enemies, the military clique." McLaren, *Political History,* pp. 254, 268, 299. See also Miyake, "Ōkuma haku," p. 125; Hackett, "Yamagata," pp. 322, 335; Olson, "Hara," p. 136.

2. Meaning, of course, members of the two major parties. Itō, it should be recalled, was dealing with politicians of the Kokumin kyōkai in his second attempt to form a party.

3. For a detailed discussion of the cabinet, see Lebra, "Ōkuma, Modern Statesman," Chap. 7: "The Kenseitō Cabinet."

4. *Ibid.,* p. 206; Scalapino, *Democracy,* pp. 175–176; Yanaga, *Japan since Perry,* p. 262; Cody, pp. 271–281.

5. Miyake, *Jidai shi,* III, 150–151. Watanabe Ikujirō also is convinced that the lack of Itō's support caused the failure of the Ōkuma-Itagaki cabinet. Watanabe, *Ōkuma Shigenobu,* p. 225. See also Masumi, "1890 nendai no seitō soshiki," p. 71, where he cites Okazaki Kunisuke, an important politician of this period.

6. When Itō, Ōkuma, and Itagaki met on June 30, Itagaki could scarcely conceal his surprise at the sudden development which would place them in power. He admitted that

up to that date he had had only one talk with Ōkuma, and he also candidly admitted that they had no precise notions on how they were to conduct state affairs.

7. Ozaki, *Minken tōsō,* p. 96; Isa, p. 587; Furushima, p. 161. Furushima Kazuo was a newspaperman/politician whose career spanned the Meiji, Taishō, and Shōwa eras.

8. Kurihara, I, 399–400; cf. account in Yamazaki Rintarō, "Hoshi Tōru no hammen" (A profile of Hoshi Tōru), *CK,* 49:151 (Aug. 1934).

9. Robert Butow, in his *Japan's Decision to Surrender,* examines this concept critically and at length. According to him, a person who resorts to *haragei* is essentially one "who says one thing but means another" (pp. 70–71, and Index, under *haragei*). Cf. concepts of strict and broad mental reservations in Catholic ethics. Austin Fagothey, S.J., *Right and Reason: Ethics in Theory and Practice* (St. Louis, 1959), pp. 317–319.

10. Isa, p. 664, quoting Ozaki's *Nihon kensei shi wo kataru.* Tokutomi says that Itō explicitly cautioned Seiyūkai members against "arbitrarily" opposing the government. Tokutomi, *Katsura,* II, 8. But Katsura, in his autobiography, states: "Although I received the mandate to form a cabinet, it was natural that Itō was not truly happy about it. And it was clear as day that Itō was going to have the Seiyūkai adopt an attitude of hostility toward the cabinet." Quoted in Tokutomi, *Katsura,* I, 976. See also Oka, *Kindai Nihon no seijika,* p. 24.

11. Isa, p. 588, quoting from Ozaki's *Nihon kensei shi wo kataru.*

12. Itō Miyoji, in a conversation with Maeda Renzan, revealed that the Jiyūtō had asked the Shimpotō to give the post of foreign minister to him. He further told Maeda: "[Those from the Jiyūtō] said that Matsuda (the finance minister) was plainly an introverted person with a philosophical bent. Hayashi [the communications minister] was an artless, good-natured man who had an undeserved reputation as a wire-puller. To offer any kind of opposition to Ōishi and Ozaki from the Shimpotō, they insisted that they had to have me in the cabinet. When I discussed this with Itō, Itō replied that this was the first time in Japan, and for that matter anywhere, that a cabinet was organized with the expectation of fighting within the cabinet." Itō Miyoji then told Maeda that he refused the Jiyūtō request on the ground that he did not want to enter that cabinet as a fighting "champion." Maeda, *Hoshi Tōru,* p. 301. Saigō also predicted an early break between the two groups. See Ōtsu, IV, 821.

13. Ōkuma concurrently held the prime minister's and foreign minister's posts. Shimpotō members also held the justice, education, and agriculture and commerce portfolios. The Jiyūtō was allocated the home, finance, and communications ministries. See comments in Lebra, "Ōkuma, Modern Statesman," p. 205.

14. Quoted in Tokutomi, *Katsura,* I, 804. The Jiyūtō also could not have been unaware of the implications of the election returns of the sixth general election held on August 10, 1898. The Shimpotō won more seats than the Jiyūtō for the first time. The Kenseitō captured a total of 260 seats. Out of this number, the Shimpotō won 110 and the Jiyūtō claimed 95. Ōtsu, IV, 818. See also Lebra, "Ōkuma, Modern Statesman," p. 198. "Among the leaders of the Jiyūtō, there was a fear that if the Ōkuma-Itagaki cabinet enjoyed any measure of long life, this would result merely in enlarging Ōkuma's influence and bringing about a natural decrease in the [power] of the Jiyūtō. Actually, Matsuda Masahisa and Sugita Teiichi, who occupied positions as 'elder statesmen' of the Jiyūtō, looked upon Ōkuma with something akin to veneration." Baba, "Itō Miyoji ron," p. 210.

15. Saionji, writing to Itō on November 8, revealed that both the Jiyūtō and the Shimpotō were seeking a working arrangement with Itō. He wrote: "What the Jiyū and Shimpo factions both ardently desire is to combine [forces] with you. This situation, I believe, is already well known to you. However, it is extremely doubtful that the two factions desire to rely on your statesmanship because they have undergone sudden enlightenment. Their range of vision does not extend outside their diverse party interests." Quoted in Kaneko, *Itō den,* III, 406.

16. Quoted in Miyake, *Jidai shi*, III, 154. Hoshi, the politician, obviously shared the impatience of the younger bureaucrats with the continuing dominance of the oligarchs.

17. Ichijima, II, 311; Ozaki, *Minken tōsō*, p. 99. Itō Miyoji also wrote the draft of Itagaki's resignation. Kurihara, I, 304–305. See also, Kawada, p. 745. On August 22, 1898, Ozaki Yukio, then a relative youngster of thirty-nine, delivered a speech in which he drew up a hypothetical situation of a republican Japan that would inevitably see men from the Mitsubishi and Mitsui companies run for president. Although he was careful to preface his remarks with the statement that there was absolutely no chance that Japan would ever have a republican form of government, he was vehemently attacked by groups within and without the government for even uttering the words. It should be noted that Ozaki says that there were actually two stages in the incident. The initial flare-up diminished with Ozaki none the worse for wear. Ozaki believes that the affair was resurrected by Itagaki followers as a red herring. Itagaki, when this happened, was the center of an embarrassing controversy for granting permission to have Christian ministers serve as prison chaplains where previously only Buddhist priests had served. Ozaki, *Minken tōsō*, pp. 99–101; Isa, pp. 596–616.

18. Hackett, "Yamagata," pp. 284–286; Ozaki, *Minken tōsō*, p. 99. Miyake reveals what appears to be an authentic case of *haragei* in this connection. "Yamagata," he writes, "could not directly attack the cabinet, but his subordinates, observing his countenance, created conditions for the breakup of the [Ōkuma-Itagaki] cabinet." Miyake, *Jidai shi*, I, 151.

19. Itō was in China when he received the telegrams from Grand Chamberlain Iwakura Tomosada and Ōkuma on the cabinet crisis. He cut his trip short and returned to Nagasaki on November 7. Before he could leave Nagasaki the other *genrō* had nominated Yamagata. For details on the last days of the Ōkuma-Itagaki cabinet, see Ozaki, *Minken tōsō*, pp. 101–102; Tokutomi, *Katsura*, I, 829–830; Ozaki, "Itō, Ōkuma, Itagaki to watakushi," p. 357; Kaneko, *Itō den*, III, 403–404; Hayashida, *Seitō shi*, II, 24.

20. Tokutomi, *Katsura*, I, 836; Mumeishi, p. 36. Ōkuma believed that he could form a new cabinet based only on the Shimpotō.

21. Hayashida, *Seitō shi*, II, 27–28; *Hara nikki*, II(a), 254–255.

22. The Jiyūtō faction of the Kenseitō unilaterally dissolved the Kenseitō on October 29 and retained the name Kenseitō. The Shimpotō faction "reorganized" shortly thereafter and called itself the Kenseihontō (Orthodox Kenseitō). Many of the contemporary sources continued to use Jiyūtō and Shimpotō when referring to the two parties. This practice will be followed when these sources are quoted.

23. Idditti (p. 322) writes: "He [Itō] seems to have felt a godfather's love for the Ōkuma cabinet at whose birth he had assisted." Saionji, in the letter to Itō quoted above, continues: "I secretly rejoice that you did not form the present cabinet." Kaneko, *Itō den*, III, 406.

24. Yamagata postponed the opening ceremonies on the ground that he had to accompany the emperor to witness the grand maneuvers in the Osaka area. The first of the series of conversations is sometimes referred to as the "Osaka kaigi." Baba, "Itō Miyoji ron," p. 210.

25. It is also said that at this time the government paid 300,000 yen to the party. Cody p. 281.

26. Among other things, the Kenseitō platform called for electoral reform, extension of the franchise, and the nationalization of the railways. Uyehara, *Political Development*, p. 241. For information on the prolonged negotiations, see Hayashida, *Seitō shi*, II, 28–31; Tokutomi, *Katsura*, I, 853–858; Tokutomi, *Yamagata*, III, 348–357; Maeda, *Hoshi Tōru*, p. 316; Kurihara, pp. 307–308; Ōtsu, IV, 19; *Hara nikki*, II(a), 256; Clement, "Fifty Sessions of the Japanese Imperial Diet," p. 6.

27. *Hara nikki*, II(a), 256. Uyehara writes: "Of course, Itō largely contributed to the formation of this alliance." Uyehara, *Political Development*, p. 241.

28. In *Osaka asahi*, quoted in the *Kobe Weekly Chronicle* (Nov. 12, 1898), p. 400. When Hoshi concluded the pact with Yamagata, he made the great general pause in amazement with a typically cocky, but realistic, assessment of their respective strengths in the Lower House: " . . . at the very least I control 40 men. Pray, tell me, how many soldiers can you mobilize [in the House of Representatives?]." Quoted in Masumi, "1890 nendai no seitō soshiki," p. 67. Cf. Scalapino, *Democracy*, p. 177.

29. This was not the first time that this proposal was made. A resident foreigner, writing in 1895, said that, before and after the Sino-Japanese War, there was talk of suspending the constitution. On April 10, 1897, Sasaki Takayuki made a similar recommendation in a conversation with the Meiji emperor. See "Japanese Constitutional Crisis and the War," pp. 457, 476; and Watanabe Ikujirō, *Meiji tennō no seitoku: Seiji* (The virtues of the Meiji emperor: Politics; Tokyo, 1942), pp. 303–304. Katsura is also credited with suggesting, on June 24, 1898, that the postwar development projects be carried out even at the cost of suspending the constitution. Yamagata's "organ," *Keika nippō*, made public the thesis of repeated dissolutions, thus giving it at least semiofficial blessing. See *Itō Hirobumi hiroku*, p. 295; Tokutomi, *Katsura*, I, 787–788; Kaneko, *Itō den*, III, 376–377, 390; *Kobe Weekly Chronicle* (July 9, 1898), p. 10; *ibid.* (July 2, 1898), p. 584; *ibid.* (Nov. 18, 1898), p. 416; Watanabe, *Meiji shi*, p. 338.

30. Mumeishi, p. 35; Hackett, "Yamagata," pp. 289–290. According to Hackett, the "policy of assaulting the center" involved driving a wedge between the parties and keeping them apart. Katsura, however, envisaged the possibility that in spite of the government's efforts the two parties might still combine against the government. One source credits Katsura with political acumen and talent from the time of the first Diet session. At that time he persuaded the budget committee members to limit the reduction of the army's requests to a mere 300,000 yen. Mumeishi, p. 28. The anonymous writer of this lengthy article apparently was Tokutomi.

31. Hackett, "Yamagata," p. 314. Earlier, on June 27, 1898, Yamagata wrote to Tanaka Kōken, minister of the Imperial Household. Tanaka was instructed to advise the emperor that when Ōkuma and Itagaki were given the imperial command to form their cabinet, the command was not to include the positions of the service ministers. Yamagata's aim was to make it abundantly clear that the service ministers were entering the cabinet under special circumstances. Hackett, "Yamagata," pp. 282–283. See also Tokutomi, *Katsura*, I, 795.

32. Scalapino, *Democracy*, pp. 174–175 and 175n72. Yanaga is much more emphatic. He states: "No other legal provision so strengthened the position of the bureaucracy and the military and so retarded constitutional progress as the Imperial Ordinance [*sic*] of May 1900 . . . This gave the Army and Navy the power of life and death over the government since either one could wreck any existing cabinet or prevent the formation of a new one by withdrawing its Minister or by refusing to recommend one. It gave the military the power to manipulate the exercise of sovereignty, inasmuch as no cabinet could exist without the consent and cooperation of the military." Yanaga, *Japan since Perry*, p. 266. See also Colgrove, "The Japanese Constitution," p. 1028n4; Borton, *Japan's Modern Century*, p. 146.

33. Hackett, "Yamagata," pp. 307–309; Yanaga, *Japan since Perry*, p. 264.

34. Hackett, "Yamagata," p. 313. This is the Yamagata who, in 1893, as president of the Privy Council, expressed strong doubts that the organ's reviewing power extended beyond its right to interpret constitutional questions and laws. When he stated these views in 1893 it was obvious that he wanted to embarrass Itō, who was seeking a ruling on a memorial submitted by the Lower House impeaching the government. Kaneko, *Itō den*, II, 929–933. The expansion at this time of the powers of the Privy Council is also discussed in Arthur E. Tiedemann, "The Hamaguchi Cabinet, First Phase July 1929–February 1930: A Study in Japanese Parliamentary Government," Ph.D. thesis (Columbia, 1959), pp. 21–23, 33.

35. It should be recalled that Matsukata had very early attempted to tamper with the rule that only generals could serve.

36. Tokutomi, *Katsura,* I, 848–849. See also, Tokutomi, *Sohōjiden,* pp. 357–358. Katsura also represents the tendency of subordinates to suggest more radical steps than those in responsible positions are willing or able to take. Sasaki Takayuki recorded that Itō, in March 1881, told him that he was troubled by the radical views of the (young) secretaries. Sasaki replied that Itō's views had changed greatly from those he had held five or six years previously. Itō laughed, and admitted that he, too, had caused his seniors some anxiety with his radical views five or six short years ago. Quoted in Osatake, *Nihon kensei shi taikō,* II, 486. Itō was described by the *Chicago Times* in 1872 as "somewhat radical." See Brown, "Kido Takayoshi," p. 200; also, pp. 179, 208.

37. Tokutomi, *Katsura,* I, 954–956. Cf. Tokutomi, *Yamagata,* III, 362–363. The sale of bonds was meeting spectacular failure. The amount called for, but still unsubscribed by the time the 1899 budget was compiled, was 125,000,000 yen. Tokutomi, *Katsura,* I, 956.

38. Tokutomi, *Yamagata,* III, 363–368; Ichijima, II, 334–337; Yanaga, *Japan since Perry,* p. 264; Hayashida, *Seitō shi,* II, 31. The amount realized through these increases was some 43,000,000 yen. Besides, the government succeeded in floating a sterling loan for 100,000,000 yen and collected 86,000,000 yen. Tokutomi, *Katsura,* I, 956. The Kenseitō received at least some concrete repayments for its cooperation. The government introduced a measure increasing the salaries of the presiding officers of the two houses from 4,000 to 5,000 yen. The vice-presidents' salaries were increased from 2,000 to 3,000 yen, and other Diet members' salaries from 800 to 2,000 yen. Yanaga, *Japan since Perry,* p. 264; Hayashida, *Seitō shi,* II, 31.

39. The *Kobe Weekly Chronicle* (July 2, 1898), pp. 577–578. Mayo makes the following observations: "Thus almost from the beginning of their assumption of power, once they had been able to agree on principles, then on the wording and timing of an initial announcement, the Meiji authorities had joined their confirmation of the treaties to an open desire for revision." The first attempt at revision in February 1869 was a call to the foreign powers to designate accurately the Japanese authority responsible for making treaties—the emperor. In April 1869 Iwakura set down his views on the treaties in a memorandum, and though he did not touch on tariff autonomy, "he was helping to shape arguments against the legal provisions of the treaties into the form which was to prevail in later years." Mayo, pp. 50, 53, 62–66.

The treaty signed with Britain on July 16, 1894, as the first step in abolishing the unequal treaties, stipulated that the provisions would go into effect five years later, in 1899. Yanaga, *Japan since Perry,* p. 196.

40. See, Scalapino, "Japan: Between Traditionalism and Democracy," p. 316.

41. Tokutomi reports that Katsura himself was willing to compromise on the army budget when he was asked to reduce army requests under the Ōkuma-Itagaki cabinet. Tokutomi, *Katsura,* I, 810–811.

42. Quoted in Mizuno, p. 157. When Itō was about to take over the Kenseitō, the *Japan Weekly Mail* asserted: "Although the Marquis cannot be persuaded to accept the leadership of the Liberals as at present constituted, he realizes the importance of party cooperation in constitutional government" (June 30, 1900; p. 638).

43. Hayashida, *Seitō shi,* II, 32; Yanaga, *Japan since Perry,* p. 264; Ōtsu, V, 56.

44. Maeda, *Hoshi Tōru,* p. 331. Some allowances for errors and exaggeration by Maeda should be made, for he is guilty of both in this biography. Cf., for example, Kurihara, I, 313 and Miyake, *Jidai shi,* III, 170.

45. Maeda, *Hoshi Tōru,* p. 331.

46. Quoted in Tokutomi, *Katsura,* I, 797. Miyake says that when Itō became president of the Seiyūkai, he wanted to abolish the local branches. Hoshi, according to Miyake,

reminded Itō that the existence of these branches was intimately related to party strength. Miyake, *Jidai shi*, III, 212. See also Masumi, "1890 nendai no seitō soshiki," p. 68.

47. Quoted in Tokutomi, *Katsura*, I, 865; see also, pp. 865–869.

48. Maeda, *Hoshi Tōru*, p. 321.

49. Letter dated September 8, 1899, quoted in Tokutomi, *Yamagata*, III, 377–378. The shift in strength is all the more striking because the Kenseihontō had, only in the previous general election for Diet members, elected more representatives to the Diet than the Kenseitō.

50. Ōkuma, "Nihon no seitō," p. 159. The passage of an election reform law during the fourteenth session (November 20, 1899–February 24, 1900) may be said to have been another payment for Kenseitō support. Under this law, tax qualification for suffrage was reduced from fifteen yen to ten yen and the system of secret ballot was adopted. The number of representatives was also raised by sixty-nine, the total then becoming 369. See Yanaga, *Japan since Perry*, p. 265; Norman, *Japan's Emergence*, p. 189; Maeda, *Hoshi Tōru*, p. 332.

51. Itagaki had very early, in March 1892, stated that the ideal party should concentrate its activities in the Diet through representatives who would represent the national interests rather than a single district. Cody, p. 234.

52. The *Japan Weekly Mail* (June 9, 1900), p. 561. Hoshi, Kataoka Kenkichi, Matsuda Masahisa, and Hayashi Yuzō of the Jiyūtō called on Itō on June 1, 1900, to ask him to lead the Kenseitō. Hayashida, *Seitō shi*, II, 44–46; Kaneko, *Itō den*, III, 443. See also Okazaki Kunisuke's recollection of the time in *Itō Hirobumi hiroku*, pp. 174–175.

53. Scalapino, *Democracy*, p. 179. See also Oka Yoshitake, "Gaikanteki rikkensei ni okeru seitō: Seitō seijika to shite no Hara Kei" (The political parties in a superficial constitutional system: Hara Kei as a party politician), *Shisō*, No. 333:32 (Mar. 1953). Itō had declined the first Kenseitō offer to place itself under his leadership. On July 1, however, he had written a draft of the policy of the party he planned to organize. By August 23 the Kenseitō "unconditionally" offered to dissolve itself and to place the "party" at Itō's disposal. On August 25 an inaugural committee was created to establish the new party. For some details on these events, see Kaneko, *Itō den*, III, 442–462; Maeda, *Hoshi Tōru*, pp. 338–340; Hayashida, *Seitō shi*, II, 42–66; Isa pp. 633–643; "Itō nyūtō mondai" (The question of Itō's entry into a political party), *CK*, 15:44–45 (July 1900); Ōtsu, V, 116–131; Kurihara, I, 316–323; Hackett, "Yamagata," p. 322; *Hara nikki*, II(a), 286; Itō Masanori, *Kato Takaaki* (Tokyo, 1929), I, 465.

54. The most conspicuous aspect of the regulations of the Seiyūkai was the great power concentrated in the president of the party, in this case Itō. Among other things, the president was empowered to appoint members of the executive committee and to determine the number of members. He could appoint and direct the heads of the various sections o the party. He could summon meetings of the Diet members of the party when the Diet was in session. See Hayashida, *Seitō shi*, II, 106–108; *Japan Weekly Mail* (Sept. 22, 1900), p. 303.

55. Quoted in *ibid.*, (Sept. 1, 1900), p. 224. Watanabe Ikujirō's interpretation is that the handing over of the Kenseitō to Itō was the result of "profound" political thinking on the part of Hoshi and the others in the party. They felt, according to Watanabe, that in the world of political parties those who possessed *de facto* power won. So long as the Kenseitō faction remained the majority, they believed, the new party would automatically come under its control. Hence, Watanabe concludes, the Kenseitō leaders felt that there was no need to "adhere to such matters as honor." Watanabe, *Meiji tennō: Seiji*, p. 314. Miyake goes further and says that with this speech Hoshi served notice to both the Kenseitō and Itō that he was *de facto* party head. Miyake, *Jidai shi*, III, 209; see also Hayashida, *Seitō shi*, II, 85.

56. Quoted in *Itō Hirobumi hiroku*, p. 154. Ozaki Yukio says that the Hoshi faction was

powerful in the Seiyūkai and that "the authority of President Itō was hardly effective." Ozaki, *Minken tōsō*, p. 109. Maeda's description of the tight control Hoshi wielded over one budget deliberative conference between party men and cabinet ministers also illustrates Hoshi's real power in the Seiyūkai. See Maeda Renzan, *Hara Kei den* (A biography of Hara Kei, Tokyo, 1943), I, 440–442; see also Ōtsu, V, 130–131. Hattori writes: "The despot in the party and the Lower House was not Itō, but Hoshi." Hattori Yukifusa (Shisō), "Meiji no dokusaisha" (Autocrats of the Meiji), *Kaizō*, 35.10:96–97 (1954). Cf. Scalapino, *Democracy*, pp. 179–180, and n. 84.

57. Hayashida, *Seitō shi*, II, 65–66. Ōtsu (V, 140) gives the number as 15. As Maeda observed, "So while [the Seiyūkai] may be called a new party, it was really the Kenseitō." Maeda, *Hoshi Tōru*, p. 348. Ozaki Yukio and nine others from Ōkuma's Kenseihontō were among those not from the Kenseitō. Ozaki, *Minken tōsō*, p. 108.

58. As stated in chapter IX, the combination of the Kenseitō and Itō set the pattern for subsequent government parties of an open alliance between bureaucrats and politicians. When the Liberal-Democratic party sought to determine the successor to Prime Minister Kishi Nobusuke in July 1960, one of the cleavages in the party occurred between "party men" and "bureaucrats." See *Tokyo shimbun* (July 13, 15, 1960), and *Mainichi shimbun* (July 14 and 15, 1960).

59. *Jimmin* (Mar. 16, 1899). Itō, moreover, still was not able to get the wholehearted support of the industrialists. Shibusawa Eiichi, for instance, refused to join the projected party. Itō is described by Shibusawa as becoming "greatly angered." Only Inoue Kaoru's intercession prevented the rupture of a friendship of thirty years' standing. *Itō Hirobumi hiroku*, p. 10. See also Uno Shun'ichi, "Itō Hirobumi: Rikken seiyūkai kessei no zentei jōken wo chūshin ni" (Hirobumi Itō: A problem on the organization of the Rikken Seiyū party), *RK*, No. 253:48 (May 1961).

60. The *Japan Weekly Mail*, though not fully convinced that a merger would take place, stated: "If he [Itō] ever does consent to take the leadership of a party—which is doubtful—there can be no question as to the choice he will make" (Apr. 15, 1899; p. 365).

61. The *Kobe Weekly Chronicle* (Jan. 18, 1899). Itō's advice to Hoshi in Kobe in November 1898 should also be recalled. Itō's supporters were divided into two factions on the subject of combining with the Kenseitō. Itō Miyoji led the group that strongly urged Itō to accept the Kenseitō offer to place the party under Itō. Hayashida opposed the idea that Itō should work with the Kenseitō. Hayashida's reason was that since the Kenseitō was nothing more than the Jiyūtō in a new guise, it would damage Itō's moral stature to head the party. Itō Miyoji insisted that if Itō accepted the Kenseitō offer he would be leading a party that was established and one that had a "firm and solid" basis. Itō Miyoji stressed that this foundation was not and could not be built up in a day. When Itō finally decided to make use of the Kenseitō, Hayashida "cut off relationship" with Itō. Hayashida, *Seitō shi*, II, 58, 66.

62. Quoted in *Itō zenshū*, II, 280.

63. Itō opened his campaign with two speeches in Nagano in April 1899. He returned to Ōiso and then proceeded to the Kansai area, speaking in Osaka on May 8. He spoke successively in Kōchi, Kobe, and Shimonoseki. He then crossed over to Kyushu and spoke at Ōita and Fukuoka. He doubled back to Honshu, where he addressed crowds at Yamaguchi and Hiroshima. On June 16 he returned to his Ōiso residence via Nagoya. He spoke over twenty times in all. Four months later, in October, he began his swing into northern Japan. See Kaneko, *Itō den*, III, 411–416.

64. Article XIX of the Meiji constitution reads: "Japanese subjects may, according to qualifications determined in laws or ordinances, be appointed to civil or military or any other public office equally." Quoted in Quigley and Turner, p. 417.

65. Quoted in *Itō zenshū*, II, 173–178.

66. Quoted in *ibid.*, II, 168–171. The citations from *Itō zenshū* are from speeches Itō

made during the tour. For restatements of his basic ideas in English, see the *Japan Weekly Mail* (Sept. 1, 1900), p. 230; Itō Hirobumi, "The Duties of Political Parties," pp. 72–75.

67. *Itō zenshū*, II, 113–117.

68. Yamagata saw the successful conclusions of the thirteenth (November 7, 1898–March 10, 1899) and the fourteenth (November 20, 1899–February 23, 1900) sessions of the Diet, mainly on the strength of Kenseitō support.

69. Hayashida, *Seitō shi*, II, 44–52; Tokutomi, *Yamagata*, III, 426.

70. Quoted in Kaneko, *Itō den*, III, 464. When Yamagata indicated his desire to resign for the first time, he asked Katsura to be his successor since none of the other genrō would accept the position. Tokutomi, *Katsura*, I, 886–887.

71. *Ibid.*, I, 935; Hayashida, *Seitō shi*, II, 115; Miyake, *Jidai shi*, III, 204–205; Itō Masanori, I, 373; Hackett, "Yamagata," p. 323. Cf. Komatsu, *Itō to Yamagata*, pp. 95–100; Kaneko, *Itō den*, III, 466.

72. Suzuki, *Hyōden Itō*, p. 303; see also Ozaki, *Minken tōsō*, p. 33.

73. *Ibid.*, p. 34. Ōkuma, Itō's other rival, declared right after Itō's death that while ambition is essential in the make-up of a politician, Itō's political actions were inevitably motivated by one test, that of the nation's welfare. Itō, according to Ōkuma, was never prompted by ambition, and never willfully engaged in grasping for power. Ōkuma Shigenobu, "Seijika to shite no Itō kō" (Prince Itō as a politician), *Taiyō*, 15:162 (Nov. 1909). Cf. translation appearing in the *Japan Weekly Mail* (Nov. 27, 1909), p. 698. See also Komatsu, *Itō to Yamagata*, p. 69; Suzuki, *Hyōden Itō*, p. 303; *Ajiya* (Sept. 1, 1893), Vol. 1, No. 10; *Japan Weekly Mail* (Mar. 24, 1906), pp. 314–315. The loosening of ties between Itō and his closest followers is also indicative of his indifference to empire-building. Itō and Itō Miyoji, as we have noted, were estranged for a period after 1898. It also appears that Inoue Kowashi drifted away from Itō and into Yamagata's camp after 1890 or 1891. Tokutomi, "Itō, Ōkuma, Yamagata," p. 284. Ozaki regards this as a basic cause for Itō's eventual failure as a party leader. Ozaki writes: "Itō, when he was impressed by say, a bureaucrat, would enthusiastically make use of him. However, once the person in question had served Itō's needs, Itō would indifferently and without a second thought cut off relations. In this respect he differed greatly from Hoshi and Hara. Once someone close to Itō remarked, 'Inukai and Hoshi have quite a number of devoted and loyal supporters.' Itō's answer was, 'Such is not the case with me. Not making supporters is my special virtue.' Because he thought this way Itō could not create a faction. There was no such thing as an Itō clique; there was only a body of admirers. There were none who would stick by Itō through thick or thin. Japanese parties in truth are not public parties but factions. Hence a person like Itō could not be expected to have any measure of success in controlling [a party]." Ozaki, "Itō, Ōkuma, Itagaki, to watakushi," p. 352.

74. "The files of the *Japan Weekly Mail* are an almost indispensable source book for the history of the Meiji era. After 1900 their value rapidly diminished, however, for the editor [Captain Frank Brinkley, R.A.] about that time was offered and accepted a subsidy from the Japanese Government, and thereafter became a thick and thin supporter of the Administration and its measures." McLaren, *Political History*, p. 157n1.

75. *Japan Weekly Mail* (Apr. 15, 1899), p. 365.

76. *Ibid.*, (July 22, 1899), p. 82; (July 1, 1899), p. 10; (Mar 24, 1900), p. 280.

77. Quoted in *Itō zenshū*, II, 235. See also Itō Hirobumi, *Marquis Itō's Experience*, tr., Kuramata Teizō (Nagasaki, 1904), p. 125; and Ōkuma Shigenobu, "Itō kō wo tsuitō suru" (Eulogizing Prince Itō), in *Ko Itō kōshaku tsuitōe enzetsu* (Eulogies to the late Prince Itō), Special issue of *KGZ*, No. 281:1007 (July 1910).

78. Speech delivered at the inaugural ceremony of the Okayama branch of the Seiyūkai, July 15, 1901, quoted in *Itō zenshū*, II, 358. See also, Itō's statements in *KGZ*, 13.154:6 (1899); *Nichi nichi shimbun* (Dec. 21, 1900). Ozaki Yukio substantiates Itō's professed lack of personal ambition in conducting state affairs. He recalls: "From childhood I was taught

to look upon Itō as a political enemy . . . [Later] I clearly discerned that Itō might have made mistakes . . . but that he never had any malicious intentions. In short, he conducted state affairs from a fair and just position . . . He can be classed as a great statesman because of this characteristic." Ozaki, *Minken tōsō*, p. 33. See also Uyehara Etsujirō, "Katsura kō to Itō kō" (Prince Katsura and Prince Itō), *Kokka oyobi kokkagaku* (The state and statecraft), 1:13–14 (Nov. 1913); Matsukage Sanjin, "Yamagata kō to rikken seiji" (Prince Yamagata and constitutional government), *ibid.*, 1:15–16 (Mar. 1913).

79. For example, *Itō zenshū*, II, 109–235. Another motive has been suggested for the formation of the Seiyūkai. This is that Itō wanted to create a unified body politic so that Japan could participate with the capitalistic nations of the west in the carving of the Chinese melon. The first step toward this goal, according to this view, was the creation of the Seiyūkai. Uno, pp. 46–47.

CONCLUSIONS

1. Scalapino, *Democracy*, p. 346; also his "Japan: Between Traditionalism and Democracy," p. 317.

2. James B. Crowley may have started a long-needed revisionist trend in the interpretation of the 1930's. See, for example, his view of the characterization, "government by assassination," in "Japan's China Policy," pp. 110–111; see also *ibid.*, pp. 79–83, 318–319, and his "A Reconsideration of the Marco Polo Incident," *Journal of Asian Studies*, 22:277–291 (May 1963).

3. Richard Storry, *A History of Modern Japan* (London, 1960), p. 18; Yoshino Sakuzō, "Fascism in Japan," *Contemporary Japan*, 1:185 (Sept. 1932).

4. Paul Clyde is correct in differentiating between Anglo-Saxon/American studies on Japan and those from continental Europe. Paul H. Clyde, "Japan's March to Empire: Some Bibliographical Evaluations," *Journal of Modern History*, 21:333–335 (Dec. 1949). To his first category, Canadian should be added.

5. Scalapino, *Democracy*, p. 346.

6. This thesis has been brilliantly articulated by Scalapino in *ibid*. See also his "The Japanese Diet Today," *Parliamentary Affairs*, 5:347–349 (Summer 1952). Earlier exponents are E. H. Norman in his *Japan's Emergence as a Modern State*, Chap. 6: "Parties and Politics," and T. A. Bisson, "Japan as a Political Organism," *Pacific Affairs*, 17:392–420 (Dec. 1944). The heritage of failure is forcefully and ably traced from the Restoration to the years before 1890 by Ike in *Political Democracy*, and by Beckmann in *Making of the Meiji Constitution*. See also Beckmann's "Political Crises and the Crystallization of Japanese Constitutional Thought, 1871–1881," *Pacific Affairs*, 23:259–270 (Aug. 1954). For Hugh Borton, in the period " . . . from the restoration of Emperor Meiji in 1868 to the surrender . . . on September 2, 1945, conservatism, absolutism and a strong centralized autocracy were the guiding political principles of Japan." "Past Limitations and the Future of Democracy in Japan," *Political Science Quarterly*, 70:412 (Sep. 1955). This statement reflects his approach in *Japan's Modern Century*. There is also the dichotomous approach which highlights the "democratic" postwar Japanese scene by contrasting it with a "despotic" prewar Japan. See, for example, Justin Williams, "The Japanese Diet under the New Constitution," *American Politican Science Review*, 42:927–939 (Oct. 1948). Williams was chief of the Legislative Division, Government Section, SCAP. For a recent vigorous exposition of this approach see John M. Maki, *Government and Politics in Japan: The Road to Democracy* (New York, 1962). It would be dangerous, of course, to state that the dismal view of prewar Japanese politics resulted only from looking at the Japan of the 1930's and the Pacific War. One of the earliest and fullest expositions in the pessimistic school is McLaren's *Political History*. In his preface (pp. 8–9) McLaren provides a hint to the reason for his viewpoint: "My main criticism of their system is directed against the appalling lack of principle dis-

played, not only in connection with their domestic but also their foreign policy. That there is a tendency toward an increase rather than a diminution of unprincipled action, and that a remedy will not be found except in an abatement of the intense chauvinism of the race, *especially of the ruling military caste,* is my settled conviction." Clyde suggests another when he states that McLaren's work is "marred by a regrettable tendency to moralize." Clyde, "Japan's March to Empire," p. 337.

7. During the Pacific War it was asserted by some that the Japanese were not only political deviants but that they suffered from national psychological and character disorders bordering on the psychotic. The classic studies are Geoffrey Gorer, "Themes in Japanese Culture," *Transactions of the New York Academy of Science,* 5:105–124 (Jan. 1943); Weston La Barre, "Some Observations on Character Structure in the Orient: The Japanese," *Psychiatry,* 8:319–342 (Aug. 1945); Herman Spitzer, "Psychoanalytic Approaches to the Japanese Character," in Geza Roheim, ed., *Psychoanalysis and the Social Sciences* (New York, 1947), I, 131–156.

8. O. Eltzbacher, "How Japan Reformed Herself," *Nineteenth Century and After,* 56:41 (July 1904). He also stated (p. 28), " . . . the world has learned to respect and admire Japan for her splendid achievements in every province of human activity."

9. T. A. Bisson, *Japan in China* (New York, 1938).

10. Ralph E. Minger, "Taft's Missions to Japan: A Study in Personal Diplomacy," *Pacific Historical Review,* 30:280 (Aug. 1961). For a readable account of the changes in the American views of Japan, see William L. Neumann, *America Encounters Japan: From Perry to MacArthur* (Baltimore, 1963). China, too, has been the object of wildly fluctuating generalizations. In the eighteenth century Voltaire depicted China as "the finest, most extensive, most populous, and most civilized Kingdom in the Universe." Voltaire, "A Conversation with a Chinese," *Works of Voltaire* (Ohio, 1905), IV, 32. In the next century another Westerner declared with equal passion, "The state of China since time immemorial is one of the bestial degeneracy of nearly all the most noble faculties of mankind." J. B. Aubry, *The Chinese At Home,* quoted in Edward Eyre, ed., *European Civilization* (New York, 1939), III, 717.

11. It would also appear that this way of viewing nations is a rather common phenomenon. Edward Crankshaw, discussing his approach to the study of Russian affairs, writes: "One of our difficulties when it comes to understanding foreign countries is that we think of them almost exclusively in terms of foreign policy, whereas they are thinking of themselves much more in terms of domestic policy. This is natural and inevitable; but it is also unfortunate. It means, for example, that the Soviet Union is seen by us always in relation to our problems and hardly at all in relation to its own. To hear people talk, to read the Western newspapers, one would think that the Soviet Government devotes nine-tenths of its energies and ingenuity to making trouble for us, whereas in fact it is spending most of its time in trying to make the Soviet Union work . . . Hence the fundamental unreality which permeates the study of foreign countries . . . we are so taken up by what the Russians say about us, which is usually vicious, and so little interested in what they say about themselves." Crankshaw, *Khrushchev's Russia* (Baltimore, 1959), "Foreword."

12. Harold R. Isaacs, *Scratches on Our Mind: American Images of China and India* (New York, 1958), p. 107, and n. 27, pp. 107–108.

13. He also argues that " . . . the pattern of history is what is put there by the historian." Edward Hallet Carr, *The New Society* (London, 1951), pp. 11, 12.

14. Pittau suggests " . . . the best interpretation of the Meiji political system still remains that given by Meiji thinkers." Pittau, "The Meiji Political System," p. 122.

15. Tsunoda Ryūsaku, William Theodore de Bary, and Donald Keene, comps., *Sources of Japanese Tradition* (New York, 1958), p. 666. See also Beckmann, *Making of the Meiji Constitution,* pp. 111–112; Pittau, "Ideology," pp. 303–304.

16. Osatake, *Nihon kensei shi no kenkyū,* p. 323; Itō Hirobumi "Some Reminiscences of

the Grant of the New Constitution," in Ōkuma Shigenobu, ed., *Fifty Years of New Japan* (London, 1909), I, 130, also, p. 126.

17. Hane, "English Liberalism," p. 241. This was also not an uncommon position to take in England at this time. "Perhaps the most remarkable feature of this instrument [the Meiji constitution] is to be found in the safeguards by which the executive is protected from the encroachments of the representative bodies which it has called into existence. The statesmen of Japan, with all the political experience of the Western world to draw upon for their instruction, appear to have been impressed at least as much by the disadvantages and dangers as by the benefits of popular government." "The Japanese Revolution," *Quarterly Review,* 200:300 (July 1904).

18. Tsunoda *et al.,* pp. 730, 737, 728. "And that aspect of Confucianism known as *min-pen-chu-i* (Japanese, *mimpongshugi*) principle of the people as the basis [of the state] *should never be equated to democracy.*" Scalapino, *Democracy,* p. 7 (italics mine).

19. Robert E. Ward, "Political Modernization and Political Culture in Japan," *World Politics,* 15:575–577 (July 1963).

20. I am aware that there were various schools of Confucianism in the Tokugawa period; that Tokugawa Confucianism may differ from the Confucianism of the Meiji leaders, which in turn may differ from the Confucianism of Yoshino. Pittau, for example, has shown the differences between the *kokutai* (national polity) of the Tokugawa, Meiji, and Showa periods and between different groups of Meiji leaders. While he points to the importance of continuity, he seems also to underplay the influence of Tokugawa Confucian thought on the Meiji leaders. Pittau, "Ideology," pp. v, 55–57; 302–303, Chap. 2: "Political Thought in Pre-Meiji Japan."

21. Craig, *Chōshū in the Meiji Restoration,* p. 144, see pp. 143–164; Jansen, *Sakamoto Ryōma,* p. 95; Tsunoda *et al.,* pp. 638–643, 662–679, 702–713; Itō, "Reminiscences," pp. 123–124.

22. Bisson, "Japan as a Political Organism," pp. 393–401. See also Scalapino, *Democracy,* Chap. 1: "The Tokugawa Background." McLaren clearly oversimplified the nature of the Confucian ideology when he dismissed it with: "Chinese political philosophy, which had been adopted by the Japanese along with so much else that was Chinese can be summarized in a sentence—it is the duty of the governors to rule, and of the governed to obey." McLaren, *Political History,* p. 107.

23. McLaren, "Documents," p. 575, also p. 572. A strong echo of this account is found in the words of William G. Sumner who wrote in 1883: "So far as I can find out what the classes are who are respectively endowed with the rights and duties of posing and solving social problems, they are as follows: Those who are bound to solve the problems are the rich, comfortable, prosperous, virtuous, respectable, educated and healthy; those whose right it is to set the problems are those who have been less fortunate or less successful in the struggle for existence. The problem itself seems to be, How shall the latter be made as comfortable as the former? To solve this problem, and make us all equally well off, is assumed to be the duty of the former class; the penalty, if they fail of this, is to be bloodshed and destruction." Quoted in Ray Allen Billington, *et al.,* eds., *The Making of American Democracy: Readings and Documents* (New York, 1962), II, 73–74. We shall see, however, that the Meiji leaders differed with Sumner on the critical point of the roles and goals of government.

24. Beckmann, *Making of the Meiji Constitution,* pp. 132–133.

25. Tsunoda *et al.,* pp. 709, 713.

26. McLaren, "Documents," p. 576; Beckmann, *Making of the Meiji Constitution,* p. 111; Itō, "Reminiscences," p. 129. The Meiji leaders therefore anticipated Yoshino's views on the dangers of "oligarchic" government. Tsunoda *et al.,* pp. 737–738.

27. McLaren, "Documents," pp. 621, 622, 576, 439; Tsunoda *et al.,* p. 709.

28. McLaren, "Documents," p. 622. See also Ōkubo's views in Tsunoda *et al.,* p. 666.

Here again, the Meiji leaders anticipated Yoshino who contended that "There is absolutely no contradiction nowadays between 'the interest of the Imperial Family' and the interest of the nation, [an interest] which stands at the very top of the people's well-being." *Ibid.*, p. 732.

29. George B. Sansom, *Japan: A Short Cultural History* (New York, 1943), pp. 104, 111. See also Edwin O. Reischauer, "Our Asian Frontiers of Knowledge," *University of Arizona Bulletin Series*, 29:18 (Sept. 1958). It should be noted that in the Tokugawa period certain Japanese Confucian scholars were advocating the principle of vertical mobility. Ogyū Sorai and Nakae Tōju may be cited as examples. See Tsunoda *et al.*, pp. 433 and 382.

30. McLaren, "Documents," p. 622.

31. Itō, "Reminiscences," pp. 123–125. Itō's statement reminds us of Chang Chih-tung's rallying cry: "Chinese learning for the fundamental principles, Western learning for practical application." See Teng Ssu-yu, and John K. Fairbank, *China's Response to the West: A Documentary Survey, 1839–1923* (Cambridge, Mass., 1954), pp. 164–165.

32. Tsunoda *et al.*, p. 666. Itō parrots the words by calling for "adapting the principle [of constitutional politics] to our national characteristics, manners, and customs." McLaren, "Documents," p. 621.

33. Those administering American economic aid to underdeveloped countries are cautioned, on the basis of studies by social scientists working with them, "Beware of changes that conflict with religious beliefs or practices"; "Don't assume that material values necessarily outweigh other values people find in their lives"; or "Don't apply the economic syllogisms of a highly developed market exchange economy to the largely non-pecuniary economic activities of underdeveloped areas." Samuel P. Hayes Jr., "Personality and Culture Problems of Point IV," in Bert F. Hozelitz, ed., *The Progress of Underdeveloped Areas* (Chicago, 1952), p. 203. See also in *ibid.*, "Economic Backwardness in Historical Perspective," by Alexander Gerschenkron, who says: "What can be derived from a historical review is a strong sense for the significance of the native elements in industrialization of backward countries" (p. 26).

34. Kaneko, "Kempō seitei kaikyū dan," pp. 3–4. The date of this advice is highly important since it is still another indication of general government interest in constitutionalism antedating the "great surge" in the movement for parliamentary government.

35. Baron Kentarō Kaneko, "The Magna Charta of Japan," *Century Magazine*, 68:486 (July 1904). Actually, Spencer gave very conservative advice and was piqued that his advice was not taken to heart, and stressed that the Japanese were consequently "experiencing the evils arising from too large an installment of freedom." See letter to Kaneko, quoted in Nagai Michio, "Herbert Spencer in Early Meiji Japan," *Far Eastern Quarterly*, 14:58 (Nov. 1954).

36. McLaren, "Documents," p. 574.

37. Itō in McLaren, "Documents," p. 621. It should not be forgotten that even the opposition press pointed to this factor with undisguised satisfaction.

38. On this, too, the influence seems pervasive. "There is still a residual legacy that is deep rooted traditional disapproval if not abhorrence of division, disruption, and factionalism which political parties reflect. Consequently, parties to an average Japanese symbolize clashes and cleavages that are detrimental to social harmony and inimical to national well-being." Yanaga Chitoshi, "Japanese Political Parties," *Parliamentary Affairs*, 10:266 (Summer 1957).

39. Itō, "Reminiscences," p. 129. It is conceivable that what Itō called socialistic ideas is what Yoshino called *heimin shugi* (democracy). "*Heimin shugi* implies an opposition between the common people *(heimin)* and the nobility, and there is the risk it will be misunderstood to mean that the nobility is the enemy and the common people are the friendly forces. By themselves the words *minshū shugi* are not liable to such a misinterpretation, but they smack of overemphasis on the masses *(minshū)*." Tsunoda *et al.*, p. 728.

40. Horie Yasuzō, "Confucian Concept of State in Tokugawa Japan," *Kyoto University Economic Review*, 32:34–35 (Oct. 1962).

41. "There is a widely held view in the United States that social welfare makes a country 'soft' and attention is drawn to Britain, Sweden, and New Zealand. Leaving aside the question whether any of these countries is truly 'soft,' the facts are somewhat different from what this picture would suggest. After all, the originator of the social security state was none other than Bismarck, the Great German chancellor who transformed Germany into one of the most powerful modern nations." D. W. Brogan and Douglas V. Verney, *Political Patterns in Today's World* (New York and Burlingame, 1963), p. 108. Siemes (p. 7) says that Bismarck's social legislation was inspired by the ideas of "social monarchy." Itō firmly believed that Japan's defeat of Russia in 1905 was the result of a "slowly but steadily constitutionalized" monarch. Itō, "Reminiscences," p. 126. The opposition endorsed Itō's views, but naturally with stress on the Diet. Ōtsu, for example, writes: " . . . a primary reason for the victory in the Russo-Japanese War is the Diet which made clear the efficacy of constitutional government. The same may be said for the Sino-Japanese War." Ōtsu, V, 855.

42. Siemes, p. 7. I am grateful to Father Siemes for sending me a reprint of this article, which I should otherwise surely have missed reading. I am indebted to Father Pittau also for sending from Tokyo a copy of his manuscript. Readers will undoubtedly notice the influence of these two works in these pages. For a discussion of Roesler, Stein, and Gneist, see Pittau, "Ideology," Chap. 7: "The German Influence: Roesler and the Making of the Constitution."

43. Siemes, pp. 6–7.

44. *Ibid.*, p. 7.

45. *Ibid.*, p. 8. Roesler's ideas stemmed from a reaction against the classical liberal theory of the nineteenth century. Another voice crying against this liberalism belonged to Richard Oastler (1789–1861) of England. Itō would also have greatly appreciated some of Oastler's views which included the following beliefs: there was a period in England's past when "social harmony" existed; "wise gardeners" had a responsibility to tend the "garden" which was society (a benevolent elitism in a God-ordained hierarchical society); the responsibility of the "gardeners" (statesmen) lay in regulating "the multifarious activities of society to the end that the general welfare of the whole might be secured" on the basis of *ordered* liberty; and, "institutions of fellowship" alone make possible the fulfillment of human capacities which is character. Itō, however, would have been repelled by Oastler's calls to direct action and his belief that the throne, aristocracy, and church were not immune to attack if they stood in the way of the social state based on ordered liberty. Cecil Driver, *Tory Radical: The Life of Richard Oastler* (New York, 1946), Chap. 32: "The Faith of a Tory."

46. Siemes, pp. 8, 2–3; Pittau, "Ideology," pp. 227, 231–234.

47. Itō, "Reminiscences," p. 126. Siemes says that Stein and Gneist had the concept of "social monarchy" in mind when they talked about the role of the monarch in a constitutional system with Itō. Siemes, 7.

48. For a discussion, see Pittau, "Ideology," pp. 252–253, 282–285, 290.

49. Nakayama Yoshisuke, I, 186. In other areas too, we see this fusion. Yano Ryūkei (Fumio) wrote *Keikoku bidan* (The saga of a classical country), in which he talks of a government described as "a Confucian democracy." Horace Z. Feldman, "The Meiji Political Novel: A Brief Survey," *Far Eastern Quarterly*, 9:247–248 (May 1950). This is the same Yano who drafted Ōkuma's memorandum of 1881.

50. Silberman, pp. 317, also p. 322.

51. Charles S. Terry, "Taking Exception," *Japan Society Forum* (Dec. 15, 1961).

52. Itō, "Reminiscences," pp. 128, 130. Siemes, pp. 46–60. It is difficult to pinpoint these Confucianists. Motoda Eifu is usually cited as an example. For a discussion of the

conflicts between Itō, Inoue Kowashi, and Motoda, see Warren W. Smith, Jr., *Confucianism in Modern Japan: A Study in Japanese Intellectual History* (Tokyo, 1959), pp. 68–88; Pittau, "Ideology," pp. 258–262, 281–282, 300–301. In the Meiji period, however, it is especially foolhardy to pin labels. For example, Nakamura Keiu was a prominent Confucian, yet he was also well known for his translations of the American constitution, Washington's Farewell Address, John Stuart Mill's *On Liberty,* and Smiles's *Self Help* and *Conduct.* Smith's evaluation of Nakamura is pertinent: "He represents, rather, a continuation of that group of Confucianists of the Tokugawa days who advocated a complementary fusion of Western knowledge and Confucian ethics. And in general his position even in this regard was most moderate, for he did not differentiate on the basis of Western material civilization versus Eastern spiritual civilization, but recognized Western ethical theories as existing and having value." Smith, *Confucianism,* pp. 53–54.

53. Quoted in Inada Masatsugu, *Meiji kempō,* II, 529. See also Kido's views in McLaren, "Documents," pp. 573–574, and Ōkubo's in Beckmann, *Making of the Meiji Constitution,* pp. 116–117. See also Siemes, pp. 21–33.

54. Speech on June 18, 1888, quoted in Kaneko, *Itō den,* II, 614–616. See also letter from Itō to Matsukata, dated January 8, 1883, in *ibid.,* II, 335–338. Baelz' remarks in 1880 that the people took little interest in the emperor should be recalled.

55. "Economic Backwardness in Historical Perspective," pp. 23–24. There is, it is true, something to be said for the view that nationalism and the awe and trepidation that the oligarchs fostered contributed to creating the narrow jingoism of the 1930's. It may be argued, however, that in the context of their age and the goals they had set for Japan, their stress on nationalism and the emperor was understandable and even imperative. The question of historical responsibility, unfortunately is one which eludes simple answers.

56. Yoshino Sakuzō, "In the Name of the People," *Pacific Affairs,* 4:193–198 (Mar. 1931); also by the same author, "Kempō to kensei no mujun" (Contradictions between the constitution and constitutional government), *CK,* 44:83–84, 98 (Dec. 1929). See also Kenneth Colgrove, "Parliamentary Government in Japan," *American Political Science Review,* 21:852 (Nov. 1927). Harold S. Quigley, "Privy Council vs. Cabinet in Japan," *Foreign Affairs,* 9:503 (Apr. 1931).

57. Colgrove, "The Japanese Privy Council," Pt. 2, p. 905. A conclusion shared by H. Vere Redman in his "How the Cabinet is Controlled," *Contemporary Japan,* 1:406–407 (Dec. 1932). Hozumi Yatsuka, the conservative constitutional scholar, was one of those Itō consulted when he worked on the *Commentaries.* Siemes, p. 12.

58. In a sense Itō's attitude reminds us of Tseng Kuo-fan's conviction that although dealing with barbarians was a difficult matter, "the basic principles are no more than the four words of Confucius: *chung, hsin, tu,* and *ching*—faithfulness, sincerity, earnestness, and respectfulness." Quoted in Teng and Fairbank, p. 63.

59. Itō, "Reminiscences," pp. 126–127. One of the best statements of the organ theory was found among Itō's papers. "The monarch is not the ruler of the state [but] is an organ of the state . . . However, the monarch occupies the highest position in the state. Besides, he possesses the public power . . . The fact that the monarch is the possessor of the nation's constitution definitely does not mean that his rights and powers are unlimited. The monarch, in the exercise of his powers under a constitutional system, must first conform to fixed usages, and second, must accept the participation of other organs." Itō, *Hisho ruisan: hōsei kankei shiryō* (Private papers: Materials on the legal system), quoted in Osatake, *Nihon kensei shi no kenkyū,* pp. 321–322. Osatake hesitates to commit himself on the extent of Itō's adherence to the organ theory and merely states that it is "intriguing to note that substantially this view was similar to the concept propounded by a 'certain professor'" and that undoubtedly Itō was one of the earliest to introduce the organ theory to Japan. It should be noted that Osatake was writing in the early 1940's.

60. This argument is developed by Kawai Kazuo in "Sovereignty and Democracy in

the Japanese Constitution," pp. 670–671; see also Ardath W. Burks, *The Government of Japan* (New York, 1961), p. 18; Siemes, pp. 13–16. In Roesler's *Commentaries* are found the following words: "The practical effect of this principle is that the Emperor, in the deliberation of rules of law, is served and assisted by the national intelligence and wishes at large, instead of by his governmental advisers only." Siemes, p. 27.

61. Kaneko, *Kempō seitei to Ōbeijin no hyōron*, p. 174. And Kaneko must have been pleased when he found support for his position from the distinguished scholar on English law, Sir William Anson (1834–1914), for he underlined Anson's remarks that " . . . no matter what government is involved, once a constitutional system is adopted the government cannot by itself, standing aloof and above parties, carry out the administration of the country." *Ibid.*, pp. 271–272.

62. Speech before the presidents of the prefectural assemblies, February 21, 1889, quoted in Miyake, *Jidai shi,* II, 368. For a rather intriguing incident involving Itō and Ōkuma, bordering on *haragei* and indicating that the two saw eye-to-eye on the effects of the constitution, see Idditti, p. 252; and Kaneko, "Teikoku kempō seitei," pp. 27–28.

63. This is the warning General Mazaki Jinzaburō gave some young officers who sought to carry out a *coup d'état* in the wake of Inukai's assassination. Richard Storry, *The Double Patriots: A Study of Japanese Nationalism* (New York, 1957), p. 123.

64. A biographer of Ozaki Yukio states that "The constitution . . . was far more progressive than the leaders of the opposition had thought it would be." Isa, p. 393.

65. Pittau feels that even the *Commentaries* were not so illiberal. Pittau, "Meiji Political System," pp. 100–101. In Roesler's *Commentaries* are some sentiments which indicate that he was also aware of political realities. "The right of voting laws and taxes is the constitutional center towards which all other political rights gravitate." Siemes, p. 19.

66. Colgrove, "Powers and Functions of the Japanese Diet," Pt. 1, p. 889. " . . . so far as the constitution is concerned, there are no legal limitations upon the legislature that bar its way toward the attainment of dominance in the political field." *Ibid.*, Pt. 2, p. 39. And again, "Like the constitution of the United States, the supreme law of Japan is worded in very general terms, permitting a wide latitude of interpretation and allowing expansion by legislative acts and administrative ordinances. . . . Thus it is entirely possible to have a liberal development in Japan without formal amendments to the constitution." "The Japanese Emperor," Pt. 2, p. 844.

67. Quigley, *Japanese Government and Politics,* p. 42. He has consistently held this viewpoint. After the Pacific War he asserted: "Since imperial absolutism is as alien to its people as republicanism, the natural line of development is toward constitutional monarchy." Harold S. Quigley, "How New is the New Japan?" *Virginia Quarterly Review,* 33:19 (Winter 1957). Colgrove was also convinced that there was "a pronounced parliamentary trend prior to the invasion of Manchuria in 1931" ("The Japanese Cabinet," p. 923). He substantiates his opinion by noting that even in the matter of control over the foreign office, where constitutional development moves more slowly than in other areas of public law, the government is "falling more and more into the control of the House of Representatives . . . " Kenneth Colgrove, "Treaty-Making Power in Japan," *American Journal of International Law,* 35:270–297 (Apr. 1931). Some years after the organ theory controversy Minobe argued against scrapping the Meiji constitution and substituting for it the new constitution, feeling that "democracy could advance under it if it were properly enforced." Harold S. Quigley, "Japan's Constitutions: 1890 and 1947," *American Political Science Review,* 41:847 (Oct. 1947).

68. John F. Embree, "Democracy in Postwar Japan," *American Journal of Sociology,* 50:206 (Nov. 1944). Cf. Ward, "Political Modernization in Japan," pp. 592–593.

69. See, for example, Scalapino, *Democracy,* pp. 83–87.

70. Bisson, "Japan as a Political Organism," pp. 401, 417.

71. John M. Maki, "The Role of the Bureaucracy in Japan," *Pacific Affairs*, 20:395 (Dec. 1947).

72. Colgrove, "The Japanese Cabinet," p. 913. Pittau puts it this way: "The fact that the articles of the Constitution, because of their brevity, were supplemented by other laws, and the further fact that the praxis of constitutional government changed from the initial form of 'transcendental cabinet'—by definition a cabinet outside and above political factions—to the form of a party cabinet exerted an important influence upon the theories of the Constitution and the Meiji political system." Pittau, "The Meiji Political System," p. 105.

73. One of the reasons that Yoshino proposed his theory of *mimponshugi*—a theory that in many respects resembles the ideas held by the Meiji leaders—was that he saw the rise of a new "plutocracy" following the Sino-Japanese and Russo-Japanese wars and wanted to cry out against the abuses of its political powers. Tsunoda *et al.*, pp. 733–734.

74. *Ibid.*, pp. 652–653.

75. McLaren, "Documents," p. 439. Pittau says that Katō faithfully reflected the government's every mood and change. He emerges from Pittau's characterization as a rather enlightened man with "progressive" views. Pittau, "Ideology," pp. 130–137.

76. McLaren, "Documents," pp. 272–276.

77. Masumi discusses the problems caused by the provincial assemblies and observes: "Generally, the government had a tendency to set up systems which were based on conceptions far removed from reality. And there arose confusion and disorder based on the adverse reactions to and maladjustments resulting from this great gap between reality and the systems." Masumi, "1880 nendai no fu-ken kai," pp. 22–23.

78. McLaren, "Documents," pp. 331–404; see also Tsunoda *et al.*, pp. 708–710.

79. Ernest W. Clement, "Local Self-Government in Japan," *Political Science Quarterly*, 7:294 (June 1892). The trend appears to have been a continuous one, for years later it was noted: "Coming down, now to the local government at the town and village level, we find a really democratic type of government. Japanese towns and villages are governed by locally elected councils, and these councils in turn appoint their own mayors or headman. Such mayors are usually local men, respected by the people and responsible to them." Embree, "Democracy in Postwar Japan," p. 207.

80. Yanaga, *Japan since Perry*, p. 101.

81. The writer of the following words, written in the 1870's was imprisoned for two months and fined twenty yen. "Our government is a tyranny and our authorities are brutal; therefore we must destroy this government and punish the officials with death." Another advocated the assassination of government authorities and was sentenced to two months in prison and fined 30 yen. Kawabe Kisaburō, *The Press and Politics in Japan: A Study of the Relations between the Newspaper and the Political Development of Modern Japan* (Chicago, 1921), p. 63; see esp. Chap. 8: "Political Journals and the Movement for a Constitutional Government."

82. Pittau gives the details in his "Ideology," Chap. 6: "The Debate on Sovereignty and Natural Rights." Interesting comparisons can be made with Russia, a contemporaneously "backward" society. Fischer writes: "This Russia was still a largely pastoral society, half welcoming half repulsing modernization. Islands of the latest culture and technology grew steadily but tortuously and unevenly in a sea of medieval and feudal backwardness. And government chicanery and suppression coexisted with a most untotalitarian leeway for oppositional thought and activity." George Fischer, *Russian Liberalism: From Gentry to Intelligentsia* (Cambridge, Mass., 1958), p. 203. A crucial difference between Russia and Japan, it seems, was that the Meiji leaders were consistently seeking to modernize and in their own way, were propounding and putting into practice political programs being advocated by the "liberal" opposition.

83. C. B. Roylance-Kent, "The New Japanese Constitution," *MacMillan's Magazine*,

70:420–421 (Oct. 1894). Another speaker, disparaging the idea that the Chinese immigrant was capable of taking part in American political life, categorically stated before the Social Science Association of America, " . . . ethnologists declare that a brain capacity of less than eighty-five inches is unfit for free government, which is considerably above that of the [Chinese] coolie . . . " Quoted in California State Senate, Special Committee on Chinese Immigration: *Report* (Sacramento, 1876); see esp. pp. 297–301.

84. Carr, p. 62.

85. Brogan and Verney, pp. 105–106.

86. Norman Thomas, "Rethinking Socialism," *Virginia Quarterly Review,* 34:46–47 (Winter 1958). Carr's description of the rise of "mass democracy" in England is interesting, especially in the face of our earlier discussion on "social monarchy" and the Confucian ideals of the Meiji leaders: "The flagrant absence of a harmony of interests between competing and conflicting classes more and more urgently called for state intervention. The state could no longer be content to hold the ring; it must descend actively into the arena to create a harmony which did not exist in nature. Legislation, hitherto regarded as an exceptional function required from time to time to clear up some misunderstanding or to rectify some abuse, now became normal and continuous. It no longer sufficed to interpret and apply rights conferred on the individual by the laws of nature. What was expected of the state was positive and continuous activity—a form of social and economic engineering . . . The functions of the state were no longer merely supervisory, but creative and remedial." Carr, pp. 66–67.

87. Robert L. Heilbronner, *The Future as History: The Historic Currents of Our Time and the Direction in Which They are Taking America* (New York, 1959), pp. 85–86.

GLOSSARY

Abei Iwane 安部井磐根
Aikokukōtō 愛国公党
Aikokusha 愛国社
Aoki Shūzō 青木周蔵
Arai Shōgo 新井章吾
Arisugawa Taruhito 有栖川熾仁
Asano Chōkun 浅野長勲

"Bunkan bungen rei" 文官分限令
"Bunkan chōkai rei" 文官懲戒令
"Bunkan nin'yō rei" 文官任用令

chokkan giin 勅勘議員
chokunin 勅任
chokusai 勅裁
chōzen naikaku 超然内閣
chūō tokkan no saku 中央突貫の策

Dai Nihon kyōkai 大日本協會
"Daiichi naikaku kiyaku" 第一内閣
　規約
daikan 代官
"Daikōryō" 大綱領
Daishin-in 大審院
dajōdaijin 太政大臣
Dajōkan 太政官
Dōmei kurabu 同盟倶楽部

Enomoto Takeaki 榎本武揚
eta 穢多
Etō Shimpei 江藤新平

fu-ken kai 府縣會
Fukuoka Kōtei 福岡孝弟
Furuzawa Shigeru 古沢滋

genkun 元勲
genkun naikaku 元勲内閣
genrō 元老
Genrō-in 元老院
genrō kaigi 元老會議
Gikai kisei dōmei kai 議會期成同盟會
Gō Junzō 郷純造
Godai Tomoatsu 五代友厚
gōnō 豪農
Gōnō minken undō 豪農民權運動
gōshi 郷士

hambatsu seifu 藩閥政府
han 藩
hannin 判人
haragei 腹藝
Hatoyama Kazuo 鳩山和夫
Hayashi Yūzō 林有造
heimin 平民
heimin shugi 平民主義
Hirata Tōsuke 平田東助
Hozumi Yatsuka 穂積八束

"Iken" 意見
Iwabashi Tetsusuke 岩橋徹輔
Iwakura Tomomi 岩倉具視
Iwakura Tomosada 岩倉具定
Iwamura Michitoshi 岩村通俊
Iwasaki Yanosuke 岩崎弥之助
Iwasaki Yatarō 岩崎弥太郎

Jijosha 自助社
jimmin 人民
Jiyū minken undō 自由民權運動
Jiyūtō 自由党

jō-i 攘夷

Kabayama Sukenori 樺山資紀
kaiin shiki 開院式
Kaishintō 改進党
Kaitakushi 開拓使
kangaku 漢學
Katō Hiroyuki 加藤弘之
Katsura, Princess 桂宮
Kawahara Shigesuke 川原茂輔
Kawakami Sōroku 川上操六
Kawamura Sumiyoshi (Jungi) 川村
　純義
Keiho kyoku chō 警保局長
Keiō gijuku 慶應義塾
Keishi sōkan 警視總監
kempō 憲法
Kempō torishirabe jo 憲法取調所
Kenseihontō 憲政本党
Kensei shiryō shitsu 憲政資料室
Kenseitō 憲政党
Kinnōtō 勤王党
Kishi Nobusuke 岸信介
Kitabatake Harufusa 北畠治房
Kōfuku anzen sha 幸福安全社
Kōjunsha 交詢社
"Kokkai giin tetsuzuki torishirabe"
　國會議員手続取調
Kokkai kisei dōmei kai 國會期成
　同盟會
Kokkai kisei kai 國會期成會
kokken 國憲
"Kokken-an" 國憲案
"Kokken sōan" 國憲草案
kokugaku 國學
kokuhō kaigi 國法會議
"Kokuhō kaigi no gian" 國法會議の
　議案
Kokumin kyōkai 國民協會
"Kokusei kaikaku an" 國政改革案
kokusuishugisha 國粹主義者
kokutai 國体
Komatsu Akira 小松彰

Komatsu, Princess 小松若宮妃
Komiya Mihomatsu 小宮三保松
Kōmuchi Tomotsune 神鞭知常
Komuro Nobuo 小室信夫
Kondō Isami 近藤勇
Kōno Togama 河野敏鎌
"Kōryō" 綱領
kuge 公卿
kurai tanima 暗い谷間
kuromaku genrō 黒幕元老
kuromaku naikaku 黒幕内閣
Kusumoto Masataka 楠本正隆
Kyōson dōshū 共存同衆

Maebara Issei 前原一誠
Magoshi Kyōhei 馬越恭平
Maruyama Masakura 丸山作樂
Matsuda Masahisa 松田正久
Matsuoka Tokitoshi 松岡時敏
Mazaki Jinzaburō 真崎甚三郎
"Meiji shinki kiji" 明治辛己紀事
Meirokusha 明六社
metsuke 目付
mimponshugi 民本主義
min-pen-chu-i 民本主義
minshin 民心
minshū 民衆
minshū shugi 民衆主義
mintō 民党
Miura Gorō 三浦梧樓
Mizuno Echizen-no-kami 水野越前
　守
Mizuno Torajirō 水野寅次郎
Mori Arinori 森有禮
Motoda Eifu 元田永孚

Nabeshima Naomasa 鍋島直正
"Naikaku giketsusho" 内閣議決書
Nakae Tōju 中江藤樹
Nakai Hiroshi 中井弘
Nakajima Nobuyuki 中島信行
Nakamura Keiu 中村敬宇
"Nihon kokken an" 日本國憲案

Ni shichi kai 二七會
Ninomiya Kumajirō 二宮熊次郎
Nirei Kagenori 仁禮景範
Nishi Amane 西周
Nōmin minken undō 農民民權運動
Nomura Yasushi 野村靖
Numama Morikazu (Moriichi) 沼間守一

Oguri Tadamasa 小栗忠順
Ogyū Sorai 荻生徂徠
Ōi Kentarō 大井憲太郎
Ōishi Masami 大石正己
Okamoto Kenzaburō 岡本健三郎
Ōki Takatō 大木喬任
Ōkubo Ichiō 大久保一翁
Ōmeisha 嚶鳴社
Osaka kaigi 大阪會議
Ōtake Kan'ichi 大竹貫一
Ōtori Keisuke 大鳥圭介
Ōyama Iwao 大山巌

Rikken kakushintō 立憲革新党
Rikken seiyūkai 立憲政友會
Rikken teiseitō 立憲帝政党
"Rikkokuken gi" 立國憲議
Risshisha 立志社

Saigō Takamori 西郷隆盛
Saigō Tsugumichi 西郷従道
Sa-in 左院
Saionji Kimmochi 西園寺公望
Sakamoto Ryōma 坂本龍馬
sandaijin 三大臣
sangi 参議
Sanjō Sanetomi 三條實美
Sano Tsunetami 佐野常民
Sasaki Takayuki 佐々木高行
Seido torishirabe kyoku 制度取調局
Sei-in 正院
seiki 政規
Seimubu 政務部
Seitaisho 政体書

Seiyū yūshi kai 政友有志會
sengo keiei 戰後經營
shi 士
Shimada Saburō 島田三郎
Shimazu Hisamitsu 島津久光
Shimpotō 進歩党
Shimpūren 神風連
Shinsengumi 新撰組
Shirane Sen'ichi 白根專一
Shizoku minken undō 士族民權運動
shōchoku 詔勅
Shomin 庶民
shōshū 召集
Soejima Taneomi 副島種臣
sōnin 奏任
Sugita Seikei 杉田成卿
Sugita Teiichi 杉田定一
Suzuki Mosaburō 鈴木茂三郎

Taigai kō ha 対外硬派
Taiseikai 大成會
Takahashi Kenzō 高橋建三
Takashima Tomonosuke 高島鞆之助
Takeuchi Tsuna 竹内綱
Tanaka Fujimaro 田中不二麿
Tani Kanjō 谷干城
Tani Shigeki 谷重喜
Teikokutō 帝國党
Tokudaiji Sanenori 徳大寺實則
Torio Koyata 鳥尾小弥太
Tōyō jiyūtō 東洋自由党

udaijin 右大臣
Ueki Emori 植木枝盛
Uesugi Shinkichi 上杉慎吉

Watanabe Kōki 渡辺洪基
Watanabe Kunitake 渡辺國武

Yada Isa 矢田績
Yamada Akiyoshi 山田顕
Yamazaki Naotane 山崎直胤
Yoshida Shigeru 吉田茂

Yoshikawa Kensei 芳川顕正
Yuri Kimimasa 由利公正

Zeisho Atsushi 税所篤

Index

HARVARD EAST ASIAN SERIES